Onwards and Upwards Publ
Berkeley House, 11 Nightingale Crescei
Surrey, KT24 6PD.
www.onwardsandupward

222 Publications

Printed in the UK.

ISBN: 978-1-907509-63-6

Typeface: Sabon LT

Graphic design: Leah-Maarit

Acknowledgements

We want to thank all those who have helped us to create and publish this book.

First to Pete Worthington who gave us the vision at the beginning and the members of Living Waters Church who inspired us to keep going.

To Corinne Wijsman who checked the script very carefully and made sure the Bible references were accurate.

To Mark, Di and Luke Jeffery – our publishers – and to Leah Jeffery who designed the cover.

JANUARY

"I've Pitched My Tent in the Land of Hope"

These words from Acts 2:26 in The Message are spoken by David in Psalm 16 and quoted by Peter on the day of Pentecost. Peter and the disciples have just experienced the outpouring of the Holy Spirit, seen the evidence of speaking in tongues, and been released into joy and praise. Peter then quotes David and identifies with his fearless declaration, which in my words, is, **"I will live by promise and not by circumstances."**

There is an attitude of resolution: **"I've made my choice; for me there is no other way. Do whatever you will, but I have decided to follow Jesus."** This is the result, as stated in the NIV translation: **"Therefore my heart is glad and my tongue rejoices; my body will also live in hope."** Other devout Jews, now followers of Jesus, see the evidence, hear the words and make the same decision.

Then there is the backlash from circumstances and religious authorities as they are imprisoned and persecuted. However, their internal choice enables these early disciples to overcome, remain joyful, and face very challenging issues with boldness and joy.

When your heart rejoices and trusts in God, when your mouth speaks hope and not misery, your body will reflect what is going on both emotionally and mentally. This will show itself in peace within and health without.

We are living in challenging days; the atmosphere around us is full of negativity, fear, gloom and despondency. Depression, hopelessness and helplessness are on many lips.

Where have you pitched your tent? Under the shadow of the Almighty and the promises of God? Or under the negative atmosphere and spirit that dominates our nation?

God has promised you His presence, His help, His wisdom, His love, His resources. You are not alone in a sea of darkness. You are in the family of God; you are His child and His eye is upon you.

Live in hope today!

Joyce

One Year Plan : Psalm 1, Matthew 1, Genesis 1 - 2
Two Year Plan : Psalm 1, Matthew 1, Genesis 1 (Yr 1)
1 Samuel 1 (Yr 2)

The Promise Before You

"When you walk with God, the promise before you is always greater than the pain behind you." *(Words written by Bob Gass.)*

Starting a New Year with all its potential and promise can be like opening up a new notebook, unused, and containing no spoiled pages or messy writing. However, it is possible to be so dominated by past failures and present disappointments that the future is already marred before it has begun.

While meditating on the opening statement, I thought about the verses in Revelation 21:3-4 which say, **"Now the dwelling of God is with men, and he will live with them. They will be his people, and God himself will be their God. He will wipe away every tear from their eyes."** Although these verses speak of our final destination in heaven, I believe they can be a promise for today.

As we enter a New Year, God has promised to be with you. He wants to make you His dwelling place – to live within you, to fill you with His love and power, and by His Holy Spirit to empower you to do His will. I find that encouraging and exciting.

To return to my analogy of the new notebook, the passage in Revelation continues, **"He who was seated on the throne said, 'I am making everything new!'"** Again, I believe this is a promise for today; it does not matter what has happened in the past, God always wants to give us a fresh start. The Lord says, **"I will forgive their wickedness and will remember their sins no more."** (Jeremiah 31:34)

So as we enter a New Year, remember that God is your Father and He wants to have His dwelling place in your heart. God is the One who wipes every tear from your eyes; He is the One who comforts and heals the pain of the past. God is the One who makes everything new.

Charles

One Year Plan : Psalm 2, Matthew 2, Genesis 3 - 4
Two Year Plan : Psalm 2, Matthew 2, Genesis 2 (Yr 1)
1 Samuel 2 (Yr 2)

Prayer and Fasting

We had set aside three days when we called our people at Living Waters Church to pray, fast and to seek God for direction and focus for the coming year. We did our normal daytime work, but as many as possible gathered together in the evening to worship, pray and hear from God.

We probably had no higher expectation than to hear prophetic words that would give clarity and direction for the various activities of the church. God had other ideas; He began to speak to us about holiness and revival.

At the end of the first evening, as God had surprised us and started speaking to us about holiness, one of our people drew my attention to an extract from the devotional he read each day.

This is what it said: **"After a successful crusade someone asked Billy Graham, 'Is this revival?' 'No,' he replied. 'When revival comes we'll see two things we haven't seen yet: (1) A fresh sense of God's holiness; (2) a heightened sense of our own sin and carnality.'"**

We realised how easily we become complacent. We were reminded of Isaiah's encounter with God in Isaiah 6, when Isaiah was probably quite content with his relationship with God until **"He saw the Lord, high and lifted up."** He could only respond, **"Woe is me!"**

God spoke to us about leaving our comfort zones to venture into His finest purposes. He spoke about broken relationships, criticism, backbiting and half-heartedness. There were tears and reconciliation but also the overwhelming desire to go deeper and to seek God with all our hearts.

We found ourselves praying the same words as King David: **"Teach me your way, O Lord, and I will walk in your truth; give me an undivided heart that I may fear your name."** (Psalm 86:11)

Charles

One Year Plan : Psalm 3, Matthew 3, Genesis 5 - 6
Two Year Plan : Psalm 3, Matthew 3, Genesis 3 (Yr 1)
1 Samuel 3 (Yr 2)

The Swedish Calendar

In our Christmas mail we received the gift of a Swedish Calendar, which we hung in the traditional spot in the downstairs toilet!

There is a Bible verse for each month, so as I turn the page each month I try to figure out the scripture verse, even though it is written in Swedish.

I have also discovered from this calendar that the Swedes attach a name or a couple of names to each day so that in addition to a birthday everyone can celebrate their 'name day'.

"Bara hos Gud finner jag ro" was the verse for the month (Psalm 62:1). I had no idea what those words meant so I looked up the verse in my Bible. The translation given is **"My soul finds rest in God alone."** It is a game I played with myself each month, so after all that effort I began to meditate on the scripture.

At that time we had just come through a very busy weekend. We had a been involved in a wedding on the Saturday, our house had been full of people who had come for the celebration; my car had broken down and I had had to be rescued by the AA, which had made it an eighteen hour day; and my computer had crashed!

What a mixture of joy, celebration, exhaustion and frustration, and yet my verse for the month said, **"My soul finds rest in God alone."**

In the middle of all the demands of life God is there; He knows and He cares and He will give deep rest beyond the natural.

Sleep is only part of the answer; anger does not help; it is at these moments that I need to go the God. **"My soul finds rest in God alone."**

Where are you going to find the resources you need for today?

Charles

One Year Plan : Psalm 4, Matthew 4, Genesis 7 - 8
Two Year Plan : Psalm 4, Matthew 4, Genesis 4 (Yr 1)
1 Samuel 4 (Yr 2)

Sleepless at Midnight

Psalm 63:6 in The Message says, **"If I'm sleepless at midnight, I spend the hours in grateful reflection."** Shortly after I had received Jesus as Saviour and friend, I went on a Summer Camp where we sang extensively from a selection of catchy choruses compiled by the CSSM. Returning home was not easy and I remember lying in bed waiting for sleep to take over, so I developed a habit of 'singing through the alphabet' using these choruses, e.g.

A – '*Absolutely tender, absolutely true...*'

B – '*By blue Galilee, Jesus walked of old...*'

C – '*Cleanse me from my sin Lord, put Thy power within Lord...*'

By the time I reached 'E' or 'F', I was usually gone!

It is good to give thanks, and if I am awake and anxious about a situation, I turn those thoughts into prayer and then thank God for His loving care in so many other situations – I seldom run out of things to be thankful for! There are times too when I am aware that I need to get up and really pray and intercede for a particular situation.

I used to wonder, when I had spent time in this way, if I would have enough resources for the next day. Over and over the Lord reassured me that He could supply supernatural refreshment, which means that if I miss two hours of sleep, the fact that I am in His presence will compensate.

One day I was due to speak at a Ladies' Conference, and on the night before I simply could not sleep. I was not anxious – I knew what the Lord had given me to share. I wanted to sleep but heard the Lord say to me, **"Just rest in my arms; I will give you all you need."** I lay still, at peace, but watched the clock register each hour.

I was up early the next morning, drove a hundred and fifty miles, spoke three times and returned home without any tiredness, although I had not slept a wink. This took from me any fear of sleeplessness. I am not an insomniac, but I felt the Lord was showing me that strength and refreshment can come supernaturally from Him as well as physically from sleep.

Joyce

One Year Plan : Psalm 5, Matthew 5, Genesis 9 - 10
Two Year Plan : Psalm 5, Matthew 5:1-20, Genesis 5 (Yr 1)
1 Samuel 5 (Yr 2)

A Life-Giving Spirit

Paul writes, **"The first Adam became a living being, the last Adam, a life-giving spirit."** (1 Corinthians 15:45) The message of Jesus is clear: He came to enable us to know Him, connect to Him and introduce us to a supernatural lifestyle, not to try and educate us to a better way of life.

One of the reasons Jesus came was to baptise His people in the Holy Spirit because He came not to improve us but to connect us to supernatural power. That is the secret of life in Jesus. He consistently pointed to the One who would continue in us the 'God life' He had demonstrated.

He told His disciples, **"I am going to send you what my Father has promised; but stay in the city until you have been clothed with power from on high."** (Luke 24:49) Don't move until you have received this **life-giving Spirit**. You can't live out of your own resources.

Paul wrote to the Romans, **"And if the Spirit of him who raised Jesus from the dead is living in you, he who raised Christ from the dead will also give life to your mortal bodies through his Spirit, who lives in you."** (Romans 8:11) The power of the indwelling Spirit has a beneficial effect on every part of our life, even on our physical bodies.

In Ephesians 5:18, Paul contrasts the effect of drinking too much wine to being filled with the Spirit when he says, **"Do not get drunk on wine, which leads to debauchery. Instead be filled with the Spirit."** One kind of intoxication leads to a destructive lifestyle; the other kind to exuberant praise, a joyful heart, overflowing thanksgiving and powerful living.

Jesus came as the **life-giving Spirit** and demonstrated that everything that comes into contact with that supernatural power is transformed. Galatians 5:16 says, **"So I say, live by the Spirit, and you will not gratify the desires of the sinful nature."**

Live by the Spirit; it will protect you from sin, make you healthier, more joyful and spread life and Jesus, wherever you go!

Charles

One Year Plan : Psalm 6, Matthew 6, Genesis 11 - 12
Two Year Plan : Psalm 6, Matthew 5:21-48, Genesis 6 (Yr 1)
1 Samuel 6 (Yr 2)

Superheroes

In the past many of us enjoyed watching films like Superman, and now for this present generation we have The Incredibles. Whatever our age, there is something very exciting about watching a mild and unassuming person become a superhero and perform great life-saving acts of bravery.

Do you realise that those who belong to Jesus are superhuman? Paul declared that he had been given an amazing message to give to God's redeemed people; he called it **"the mystery"**. And what was that mystery? Paul states it clearly in Colossians 1:25-27: **"God has chosen to make known among the Gentiles the glorious mystery, which is Christ in you, the hope of glory."**

To have received the life of Jesus through faith does not improve our old flesh life; it gives us a brand new life and a new power within. You are a superhero; Christ lives in you with all His resurrection power at your disposal.

This theme runs throughout the New Testament, not only from Paul but from all the writers. We read in 1 John 4:4, **"You, dear children, are from God and have overcome them, because the one in you is greater than the one who is in the world."** We are promised constant victory over the devil.

Paul told the Corinthians, **"The weapons we fight with are not weapons of the world. On the contrary they have divine power to demolish strong-holds."** (2 Corinthians 10:4) We are promised victory in our thought life over every argument that sets itself up against the knowledge of God.

Galatians 2:20 states, **"I have been crucified with Christ and I no longer live, but Christ lives in me."** Consequently we have victory over the flesh life and can live a life of faith every day.

Be a superhero today! Live in victory over the devil, victory over your thought life and victory in every area of life.

You are not just human; you are superhuman!

Charles

One Year Plan : Psalm 7, Matthew 7, Genesis 13 - 14
Two Year Plan : Psalm 7:1-9, Matthew 6 , Genesis 7 (Yr 1)
1 Samuel 7 (Yr 2)

Are you Able to Receive?

Giving and receiving are spiritual principles. You need faith to give, but you also need faith to receive.

"Give and it will be given to you. A good measure, pressed down, shaken together and running over, will be poured into your lap." (Luke 6:38)

"...and with the measure you use, it will be measured to you." (Matthew 7:2)

The principle of sowing and reaping runs throughout the Bible – seedtime and harvest. You reap in kind: sow wheat and reap wheat; sow kindness and reap kindness. We are encouraged to be sowers and givers but also reapers and receivers.

A farmer expects a harvest and could never think of sowing without the expectation of multiplication and harvest.

- For every seed sown in prayer expect a harvest.
- For every kindness sown expect kindness in return but not necessarily from the same source.
- For every tithe and offering expect the windows of heaven to open.
- For every up-building word expect to be encouraged in the same way.
- Bless others and be blessed.

I have recently spent time with some people who cannot receive. They like to give but don't expect to receive – and don't want to! A very odd situation!

Giving without receiving can be self-protective or it can be a symptom of total independence. It can also be a statement of pride which says, **"I need nothing from you or anyone else."**

God longs to be gracious to you and me, to give to us, to bless us, to provide abundantly for His children. How sad it is when we won't receive from Him.

- He is waiting for you to receive salvation in the widest sense.
- He is longing to answer your prayers.
- He wants you to receive all you need in every area of life.
- He longs for you to receive an abundant harvest so you will have more seed to sow.

Receiving makes you vulnerable – but blessed.

Joyce

One Year Plan : Psalm 8, Matthew 8, Genesis 15 -16
Two Year Plan : Psalm 7:10-17, Matthew 7, Genesis 8 (Yr 1)
1 Samuel 8 (Yr 2)

Touched and Tempted

When we are going through difficult times, we need to know there is someone who really understands and cares. For me the person who most fully fits that role is Jesus.

Hebrews 4:15-16 says, **"For we have not a high priest which cannot be touched by the feeling of our infirmities; but was in all points tempted like we are, yet without sin. Let us therefore come boldly to the throne of grace that we may obtain mercy, and find grace to help in time of need."**

In the Message, the same verses say, **"We don't have a priest who is out of touch with our reality. He's been through weakness and testing, experienced it all – all but the sin. So let's walk right up to him and get what he is so ready to give. Take the mercy, accept the help."**

I like the word **'touched'** because it speaks of someone who is able to enter fully into our situation. Jesus is the one who comes alongside you when you are feeling your worst, but He does not leave you struggling and alone. He invites you to come boldly, to walk right up to Him and receive from Him exactly what you need. It may be healing, comfort, strength – anything.

The Message says, **"He's been through weakness and testing,"** and the King James Version says, **"He has been tempted like we are."** Jesus experienced weakness, testing and temptation and He came through undefeated. In 1 Corinthians 10:13 it says, **"No temptation has seized you except what is common to man. And God is faithful; he will not let you be tempted beyond what you can bear. But when you are tempted, he will also provide a way out..."**

I find great reassurance in the fact that Jesus has experienced everything that I am experiencing so that He can bring His mercy and grace and set me free from the circumstances that are threatening to overwhelm me.

Are you going through it at this time? **He understands; let Him help you.**

Charles

One Year Plan : Psalm 9, Matthew 9, Genesis 17 - 18
Two Year Plan : Psalm 8, Matthew 8, Genesis 9 (Yr 1)
1 Samuel 9 (Yr 2)

Put your Money Where your Mouth is!

Once you have declared a thing, stand by it, and back what you have said with action – that's what Ezra had to do. He declared to a foreign king, ruler of Persia, that God would lovingly care for, protect and watch over a group of exiles travelling back to Jerusalem to rebuild the temple.

Ezra, his small group of people and their families, had more than a thousand miles to travel, and they were loaded with silver and gold – a sitting target for bandits and robbers – but having declared that God would protect them, Ezra was too embarrassed to ask the king for a bodyguard. Instead, we read, **"I proclaimed a fast, so that we might humble ourselves before our God and ask him for a safe journey for us and our children with all our possessions."** (Ezra 8:21)

He got what he asked for and having arrived stated, **"The hand of our God was on us, and he protected us from enemies and bandits along the way."** (Ezra 8:31) Living in a fear-filled society can affect us, and we find ourselves worrying instead of trusting God. Ezra wasn't unrealistic about the potential dangers, but he knew his God. Don't let fear cause you to cower – deliberately place yourself and those you love under God's protection. We live in a dangerous world, but God is with us, has promised His protection and can deal with every potential attack against us and our families.

Notice that Ezra didn't assume that God would protect them; he deliberately prayed, fasted and committed his journey to God. He also acted wisely, dividing the valuables between the group and letting individuals take responsibility for their share.

We seek to act wisely, lock our house, have a burglar alarm, put valuables out of sight, leave lights on, and check doors and windows when we go away, but we also commit our home, family and possessions to God's care and believe He is able to protect us from all harm.

Don't come under the spirit of the age – entrust yourself and your family to God. **Pray and be vigilant!**

Joyce

One Year Plan : Psalm 10, Matthew 10, Genesis 19 - 20
Two Year Plan : Psalm 9:1-10, Matthew 9:1-17, Genesis 10 (Yr 1)
1 Samuel 10 (Yr 2)

Poison or Peace

The tongue is the most unruly member of our body, described in graphic detail in the book of James, chapter 3. It can almost feel, as you read the chapter, that we are helpless to do anything about the things we find ourselves saying. He tells us that **"no human being can tame the tongue" - but God can.**

Verses 9 and 10 say, **"With it we bless our Lord and Father, and with it we curse people who are made in the likeness of God. From the same mouth come blessing and cursing. My brothers, these things ought not to be so."**

But we have a choice. We can succumb to our own humanity and let rip in each and every situation, so that the words that we speak could be described in the words of James as **"...a restless evil, full of deadly poison"**, or we can reach out to God and seek the power of His Holy Spirit to come and transform our words.

The chapter ends with an explanation of the contrast between worldly and godly wisdom. Verses 17 and 18 say, **"But the wisdom from above is first pure, then peaceable, gentle, open to reason, full of mercy and good fruits, impartial and sincere. And a harvest of righteousness is sown in peace by those who make peace."**

Both passages quoted refer to the outcome of our words: if we let it tumble out **"in the flesh"** then our words can be described as **"a deadly poison"**; if we speak with godly wisdom borne out of a life filled with the Holy Spirit then our words will produce **"a harvest of righteousness, sown in peace by those who make peace"**.

It is not easy and cannot be produced by one quick prayer; King David had the same battle with his tongue and so consequently prayed, **"May the words of my mouth and the meditation of my heart be pleasing in your sight O Lord, my Rock and my Redeemer."** (Psalm 19:14)

Today, will you sow poison or peace?

Charles

One Year Plan : Psalm 11, Matthew 11, Genesis 21 - 22
Two Year Plan : Psalm 9:11-20, Matthew 9:18-38, Genesis 11 (Yr 1)
1 Samuel 11 (Yr 2)

God Always Has the Last Word

When I listen to the media and hear reports on the world situation, it's easy to sink into despair. Governments in disarray, fighting, killing, all kinds of depravity and violence – these things can so easily induce fear. We may also be surrounded by personal issues that are unresolved.

It was no different in Isaiah's day; two kings had made a failed attack on Jerusalem, everyone was jittery and fearful, uncertain about their future and dreading the worst. But what does God say? Isaiah is told to go and meet King Ahaz, to tell him not to panic but to calm down, not be afraid and to hear from God. He counters the threats and rumours with the authoritative words, **"It will not take place, it will not happen..."** (Isaiah 7:3-9)

When everyone around you is giving way to fear and helplessness, you need to hear what God says about the situation. Isaiah needed to hear from God in another situation which is recorded in Chapter 8:12 – this is what he heard: **"Don't be like the people around you, don't fear what they fear, don't take on their worries."**

The answer, however, seems to be taking a long time, but Isaiah's response is, **"While I wait for God as long as he remains in hiding, while I wait and hope for him I stand my ground and hope..."** (Isaiah 8:17, The Message)

Are you waiting for answers in your own personal situation? Are you waiting for God's power and love to be seen again in our nation? Are you expecting Him to move in revival? Are you praying that those you love will turn from pleasure-seeking and material satisfaction and realise again they need to be in living connection with God?

God has a divine plan for you, those you love, for our land, mainland Europe and the other nations; what He purposes will happen.

Wait for God and don't be afraid.

Joyce

One Year Plan : Psalm 12, Matthew 12, Genesis 23 - 24
Two Year Plan : Psalm 10:1-11, Matthew 10:1-23, Genesis 12 (Yr 1) 1 Samuel 12 (Yr 2)

What He does... NOT – What we do!

We, as ordinary human beings, have the habit of constantly examining the consequences of our actions as a measure of the blessing or success happening around us. As believers we keep asking, **"Have I prayed and read my Bible enough?" "Have I been kind to my family?" "Is there anyone who I need to forgive?"**

These are all good, but David saw it another way. He saw that the blessing, protection and success he experienced were because of God, who He is and what He does!

Psalm 18 is a declaration of what God can do, so David declares boldly, **"The Lord is my rock, my fortress and my deliverer; my God is my rock, in whom I take refuge. He is my shield and the horn of my salvation, my stronghold."** (verse 2)

David continues to declare what God is doing for him: **"He reached down from on high and took hold of me; he drew me out of deep waters. He rescued me from my powerful enemy, from my foes, who were too strong for me."** (verses 16-17)

"He brought me into a spacious place; he rescued me because he delighted in me." (verse 19)

David does speak of his commitment to God, that he has sought to live right and act right, but this is not the reason God is working so powerfully on his behalf. God longs to bless us and to be gracious to us, but so many times we find it difficult to receive.

David continues, **"You, O Lord keep my lamp burning; my God turns my darkness into light. With your help I can advance against a troop, with my God I can scale a wall."** (verses 28-29)

Do you need a rock, a stronghold? Do you need to be saved from your enemies? Do you feel trapped and need a spacious place? Do you need a light in a dark place?

Go to God; and remember, it does not depend on what you do for Him but on what He does for you!

Charles

One Year Plan : Psalm 13, Matthew 13, Genesis 25 - 26
Two Year Plan : Psalm 10:12-18, Matthew 10:24-42, Genesis 13 (Yr 1)
1 Samuel 13 (Yr 2)

Holding On to a Promise

2 Peter 3:9 says, **"The Lord is not slow in keeping his promise, as some understand slowness. He is patient with you, not wanting anyone to perish, but everyone to come to repentance."**

The people to whom this message was written were waiting for Jesus' second coming, convinced that they were living in the 'last days', and they were getting impatient. God is holding back because He doesn't want anyone lost. He's giving everyone space and time to change.

God's timescale is not ours! Several times Jesus speaks of **the time not being right** and **"my time has not yet come"**. He is in touch with the heavenly calendar and clock!

In reading Genesis, I was challenged again by how long Abraham and Isaac had to wait to see God's promises fulfilled. Abraham waited twenty-five years for Isaac. Isaac was forty when he married Rebecca and sixty when the twins were born. A lot of praying and a lot of waiting – lots of questions, doubts from within and without.

You may be holding on to a promise as yet unfulfilled – and it's tough! Another year and you are hoping, longing, that this year you will see the promise become a reality. Don't give up. Wait, and keep trusting His word. He understands; we don't. There are so many factors and intricate details He is working out. We think He is indifferent; He never is. His nature is compassionate and tender-hearted.

I waited nearly fifty years to see my own father come to personal faith in Jesus. God had told me he would believe and he did, just two years before he died. I don't know why there were all those seemingly wasted years. I do know his story has helped many not to give up praying for their family members.

If God makes you a promise that you have received in your innermost being and it is backed by His Word, then it is **done**.

Keep trusting until it becomes a reality.

Joyce

One Year Plan : Psalm 14, Matthew 14, Genesis 27 - 28
Two Year Plan : Psalm 11, Matthew 11, Genesis 14 (Yr 1)
1 Samuel 14 (Yr 2)

No Blame, No Bitterness

Whilst reading about the life of Joseph, I was struck by the verses in Genesis 39:2-4, which say, **"The Lord was with Joseph and he prospered, and he lived in the house of his Egyptian master. When the master saw that the Lord was with him and that the Lord gave him success in everything he did, Joseph found favour in his eyes."**

How did this happen? Joseph had been roughly treated by his brothers, sold to the Ishmaelites and now handed over to Potiphar. He could have acted with stubbornness, bitterness and anger – but he didn't. What were the qualities that brought the blessing of God on his life?

Joseph did not lose the sense of destiny he had received through his dreams, even though when he shared them with his family this had prompted such negative reactions. He had complete faith that God's hand was upon his life for good and not for evil.

He continued to live righteously and with integrity within a heathen culture and refused to compromise his purity by succumbing to the sexual advances of Potiphar's wife.

He refused to become bitter despite all the injustice he experienced. After false accusation landed him in prison, it is recorded, **"But while Joseph was in prison, the Lord was with him..."** Even at the end of his life when his brothers thought he would get even with them for all the cruel things they had done to him, Joseph said, **"Don't be afraid. Am I in the place of God? You intended to harm me, but God intended it for good to accomplish what is now being done, the saving of many lives."** (Genesis 50:19-20)

Hebrews 11:22 says, **"By faith Joseph, when his end was near, spoke about the exodus of Israel from Egypt and gave instructions about his bones."** Right at the end of his life Joseph still did not regret the past but focussed on destiny.

There are keys here to help us imitate Joseph's example and live under God's favour – living lives of faith and integrity with no blame and no bitterness.

Charles

One Year Plan : Psalm 15, Matthew 15, Genesis 29 - 30
Two Year Plan : Psalm 12, Matthew 12:1-21, Genesis 15 (Yr 1)
1 Samuel 15 (Yr 2)

Extravagant Love

Many years ago I had contact with a young woman who had just moved into the area where we were living. The day after she moved, when the van had just been unloaded and before any boxes had been unpacked, her husband drove his mother to her home some thirty miles away, taking his thirteen-year-old son for the ride and leaving his wife, daughter and small baby in the new house.

Tragically, on that journey he was killed in an accident together with his mother; the son sustained severe injuries from which he died a few days later. It's hard to imagine how anyone copes, even when surrounded by friends, family and community. This woman was in a new house, in a new part of the country, knew no-one, and her remaining family were miles away.

In her desperate need she cried out to God, who previously she had had no time for and didn't believe in! He put His arms around her in an amazing way. She told me she had felt as if she had been wrapped in warm cotton wool, placed in a bubble, and all she could understand was that she was not alone and it would be alright. I believe what she experienced was **pure love**, freely poured out into her situation and extreme need.

It was supernatural; she was comforted and able to deal with the chaos that confronted her. Over time she was able to forgive the drunken driver – leaving him to God's justice.

You and I were designed to be recipients of this same **extravagant love** of God, to feel His closeness and help, to understand His nearness and unconditional acceptance; not only to receive it but also to be able to give it away – loving and being loved.

It is a wonderful thing to know human love and acceptance, but God's love is something else, the best of human love being only a pale reflection of the divine. John wrote in his letter, **"How great is the love the Father has lavished on us, that we should be called children of God! And that is what we are!"** (1 John 3:1)

Joyce

One Year Plan : Psalm 16, Matthew 16, Genesis 31 - 32
Two Year Plan : Psalm 13, Matthew 12:22-50, Genesis 16 (Yr 1)
1 Samuel 16 (Yr 2)

The Truth will set you Free

I often attend a gathering of business people who meet regularly to network and exchange ideas. At one particular time I was amazed, but most encouraged, to find that the two recurring themes of our discussions were the need to maintain a good work-life balance and the value of truth and integrity.

One businessman told how being utterly truthful with his customers had benefited his business. He would not promise a delivery or job completion he was not able to fulfil.

This was not specifically a gathering of Christian business people, and I came away thinking deeply about what I had just witnessed. Is there a reaction against the loss of values and integrity in today's society?

I then looked again at the book of Proverbs and was impacted by the values it extols.

"Let love and faithfulness never leave you; bind them around your neck, write them on the tablet of your heart. Then you will win favour and a good name in the sight of God and man." (Proverbs 3:3-4)

"Do not be wise in your own eyes; fear the Lord and shun evil. This will bring health to your body and nourishment to your bones." (Proverbs 3:7-8)

"The man of integrity walks securely, but he who takes crooked paths will be found out." (Proverbs 10:9)

These words were written thousands of years ago. Why do so many people reject them and still believe that this will not harm them?

Might not this be an antidote to the pressure, stress, self-seeking, which today is deemed part of normal lifestyle?

God's ways work!

Charles

One Year Plan : Psalm 17, Matthew 17, Genesis 33 - 34
Two Year Plan : Psalm 14, Matthew 13:1-30, Genesis 17 (Yr 1)
1 Samuel 17 (Yr 2)

Unlimited Resources

Whilst travelling to church one Sunday I was thinking what I would do if I had unlimited resources in my bank account. I imagined giving to various people and causes, when... suddenly the Holy Spirit broke into my musing and said, **"You do have unlimited resources, but you don't believe it."**

He had my attention and began to challenge me afresh about the promises that are available when we use the name of Jesus. Words and phrases came to mind – **"anything", "what you wish", "whatever you ask"** – and the promise of immediate action by Jesus and the Father... Wow! I still needed to face the challenge of believing.

I looked again at the scriptures in John's gospel and prayed that unbelief would be eradicated from my heart and I would have a new revelation of faith.

We who are children of God are privileged ones who, in Jesus, can approach God's throne; His sceptre is outstretched as a sign of His favour and willingness to grant our requests.

We come, we ask, we speak, we decree, we declare, we believe, we receive... **"as it is in heaven so on earth."**

God now goes into action to fulfil his promises.

"I tell you the truth, anyone who has faith in me will do what I have been doing. He will do even greater things that these, because I am going to the Father." (John 14:12)

"If you remain in me and my words remain in you, ask whatever you wish, and it will be given you." (John 15:7)

"Until now you have not asked anything in my name. Ask and you will receive, and your joy will be full." (John 16:24)

As we have faith, remain in Him and ask, we will receive. Surely there is nothing compared with the privilege of drawing off the bank of heaven.

Joyce

One Year Plan : Psalm 18, Matthew 18, Genesis 35 - 36
Two Year Plan : Psalm 15, Matthew 13:31-58, Genesis 18 (Yr 1)
1 Samuel 18 (Yr 2)

Is the River Flowing?

Psalm 46:4 says, **"There is a river whose streams make glad the city of God."** Jerusalem has no river, so this cannot be talking about the city in a natural way. This refers to how God is continually pouring out His refreshing streams and blessings on His people.

There is something very wonderful about a flowing river; it is so full of life and yet often the source is hidden. As you stand on the bank you may not know what is feeding it upstream, but as it passes, you know that everywhere it goes it will bring life and nourishment.

As I read this psalm, God began to speak to me about my life which He wants to be like a river, with something new and alive always flowing into it, and like refreshing powerful streams flowing out to others.

Jesus said, **"If anyone is thirsty, let him come to me. And let him drink who believes in me, as the Scripture has said, streams of living water will flow from him. By this he meant the Spirit, whom those who believed in him were later to receive."** (John 7:37-39) I so much need the living water of the Holy Spirit to flow into my life each day. That stream needs to be fed by the word, prayer and worship – not just filled up like a reservoir but sourced like a river that is always on the move. If a river is not constantly supplied, it will dry up, and there is nothing sadder than a dry river bed.

Jesus said that the river would flow from within so that it pours out into the lives of others. Another psalm speaks of the way God nourishes His people: **"They feast on the abundance of your house; you give them drink from your river of delights. For with you is the fountain of life; in your light we see light."** (Psalm 36:8-9)

Are you dry? Then go to the source of living water and drink.

Are others needing to be refreshed? Then let your river flow out to them.

Charles

One Year Plan : Psalm 19, Matthew 19, Genesis 37 - 38
Two Year Plan : Psalm 16, Matthew 14:1-21, Genesis 19 (Yr 1)
1 Samuel 19 (Yr 2)

God, You Can Do All Things

At the end of the book of Job, after he had experienced loss, pain, frustration, anger and remorse, Job speaks to God and says, **"I know that you can do all things and no plan of yours can be thwarted."** (Job 42:2)

How did Job get this revelation? How did he gain this understanding of who God is and what He is able to do?

God had spoken to him in the middle of his crisis and pain; He had caused him to think again about the created world, the order in the universe, the detail and beauty of created things. As Job listened he began to realise his inability to create anything, he began to see God's greatness and his own smallness – and to worship.

Once these truths broke into Job's understanding, it did not take long for God to restore all that he had lost and give him twice as much as he had before. It is recorded that the Lord blessed the latter part of Job's life more than the first.

It's so easy to lose sight of the greatness, the power and the ability of our Father God – and when we do, the problems of life become overwhelming.

In Isaiah 59:1, the prophet says, **"Surely the arm of the Lord is not too short to save, nor his ear too dull to hear."**

Our Father is King of Kings, Lord of Lords, Maker of heaven and earth, and nothing is impossible for Him.

Today ask for a new glimpse of His power, splendour and majesty. As you see His glory, faith will be released and you will say with Job, **"I know that you can do all things."**

Joyce

One Year Plan : Psalm 20, Matthew 20, Genesis 38 - 40
Two Year Plan : Psalm 17:1-5, Matthew 14:22-36, Genesis 20 (Yr 1)
1 Samuel 20 (Yr 2)

David's Daily Checklist

Reading Psalm 101 in the New Living Translation has impacted me in a fresh way. David was setting out his plan of action for the day describing his lifestyle. So here it is, with my added reflections:

I will sing of your love and justice.
I will praise you, Lord, with songs.

I am going to start my day with praise on my lips and a song in my heart.

I will be careful to live a blameless life.
When will you come to my aid?

I am going to seek to live in a way that is pleasing to the Lord; not that I am perfect, but I will repent when I get it wrong. I can't do it without your help, Lord, so I will be asking you to come alongside and help me.

I will lead a life of integrity in my own home.

I know that my home is the place where I need to show my whole family that I can live life with love, compassion and helpfulness.

I will refuse to look at anything vile and vulgar.

I will be careful to watch what I read and what I look at on the television.

I hate all crooked dealings;
I will have nothing to do with them.

I will act honestly in all my business transactions and hand back the change if the shop gives me too much.

I will reject perverse ideas and stay away from evil.

I will not be drawn into wrong action and alliances in my work.

I will not tolerate people who slander their neighbours.
I will not endure conceit and pride.

I am not going to get trapped into gossiping, and I am going to seek to act with grace and humility.

Charles

One Year Plan : Psalm 21, Matthew 21, Genesis 41 - 42
Two Year Plan : Psalm 17:6-15 , Matthew 15:1-20, Genesis 21 (Yr 1)
1 Samuel 21 (Yr 2)

Ask God to be Your Teacher

Take an average twelve-year-old; can you imagine yourself marvelling at their depth of understanding and insight into spiritual subjects? At the age of twelve, Jesus astounded the teachers of Israel with His understanding, His questions and His answers as He sat in the temple courts debating, causing them to ask, **"Who taught Him?"**

Isaiah 50:4 explains that the Sovereign Lord taught Him, opened His ears, and brought revelation by His Spirit. Jesus was no doubt encouraged to obey the command given in Joshua 1:8 to **"meditate on the law of the Lord day and night"** and to be careful to do what was said. This resulted in wisdom that was recognised by scholars and ordinary people as they listened to Him and learned truth expressed in ways they could understand and accept.

It is recorded in John 7:46, **"No one ever spoke the way this man does."**

In the same way the Holy Spirit wants to teach you, bring you revelation and understanding. He uses anointed Bible teachers, but He will also bring understanding as you read the Word on a daily basis.

So, when were you last excited about some **new-to-you** truth from God's Word?

In many places in the world, the Bible is regarded as a priceless treasure, greatly valued and honoured. To own such a wonderful book is to be rich beyond measure. It is not left on a shelf to gather dust but is hungrily devoured like daily bread, copied for others, discussed and shared.

Pick up your Bible today; ask Jesus to be your teacher and give you instruction and understanding.

Joyce

One Year Plan : Psalm 22, Matthew 22, Genesis 43 - 44
Two Year Plan : Psalm 18:1-6, Matthew 15:21-39, Genesis 22 (Yr 1)
1 Samuel 22 (Yr 2)

Certainties

When surrounded by things that may be difficult, situations that seem to be going wrong, it is good to remind ourselves of our certainties.

You are probably familiar with the story of Job. He had lost everything, was suffering badly with health issues, and had friends who were accusing him of sin and placing the blame for his problems firmly on him. In the middle of all these trials and dilemmas, Job declares his certainties: **"I know that my Redeemer lives, and that in the end he will stand upon the earth. And after my skin has been destroyed, yet in my flesh I will see God; I myself will see him with my own eyes – I and not another."** (Job 19:25-27) He did not have to wait until after he died to see God's goodness. At the end of the story, we see Job restored to health, with children and possessions. Job 42:12 says, **"The Lord blessed the latter part of Job's life more than the first."**

When Paul was writing to the church at Philippi, he was imprisoned and under great pressure, and yet he was able to write, **"I know that through your prayers and the help given by the Spirit of Jesus Christ, what has happened to me will turn out for my deliverance."** (Philippians 1:19) Paul expressed great confidence in the prayers of the believers. Let us remain faithful in praying for those in difficult circumstances; God hears and answers.

In the final letter that Paul wrote to Timothy, once again his confidence in God shines through. He speaks of being in great difficulties: **"That is why I am suffering as I am. Yet I am not ashamed, because I know whom I have believed, and am convinced that he is able to guard what I have entrusted to him for that day."** (2 Timothy 1:12)

Keep declaring your certainties; it will strengthen your faith.

Charles

One Year Plan : Psalm 23, Matthew 23, Genesis 45 - 46
Two Year Plan : Psalm 18:7-15, Matthew 16, Genesis 23 (Yr 1)
1 Samuel 23 (Yr 2)

Words Have Power

Words can create or destroy. They are never neutral: they build up or they tear down; they bring hope or instill fear. Our very world was created by the word and command of God (2 Peter 3:5). He spoke and it happened, such was His power and authority. Romans 4:17 declares, **"The God who gives life to the dead and calls things that are not as though they were."**

We hear a lot of negative speech about things in the world around us – like the economy, health worries, and epidemics – but we need to be people who have not allowed those negatives to shape their destiny.

I am looking to see the glory of God manifest in this world – not gloom and doom but a greater revelation of the majesty and power of Jesus and individually an increasing understanding of just who lives in us by His Spirit.

You have God-given authority in your family, workplace and church. Take a few moments and speak into being blessing, protection, and prosperity:

- Blessing on family – **"I will pour out my Spirit on your offspring, and my blessing on your descendants."** (Isaiah 44:3)
- Blessing on your soul – **"I pray that you will enjoy good health and that all may go well with you, even as your soul is getting along well."** (3 John 2)
- Blessing and rejoicing, whatever the circumstances – **"Though the fig tree does not bud and there are no grapes on the vines, though the olive crop fails and the fields produce no food ... yet I will rejoice in the Lord, I will be joyful in God my Saviour."** (Habakkuk 3:17-18)

As a child of the King of Kings, you are part of His reign on earth. Wherever He has placed you, exercise His authority and speak into being the Kingdom of God – **pray it on earth as it is in heaven.**

Joyce

One Year Plan : Psalm 24, Matthew 24, Genesis 47 - 48
Two Year Plan : Psalm 18:16-24, Matthew 17, Genesis 24 (Yr 1)
1 Samuel 24 (Yr 2)

A Restoration Project

I was in my late teens when, at the great cost of £15, I became the proud owner of a 1933 Riley 9 Monaco Saloon. It was a sad sight, it was shabby and neglected. I set about the restoration project with youthful energy. Soon the wire wheels were painted, the aluminium bodywork polished, and the fabric roof renewed. After receiving a new set of pistons, there it was – my pride and joy.

God is in the restoration business and so are we.

Do you remember how you felt when you first met God? The emotions that flowed through you as you first received the love and forgiveness of Jesus? Have those feelings subsided? Has life become wearisome and humdrum? Has sin separated you from fellowship with God? Then you will identify with King David as he cried out to God, **"Restore to me the joy of my salvation."**

In Psalm 23, David declares confidently that the Lord cares for His people like a shepherd cares for his sheep. **"He makes me to lie down in green pastures, he leads me beside still waters, he restores my soul."**

Paul, when writing to the church in Galatia, said, **"If someone is caught in a sin, you who are spiritual should restore him gently."** (Galatians 6:1) When somebody has been caught trying to hide their sin, how do you respond? Would you condemn or restore? Would you destroy or seek to heal?

God can bring the joy back when your relationship with Him has grown dull and boring; He can rescue you from pain and failure. He also wants to lead you out of your busyness and give you new strength and refreshment.

Charles

One Year Plan : Psalm 25, Matthew 25, Genesis 49 – 50
Two Year Plan : Psalm 18:25-36, Matthew 18:1-20, Genesis 25 (Yr 1)
1 Samuel 25 (Yr 2)

The Futility of Going It Alone

Jesus had been teaching the crowd for several days. They had followed Him to the far side of the lake, mainly because He had been healing the sick, and now they were hungry and needed feeding. After the miraculous multiplication of food, the people were intent on making Jesus king, and to avoid this, Jesus withdrew to a mountain while the disciples entered a boat and set off across the lake without Him.

We are probably familiar with this story, but what caught my attention was the behaviour of the disciples, which led me to ask a number of questions. (John 6:16-21)

Why didn't they wait for Jesus? They knew where He was, and yet they proceeded to go ahead of Him. They had been well fed; it wasn't hunger that drove them back across the lake.

Was it independence? Or, were they having to follow their normal routine?

Was it the fear of the unknown – camping in unfamiliar territory?

Was the crowd still demanding healing, more food, more prayer, more anything?

Was it a 'get me out of here' reaction?

Whatever the reason, they chose to go back without Jesus, and the result of that decision could have been disastrous. They found themselves battling against a strong wind and rough sea and not making a lot of progress. Fear was rising; it was dark. Perhaps they questioned why they hadn't waited; perhaps they blamed each other. Whatever was going on, they needed Jesus.

There is no record of them praying, but Jesus was watching them and came to their rescue. Their fear was calmed; He brought supernatural resources to bear upon natural circumstances. He came on board and immediately they reached their destination.

Contrast the toil of rowing three and a half miles against the wind with arriving immediately at your destination when He is in the boat! Don't be tempted to go ahead of Jesus. His timing is always perfect.

Independence is encouraged by the world around us but not in the Kingdom of God. **Why live with human resources when you can have access to heavenly ones?!**

Joyce

One Year Plan : Psalm 26, Matthew 26, Job 1 – 2
Two Year Plan : Psalm 18:37-50, Matthew 18:21-35, Genesis 26 (Yr 1)
1 Samuel 26 (Yr 2)

Waiting

I do not like waiting! If I have an appointment with the doctor or dentist, I like to arrive as my name is called. If I have ordered something on Amazon, I want it to arrive the very next day.

God's timing is different and will be the **right time**; it is more reliable because He will never let us down. Perhaps you are waiting for an answer to prayer or for a vision or prophecy to be fulfilled. I have good news for you. Numbers 23:19 says, **"God is not a man that he should lie, nor a son of man that he should change his mind. Does he speak and then not act? Does he promise and not fulfil?"** Don't let **waiting** undermine your faith.

Perhaps God has placed a vision on your heart and you are wondering how long it is going to take for it to become reality. Habakkuk 2:2-3 says, **"Write down the revelation (vision, prophecy) and make it plain on tablets so that a herald may run with it. For the revelation awaits an appointed time ... though it linger wait for it; it will certainly come and will not delay."**

Some of you are waiting for loved ones to come to living faith in Jesus; be encouraged with these words: **"The Lord is not slow in keeping his promise, as some understand slowness. He is patient with you, not wanting anyone to perish, but everyone to come to repentance."** (2 Peter 3:9)

George Muller prayed for many years for four specific friends to come to know Jesus. Two came through quickly, another after many years and the final one after George had died. However, he never left his position of faith and was like those in Hebrews 11:13. It says there that, **"All these people were still living by faith when they died. They did not receive the things promised; they only saw them and welcomed them from a distance."**

Don't let time and weariness erode your faith. **Keep waiting, keep trusting; God is faithful.**

Charles

One Year Plan : Psalm 27, Matthew 27, Job 3 - 4
Two Year Plan : Psalm 19:1-6, Matthew 19, Genesis 27 (Yr 1)
1 Samuel 27 (Yr 2)

Trusting God under Pressure

How do you trust God when your whole being seems under threat? During the devastating earthquake in Haiti, some of the victims were asked, somewhat cynically, **"Where was God when this happened?" "We can't answer that,"** they replied, **"God is Almighty and does whatever He wants, but we are happy because He protected us. God has a plan for us and He will send help."** Others answered, **"God is with us and is helping us."**

Your circumstances may be very different, but in the midst of pain, frustration and anger, God wants to help you – to be 'in it' with you and lead you on.

King David voiced some of this emotion when he was fleeing from Absalom. His world had fallen apart; God's promises seemed empty words, his own son had betrayed him and was now leading a rebellion, hounding David out of the land God had promised to him as an inheritance.

In Psalm 61 David prays, **"Hear my cry, O God; listen to my prayer ... lead me to the rock that is higher than I ... I long to take refuge in the shelter of your wings."** Later he expresses confidence that God has heard: **"For you have heard my vows, O God; you have given me the heritage of those who fear your name."**

When everything looks black and you feel at rock bottom, there is only one place to go – up – into the arms of the only One who can give perspective and make sense of what appears senseless. **"Lead me to the rock, take hold of me, bring me under the shelter of your wings!"**

Jesus looked over Jerusalem and saw the people were harassed and helpless; He saw the future destruction of that city, and His heart was broken. He cried out, **"O Jerusalem, Jerusalem, how often I have longed to gather your children together, as a hen gathers her chicks under her wings, but you were not willing."** (Matthew 23:37)

Today, however much you are hurting, fearful or disappointed, run to the shelter of the Lord's waiting arms and **find His resources to give you help and hope.**

Joyce

One Year Plan : Psalm 28, Matthew 28, Job 5 - 6
Two Year Plan : Psalm 19:7-14, Matthew 20:1-16, Genesis 28 (Yr 1)
1 Samuel 28 (Yr 2)

Rest on Every Side

King Asa was a good king who commanded his people to seek the Lord, and they testified, **"We have sought the Lord our God, and he has given us rest on every side."** (2 Chronicles 14:7)

The people enjoyed this **rest** because Asa restored the right priorities to his people. They removed the foreign altars and high places and cut down the Asherah poles; worshipping the wrong things makes us rest-less. For these people it was heathen worship; for us it may be the worship of things and being too occupied with our own image or reputation.

When they were under pressure from their enemies, Asa called to the Lord his God and said, **"Lord, there is no one like you to help the powerless against the mighty. Help us, O Lord our God, for we rely on you, and in your name we have come against this vast army."** He was at rest because God was fighting for him. You may be under attack in your work situation or even within your family. **Rest** comes from knowing that God helps the **"powerless against the mighty"**.

We are living at a time of great restlessness and turmoil, and there are many suggested answers and remedies; however, God's answer is the only one that will really work. David wrote in Psalm 62:1, **"My soul finds rest in God alone, my salvation comes from him. He alone is my rock and my salvation; he is my fortress, I will never be shaken."**

Rest is a wonderful gift; it is the result of living with God's agenda and not of trying to resist pressure and the demands of life. In Hebrews 4:9-10 it says, **"There remains, then, a Sabbath-rest for the people of God; for anyone who enters God's rest also rests from his own work."**

Charles

One Year Plan : Psalm 29, Acts 1, Job 7 - 8
Two Year Plan : Psalm 20, Matthew 20:17-34, Genesis 29 (Yr 1)
1 Samuel 29 (Yr 2)

Filled with Glory!

Jesus emptied himself of glory and took on flesh. He wants you to empty yourself of flesh and take on glory!

He emptied himself – left His Father's presence and became a helpless human baby, living a human life, as part of the human family, experiencing everything common to humankind – except sin.

Then at Calvary He became the sin-bearer, received judgement for every criminal act, murder, rape, violence, shame, abuse, cruelty. He took upon himself the sin and sins of the world and received the penalty and punishment that these crimes warrant.

...In my place, condemned he stood,
Sealed my pardon with His blood...

But God raised Him to a new life, a life He wants to give to you and me: glory life, resurrection life; His very own life lived out in many bodies – millions of Jesus's doing what the Father commands, hearing the voice of God's Spirit, being directed as Jesus Himself was by heaven.

"...because those who are led by the Spirit of God are sons of God." (Romans 8:14)

"No eye has seen, no ear has heard, no mind has conceived what God has prepared for those who love him – but God has revealed it to us by his Spirit." (1 Corinthians 2:9-10)

"And we, who with unveiled faces all reflect the Lord's glory, are being transformed into his likeness with ever-increasing glory, which comes from the Lord, who is the Spirit." (2 Corinthians 3:18)

Jesus prayed for you and me that we would see His glory. Paul prayed that our eyes would be opened in order to see the riches we have been given: **"Christ in you, the hope of glory"** (Colossians 1:27).

Today see yourself as a container of **glory,** carrying the living Jesus wherever you go. Less of me – more of Him.

Channels only, blessed Master
But with all Thy wondrous power
Flowing through me,
Thou canst use me
Every day and every hour

Emptied of flesh and self – filled with glory!

Joyce

One Year Plan : Psalm 30, Acts 2, Job 9 - 10
Two Year Plan : Psalm 21, Matthew 21:1-22, Genesis 30 (Yr 1)
1 Samuel 30 (Yr 2)

Do Not Be Deceived!

The problem with deception is that the person who is deceived is the last person to realise it. In my dictionary one of the definitions of the word 'deceive' is: **"To cause to believe what is false, to lead into error, to delude."**

It is plain for us to see how Eve was deceived by the serpent. Because of her pride and independent action, as well as being flattered by the serpent, she failed to consult Adam, and she deliberately disobeyed God. It only took a moment in time for God to expose this trick, and then Eve suddenly saw her folly: **"The serpent deceived me, and I ate."** (Genesis 3:13)

In Galatians 6:7 it says, **"Do not be deceived: God cannot be mocked. A man reaps what he sows."** To believe that there are no consequences to our words and actions is deception. Whatever we sow, we will reap. If you sow unforgiveness you will reap bitterness. If you sow love and kindness you will reap love and acceptance. If you sow anger you will reap retaliation. If you sow generosity you will reap abundance and blessing. The list is endless.

James 1:22 says, **"Do not merely listen to the word, and so deceive yourselves. Do what it says."** And Jesus said, **"You will know the truth, and the truth will set you free."** (John 8:32)

I am amazed that there are so many so-called Christians who seldom read the Bible. Consequently, they can easily be deceived by circumstances that are totally contrary to the Word of God. In the Psalms we read, **"Great peace have they who love your law, and nothing can make them stumble."** (Psalm 119:165); and **"I have hidden you word in my heart that I might not sin against you."** (Psalm 119:11)

Are you deceived because you are living in pride and independence? Are you deceived because you do not think that you will reap what you sow? Are you deceived because the Word is having no impact on your life?

Charles

One Year Plan : Psalm 31, Acts 3, Job 11 – 12
Two Year Plan : Psalm 22:1-8, Matthew 21:23-46, Genesis 31 (Yr 1)
1 Samuel 31 (Yr 2)

FEBRUARY

An Exhilarating Ride

Many years ago I had an extremely clear dream; it involved the choice of reaching a destination by two different ways. The first way was to walk down a railway track, which was very predictable and measured; you had to watch your feet in order to tread on the sleepers and, really, it was a drudge. The second way was full of life and adventure, for in my dream I was invited to climb onto the pillion of a motor bike for a thrilling, scary ride.

The route the rider chose was through a beautiful forest, and he rode confidently and quickly; I simply had to hold on as tight as I could. It was an emotional roller coaster and when we arrived at our destination he asked which I had enjoyed the most – riding the bike or walking the track. I had no doubts; the bike ride was much more exciting – but far less predictable.

The dream was extremely real, and on waking I began to pray about it. Instinctively I knew the choice before me concerned letting Jesus lead my life or taking control myself. I also had no doubt that I wanted to let Jesus lead and choose not only the destination but the route. This was going to be far better than the other option – my way.

His way is always unusual but purposeful, and always involves holding on tight. In my personal experience I've found following Jesus challenging, exciting, scary, but never boring or predictable.

When God was giving life instructions to Joshua he said, **"Don't get off track, either left or right, so as to make sure you get to where you're going. And don't for a minute let this Book of The Revelation be out of your mind. Ponder and meditate on it day and night, make sure you practise everything written in it. Then you'll get where you're going; then you'll succeed. Don't be timid; don't get discouraged. God your God is with you every step you take."** (Joshua 1:7-9, The Message)

Joyce

One Year Plan : Psalm 32, Acts 4, Job 13 - 14
Two Year Plan : Psalm 22:9-18, Matthew 22:1-22, Genesis 32 (Yr 1)
2 Samuel 1 (Yr 2)

Covenant

When you sign a legal document you have to use a special pen which is filled with indelible ink. The reason for this is to prevent the signature being erased or altered. In our imperfect world, even then some covenants and contracts are broken. When God made a covenant with us He did not sign it with indelible ink but with the blood of His Son, and this covenant is permanent and can never be altered.

It is possible to have a contract in our possession and not to benefit from the promises contained therein. It is possible to have received Jesus into our lives and not to be benefitting from our New Covenant blessings.

Through the Covenant we are free from condemnation. Paul writes, **"He forgave us all our sins having cancelled the written code, with its regulations, that was against us and that stood opposed to us; he took it away nailing it to the cross."** So, don't let guilt and past sin weigh you down and rob you of peace. Paul continues, **"And having disarmed the powers and authorities, he made a public spectacle of them, triumphing over them by the cross."** You are assured of victory over every device of the evil one because the devil has already been defeated. (Colossians 2:13-15)

These verses in Hebrews have made a great impact on me: **"May the God of peace, who through the blood of the eternal covenant brought back from the dead our Lord Jesus, that great Shepherd of the sheep, equip you with everything good for doing his will, and may he work in us what is pleasing to him, through Jesus Christ, to whom be glory forever and ever. Amen."** (Hebrews 13:20-21)

The New Covenant gives peace, cleansing, forgiveness, healing, victory over the enemy, equips us to do His will and to live lives that are pleasing to Him.

It's a great covenant; live it, enjoy it, and don't live on a lower level.

Charles

One Year Plan : Psalm 33, Acts 5, Job 15 - 16
Two Year Plan : Psalm 22:19-31, Matthew 22:23-45, Genesis 33 (Yr 1)
2 Samuel 2 (Yr 2)

Taken from the Trash

Can you imagine the helplessness and horror of a nine year-old boy, chained like a dog and abused in so many different ways? Or that of a seven year-old girl, sexually abused to the point of severe physical damage? These are real children in Mongolia – rescued by Christians, housed, fed and being healed. The seven year-old was heard to say, **"I've never been happy before today."**

Only Jesus can heal such wounds and give hope to the helpless, and He is doing just that all over our broken world.

Psalm 113:7 says, **"He raises the poor from the dust and he lifts the needy from the ash heap; he seats them with princes."**

Psalm 9:12 says, **"He does not ignore the cry of the afflicted,"** and in verse 18 we are told, **"The needy will not always be forgotten, nor the hope of the afflicted ever perish."**

Your circumstances may not be as dire as those of the children I have spoken about; but be assured that if you feel you are in a pit, thrown out with the rubbish, forgotten, abused or abandoned, God is not going to forget you. He has heard your cry and is at work to bring deliverance. Take heart; but remember, God uses people like us to be His hands and feet. Keep your eyes open to the pain of those you interact with – you may well be God's servant to bring the deliverance they are silently crying out for!

A young woman I know very well experienced God's help during a painful marriage breakdown, and despite her own pain she reached out to a friend who was very broken and battered. Over the past year this lady too has received total life transformation; there is still a lot to work through, but she knows that she has Jesus, and He makes her radiant and able to point others to her rescuer!

God can lift you up; you can lift up others.

Joyce

One Year Plan : Psalm 34, Acts 6, Job 17 - 18
Two Year Plan : Psalm 23, Matthew 23:1-22, Genesis 34 (Yr 1)
2 Samuel 3 (Yr 2)

You Need a Bucket, not a Water Tap

We had been watching videos of the life of the indigenous people who live in Chad on the edge of the Sahara desert, in a very remote part of the world. We were particularly interested as part of our family were at that time living and working in Chad.

The method of drawing water from wells was amazing. Many of these wells are over a hundred feet deep, and donkeys are used to pull up the bucket from the depths of the ground. It is a daily task which is essential to life.

Here in England we turn on our taps without a thought as to the engineering required to deliver water into our homes. If the system fails, we complain bitterly. It's too easy.

I was thinking of the verse in Isaiah 12:3: **"With joy you will draw water from the wells of salvation."** What picture does it bring to your mind? Perhaps of a charming rural scene with someone gently winding the handle of the well? It all looks so easy.

I believe that the **well of salvation** contains everything we need to live our lives in joy, peace and victory – but it is not a **'turn the tap'** quick fix answer. I believe that we need to let down our bucket into the depths of God's Word, to reach deeply into His love and to stretch our faith muscles; we will then find that God has the resources for our every need.

We live in a fast food world where we want everything instantly and without effort. But the **well of salvation** does not have a tap; it has a bucket.

Today, reach deeply into God's unlimited resources because He has the answer to your need.

Charles

One Year Plan : Psalm 35, Acts 7, Job 19 - 20
Two Year Plan : Psalm 24, Matthew 23:23-39, Genesis 35 (Yr 1)
2 Samuel 4 (Yr 2)

Watch Yourself & Care for Others

It's possible to think that the early Church was free from the problems we experience in the 21st Century. If you want to have a snapshot of the Church during that time, read the book written by Jude, thought to have been the brother of Jesus.

Jude 1:11-13 tells of rebellion, greed, selfishness, false teaching and immorality. As an antidote or precaution Jude tells the believers to:

- **Build yourselves up in your faith.**
- **Pray in the Holy Spirit.**
- **Keep yourselves in the love of God.**

First the instruction is to watch yourself, take care and actively monitor how you are growing in your walk with God, but at the same time Jude tells us:

- **Be merciful to those who doubt.**
- **Snatch others from the fire and save them.**
- **Be aware of the corrupting influence of sin.**

It is possible for us to follow the first instructions but to ignore mercy and rescuing those in danger.

The letter ends with these amazing words: **"God is able to keep you from falling and to present you before his glorious presence without fault and with great joy."** (Jude 1:24)

Give attention to strengthening your own faith, but also pray for those you know are battling with doubt and temptation. What can you do to show mercy? How can you snatch them from danger?

Be practical:

- **Watch over yourself.**
- **Watch out for your brothers and sisters.**
- **Be kind and merciful.**

Read the book of Jude **now;** it will take less than five minutes!

Joyce

One Year Plan : Psalm 36, Acts 8, Job 21 - 22
Two Year Plan : Psalm 25:1-7, Matthew 24:1-29, Genesis 36 (Yr 1)
2 Samuel 5 (Yr 2)

Those Shoes are made for Walking

A friend of mine who is an expert in healthy living told me that twenty minutes of brisk walking twice a day is the very best exercise possible. It is much better than jogging, which jars your bones, and even better than going to the gym (which is just as well as we gave up the gym because we weren't using it enough to justify the expense!)

Enoch was a man who enjoyed walking, and he chose God as his walking companion. It seems that one day they had walked so far that God said to Enoch, **"I think we are nearer to where I live than where you live, so you had better come home with me!"** You can read about it in Genesis 5:21-24.

Life is a journey, and it is important that we make progress every day in our walk of faith. When you walk, your surroundings are constantly changing and you are always getting closer to your destination. Standing still can be very tiresome and tedious. It is important that in our relationship to God we do not stand still.

So how do we take steps along the journey of life? Here are a few ideas. Every day, seek to learn more of God through worshipping Him and reading and meditating on His Word. Talk to Him in prayer and lay specific issues before Him, expecting to receive answers. Reach out in love to someone in need; it may mean making a phone call or sending an e-mail; it might involve going to visit someone in need. Spend some time listening to God's voice and receiving vision for your future.

As you look back on each day, ask yourself, **"What have I done today that has advanced my journey of faith? How has my personal scenery changed? Have I made significant steps towards my goal?"**

Paul put it like this: **"Forgetting what is behind and straining toward what is ahead, I press on toward the goal to win the prize for which God has called me heavenwards in Christ Jesus."** (Philippians 3:13-14)

Charles

One Year Plan : Psalm 37, Acts 9, Job 23 - 24
Two Year Plan : Psalm 25:8-15, Matthew 24:30-51, Genesis 37 (Yr 1)
2 Samuel 6 (Yr 2)

God was With Him

Joseph didn't know how to keep out of trouble. There seems to have been a 'Pollyanna' type of innocence about him – spilling out all that he thought and felt! It might have been wiser to keep his mouth shut or simply ponder the dreams in his heart – but he didn't. His bad reports alienated his brothers, and when he shared his dreams and their interpretations, his father joined with the brothers in rejecting them as 'visions of grandeur'. This ultimately led to Joseph ending up in Egypt, rejected and abandoned – but **"God was with him."**

God had His plans for this dreamer as Potiphar swiftly endowed him with trust and responsibility; however, the pathway to blessing was not without its difficulties. Potiphar's wife tried to seduce him, and he landed in prison – but **"God was with him."** Once again he became a trusted servant, a man of integrity and for the second time he was given massive responsibilities; he was so trusted that no-one felt the need to check on him! Amazing! He is then forgotten by the cupbearer who he was expecting to use his influence to get him released.

Eventually, at the **right time**, he is remembered and called to come before Pharaoh to interpret dreams that are beyond the wisest in Egypt. Joseph simply states that God is the dream giver and God will give the interpretation because **God is with him** – and again he rises to a place of rulership.

We see Joseph as a man of integrity – he is trustworthy, pure and truthful – but these were not natural virtues in themselves; they were part of a life lived walking with God and leaning on Him. Over and over again he declares his success is totally dependent on God, and he constantly acknowledges that without God he would be nothing.

As Christians, we are more blessed than Joseph for Jesus lives, by His Spirit, within us. The more we understand this privilege, the more we know and love Jesus, the more like Him we will become. Just as He received favour during His time on earth from God and man, so will we!

Expect this – live life to the full with love, honesty and integrity as life's foundations – and goodness and mercy will follow you; favour will be yours because **God is with you**.

Joyce

One Year Plan : Psalm 38, Acts 10, Job 25 - 27
Two Year Plan : Psalm 25:16-22, Matthew 25:1-30, Genesis 38 (Yr 1)
2 Samuel 7 (Yr 2)

Joy and Laughter

It had just been announced that Ronnie Barker had died. Many of us had enjoyed his comedy performances over the years in 'The Two Ronnies' and 'Porridge' as well as in many other shows. Why do we enjoy watching comedy? Is it because it is good to laugh, or is it because we want to cover over deep sadness within?

Proverbs 17:22 says, **"A cheerful heart is good medicine, but a crushed spirit dries up the bones."** Laughter has been proven to have beneficial effect upon health. However, the best kind of laughter flows out of joy that is deep within. Happiness is dependent upon happenings, but joy comes from what is going on inside of us.

When we know Jesus and have received His life, there is a deep joy within us that cannot be undermined by circumstances.

Jesus spoke these words to His disciples shortly before He went to the cross: **"Now is your time of grief, but I will see you again and you will rejoice, and no one will take away your joy."** (John 16:22)

Peter wrote, **"Though you have not seen him [Jesus] you love him; and even though you do not see him now, you believe in him and are filled with an inexpressible and glorious joy, for you are receiving the goal of your faith, the salvation of your souls."** (1 Peter 1:8)

Nehemiah, when he sent the people back to their homes, gave them these words of encouragement: **"The joy of the Lord is your strength."** (Nehemiah 8:10)

What is the source of your joy?

Charles

One Year Plan : Psalm 39, Acts 11, Job 28 - 29
Two Year Plan : Psalm 26, Matthew 25:31-46, Genesis 39 (Yr 1)
2 Samuel 8 (Yr 2)

Do You Need to Be Circumcised?

I am not talking about the cut of a foreskin but the cut that consecrates our hearts, our ears and our lips.

When Stephen was addressing the Sanhedrin, who would soon put him to death, he said, **"You stiff-necked people with uncircumcised hearts and ears!"** (Acts 7:51)

When God is speaking to Jeremiah, He says, **"To whom can I speak and give warning? Who will listen to me? Their ears are closed [un-circumcised] so that they cannot hear."** (Jeremiah 6:10)

When Moses is being challenged by God to go and confront Pharaoh and liberate the Hebrew nation, he says, **"Why would Pharaoh listen to me, since I speak with faltering [uncircumcised] lips?"** (Exodus 6:12)

There are several occasions where Moses and Jeremiah describe the Israelites as having hearts that are calloused and uncircumcised. Jeremiah 4:4 records words from the Lord: **"Circumcise yourselves to the Lord, circumcise your hearts you men of Judah and people of Jerusalem."**

God is calling for lips consecrated afresh to Him; lips that speak truth and are instruments that He can use – purified, touched by fire. He wants hearts that are soft, vulnerable and responsive. Jesus' disciples could not understand the miracle of the feeding of the five thousand because their hearts were hardened.

We will not hear clearly when our ears are closed; we literally become sense-less. It is time to ask Jesus to circumcise us again, to sensitise us and make us tender, able to feel, able to hear, able to speak, with God's compassion and authority, showing that we are, **"a chosen people, a royal priesthood, a royal nation, a people belonging to God, that you may declare the praises of him who called you out of darkness into his wonderful light."** (1 Peter 2:9)

Joyce

One Year Plan : Psalm 40, Acts 12, Job 30 - 31
Two Year Plan : Psalm 27:1-6, Matthew 26:1-30, Genesis 40 (Yr 1)
2 Samuel 9 (Yr 2)

How Much Thanksgiving is in your Life?

"How much thanksgiving is there in your life?" was the question asked in a book containing the following testimony.

The author was sitting in a church in Africa. It was hot and stuffy, the bench he was sitting upon was hard, and the service was lasting forever! Then, an African lady came to the front of the church and said, **"For the past three months I have been asking God to provide me with a pair of shoes, and this week He has."** The shoes were waved in front of the eager and rejoicing people; but the author of the book was sitting there deeply ashamed. He thought, **"I've never prayed for a pair of shoes – I just bought them when needed – and I have never thanked God for them either."**

Romans 1:21 states, **"For although they knew God, they neither glorified him as God nor gave thanks to him, but their thinking became futile and their foolish hearts were darkened."** This indicates that thanksgiving and glorifying God prevents my thinking from becoming futile and my heart being darkened. A lack of thankfulness will lock me into the mistakes and failures of my past and stop me seeing the future God is preparing for me.

Psalm 50:23 says, **"He who sacrifices thank-offerings honours me, and he prepares the way so that I may show him the salvation of God."**

I have found this to be a very salutary reminder to check my thanksgiving levels. Do I greet each day with a heart overflowing with thankfulness to a God, who cares, gives me strength, and who provides for my every need, or do I get up each day with moaning, complaining and heaviness?

The psalmist says, **"Enter his gates with thanksgiving and his courts with praise; give thanks to him and praise his name. For the Lord is good and his love endures forever; his faithfulness continues through all generations."** (Psalm 100:4-5)

Charles

One Year Plan : Psalm 41, Acts 13, Job 32 - 33
Two Year Plan : Psalm 27:7-14, Matthew 26:31-56, Genesis 41 (Yr 1)
2 Samuel 10 (Yr 2)

Have you Cursed Yourself?

Peter not only denied Jesus but **"he called down curses upon himself"** (Matthew 26:74). Even as he was speaking, he heard the cock crow, remembered Jesus' warning and prediction, and found himself weeping bitterly. Imagine the self-hatred, condemnation, loss, shame, and isolation he undoubtedly experienced. Add to this a curse, carrying with it a demonic dimension of despair, death and destruction.

This threw Peter into a state of merely functioning, of scarcely feeling alive, cut off from his life source in Jesus. He was only going through the motions; he was physically present at the crucifixion and at the empty tomb but inside experiencing a hell of turmoil, anguish and agony.

It is in the middle of this crisis that Jesus reveals Himself to Peter on Easter Sunday, even before he had walked the road to Emmaus. We know nothing of the context, only that he appears to Peter alone (1 Corinthians 15:5). Jesus knows everything that has happened, everything that has been said. He knows all the pain in Peter's heart but comes to him offering Himself, His love, His forgiveness, His friendship, His restoration and the potential of wholeness. Is Peter able to receive all that is proffered?

Jesus met Peter a number of times in the group, but He wanted to make sure Peter had escaped the curse. On the beach, over breakfast, He asks not once but three times, **"Do you love me?"** We are able to love only because we have received love. Peter is still aware of the wounds in his heart. Will he let go of the pain and failure and look forward?

We know Peter was healed because many years later he was able to write these words: **"And the God of all grace, who called you to his eternal glory in Christ, after you have suffered a little while, will himself restore you and make you strong, firm and steadfast."** (1 Peter 5:10)

If you have failed, cursed yourself, distanced yourself from Jesus – for whatever reason – ask Him to come to forgive, heal, restore and break every curse.

Joyce

One Year Plan : Psalm 42, Acts 14, Job 34 - 35
Two Year Plan : Psalm 28, Matthew 26:57-75, Genesis 42 (Yr 1)
2 Samuel 11 (Yr 2)

A Prison of the Past

I am always saddened when I meet people who have become trapped by hurtful experiences from their past. One of the greatest benefits of our Christian faith is the knowledge that the past can be forgiven and healed and we can have hope for the future.

The most common reason you become a prisoner of your past is unforgiveness. If someone hurts you, mistreats you, or betrays you, and you cannot forgive or release them from your anger and bitterness, your resentment does not necessarily harm them but it most certainly can damage you.

If you have made a severe error of judgement in your past (something you expected to bring fulfilment and joy but which turned sour and you cannot forgive yourself) you ask yourself what might have happened if you had made a different decision. That question becomes your prison cell.

Were you overlooked when you thought you ought to have been promoted in your work? Were you rejected by someone you loved? Have your children grown up, walked out of your life, and lost contact with you? Such things cause unbearable pain.

Jesus said, **"The thief comes only to steal and kill and destroy, I have come that they might have life, and have it to the full."** (John 10:10)

Ephesians 4:32 says, **"Be kind and compassionate to one another, forgiving each other [including yourself], just as God in Christ forgave you."**

There is a way out of the prison cell through forgiveness, drawing a line on the past, and allowing the victory of Jesus on the cross and His power and love to give you a new beginning.

Unforgiveness is like a deep-seated thorn that keeps tormenting you. Remove it today.

Charles

One Year Plan : Psalm 43, Acts 15, Job 36 - 37
Two Year Plan : Psalm 29, Matthew 27:1-31, Genesis 43 (Yr 1)
2 Samuel 12 (Yr 2)

Believe the Promise

In Isaiah Chapter 11 a prophetic picture of the Messiah is given, fulfilled hundreds of years later in Jesus. Verse 3 states, **"He will not judge by what he sees with his eyes, or decide by what he hears with his ears."** Jesus confirms this in John 12:49-50, where He explains that His words and actions are defined by what He has seen and heard from heaven.

As I read through the Old Testament, I have been impacted by the many times prophets spoke to their nations and people, telling them what they had heard from heaven. God's words through them were life-giving, circumstance-changing, and counteracting voices of unbelief, rational thinking and cynicism; when God speaks He will always have the last word.

When Israel had been besieged by the King of Aram, famine was rampant and the people and rulers were at their wits' end. Then God spoke through Elisha: **"The famine is over."** Few, if any, believed him. One of the King's advisors voiced the unbelief: **"You expect us to believe that? Trapdoors opening in the sky and food tumbling out?"** Elisha's reply was, **"You will watch it with your own eyes, but you will not eat so much as a mouthful!"** (2 Kings 7:2, The Message)

God is speaking through many prophets about visiting the UK with a fresh outpouring of His Spirit, His mercy and His healing power. He has said He has not forgotten Great Britain. Do you believe God can visit us with revival and satisfy the hungry, hurting hearts with His love and mercy? Or, do you refuse to listen and choose rather to dwell on the downward spiral we are seeing in all areas of national life?

I choose to be a believer, to expect God's help, to thank Him that we still live in the day of His mercy, that we not only need His help but believe He has promised to respond to prayer and help us.

Pray today for God to fulfil His word and pour out His Holy Spirit on this dry and thirsty land.

Joyce

One Year Plan : Psalm 44, Acts 16, Job 38 - 39
Two Year Plan : Psalm 30, Matthew 27:32-66, Genesis 44 (Yr 1)
2 Samuel 13 (Yr 2)

Who do you think you are?

The television series **'Who do you think you are?'** makes compelling viewing for those who find fascination in seeing a famous person discover their ancestry. There is great joy in discovering wonderful people in the past and tears as tragedy and shame are uncovered.

As I began reading Matthew's Gospel, I was tempted to skip the genealogies, but then began to notice the **skeletons in the cupboard** of Jesus' ancestry. In most genealogies it only mentions the men but here five mothers are included. In every case, except for Mary's, a dark secret is uncovered.

- Judah fathered Perez by Tamar his daughter-in-law – a forbidden relationship!
- Rahab, the prostitute from Jericho, is the mother of Boaz.
- Obed's mother is Ruth, who was a Moabitess, not one of the children of Israel.
- The birth of Solomon to David and Bathsheba is surrounded by both adultery and murder!

Why has all this been recorded in scripture? I believe it demonstrates that God is a gracious and merciful God. The devil wants to hold believers captive because of the sins of the past, but God wants you to live in freedom. There are many people whose lives have been blighted because of sin and shame in their past lives.

In 1 Corinthians 6:9-11 there is a list of those whose past would seem to bar them from God's blessing; the list includes the sexually immoral, adulterers, and male prostitutes. Paul then speaks of the power of the redeeming grace of God and continues, **"But you were washed, you were sanctified, you were justified in the name of the Lord Jesus Christ and by the Spirit of God."**

In Colossians 1:21-22, Paul again describes the amazing grace of God as he says, **"Once you were alienated from God ... but now he has reconciled you ... to present you holy in his sight, without blemish and free from accusation."**

Who are you then? If you are a believer in Jesus, you are not a captive to your past **but chosen by God, forgiven, made righteous and in a family line of peace and blessing.**

Charles

One Year Plan : Psalm 45, Acts 17, Job 40 - 42
Two Year Plan : Psalm 31:1-8, Matthew 28, Genesis 45 (Yr 1)
2 Samuel 14 (Yr 2)

What is Your Jesus Like?

Recently I heard of a man who described himself as a **reluctant atheist**. He longed to know a God who is real, personal, relevant and tangible – but he could not believe that such a person could exist.

During the Second World War, when working as a military chaplain, David Pawson was assigned to those who were non-conformists, atheists or agnostics. Before active combat he had to interview each man to ascertain his funeral arrangements were in place, should he die on the battlefield. Many of the atheists declared that they did not believe in God or an afterlife. **"If that is the case, at your burial there will be no service, no prayers, no mention of God; you will simply be placed into the grave,"** were David's words to these men. On many occasions this caused a certain amount of distress and second thoughts.

David would then ask them, **"Tell me about the God you do not believe in."** Many would speak in anger of a cruel, unjust, unloving God – such a distorted and un-biblical picture. David's response was, **"I don't believe in a God like that either."** He would then tell them about Jesus, after which many changed their whole attitude and put their faith in Him.

In Mark 5, we read about the man possessed by demons who caused him to be violent and a danger to himself and those around him. He needed a power encounter with someone stronger than the evil that was destroying him. He lived in the hills, isolated and in great need. What drew him to Jesus? Did he see the little boat battered by the waves and the unexpected calm when Jesus rebuked the wind? Something caused him to want to meet Jesus as He came ashore; he ran to meet him and to get closer. **His meeting with Jesus changed his life** – the mighty Son of God, the All-Powerful One, sent the demons packing and restored him to his right mind. Peace instead of torment.

Let Jesus demonstrate His love and power through you today.

Joyce

One Year Plan :	Psalm 46, Acts 18, Exodus 1 - 2
Two Year Plan :	Psalm 31:9-18, Acts 1, Genesis 46 (Yr 1)
	2 Samuel 15 (Yr 2)

Who is in your Heart?

I was reading in Paul's second letter to the Corinthians and the phrase **"Make room for us in your hearts"** jumped off the page and set me thinking. Who is in my heart and what does it mean? I know that my wife and family are strongly in my heart, but who else? Why is it important?

In Philippians 1:4-7, Paul speaks of his heart for the believers in Philippi: **"In all my prayers for all of you, I always pray with joy ... being confident of this, that he who began a good work in you will carry it on to completion ... it is right for me to feel this way about all of you, since I have you in my heart."**

When someone is in our heart they will be in our prayers; we don't have to have their names written on a prayer list. We always know where our family and children are because they are in our hearts. We spontaneously pray for those in our hearts because we love them and will always pray with joy and faith.

Paul spoke of persistence in his praying: **"...being confident of this, that he who began a good work in you will carry it on to completion."** When someone is in our heart, we do not give up praying for them when things are tough or even if they seem to have distanced themselves from us.

God loves us, is for us, values His place in our heart and wants to answer our prayers. The people in our heart are those we love, whom we value and for whom we pray, expecting that God will bless and help.

When someone slips from our heart, we lose touch, we stop praying and we don't exercise our faith on their behalf. Look at who is in your heart today; if someone has slipped out, draw them back in, renew your love for them and include them in your prayers.

Charles

One Year Plan : Psalm 47, Acts 19, Exodus 3 - 4
Two Year Plan : Psalm 31:19-24, Acts 2:1-21, Genesis 47 (Yr 1)
2 Samuel 16 (Yr 2)

Underprivileged?

I once met a man who lived the life of a tramp – no home, no bed to sleep in. In extreme weather conditions he sought shelter in a derelict building, which is where I first met him. Dirty, lonely, living in an internal world cut off from humankind. After his death, I learned that he had been a man of wealth. Life had battered him, causing him to choose an existence of isolation and poverty; it seemed meaningless, sad and unnecessary. He had abundant resources but chose not to use them.

Judges 11:24 says, **"...whatever the Lord our God has given us, we will possess."** The context was this: God had helped Israel drive out her enemies, and now, former heathen kings of the territory were demanding the return of the land! Jephthah who was leading Israel replied, **"Will you not take what your god Chemosh gives you?"**

As I pondered this I felt a new desire to live in all that Jesus has purchased for me. Many live in sickness when He has purchased health, or defeat when He personally paid the price for victory over every work of the devil. Why settle for less than God's best? Why live like a pauper when heaven's riches and resources have been made available? God has promised rest – why live without it? He has given us everything we need for life and godliness: wisdom, understanding, faith and so much more.

In Romans 8:32 it says, **"He who did not spare his own Son, but gave him up for us all – how will he not also, along with him, graciously give us all things?"** which is expressed in 'The Truth' like this: **"So intent is He on seeing His plans fulfilled, He did not protect His Son from the cost of giving His life for us all, because through His grace He wanted to give us everything that belongs to Christ!"**

Today, possess your inheritance!

Joyce

One Year Plan : Psalm 48, Acts 20, Exodus 5 - 6
Two Year Plan : Psalm 32, Acts 2:22-47, Genesis 48 (Yr 1)
2 Samuel 17 (Yr 2)

Find Rest

In a busy world, getting the right amount of rest is often a real challenge. We wake up feeling the night has been too short; we take a break because our stress levels are going off the scale. However, when we've had our extra hour or two in bed, or a couple of days' break from our job, we realise they have failed to give us the rest we crave.

In Psalm 62:1 David declares, **"My soul finds rest in God alone."** So what has he found? He begins by speaking about **"my soul"** which is made up of intellect, emotions and will. He understands that to merely rest his body is not enough; there are deeper needs.

Jesus has the same message in Matthew 11:28: **"Come to me, all of you who are weary and carry heavy burdens, and I will give you rest."** Jesus is not speaking about physical burdens but the things that dominate our minds and emotions.

So when fatigue comes from the confusion and fear surrounding us, and it drains us of energy and causes us to imagine scenarios of disaster, we need to hear words from God that assure us of His presence and wisdom. Jesus often needed to speak peace to His disciples.

When our emotions are in turmoil, we need to be confident that God loves us, values us and wants the very best for us. When children are disturbed, often a mother will simply sing over them. God does that for us; Zephaniah 3:17 says, **"He will take great delight in you, he will quiet you with his love, he will rejoice over you with singing."** Let God be the one who heals your emotions as He sings over you; listen for those songs of love.

When our minds and emotions are in turmoil, we find it hard to do what is right; our decision-making is in chaos. Romans 12:2 says, **"Be transformed by the renewing of your mind. Then you will be able to know his good, pleasing and perfect will."**

There is nothing wrong with some extra sleep or a free day, but learn David's secret: **"My soul finds rest in God alone."**

Charles

One Year Plan : Psalm 49, Acts 21, Exodus 7 - 8
Two Year Plan : Psalm 33:1-11, Acts 3, Genesis 49 (Yr 1)
2 Samuel 18 (Yr 2)

Empty or Full?

Many years ago I saw a children's talk given in the open air. A container was held up, and from a jug, water was poured in until it overflowed. The question was asked, **"Is it full?"** Lots of little voices shouted, **"Yes!"** The presenter then put his fingers in the container and pulled out a stone with a label on it – 'Anger'. He threw the stone away and again asked the question, **"Is it full?"** Answer: **"No!"** So he poured more water into the container and the process continued with various sized stones labelled 'lies', 'hate', 'complaining', 'jealousy', 'criticism', and more. The more junk was thrown out, the more water could be poured in.

We need to keep our hearts empty of self and flesh and constantly filled up with Jesus and His Holy Spirit. Paul knew this way of life; he writes, **"I die daily, I go back to Calvary and see my old nature being nailed to the cross and I identify with the death of Jesus, I reckon myself dead to sin and I receive the resurrection life of Jesus and let Him live in my body by His Spirit."**

When this happens, His character will flow out: His love, His peace, His joy, His power. For too long we have been trying and failing to be like Jesus, trying to imitate His example. We can't do it and were never intended to.

The gospel that Paul preached said, **"You die and He will live the new life in you."** The early apostles preached Jesus and the resurrection – death preceding new life. They believed they needed to be born again, and they were – many Jesus's living in different shapes, sizes and genders – containers for Him to use to do His work through. **"Not I, but Christ."**

How empty are you? How full?

Joyce

One Year Plan : Psalm 50, Acts 22, Exodus 9 - 10
Two Year Plan : Psalm 33:12-22, Acts 4:1-22, Genesis 50 (Yr 1)
2 Samuel 19 (Yr 2)

Time Planner or Christ?

We all seem to be short of time. Being **stressed out** is a phrase we hear constantly. Why are we all under such pressure and unable to achieve what we want or to have adequate space and rest? Could it be because the wrong person is planning our programme?

Paul said, **"I have been crucified with Christ, and I no longer live, but Christ lives in me."** (Galatians 2:20) If we truly believe those words and have chosen to live by them, we will hand over the sovereignty of our lives to Christ!

You may say, **"My life is outside of my control."** But that is not true. We all have 168 hours per week; if we spend 56 hours sleeping, and 40 hours at our daily work, that still leaves 72 hours we can choose to use in whichever way we want. If you travel an hour each way to your work, that only uses another ten hours, so now you have 62 hours to spend as you like!

Now if **"Christ lives in me"**, why not consult Him about your use of time, on how to plan your programme? Paul did it. The Holy Spirit stopped him from going to the province of Asia but directed him to respond to the call to Macedonia. (Acts 16:6-10)

In Hebrews 4:9-10 it says, **"There remains, then, a Sabbath-rest for the people of God; for anyone who enters God's rest also rests from his own work, just as God did from his."**

When we stop planning our own programme or being pressurised by others, we can choose to ask Jesus to show us how to live our lives according to His plan.

Matthew 11:28-29 in the Message is fantastic: **"Are you tired? Worn out? Burned out on religion? Come to me. Get away with me and you'll recover your life. I'll show you how to take a real rest. Walk with me and work with me—watch how I do it. Learn the unforced rhythms of grace. I won't lay anything heavy or ill-fitting on you. Keep company with me and you'll learn to live freely and lightly."**

Charles

One Year Plan : Psalm 51, Acts 23, Exodus 11 - 12
Two Year Plan : Psalm 34:1-7, Acts 4:23-37, Job 1 (Yr 1)
2 Samuel 20 (Yr 2)

No Looking Back

Don't be tempted to look back! Remember what happened to Lot's wife; she was being rescued out of an appalling situation and commanded to keep moving forward, but she looked back and was literally turned into a pillar of salt!

Your situation may not be so extreme, but regrets, condemnation, and self–flagellation are of no value. If we fail to live up to our own expectations, recrimination will leave us immobile and lifeless.

Paul had his own past to deal with: he had been deceived; he had persecuted the emerging Church; and he had imprisoned and tortured disciples of Jesus. But after his encounter with Jesus on the road to Damascus, he knew with certainty that he had been forgiven, had received God's mercy and grace, and so he refused to look back. As he said in his own words, **"But one thing I do: Forgetting what is behind and straining toward what is ahead, I press on..."** (Philippians 3:13-14). Paul's deception and rebellion was not punished – he was simply charged with a new commission: to go to the people God sent him to and **"...open their eyes and turn them from darkness to light"**. (Acts 26:18)

Can you imagine the internal, mental struggle that Peter faced? He had denied Jesus, he had failed himself and sought refuge in the world of hard work – back to fishing; you can't be self-occupied hauling heavy nets. When he meets Jesus on the shore, there are no recriminations or analysing of past failure – rather Jesus points to the future. Self-reliance has ended, self-effort has failed, but reliance on Jesus will lead him into all that God has in mind for him.

Don't get stuck; God knew all about Peter's failure before it happened and He knows about you. His great desire is to forgive, restore, re-empower and re-direct you. In your weakness He wants you to experience His strength. **You need to forgive yourself for the failings of the past, choose to forget what is behind and strain towards what lies ahead.**

Joyce

One Year Plan : Psalm 52, Acts 24, Exodus 13 - 14
Two Year Plan : Psalm 34:8-14, Acts 5:1-16, Job 2 (Yr 1)
2 Samuel 21 (Yr 2)

The Hand of God

The phrase **'The Hand of God'** has become universally famous because of the actions of the footballer Diego Maradona whose hand ended England's chances of victory in a World Cup football match some years ago.

However, God's hand in reality is doing much more profound and wonderful things every day for those who love and trust Him. In Psalm 37:23-24 it says, **"If the Lord delights in a man's way, he makes his steps firm; though he stumble, he will not fall, for the Lord upholds him with his hand."**

When Ezra was on his way to Jerusalem to support his own people, it says in Ezra 7:8-9, **"...he arrived in Jerusalem on the first day of the fifth month, for the gracious hand of his God was on him."**

When Nehemiah went back to rebuild the walls of Jerusalem, he declared, **"I also told them about the gracious hand of my God upon me and what the king had said to me."** (Nehemiah 2:18)

Hands are a wonderful part of our bodies. We shake hands to express friendship and support. We silently hold hands to show love and unity. We use our hands to stroke the face of a child who is upset. We reach out our hand when someone near is about to stumble. We lift our hands to express our worship to God.

God's hands are always being used creatively for our good. David expressed this powerfully in Psalm 63:7-8: **"Because you are my help, I sing in the shadow of your wings. My soul clings to you; your right hand upholds me."**

Use your hands to encourage and support those around you – because God's hand is always at the ready to help you.

Charles

One Year Plan : Psalm 53, Acts 25, Exodus 15 - 16
Two Year Plan : Psalm 34:15-22, Acts 5:17-42, Job 3 (Yr 1)
2 Samuel 22 (Yr 2)

The Witness of Peace

Some years ago two people were travelling by train from West Cornwall to Plymouth. It was in the days of compartments, and conversations between strangers seemed to happen naturally.

One was a lady, Ruth, who explained she had an appointment in the hospital as she was having radiotherapy to treat cancer. Her fellow passenger, a man, wept as he listened and then told of his daughter who was also being treated for the same condition. **"But you seem so full of peace,"** he said, **"and I'm so afraid!"**

Ruth then spent the journey telling him about Jesus and how He was with her and the source of her strength. The man was a specialist in the treatment of dry-rot and 'happened' to be the consultant we had engaged to help attack a huge dry-rot problem in the house where we lived in Truro. As they conversed it came to light that he was working with us and that Ruth was our friend, and as the train passed through Truro he said, **"They have an enormous problem, but they also have what you have – peace – radiance – what is it?"**

The next time we saw him he recounted his meeting with Ruth on the train and commented again on the peace that was so visible in our friend. We again were able to tell him about the source and encourage him to meet Jesus personally.

Peace is a supernatural gift. It is beyond understanding; it comes with the presence of the Prince of Peace. If you are a believer in Jesus, you will have it.

In troubled times, with economic pressure and much fear around, your peace can be like a beacon of light causing people to ask, **"Why are you so peaceful?"** Take the opportunities that present themselves. The world around us is desperate to find **peace** and marvel when they see the real thing – not in the absence of trouble but in the midst of it.

Psalm 34:5 says, **"Those who look to him are radiant; their faces are never covered with shame."**

Joyce

One Year Plan : Psalm 54, Acts 26, Exodus 17 – 18
Two Year Plan : Psalm 35:1-10, Acts 6, Job 4 (Yr 1)
2 Samuel 23 (Yr 2)

Rejoice in Everything

In earlier times, God chose a place where His people were to worship; it was first a tent in the desert and later a temple in Jerusalem. The place is of minor importance, but what they were to do is of greater significance; these were the instructions: **"There, in the presence of the Lord your God, you and your families shall eat and rejoice in everything you have put your hand to, because the Lord your God has blessed you."** (Deuteronomy 12:7)

Every day I have the privilege to go into the presence of the Lord. I don't have to go to a special place or on a special day; God will meet with me where I am.

Each day, as I eat my food I am to rejoice because as the psalmist says, **"I have never seen the righteous forsaken, or their children begging bread."** (Psalm 37:25) We have never been without food, neither have our children lacked provision. We have been tested, but God has proved Himself utterly faithful.

As I think of my family, I am to rejoice because God has blessed me with children and grandchildren. Many years ago I had a cancer scare and was alone in Sweden battling with the symptoms and my fears, when God said to me, **"You will live to see your children's children."** (Psalm 128:6) God healed me and fulfilled His word.

As I do my daily work I am to rejoice because the Lord has blessed me. I rejoice in my work and enjoy everything I am doing. Many years ago in my younger days, if I was showing any lethargy in my work, my father would chide me, quoting Ecclesiastes 9:10: **"Whatever you hand finds to do, do it with all your might."** His words worked, and I am glad to say that I have learned to...

Rejoice in everything!

Charles

One Year Plan : Psalm 55, Acts 27, Exodus 19 - 20
Two Year Plan : Psalm 35:11-18, Acts 7:1-29, Job 5 (Yr 1)
2 Samuel 24 (Yr 2)

Are you having a Sabbath?

What is your reaction to the word **'Sabbath'**? Does it have overtones of legalism and restrictive behaviour? Does it stir negatives inside you rather than rejoicing?

Lack of Sabbath is a serious problem in today's world. One time at Spring Harvest, 55% of those when asked, **"What issues have you struggled with that have affected your personal spiritual life?"** replied, **"Fatigue!"** We desperately need Sabbath the way God intended it to be.

Some years ago, God began to show me that it was to be a day of rest in a different way – not a day to do nothing but a day to be restored, recharged, to escape from the routine of work and school; a day to reflect, to give thanks for the previous week and to prepare for the next.

My mind needed renewing in relation to Sunday and how to spend the time – to see it as God's gift; a different day, a day to spend quality time with God, family and friends.

Colossians 2:16 says, **"Therefore do not let anyone judge you by what you eat or drink or with regard to ... a Sabbath day."** Check out your attitude to Sabbath. Is it a God-given time to rest as God Himself intended? Do you value it? Do you fill it with things you haven't accomplished on the other six days?

Or, do you refresh yourself in the Lord's presence? Do you gather with believers to worship and to meet with God?

There is deep refreshing in the presence of God. Don't neglect giving time to worship and wonder, to pray and meet with other believers. People have told me they are too busy to gather with other believers in church, and my response is, **"You are too busy and need to think again about God's gift – a day of rest."**

Joyce

One Year Plan : Psalm 56, Acts 28, Exodus 21 - 22
Two Year Plan : Psalm 35:19-28, Acts 7:30-60, Job 6 (Yr 1)
Ecclesiastes 1 (Yr 2)

A Culture of Thanksgiving

As I read these words, **"I will sacrifice a thank offering to you and call upon the name of the Lord,"** (Psalm 116:17) it prompted me to look into the whole culture of thanksgiving that runs through the Bible.

In Leviticus, among the various offerings and sacrifices that were required, there was the Fellowship Offering, which was in essence a Thank Offering. Leviticus 7:12 says, **"...he offers it as an expression of thanksgiving..."** – he is then instructed as to how to make this offering.

In Psalm 50:23 the psalmist writes, **"He who sacrifices thank offerings honours me, and he prepares the way so that I may show him the salvation of God."**

Paul instructs the believers in Philippi, **"...in everything by prayer and petition, with thanksgiving, present your requests to God."** (Philippians 4:6)

Our world economics are in a mess; the word **'recession'** is constantly dominating the media, and tales of gloom abound. What are we to do? We need to be thankful because we are blessed. We in the western world are rich, and even if the recession bites hard, we will still be better off than we were ten years ago!

We must not allow a **culture of complaining** to get hold of us, nor allow **a spirit of fear** to invade our lives. We must not stop **giving and blessing others**. If we succumb to these things we will suffer and be diminished.

Thanksgiving opens the way for God to bless us. Thanksgiving makes us grateful for the small things in life. If we have food on our table and a roof over our heads we are blessed.

My son Craig, who lives in Bulgaria, once told me that some of his Jutvari Gypsy football team had come to training sessions and matches having eaten nothing all day – because they had no food!

So eliminate all complaining, fear, and misery from your speaking and **build a culture of thanksgiving – you will never regret it!**

Charles

One Year Plan : Psalm 57, Mark 1, Exodus 23 – 24
Two Year Plan : Psalm 36, Acts 8:1-25, Job 7 (Yr 1)
Ecclesiastes 2 (Yr 2)

Receiving Mercy and Grace

I had come back from Nigeria to a very busy Christmas time. We drove home from Heathrow; our Bulgarian family had arrived before us and were already in the house. It was exciting to be together as another son and daughter-in-law welcomed us with a wonderful meal. I was up early the next day to shop for food, as we had a vast crowd to feed over the coming two weeks. Our daughter was also celebrating her fortieth birthday, and we were thrilled to have all our children and their families together for the first time in ten years.

At all times the house was full of hungry, noisy adults and children. The needs ranged from those of a two-week-old baby to a ninety-seven-year-old granny. Most days we received extra visitors who had come to visit our family! I will leave you to imagine the endless cups of tea, etc.

Whilst in Nigeria we heard a very important teaching on receiving mercy for specific tasks. Not mercy for forgiveness of sins but **"...to receive mercy and find grace to help us in our time of need."** (Hebrews 4:16)

Each day I came to my Father's throne and asked for mercy for the demands ahead when so much of the responsibility would be on my shoulders – and He gave it, along with peace, amazing strength, joy and relaxation.

As our last family members left for the airport and I tackled the washing and re-ordering of our home, I praised God for the supernatural resources of these past weeks. Mercy had been asked for and received.

So come boldly to the throne of grace – asking for specific **mercy** for what you are facing right now. Stop what you are doing or planning; ask for mercy in order to receive grace to find help in your time of need.

Joyce

One Year Plan : Psalm 58, Mark 2, Exodus 25 - 26
Two Year Plan : Psalm 37:1-9, Acts 8:26-40, Job 8 (Yr 1)
Ecclesiastes 3 (Yr 2)

Living at the Cross

In a book written by Andrew Murray, he states that the mark of those who live at the cross of Jesus is: humility, helplessness and rest.

You may ask, **"How can I live at the cross?"** Jesus said, **"If anyone would come after me, he must deny himself and take up his cross daily and follow me."** (Luke 9:23). The cross is not merely an historic site where Jesus died to save us and to enable us to become children of God, it is a place where we can encounter God every day.

Jesus modelled humility as He lived His life on earth; consequently we also need to follow His example daily in our lives because **"God opposes the proud but gives grace to the humble"**. (1 Peter 5:5)

We find it difficult to see ourselves as **helpless** because we are always trying to improve our performance and boost our self-image; however, on the night before Jesus was crucified, He spoke to His disciples and said, **"Apart from me you can do nothing."** (John 15:5). God is not looking for people who will work **for Him** but for those through whom **He can work**.

The third quality that is required for those who live at the cross is **rest**. No one would deny that we are living in a very stressful and restless world, and yet the writer to the Hebrews declares, **"There remains, then, a Sabbath-rest for the people of God; for anyone who enters God's rest also rests from his own work, just as God did from his."** (Hebrews 4:9-10)

The challenge for us is this: **are we living, humble, helpless and restful lives where our self-life is diminishing and the life of Jesus is increasing?**

Christ wants to live His joyful, peaceful, victorious life through you. Will you let Him?

Charles

One Year Plan : Psalm 59, Mark 3, Exodus 27 - 28
Two Year Plan : Psalm 37:10-20, Acts 9:1-19, Job 9 (Yr 1)
Ecclesiastes 4 (Yr 2)

MARCH

Picking Fruit

In the book of Hosea, God is speaking through the prophet to a nation who has turned their back on Him. They have made and worshipped idols which have no ability to help them. However, God is still reaching out to them, to heal them, to love them freely and to be the One who meets their needs.

In Hosea 14:8 in the Message, God says, **"I am like a luxuriant fruit tree. Everything you need is to be found in me."** Reading this reminded me of a conversation I had many years ago with a friend, Francis, about the fruit of the Spirit. He explained that just as a tree produces fruit and others harvest and enjoy it, the fruit we produce in our lives is for the benefit of those around us – we do not consume it ourselves!

I find this challenging; we are encouraged to be filled constantly with the Holy Spirit and grow **love, joy, peace, patience, kindness, goodness, faithfulness, gentleness and self-control** so that others can be nourished and refreshed.

Jesus Himself grew all those fruit, and we constantly take from Him and are strengthened, refreshed and satisfied. Until the moment I was challenged by Francis, I had never understood that rather than just growing fruit that would change my character and make life easier for me, I was growing fruit for others to pick and enjoy. Jesus also declared that He came to serve, not to be served.

Today see yourself as a fruit tree, covered with attractive luscious fruit, and allow others to pick your fruit.

There is a bonus too for **"he who refreshes others will himself be refreshed"**. (Proverbs 11:25)

Joyce

One Year Plan : Psalm 60, Mark 4, Exodus 29 - 30
Two Year Plan : Psalm 37:21-31, Acts 9:20-43, Job 10 (Yr 1)
Ecclesiastes 5 (Yr 2)

Three Fires

I love lighting fires. When our children were young, one of our favourite winter leisure activities was to go to one of the beautiful Cornish beaches near our home, light a fire of driftwood and burn up all the rubbish on the beach. We were often commended for this community-spirited action. I am not sure how it would be viewed these days.

There were three significant fires in the life of the Apostle Peter.

There was the fire on the night before Jesus died; he warmed himself by a fire and at the same time denied Jesus three times. Many of us can remember a time when we messed up, let Jesus down and wondered whether there was any way back. Could it be possible that you are standing beside that fire now? (Luke 22:54-62)

The second fire was on a beach as Jesus was cooking breakfast and Peter arrived back from an unsuccessful fishing trip. It seemed like more failure; however, Jesus was not there to lay blame but to bring restoration. He had a simple question: **"Peter, do you love me?" "Yes, Yes, Yes,"** was the reply, and Jesus gave Peter a fresh start. He can give you fresh start today. (John 21:1-18)

The third fire happened on the day of Pentecost, when the Holy Spirit was given and tongues of fire came to rest on each person gathered in the Upper Room. God wants to send the same fire on His children today. We need that fire to burn up the disappointments and failures, to put power into our lives and warmth into our hearts. (Acts 2:1-4)

Don't get stuck at the wrong fire.

Charles

One Year Plan : Psalm 61, Mark 5, Exodus 31 - 32
Two Year Plan : Psalm 37:32-40, Acts 10:1-23, Job 11 (Yr 1)
Ecclesiastes 6 (Yr 2)

The Name of Jesus

Does the devil know who you are? He certainly knows who Jesus is and trembles at the very sound of His wonderful and all powerful Name.

How much are you using that Name to inflict damage on the devil's kingdom?

- You have been given the privilege of binding and loosing;
- Telling mountains of whatever kind to move;
- Rebuking sickness, disease and every work that is contrary to the kingdom of God or the will of God;

...all by using the authority which resides in the Name of Jesus.

In Acts Chapter 19, the sons of a Jewish chief priest named Sceva attempted to cast out demons by the Name of Jesus. They had no right to use that Name, as they had no personal relationship with Jesus. Recognising this, the evil spirit jumped all over them shouting, **"Jesus I know, and I know about Paul, but who are you?"** (Acts 19:15)

I hope that you can answer boldly:

- I am a child of the living God.
- I belong completely to Jesus Christ my Master.
- I am under His authority and I carry out His commands.
- I am cleansed from all sin by His blood.
- I am confident my past is in the past.
- I am in Christ Jesus.
- I am in the family of God and have authority to use the Name of Jesus who totally defeated the devil on the Cross.

Paul used this authority and, like his Master, he was known and feared by those in the kingdom of darkness.

Today, make sure the Name of Jesus is branded on your heart and life, that both heaven and hell know you. Heaven will back up everything you command or ask in the Name of Jesus – and hell will tremble.

Use your God-given authority today. Let these words be constantly on your lips: **"In the Name of Jesus"**.

Joyce

One Year Plan : Psalm 62, Mark 6, Exodus 33 - 34
Two Year Plan : Psalm 38:1-12, Acts 10:24-48, Job 12 (Yr 1)
Ecclesiastes 7 (Yr 2)

You have a Choice

Life is made up of choices, and we are fortunate to live in a free country – we select those who rule us and have a very wide range of choices – but even the lives of those in non-democratic countries are governed by choices.

We choose a career, we choose our spouse, we choose where we live, we choose how we spend our time and money, and we probably choose the number of children we will have. But choices have consequences, and we all have to live with the outcome of our actions. We also have to take responsibility for the decisions we make. You are not responsible for what others have done to you, but you are accountable for your own actions and reactions.

When things go wrong, the easiest thing is to blame someone else, but that will get you nowhere. On the other hand it is equally easy to think that nothing can be changed – wrong again!

If you are suffering under your circumstances and want to see things change, first, repent for your own actions and ask forgiveness from those you have wronged. The Bible says, **"Godly sorrow brings repentance that leads to salvation and leaves no regret."** (2 Corinthians 7:10)

Ask God to help you make right choices, however hard that may seem; this will place you in the right position to receive from Jesus, for He declared that He had come **"to heal the broken hearted, to preach deliverance to the captives, and recovery of sight to the blind, and to set at liberty them that are bruised."** (Luke 4:18)

Political choices affect us for a limited time – your personal choices could change your life forever.

Joshua said, **"Choose for yourselves this day whom you will serve ... but as for me and my household, we will serve the Lord."** (Joshua 24:15)

Charles

One Year Plan : Psalm 63, Mark 7, Exodus 35 - 36
Two Year Plan : Psalm 38:13-22, Acts 11, Job 13 (Yr 1)
Ecclesiastes 8 (Yr 2)

His Powerful Word

The writer to the Hebrews declares that among other things, Jesus is **"...sustaining all things by his powerful word."** (Hebrews 1:3)

The news media is bombarding us daily with words of alarm, gloom and potential disaster. This has the potential of filling us with fear and with thoughts of adversity and loss. What are we to do?

We need to choose the words that we are going to listen to and to live by. Words are powerful; they can threaten and disturb, or they can calm and strengthen.

After Jesus had been crucified and raised from the dead, we read about the disciples who **"...were together with the doors locked for fear of the Jews, Jesus came and stood among them and said, 'Peace be with you!'"**

The circumstances had not changed – only the words that filled their minds and hearts. Fear had been transformed to peace and **"the disciples were over-joyed when they saw the Lord."** (John 20:19-20)

At a time when David was being threatened and pursued by King Saul, who wanted to kill him, he wrote, **"My soul finds rest in God alone; my salvation comes from him. He alone is my rock and my salvation; he is my fortress, I will never be shaken."** (Psalm 62:1-2)

When Joshua was facing the pressure of having to lead the Children of Israel, God spoke to him and said, **"As I was with Moses, so I will be with you; I will never leave you nor forsake you."** (Joshua 1:5)

We can listen to all that is being spoken on our news media and be filled with fear, gloom and foreboding, or we can listen to words from God and be filled with faith, hope and the expectancy of a blessed future.

Are you being sustained by His powerful word?

Charles

One Year Plan : Psalm 64, Mark 8, Exodus 37 - 38
Two Year Plan : Psalm 39, Acts 12, Job 14 (Yr 1)
Ecclesiastes 9 (Yr 2)

Idols

What springs to mind when you see that word? Idols! Grotesque, ornate wooden images? Totem poles? Carved stone images? Anything that takes the pre-eminent place in our lives could be an idol. What do you worship? Give time and attention to? Dream about? It may not be made of wood or stone. Human beings love idols. If God is not being worshipped in our lives, something or someone else will take His place.

In the Old Testament we constantly read how God's people made and worshipped idols; they wanted visible gods like the surrounding nations.

Paul declares that behind idols there is demonic power. 1 Corinthians 10:19-20 says, **"Do I mean then that a sacrifice offered to an idol is anything, or that an idol is anything? No, but the sacrifices of pagans are offered to demons, not to God."** Be careful; idols can deceive, take over your heart, and obsess you.

Make sure today that God has His rightful place. In Exodus 20:3-4 it says, **"You shall have no other gods before me. You shall not make for yourself an idol in the form of anything..."**

Check yourself for idols – it could be another person, a hobby, an obsession with television, computer games, food or something else.

Smash them, worship God, and do not be ensnared by anything or anyone.

1 John 5:21 says, **"Dear children, keep yourselves from idols"**

As the words of an old hymn written by William Cowper (1731 – 1800) say:

The dearest idol I have known,
Whate'er that idol be,
Help me to tear it from Thy throne,
And worship only Thee.

Joyce

One Year Plan : Psalm 65, Mark 9, Exodus 39 - 40
Two Year Plan : Psalm 40:1-8, Acts 13:1-31, Job 15 (Yr 1)
Ecclesiastes 10 (Yr 2)

Getting Through

Do you ever have thoughts like these as you pick up the phone: "Will I ever get through?" "Will anybody talk to me?" "How many buttons will I have to press before I can speak to a living person?"

We are living in an impersonal world, where machines are replacing people wherever possible – because they're cheaper!

A couple of weeks ago I wanted to speak to a friend of mine who is one of the most important managers in the music industry so I picked up the phone and dialled his office. **"Can I speak to Peter** (not his real name)**?"** I asked, fully expecting to have to battle my way through receptionists, secretaries and PA's.

"I'll put you through right away," was the amazing reply. I did then speak to his secretary, who could not have been more charming or helpful. Peter was not in the office, but each person I spoke with was doing everything possible to help me make contact.

When reading Psalm 34, I pondered how God might respond if He were like so many top executives. The verse might go something like this:

I sought the Lord... and he gave me four options, and after selecting one I was offered three more, and when I selected one of those, I heard a recorded message – NO! NO! NO!

"I sought the Lord, <u>and he answered me</u>; he delivered me from all my fears." (Psalm 34:4)

"This poor man called, and the Lord heard him; he saved him out of all his troubles." (Psalm 34:6)

There is a communication system called 'Prayer' where you are listened to and receive answers.

Get on the line **now**!

Charles

One Year Plan : Psalm 66, Mark 10, Leviticus 1 - 3
Two Year Plan : Psalm 40:9-17, Acts 13:32-52, Job 16 (Yr 1)
Ecclesiastes 11 (Yr 2)

Does your Cry Reach to Heaven?

You will find this statement in 2 Chronicles 30:27: **"...and God heard them, for their prayer reached heaven, his holy dwelling place."**

Also, 2 Chronicles 32:20-21 says, **"King Hezekiah and the prophet Isaiah cried out in prayer to heaven about this. And the Lord sent an angel..."** And in verse 22 it says, **"So the Lord saved Hezekiah and the people ... He took care of them on every side."**

I found myself asking, **"Why did these prayers reach heaven, release angels and get action?"** Could it be desperation? There is something about desperate people that moves God's heart. He Himself is passionate, and He responds to such heart cries. Hannah prayed such a prayer because of her desperation to have a child and God heard.

One night a friend of ours woke in the night recalling a very disturbing dream. She saw a terrible accident involving children, both hers and ours, whilst travelling on the school bus. It was so shocking that she spent the rest of the night crying out to God for protection and safety.

Thankfully, there was no accident. So did her prayers prevent the disaster? They might well have done. As she spoke to God about this He told her, **"Because of the danger to your children you were emotionally involved. I want you to feel this kind of intensity, passion and urgency every time you pray and intercede for individuals and for the nation."**

When you are desperate, your **crying out** will take on a new compassion, a new intensity. Father responds to **heart cries** made in the Name of Jesus.

Joyce

One Year Plan : Psalm 67, Mark 11, Leviticus 4 - 5
Two Year Plan : Psalm 41, Acts 14, Job 17 (Yr 1)
Ecclesiastes 12 (Yr 2)

Repentance – The Way to a New Future

Moral lapses, sin, failure, mistakes – are these the end of the road or is there a way forward?

When Saul had been rejected as King because of his disobedience and his unwillingness to repent, God began to look for someone to replace him. David was chosen and he was described as **"a man after God's own heart"**.

David became a respected King, best remembered for the slaying of Goliath, and throughout the Bible he received many words of praise. However, he committed major sin through his adultery with Bathsheba, which also led to the murder of her husband Uriah. He survived such sin and failure because he was able to receive correction and could repent.

All sin has its consequences, and David did not escape because the child conceived through the act of adultery died, and yet there was forgiveness and redemption. The psalmist declares, **"O Israel, put your hope in the Lord, for with the Lord is unfailing love and with him is full redemption."** (Psalm 130:7)

David received the rebuke from the prophet Nathan after he had been confronted with his sin, and later wrote, **"Let a righteous man strike me – it is a kindness; let him rebuke me – it is oil on my head. My head will not refuse it."** (Psalm 141:5)

We are living in a blame culture, where we constantly want to shift the responsibility for our actions away from ourselves onto others – but God can only forgive sins, not excuses.

Adultery is the biggest cause of divorce in Britain today. I wonder how many marriages could have been saved if both parties had been prepared to admit sin, repent and seek forgiveness.

Don't let stubbornness and pride keep you in a prison – move on.

Charles

One Year Plan : Psalm 68, Mark 12, Leviticus 6 – 7
Two Year Plan : Proverbs 1:1-7, Acts 15:1-21, Job 18 (Yr 1)
1 Chronicles 1 (Yr 2)

What are you Feeding On?

It's possible to be hungry and yet not find food that **'hits the spot'** and satisfies the appetite. It's also possible not to have eaten for some time and yet be totally satisfied by something other than eating.

Many times I have come home late at night needing sleep more than food, but as the kettle boils, I have found myself grazing round the kitchen looking for food to fill that invisible, urgent need – searching for a bit of something that would satisfy, and trying increasingly ridiculous options, raiding the pantry and the fridge – then wishing I hadn't!

On the other hand, Jesus once told His disciples, **"I have food to eat that you know nothing about."** They had gone to buy some provisions and thought Jesus would be ready to enjoy the fruits of their shopping spree. Jesus tells them, **"My food is to do the will of him who sent me and to finish His work."**

Hebrews 13:9 says, **"It is good to be strengthened by grace and not by food."** In 1 Peter 2:2 we read, **"Like newborn babes, crave pure spiritual milk so that by it you may grow up in your salvation."**

Jesus describes Himself as the Bread of Life and the Living Water. The psalmist declares, **"But you would be fed with the finest of wheat; with honey from the rock I would satisfy you."** (Psalm 81:16) Of course we need food to fuel our bodies, but we also need to feed on things that will nourish our spirits and satisfy us at a deeper level than food.

It may be the comfort of Jesus that you need, or His peace, His approval. It could be rest, relaxation or sleep.

Ask Jesus today to satisfy your deepest longing. Don't turn to other substitutes. Pray for those who need healing from their prison of addiction.

Many addictions are cravings for deeper satisfaction and affirmation that can only be found in Jesus.

Joyce

One Year Plan : Psalm 69, Mark 13, Leviticus 8 - 9
Two Year Plan : Proverbs 1:8-19, Acts 15:22-41, Job 19 (Yr 1)
1 Chronicles 2 (Yr 2)

Radiation

I wonder what comes into your mind when you first read the word **'radiation'**. My guess is that you are immediately thinking of **'nuclear radiation'** – something unseen which has devastating consequences for all who come into contact with it.

We all remember Chernobyl and its dreadful aftermath. Yet in our homes we have radiant heaters which are a blessing and keep us warm in the cold, and our central heating systems have radiators to spread the heat where it is needed.

God's radiation is described as **glory**, and through it He radiates His love, power and forgiveness to all who come to Him. Psalm 19:1 says, **"The heavens declare the glory of God; the skies proclaim the work of his hands."** So in every way God wants His glory to be seen on earth. Jesus was a perfect radiator of God's glory.

So what about today – how will God's glory be seen on earth? The creation is still speaking, but what about people? Who is going to radiate God's glory to a lost and broken world? The answer is, **"We are!"**

Jesus prayed to His Father just before He died and said, **"I have given them the glory that you gave me."** (John 17:22) Paul wrote, **"Christ loved the church and gave himself up for her to make her ... a radiant church."** (Ephesians 5:25)

We all radiate something – one look into a person's face can tell you everything. You may see anger, fear, pain, depression, and sadness or you could see love, forgiveness, tenderness, joy and blessing. When the light of Jesus shines out of your face it changes you and it impacts all those you come into contact with.

It is God's plan that we should be increasingly radiating the glory of God. **"And we, who with open faces all reflect the Lord's glory, are being changed..."** (2 Corinthians 3:18)

What kind of radiation is coming out of you? What is your face displaying today?

Charles

One Year Plan : Psalm 70, Mark 14, Leviticus 10 - 11
Two Year Plan : Proverbs 1:20-33, Acts 16:1-15, Job 20 (Yr 1)
1 Chronicles 3 (Yr 2)

Be Like Alice

Alice, one of my granddaughters, was twenty months old; she hadn't seen me since she was a tiny baby, as her parents were working with Mission Aviation Fellowship and had been living in Tanzania, Africa.

Ben, Anne and Alice had been staying with us and were waiting for a new baby to arrive. I had fun with this focussed little bundle of energy who knew exactly what she wanted, and although she had as yet few words, she communicated very well. **"Boots on? Outside!"** were very clear demands. However, despite her determination, independence and spirit of adventure, about every five minutes or so she would ask, **"Where's mummy?"** She was looking for assurance that Anne was nearby. A wave or a word of encouragement would satisfy, but it wasn't long before once again we would hear the words, **"Where's Mummy?"**

Jesus wants us to have the same childlike longing – desiring His presence, looking for Him, needing Him, wanting at all times to be in vital contact. He is our life and He loves it when we call out to Him, abide in Him, talk to Him, listen to His voice and obey Him.

Most of us have moved on from those childhood days and now lead very independent lives. Jesus and His Father communicated constantly, and therefore Jesus could say, **"I only do what the Father tells me to do and I only say what I hear from Heaven."**

Let's be like Alice but change the subject of our desire and constantly say, **"Where's Jesus?"**

Let's continually connect with Jesus, feel His presence, listen to His voice, and find out what pleases Him.

Joyce

One Year Plan : Psalm 71, Mark 15, Leviticus 12 – 13
Two Year Plan : Proverbs 2:1-11, Acts 16:16-40, Job 21 (Yr 1)
1 Chronicles 4 (Yr 2)

Are You Wearing your Halo?!

Have you ever wondered why traditional religious art and paintings show the Holy Family and many of the saints and angels wearing halos?

What did the artists see when they were painting these people that caused them to place a halo around their head?

I do not believe that this artistic impression was a figment of their imagination. I believe they really saw something which they were very aware of but was not necessarily visible.

When John wrote his gospel record he described Jesus in these words: **"We have seen his glory, the glory of the One and Only, who came from the Father, full of grace and truth."** (John 1:14) What did he see? He saw glory. He saw something that he could clearly recognise and the only way he could describe it was to use the word **'glory'**.

When Paul wrote to the Church at Corinth, he tells how Moses' face was covered in glory as he returned from receiving the Ten Commandments on Mt. Sinai. But the glory was fading, and Paul believed that we as believers should have a glory that is increasing. He says this: **"And if what was fading came with glory, how much greater is the glory of that which lasts!"** (2 Corinthians 3:11)

Paul concludes this argument with these words: **"And we, who with unveiled faces all reflect the Lord's glory, are being transformed into his likeness with ever-increasing glory, which comes from the Lord, who is the Spirit."** (2 Corinthians 3:18)

What do people see when they look at you – gloom or glory?

Are you wearing your halo? Ask the Holy Spirit that today you may reflect the glory of Jesus.

Charles

One Year Plan : Psalm 72, Mark 16, Leviticus 14 - 15
Two Year Plan : Proverbs 2:12-22, Acts 17:1-15, Job 22 (Yr 1)
1 Chronicles 5 (Yr 2)

A Mystery Smell

I once heard about a Chinese lady, a believer, who was housebound because of a life-threatening illness. She kept smelling a beautiful fragrance but couldn't trace its source. **"Have you changed your aftershave?"** she asked her husband. He hadn't, nor were there any heavily scented flowers nearby.

The fragrance was strong, unusual and very sweet, and all avenues of investigation failed to reveal the source. It became a topic of daily conversation, and many who entered her room were aware of it.

A friend of mine left a copy of my book, **"Is there a Word from the Lord?"** for the lady to read. She discovered the source of the fragrance as she eagerly devoured its contents.

She had read about hearing God through the sense of smell (page 26), and suddenly realised the fragrance came from Jesus Himself. She was so grateful – in fact, quite overwhelmed – that the Lord would assure her of His nearness in this manner.

Jesus is described in the Bible as **"The Rose of Sharon"** and **"The Lily of the Valley"**. When the anointing oil was poured out on the feet of Jesus the perfume filled the house.

I found myself asking the question: what does the atmosphere smell like in my house? Does it smell of Jesus and His sweetness – or of strife, bitterness or other negative things? Is it an aroma of life or the smell of death?

2 Corinthians 2:14 in the Message says, **"Everywhere we go, people breathe in the exquisite fragrance. Because of Christ, we give off a sweet scent rising to God, which is recognised by those on the way of salvation – an aroma redolent with life."**

Joyce

One Year Plan : Proverbs 1, Romans 1, Leviticus 16 - 17
Two Year Plan : Proverbs 3:1-12, Acts 17:16-34, Job 23 (Yr 1)
1 Chronicles 6 (Yr 2)

Central Control

A newsflash was given that all UK flights had been grounded until further notice due to a computer failure. The aircraft were not incapable of taking off, but without the guidance of Air Traffic Control that was not safe. They needed direction and control, to be assured of safe passage to their destination. Despite the inconvenience, many passengers were encouraged that the authorities were not prepared to take risks with their safety.

But what about **Central Control** over our everyday lives? We so often make decisions, take action, and go places at the slightest whim, without referral to **Central Control**.

We often reserve **hearing from God** to moments of crisis, times when we are making important decisions or significant life changes, and forget that God is vitally interested in the smallest decisions of everyday life.

God wants to be involved in every detail. Psalm 48:14 says, **"For this God is our God for ever and ever; he will be our guide even to the end."**

Proverbs 4:11 says, **"I will guide you in the way of wisdom and lead you along straight paths."** God knows the way ahead, the pitfalls and the rough places.

David faced a crisis; the enemy had destroyed his city and stolen everything, including his wives. He could have panicked, but after gaining strength in God, he asked what he should do and was told, **"Pursue them ... you will certainly overtake them and succeed in the rescue."** (1 Samuel 30:8)

Paul was stopped from going to Bithynia, by the Holy Spirit; that enabled him to receive directions through a dream which took him to Macedonia, and it opened up a whole new sphere of influence and fruitfulness. (Acts 16:6-10)

You need not be grounded, stranded or confused, for God's **Central Control** computer never crashes!

Charles

One Year Plan : Proverbs 2, Romans 2, Leviticus 18 - 19
Two Year Plan : Proverbs 3:13-26, Acts 18, Job 24 (Yr 1)
1 Chronicles 7 (Yr 2)

Weak... In Order to Become Strong

I have a vivid memory of one of our granddaughters putting on outdoor clothing one winter's day. She marched to the front door muttering, **"Hat, gloves, coat, shoes."** I followed her, attempting to help, but was firmly rebuffed and told, **"I can do it,"** and she could! It took ages – she kept refusing help – but eventually we were ready, and off we went. I wanted to help, to speed up the process, to get involved – but no. Independence triumphed!

Our behaviour towards God can so often be similar to this incident. We want to do things by ourselves and therefore refuse or ignore the help the Holy Spirit.

On one occasion, I needed to spend some time praying with one of our church members who was facing a challenging situation. I was tired, short of sleep, having returned overnight from the USA, and knowing I had no human answers I cried out for the Lord's help in my weakness and lack. To my joy, He promptly supplied what He always promises: wisdom, strength and power.

The instant I said, **"I can't!"** He replied, **"But I can,"** and proceeded to give me His revelation about the situation. I received scriptures and instruction unlocking the problem – it was effortless. How foolish we are to try to do our own thing when God Himself is so willing to help us.

2 Corinthians 12:9-10 says, **"Therefore I will boast all the more gladly about my weaknesses, so that Christ's power may rest on me. That is why, for Christ's sake, I delight in weaknesses ... for when I am weak, then I am strong."** This clearly speaks of the exchange of my weakness for His strength, superior knowledge and resources.

After spending time talking and praying with this friend, light dawned in a very dark, helpless situation and we saw breakthrough. I found myself praying that I would remain helpless, weak and inadequate – so that God's power might be released moment by moment.

I want my attitude to be, **"Lord, help me!"** and not, **"I can do it myself!"** How about you?

Joyce

One Year Plan : Proverbs 3, Romans 3, Leviticus 20 - 21
Two Year Plan : Proverbs 3:27-35, Acts 19:1-22, Job 25 (Yr 1)
1 Chronicles 8 (Yr 2)

Wild Cyclamen

I was walking around my garden during one of those brief moments when the rain had stopped falling and the sun was trying to break through the clouds. To my amazement, I was greeted by a splash of life and colour; the wild cyclamen, planted in the shade under trees, had burst into life. How did they do it?

These beautiful flowers have been designed to grow in the shade, in poor soil, with little need for sunlight. The creator God has placed within this plant the power to thrive in harsh conditions. This led me to think about the amazing power that God has placed within those who are **in Christ Jesus**. When Christ comes to live in us, He gives us the power to thrive in adversity. His energy enables us to live in joy and victory, despite the pressures and problems that may surround us.

Romans 8:11 says, **"And if the Spirit of him who raised Jesus from the dead is living in you, he who raised Christ from the dead will also give life to your mortal bodies through his Spirit, who lives in you."** We are indwelt by the same power that raised Jesus from the dead!

Paul spoke to the believers in Colossae and said, **"For in Christ all the fullness of the Deity lives in bodily form and you have been given fullness in Christ, who is the Head over every power and authority."** (Colossians 2:9-10) You have been given the ability to exercise authority over everything that the enemy and life's circumstances throw at you.

So today, be a wild cyclamen, thrive in adversity, shine out of the storms and realise that **"the One who is in you is greater than the one who is in the world."**

Charles

One Year Plan : Proverbs 4, Romans 4, Leviticus 22 - 23
Two Year Plan : Proverbs 4:1-9, Acts 19:23-41, Job 26 (Yr 1)
1 Chronicles 9 (Yr 2)

Storms of Life

When the storms of life threaten to overwhelm you, don't waste your time questioning why this or that is happening – rather focus on how to get through the battle in one piece, and if others are involved, how to help them get through!

Life is not always plain sailing! Paul found himself in such a life-threatening situation. It is recorded in detail in **Acts 27**. If his advice to the captain of the ship had been heeded, the whole incident could have been avoided – but it wasn't, which left Paul and 276 others in mortal danger. The one thing that set Paul apart from the others was his **lack of fear**. He experienced the same life-threatening conditions, discomfort, and yet because he had contact with the living God, he was able to receive divine instructions which began with the command, **"Do not be afraid, Paul."** He was reminded that his life was under God's control and not at the mercy of the prevailing conditions – and he was promised his own life would be saved as well as that of those who were in the boat with him.

Once he had received the heavenly assurance himself, **he was able to speak faith and hope** to those panicking around him. He instructed them to eat, to stay with the ship, and to obey orders; consequently, although they were shipwrecked, not one life was lost and they were all cared for on the island of Malta.

Today, you may be feeling overwhelmed by the circumstances of life – storm-tossed and very uncomfortable. Listen to what heaven is saying. Ask for wisdom, for direction, what to do and how and when to do it. Like Paul, **take the lead, be bold; God wants to deliver you** and those who are in your company.

We are not promised a **storm-free life** but we are assured that Jesus will never leave us nor forsake us. He will speak if we will listen. You may be the one **fear-free person** in the storm, who has access to heavenly wisdom.

Joyce

One Year Plan : Proverbs 5, Romans 5, Leviticus 24 - 25
Two Year Plan : Proverbs 4:10-17, Acts 20:1-12, Job 27 (Yr 1)
1 Chronicles 10 (Yr 2)

There is a River

Psalm 46:4 says, **"There is a river whose streams make glad the city of God..."** However, in fact, there is no river running through Jerusalem; it is on a hill and there is no possibility of there being a river. So what is this psalm saying?

This river is God's supernatural supply of strength, joy and blessing. Your Jerusalem is who you are and where you live, and God has a river for your home and for your own situation. The verse continues, **"...the holy place where the Most High dwells. God is within her, she will not fall; God will help her at break of day."**

God is saying to you:

- There is a river of refreshment that He wants to flow through your life and the place where you live.
- He wants your home to be a holy place where the Most High dwells, for the word 'holy' means to be set apart. Make yourself a set apart place, where God is happy to make a home.
- Because you have welcomed God in this way, the verse says, **"...she will not fall."** God wants to surround you, your home, and all those who live there with blessing and success.
- Again, because of that welcome, the psalm says, **"God will help her at the break of day."** At the start of every new day God will help you, encourage and protect you.

There is a river for you. Isaiah had the same message: **"The poor and needy search for water, but there is none; their tongues are parched with thirst. But I the Lord will answer them; I, the God of Israel, will not forsake them. I will make rivers flow on barren heights and springs within the valleys."** (Isaiah 41:17-18)

Invite Him into your home, your whole environment and your personal life – and let His river flow.

Charles

One Year Plan : Proverbs 6, Romans 6, Leviticus 26 - 27
Two Year Plan : Proverbs 4:18-27, Acts 20:13-38, Job 28 (Yr 1)
1 Chronicles 11 (Yr 2)

Pray in the Holy Spirit

Jude tells us not to follow our natural instincts but to **"build ourselves up in our most holy faith and pray in the Holy Spirit"**. (Jude 1:20)

When did you last spend some time praying in this way – releasing your spirit to rise above your mind and allowing the Spirit of God to pour forth in your heavenly language? I meet many people who can **pray in tongues** but have stopped using this precious gift – to their own personal loss.

We need to **stir up** the gift given to us by the laying on of hands, to value and use tongues regularly and effectively. When we do...

- We will be built up – edified and strengthened.
- We will be interceding for situations where we don't necessarily know the specific facts – but will be yielding our voice to the One who knows everything.
- We will be maintaining intimate connection with God's Spirit, and as He flows through us, we will be blessed. Jude 1:21 says **"Keep yourself in God's love as you wait for the mercy of our Lord Jesus Christ."**

So what if you can't speak in tongues? Then ask God for this precious gift. Matthew 7:7-11 in The Message says, **"Don't bargain with God. Be direct. Ask for what you need. This is not a cat and mouse, hide and seek game we're in. If your little boy asks for bread, do you trick him with sawdust? If he asks for fish, do you scare him with a live snake on his plate? As bad as you are, you wouldn't think of such a thing. You're at least decent to your own children. So don't you think the God who conceived you in love will be even better?"** You might have had teaching that would suggest this gift died out with the early church. It didn't. Paul said, **"I thank God that I speak in tongues more than you all, and ... do not forbid speaking in tongues."** (1 Corinthians 14:18,39)

Don't neglect this precious gift. A friend of mine was feeling isolated, rather weak and quite sorry for himself. The Lord spoke to him and said, **"Pray in tongues."** He was obedient and yielded himself to God in this way; he found as he was praying with fervour that strength and perspective began to return. He was simply **building himself up** according to 1 Corinthians 14:4.

Do you need this kind of strength today? Pray in the Holy Spirit!

Joyce

One Year Plan : Proverbs 7, Romans 7, Numbers 1 – 2
Two Year Plan : Proverbs 5:1-14, Acts 21:1-26, Job 29 (Yr 1)
1 Chronicles 12 (Yr 2)

Sleeplessness

Do you find yourself waking up during the night? Does this create a problem for you? What happens to you when you are wide awake in the middle of the night?

These days, it is not uncommon for me to wake in the middle of the night. However, I have realised that I have a choice as to how I will spend my wakeful hours. Worries, concerns and burdens seek to crowd into my mind during times of sleeplessness, but I do not have to let them in.

Firstly, I have decided that I will not worry about whether I am getting enough sleep. Losing a couple of hours' sleep will not harm me. Secondly, I have decided to use this time creatively. In Psalm 42:8 it says, **"By day the Lord directs his love, at night his song is with me."** During this time of wakefulness it is good to pray and give thanks to God for all His many blessings. It is also a good time to sing praises and worship God – not too loudly; I don't want to wake Joyce up! There are times when I will listen to a worship album on my iPod. Psalm 119:148 says, **"My eyes stay open during the watches of the night, that I may meditate on your promises."** That is good advice.

In the Psalms, David speaks of how he used his wakeful times during the night. Psalm 63:6 says, **"On my bed I remember you; I think of you through the watches of the night."** In Psalm 16:7, David says, **"I will praise the Lord, who counsels me; even at night my heart instructs me."**

My word of encouragement today is this: **"Don't waste your sleeplessness."** For me, eventually I get back to sleep, but I have discovered that when I awake in the morning, I am refreshed by having used my sleepless time so creatively.

Charles

One Year Plan : Proverbs 8, Romans 8, Numbers 3 - 4
Two Year Plan : Proverbs 5:15-23, Acts 21:27-40, Job 30 (Yr 1)
1 Chronicles 13 (Yr 2)

Look Back – Look Forward

One day, I read through some old journals – they covered the years 1984-1987. At that time we were living in Sussex and our five children were between eight and eighteen years old. Life was very busy, and we were facing challenges in many areas of life.

I now have the advantage of hindsight and want to give God thanks for His utter faithfulness. He constantly told me to trust Him, not to fret, but to believe He would bless our children. He gave clear instructions on how to both train and correct them – and how also to encourage them. He told me to get out of the way, to let Him work, to trust Him and not to try and make things happen – it wasn't my energy that would change situations but His power.

At one time when we were moving to a smaller house and we were parting with many possessions, He said, **"I'm separating you from possessions and houses and especially the burden of caring for them. You may have things around you that make you happy and have special memories for you, but you are not to be weighed down by things. I want you to be mobile, and when I call you to settle down, I will provide for you in a way that will give back all you think you have missed**." He has. He made promises for our children that have been fulfilled in detail. I could go on... He is a faithful God.

I'm challenged today to trust Him even more and to rest in Him and His infinite resources. He has promised that this nation will turn back to God, that I will see revival in my lifetime, that signs and wonders will be commonplace and result in God's glory being seen and honoured.

Isaiah 30:15 says, **"In repentance and rest is your salvation, in quietness and trust is your strength, but you would have none of it."**

Don't let this be true of us. **Let us rest and trust and see the greater things.**

Joyce

One Year Plan : Proverbs 9, Romans 9, Numbers 5 - 6
Two Year Plan : Proverbs 6:1-11, Acts 22, Job 31 (Yr 1)
1 Chronicles 14 (Yr 2)

Prepared to Give an Answer

Joyce and I were walking through the beautiful cathedral town of Wells. A young man was standing on the pavement, holding a microphone, and as we went by he asked, **"Would you be willing to help me and to answer a few questions?"** He looked as though he was having difficulty in getting people to interact with him.

He explained, **"There is a proposal in Somerset that Philosophy is to be re-introduced to the school curriculum, and we at the BBC want to ask some adults the sort of questions that will be posed to the students. Can I ask you these questions?"** Our reply was, **"OK, we will have a go; what are the questions?"**

The reporter replied, **"What is truth? What is knowledge? Why are we here? And is there a God?"** Joyce began on the first question: **"Truth is a person, Jesus Christ, who declared, 'I am the way, the truth and the life.' It is impossible to know real truth without having a personal relationship with Jesus."**

The next two questions came my way. I cannot fully remember what I answered to the question about knowledge; I am sure the Holy Spirit must have crafted the words because the reporter's response was, **"That was a succinct reply."** As I responded to his next question, **"Why are we here?"** I stated, **"We are here because God made us so that He could know us and have a personal relationship with us who are His creation. He loves us and wants to know us and for us to know Him."**

Joyce's answer to, **"Is there a God?"** was clear and confident and again pointed to the fact that we can know God through Jesus and that those who have a personal relationship with Him know that Jesus lives in them and gives meaning to life.

The reporter look both stunned and pleased – he had got some answers to his questions!

In 1 Peter 3:15-16 it says, **"Always be prepared to give the reason for the hope that you have. But do this with gentleness and respect."**

Charles

One Year Plan : Proverbs 10, Romans 10, Numbers 7 - 8
Two Year Plan : Proverbs 6:12-19, Acts 23:1-22, Job 32 (Yr 1)
1 Chronicles 15 (Yr 2)

Hollow Men and Desiccated Women

Thousands of years ago a messenger of God spoke to a nation, and what he said is recorded in the Old Testament Book of Hosea. It reads like yesterday's newspaper: sex, greed, destruction, betrayal, alcohol abuse and the desire for houses and bigger houses.

It speaks of a people who once respected and obeyed God but have now decided to worship themselves – and Hosea describes the social consequences. One phrase in particular stood out to me as it described a people who had turned their back on God:

"...hollow men, desiccated women, like scraps of paper blown down the street, like smoke in a gusty wind." (Hosea 13:3, The Message)

The prophet Hosea is expecting God to act with judgement and destruction. They deserve it, but God – because He is God – decides to act with mercy and again offers forgiveness and restoration.

In Chapter 14:4 God says, **"I will heal their waywardness and love them lavishly. My anger is played out. I will make a fresh start with Israel."**

Do you see the similarities with Israel in those days and Britain today? Will you intercede and pray to God to raise up Hosea's in our day – prophets who will voice God's displeasure at what is happening in our nation but who will also declare God's remedy in ways that will be heard?

Also, pray that God Himself will once again act in mercy and not judgement and that we may become **a nation who turn back to Jesus – the Way, the Truth, and the Life.**

Joyce

One Year Plan : Proverbs 11, Romans 11, Numbers 9 - 10
Two Year Plan : Proverbs 6:20-29, Acts 23:23-35, Job 33 (Yr 1)
1 Chronicles 16 (Yr 2)

Not Guilty

Some years ago, I was privileged to pray with a friend and lead him to living faith in Jesus. He was a man in his forties, and coming to know Jesus was bringing significant change into his life. A short while after this he was visiting his doctor and the fact of his newfound faith came into the conversation.

"You have become a Christian!" was the surprised retort. **"What kind of a Christian are you then?"** he continued.

"You can only be one kind of Christian; one who has come to a living faith in Jesus," was the reply.

"What difference has it made then?" he questioned.

"I have peace and all my guilt has gone."

When he later recounted this incident to me, I was fascinated with the statement **"all my guilt has gone"**. As I pondered this I began to understand that it is only through the work of Jesus on the cross that guilt can be eradicated.

This is the message of the well-known hymn 'Rock of Ages'.

Rock of Ages, cleft for me,
Let me hide myself in Thee;
Let the water and the blood,
From Thy riven side which flowed,
Be of sin the double cure –
Cleanse me from its guilt and power.

All that I have just written was prompted by a verse in Jeremiah 50:20 which says, **"'In those days, at that time,' declares the Lord, 'search will be made for Israel's guilt, but there will be none, and for the sins of Judah, but none will be found, for I will forgive the remnant I spare.'"**

I found that scripture amazing. The book of Jeremiah is filled with the sins and rebellion of the nation of Israel and God's judgement on them for their actions; and yet God can say that their guilt can be completely removed.

That is the power of the cross and the blood: guilt can be totally removed. **No believer should be living with guilt.**

In Jesus, God has pronounced, **"Not Guilty,"** over you. **Have you received the "Not Guilty" verdict into your heart?**

Charles

One Year Plan : Proverbs 12, Romans 12, Numbers 11 - 12
Two Year Plan : Proverbs 6:30-35, Acts 24, Job 34 (Yr 1)
1 Chronicles 17 (Yr 2)

His Love Never Quits

Annually we meet with about 130 Christian leaders in Bristol; we eat a meal together and break bread as a statement of our unity with the wider body of Christ. It is a time of encouragement and fellowship – and it is good.

One year I heard of people facing challenges and yet proclaiming their faith in a God who is able to give strength and hope. There were others who had carried loads that were too heavy and had come to an end of their physical and emotional strength but who then found love, kindness and compassion as others supported and helped them get up and carry on.

There was news of new projects, fresh vision for the year ahead, and innovative ways of reaching people with the good news of Jesus – many faithful servants of God who were selflessly working in poor communities, doing what was needed; others enthusiastically planning special events – and there were many personal stories of God's faithfulness and goodness.

Psalm 136:1 says, **"Give thanks to the Lord for he is good, his love endures forever."** Or as the Message puts it, **"His love never quits!"**

Tell yourself, **"His love never quits; it endures forever"**. His kingdom is advancing. There are difficulties, disasters, encouragements and miracles – feasting and famine all going on at the same time – but God's love for you will never fail. His resources and mercies are new every morning.

If you are rejoicing, encourage those who are not. **If you are struggling**, let others help you through. We are all part of a body, and it's good to remember that the Kingdom of God is advancing – and all of us are playing our part **working and waiting for the King Himself to come.**

Joyce

One Year Plan : Proverbs 13, Romans 13, Numbers 13 – 14
Two Year Plan : Proverbs 7:1-9, Acts 25, Job 35 (Yr 1)
1 Chronicles 18 (Yr 2)

Joy and Contentment

Sometimes when I read Ecclesiastes I feel that Solomon wrote it on a rainy Monday morning after a sleepless night! However, this time I have seen something completely different.

In Chapter 8 verse 15, he says, **"So I commend the enjoyment of life, because nothing is better for a man under the sun than to eat and drink and be glad. Then joy will accompany him in his work all the days of the life God gives him under the sun."**

Work is a blessing! The first thing that God gave to Adam was meaningful work in the Garden of Eden. It was not meant to be a burden or a drudge. What is your attitude to your work? Is it a burden or a joy? In an earlier part of Ecclesiastes we are encouraged **"to find satisfaction in our toilsome labour under the sun."** Those who have suffered unemployment know that having no work is not a blessing. So today, thank God for your job; go there with joy and thanksgiving; don't moan about your boss but infuse your workplace with gratitude and contentment.

Contentment is a blessing! Chapter 5 verse 19 says, **"Moreover, when God gives any man or woman wealth and possessions, and enables him to enjoy them, to accept his lot and be happy in his work – this is a gift of God."**

Paul affirms this, when he says to Timothy, **"Godliness with contentment is great gain."** (1 Timothy 6:6)

We are living in a society which is full of negativity, criticism and complaining. If we are among those who know God – those in whom Christ lives – we are blessed, we have joy and should be at peace; **so let us be those who spread an atmosphere of thanksgiving, joy and contentment wherever we go!**

Charles

One Year Plan : Proverbs 14, Romans 14, Numbers 15 - 16
Two Year Plan : Proverbs 7:10-20, Acts 26, Job 36 (Yr 1)
1 Chronicles 19 (Yr 2)

Eternal Perspective

A friend of ours had died and gone to be with Jesus; we know, as do her family, that she is not dead, simply absent from the body, but very much alive in the presence of Jesus – full of joy and living her new life to the full.

As I was praying for her husband and daughters, the Lord drew my attention to part of a verse in Revelation 5:5: **"Do not weep! See..."** He then began to explain to me that the Apostle John was distraught and wept and wept because of the hopelessness of the vision he was looking at – until the angel said to him, **"See."** Then his eyes were opened, he saw Jesus and everything changed. He needed to see the **eternal perspective** – and so do we.

For this particular family, grieving over the loss of a wife and mother, they need to see her with the eyes of faith, to know that she is more alive than she has ever been, to see her as she is. Only Jesus can apply salve to the eyes and cause them to see beyond the sorrow and pain of sudden loss. He did just that – assured them of His understanding and help on earth and caused them to see their loved one full of joy in the presence of Jesus.

We all need **eternal perspective**; life is so busy and demanding but when evaluated with eternity in mind, some of the things that make demands on us and cause such stress seem so trivial. Prioritise with an eternal viewpoint, asking, **"Has this got eternal value?"** We can waste so much time on meaningless activity and achieve very little except exhaustion.

Today, ask Jesus to put salve on your eyes so that you see – really see, with a clarity that will cause you to become more peaceful and focussed. I see Jesus living in this kind of way, constantly in touch with the Father and consequently functioning with eternal vision.

I believe this is also possible for us – ask for heavenly vision today.

Joyce

One Year Plan : Proverbs 15, Romans 15, Numbers 17 - 18
Two Year Plan : Proverbs 7:21-27, Acts 27:1-26, Job 37 (Yr 1)
1 Chronicles 20 (Yr 2)

Determined Women

Consider the determination of two women. They had great needs, but when they heard about Jesus they crashed through every obstacle, for nothing would stop them getting to the One who could meet their need. That's faith!

The first woman had suffered with bleeding for twelve years; all her money had been spent on doctors and yet she had only got worse. The story in Mark's gospel then says, **"When she heard about Jesus..."** That was the key moment when she decided that she was going to get through to Jesus. Crowds were in the way, social protocol said she was not allowed to mix with people, and everyone seemed to be keeping her from getting to Jesus. However, she elbowed her way through the crowd, and when she got to Him, with bold faith and total confidence she simply touched His cloak. Immediately her bleeding stopped and she was completely healed. Her single-mindedness, determination and faith brought her through to the miracle she needed. (Mark 5:25-34)

The second woman was Greek, and she had a daughter who was possessed by an evil spirit. As soon as she heard about Jesus, ignoring the fact that as a Gentile she had no right of access, she still came and fell at His feet.

Jesus seemed reluctant to have anything to do with her and said, **"First let the children eat all they want, for it is not right to take the children's bread and toss it to dogs."** Not offended or deterred, the woman replied, **"Yes Lord, but even the dogs under the table eat the children's crumbs."**

Jesus was amazed at her reply and told her, **"For such a reply, you may go; the demon has left your daughter."** She went home and found her child lying on the bed and the demon gone. (Mark 7:24-30)

Most of us know these two stories from the gospels; however, are we prepared to push through every difficulty, not take **"no"** for an answer but **hold our place of faith until we see the breakthrough we need?**

Charles

One Year Plan : Psalm 73, Romans 16, Numbers 19 - 20
Two Year Plan : Proverbs 8:1-11, Acts 27:27-44, Job 38 (Yr 1)
1 Chronicles 21 (Yr 2)

Be Finished with Self-Effort

I had been very busy, not only with the circumstances of life but with many visitors, and consequently had found little time to be quiet or to have quality time with the Lord. He comforted me with these words:

"Don't you see that because I live in you, you do not need to be repenting but thanking – living in gratitude for My freedom and lack of judgement? However, when you lose the sense of My presence and get so busy with other things, then effectively you are living without My help and falling back on human ability and resources. It is that cycle I want to break; I desire a people who constantly are in touch with Me by My Spirit and who are drawing off heavenly resources in a conscious way and therefore are completely finished with self-effort."

"It is not a question of how much Bible you have read or how long you have prayed or what other 'spiritual activity' you have engaged in. No; it is rather an inner turning to Me at all times, conscious of your need for My help and resources. That's what I desire. My longing is for My people to access Me at all times: to walk with Me, talk with Me, and receive wisdom and help and to respond with thanksgiving. Your 'sin' will no longer be sinful actions and thoughts (although you can still indulge this behaviour) but rather ignoring the One who loves you, lives in you and desires to be in intimate contact. You refuse Me by your busyness and self-effort and a life with no thanksgiving. That is My complaint against you – familiarity that takes Me for granted and eventually undervalues and ignores all I have done for you!"

I also found the verses of this hymn a real help:

When satan tempts me to despair,
And tells me of the guilt within,
Upward I look and see Him there
Who made an end of all my sin.

Because the sinless Saviour dies,
My sinful soul is counted free;
For God, the Just, is satisfied
To look on Him and pardon me.

Joyce

One Year Plan : Psalm 74, Luke 1, Numbers 21- 22
Two Year Plan : Proverbs 8:12-21, Acts 28:1-16, Job 39 (Yr 1)
1 Chronicles 22 (Yr 2)

A Fading Glory

There is always a feeling of sadness whenever you see something that is fading and has lost its life and vigour; for example, flowers that are drooping and dying, an old faded photograph, a much loved piece of clothing that has been bleached by the sun.

When Moses came down from the mountain where he had met with God his face shone; however, it faded as he found himself filled with all the problems of the people. Surely, if he had stayed on the mountain the glory would have remained.

On one of our visits to Rwanda, we visited the prayer hut at Gahini where the Rwandan Revival began many years ago. Sadly we found it locked with the thatched roof deteriorating. The glory had gone; it was just a monument to a happening that had passed.

Why do revivals come to an end? First, if we get caught up with the manifestations of revival and stop looking at Jesus, the glory will fade.

Secondly, when God does something wonderful, we can try to analyse what has happened and make rules and guidelines for its preservation, without realising that revival is a gift of God's grace poured out on hungry hearts.

Thirdly, when God visits a certain group of people, it is so easy for them to become proud and believe they know the reason why God has chosen to favour them.

In the same chapter that Paul speaks of Moses' fading glory, he also speaks of an increasing glory: **"And we, who with unveiled faces all reflect the Lord's glory, are being transformed into his likeness with ever-increasing glory, which comes from the Lord who is the Spirit."** (2 Corinthians 3:18)

I believe that God wants to pour out increasing glory on all his children. Let us come to him today with hungry hearts, humble minds and open faces.

Charles

One Year Plan : Psalm 75, Luke 2, Numbers 23 - 24
Two Year Plan : Proverbs 8:22-31, Acts 28:17-31, Job 40 (Yr 1)
1 Chronicles 23 (Yr 2)

APRIL

Take Your Inheritance

"Come you who are blessed by my Father; take your inheritance, the kingdom prepared for you since the creation of the world." (Matthew 25:34)

You and I have been given a tremendous privilege. We are citizens of the Kingdom of Heaven.

- We didn't buy our citizenship;
- We didn't acquire it by natural birth;
- It was conferred on us when we were born again, as we believed in Jesus our Saviour and Lord.

What does this mean?

- We have the ear of the King of Kings; we can go to Him for help at any time. The door is never closed, and His attitude is always one of welcome.
- We have the King's authority to rule over circumstances and situations. We are told to address these in the Name of Jesus, to demand they change.
- We are to enforce our King's rule **"on earth as it is in heaven"**.
- Whatever we bind on earth will be bound in heaven. Whatever we loose on earth will be loosed in heaven.

Many Christians are found pleading with God to act of their behalf when He is waiting for us to see ourselves empowered on earth with the mandate to rule on His behalf. God is waiting and expecting us to enforce the Kingdom in our particular sphere of influence. We are to speak to the mountain and tell it to move!

You can rest today in the knowledge that you are indeed part of a Heavenly Kingdom – **a present reality and a future certainty.**

Joyce

One Year Plan : Psalm 76, Luke 3, Numbers 25 - 26
Two Year Plan : Proverbs 8:32-36, Romans 1:1-17, Job 41 (Yr 1)
1 Chronicles 24 (Yr 2)

Little England

A British lady teaching in an English Language School in Rome declared her classroom **'Little England'**. **"There will be no Italian spoken in 'Little England'. Should you forget, a fine will be placed in the charity box."** This message was reinforced by posters declaring, **"Remember, you are now in Little England!"**

We as Christians need to remember that we are part of the Kingdom of God on earth! A different atmosphere prevails here – different standards, goals, as well as language. Isaiah 51:3 states, **"The Lord will surely comfort Zion and will look with compassion on all her ruins; he will make her deserts like Eden, her wastelands like the garden of the Lord. Joy and gladness will be found in her, thanksgiving and the sound of singing."**

I see many people whose lives could be described by the words 'ruins', 'deserts', and 'wasteland' – and the atmosphere they breathe daily reinforces their lack. If that is you, God wants to comfort you and bring you into a place where He enables you to experience joy and gladness, thanksgiving and singing. God wants to bring you out of the jaws of distress into a spacious place – out of lack into plenty – out of hopelessness into expectancy.

The Kingdom of God is a reality on earth as well as in heaven. We are ambassadors of this Kingdom and should demonstrate it by the way we live our lives. In **'Little England' you speak English**, when all around you others are speaking Italian. **In the Kingdom of God you speak faith**, when others around you are speaking fear. Your life is characterised by love, joy and peace, by selflessness rather than selfishness, as you demonstrate a totally different culture.

Today consciously live **heaven on earth** and see if others around you are intrigued and attracted. A young man was brought by a friend to a prayer meeting where there was exuberant joy and great rejoicing, and asked, **"What are you lot on?"** He was then told that it was the Holy Spirit at work. His response was, **"I used to pay a lot of money to get that happy!"**

Joyce

One Year Plan : Psalm 77, Luke 4, Numbers 27 - 28
Two Year Plan : Psalm 42, Romans 1:18-32, Job 42 (Yr 1)
1 Chronicles 25 (Yr 2)

Majesty and Miracle

I was watching a video of an amazing meeting where a terminally ill cancer patient was wonderfully released from pain, touched by God, and filled with the Holy Spirit. As I watched her countenance change, all I could do was weep with joy witnessing God in action. The preacher, aware of the Majesty of God, directed the people in the auditorium to stand in awe and reverence before Almighty God.

How easily we become over-familiar with God and lose the sense of awe, wonder and privilege. Jesus is our friend, brother, lover, comforter – but He is always God.

Peter entertains Jesus in his home in Capernaum and sees his mother-in-law healed as well as many others in the neighbourhood, but at this point in time he has not been conscious of **majesty**. However, after a fruitless night of fishing he is happy to hand over his boat and for it to become a pulpit for Jesus' preaching. When He has finished, Jesus commands Peter to launch out into the deep water and let down his nets. Defying all the rules of fishing, against his own better judgement, he obeys. The resulting miraculous catch of fish causes Peter to bow, instantly acknowledging his own sin, but over and above this he experiences the presence of God, wonder, amazement, fear and a multitude of other emotions. He realises he is in the presence of **majesty**.

Luke puts it like this: **"When Simon Peter saw this he fell at Jesus' knees and said, 'Go away from me, Lord: I am a sinful man!' ... Then Jesus said to Simon, 'Don't be afraid; from now on you will catch men.' So they pulled their boats up on the shore, left everything and followed him."** (Luke 5:8-11)

He falls on his knees, submitting his life to a new future, to a new obedience, to a new reverence.

Let us do the same.

Joyce

One Year Plan : Psalm 78, Luke 5, Numbers 29 – 30
Two Year Plan : Psalm 43, Romans 2, Exodus 1 (Yr 1)
1 Chronicles 26 (Yr 2)

Renovation or Resurrection?

I had acquired a rather lovely old chest, inlaid with brass – a family heirloom, steeped in history. Sadly, when it was being transported, a corner piece was knocked off. Every time I walked past the chest, the damage shouted out to be repaired. Sometime later, I found the wood glue and proceeded to restore it to its former glory. In reality it is still an old chest bearing the many blemishes that have been inflicted through the years.

Whilst pondering this, as we were approaching the Easter weekend, I thought about the effect of the resurrection of Jesus and the incredible fact that resurrection is not renovation.

When Jesus rose from the dead He was not aiming to patch up and improve our old life with all its blemishes but to give us a brand new life, a new beginning, a new start.

In Revelation 21:3-5 it says, **"And I heard a loud voice from the throne saying, 'Now the dwelling of God is with men, and he will live with them. They will be his people, and God himself will be with them and be their God. He will wipe every tear from their eyes. There will be no more death or mourning or crying or pain, for the old order of things has passed away.' He who was seated on the throne said, 'I am making everything new!'"**

That is the message of Easter: **"I am making everything new!"** And as I preached once on Easter Day, a verse from the Proverbs kept coming to my mind: **"The path of the righteous is like the first gleam of dawn, shining ever brighter till the full light of day."** (Proverbs 4:18)

Celebrate your new life; don't be drawn in to trying to improve the old. Resurrection makes you brand new and starts you on a new day!

Charles

One Year Plan : Psalm 79, Luke 6, Numbers 31 - 32
Two Year Plan : Psalm 44:1-8, Romans 3:1-20, Exodus 2 (Yr 1)
1 Chronicles 27 (Yr 2)

Be an Ebed-Melech

I wonder if the name Ebed-Melech means anything to you. Probably not! It's the name of a Cushite working in the royal palace and living at the same time as Jeremiah, the prophet. He was a compassionate man who found himself at the right place at the right time, and he chose to act with integrity and courage on behalf of a servant of God who was in big trouble.

Jeremiah had been speaking God-given prophetic words demanding actions that the people were unwilling to take, and now the king's officials wanted to get rid of him. They lowered Jeremiah into a well and left him to die.

Ebed-Melech discovered this and chose to act on behalf of Jeremiah. He chose his moment, when the king was sitting at the gate of the city (which was like a court room in those days, where complaints were listened to and judgement executed.)

He presented his case before the King, who commanded Ebed-Melech to take thirty men and lift Jeremiah the prophet out of the cistern before he died. You can read the full account of it in Jeremiah 38:1-14.

Some time later Jeremiah was able to save the life of Ebed-Melech when the Babylonians were taking everyone captive and sending many to their death. Jeremiah sent this message to him: **"But I will rescue you on that day, declares the Lord; you will not be handed over to those you fear."** (Jeremiah 39:15-18)

A spiritual principle is operating here; it is sowing and reaping – **"Give and it will be given unto you." "He who refreshes others will himself be refreshed."**

Where you have been placed is not an accident – your job, your life, your school, your sphere of influence – it is a God-appointment!

And today you could be an Ebed-Melech!

Joyce

One Year Plan : Psalm 80, Luke 7, Numbers 33 - 34
Two Year Plan : Psalm 44:9-16, Romans 3:21-31, Exodus 3 (Yr 1)
1 Chronicles 28 (Yr 2)

When the Oil Runs Out

Some years ago, my son Ben built a kit car, of the Lotus 7 variety; it is a Raw Striker with a Toyota 1.6 litre, 20 valve engine – for those who are interested. As Ben lives in Australia with Anne and their children, I have valiantly volunteered to be the custodian of this wonderful car.

At one time the sump failed and deposited all the engine oil on the garage floor. Since that time I was left handling the saga of the new sump. I will not bore you with the details, but after over two months, I fitted the new sump and was looking forward to getting out and enjoying a blast.

I thought the job was completed, sump fitted, new oil in the engine, and ready to go, but when I started the engine there was no oil pressure. Somehow or other the oil was not circulating, and so I sought some expert advice and was told, **"The car has been unused for more than two months; all the oil has drained out and you will need to prime the oil filter in order to get the circulation going."**

As I pondered the dilemma, it seemed that I was looking at the parallel of a spiritual situation. The oil of the Holy Spirit in our lives needs to be constantly topped up and be circulating or we dry up and cannot function. In Ephesians 5:18-19 it says, **"Be filled with the Spirit. Speak to one another with psalms, hymns and spiritual songs."** Being filled with the Holy Spirit is to happen daily and to be expressed in praise to God.

The kit car is unable to function when there is insufficient oil or when it is not circulating properly. Our lives will grind to a halt if we do not make sure that we are filled with the oil of the Spirit.

How is your oil supply?

Charles

One Year Plan : Psalm 81, Luke 8, Numbers 35 - 36
Two Year Plan : Psalm 44:17-26, Romans 4, Exodus 4 (Yr 1)
1 Chronicles 29 (Yr 2)

Don't Insult the Spirit of Grace

The Lord Jesus paid for my sins and yours by becoming a sacrifice acceptable to God. He totally redeemed my life by giving His – the sacrificial Lamb of God who takes away the sin of the world.

Hebrews 10:10 says, **"We have been made holy through the sacrifice of the body of Jesus Christ once for all."** But later on, in verse 26, the writer to the Hebrews indicates the seriousness with which God views deliberate sin and disobedience: **"If we deliberately keep on sinning after we have received the knowledge of the truth, no sacrifice for sins is left, but only fearful expectation of judgement ... for the one who has insulted the Spirit of grace."**

Those who rejected the law of Moses died without mercy. What do you think will happen if we trample on God's Son, call His blood unholy and insult the Spirit of grace?

Don't mess with sin or you may find that God messes with you!

There is always forgiveness available after confession and repentance, when we acknowledge wrongdoing. Here, the writer is talking about deliberately doing things we know God has forbidden. We may even be doing them with the attitude, **"It doesn't matter; He'll forgive me anyway!"**

We always live by the grace of God, but it is not cheap grace. Jesus has made us anew so that we will live to please Him. Don't undervalue or insult the Spirit of grace.

We can be deceived; let us pray as David did, **"Search me, O God, and know my heart ... see if there is any offensive way in me and lead me in the way everlasting."** (Psalm 139:23)

Joyce

One Year Plan : Psalm 82, Luke 9, Deuteronomy 1 - 2
Two Year Plan : Psalm 45, Romans 5, Exodus 5 (Yr 1)
2 Chronicles 1 (Yr 2)

A God of Justice

I have been shocked to hear of acts of injustice and dishonesty being perpetrated by people who claim to be committed Christians. We seem to have come a long way from the statement 'My word is my bond'. The handshake that was all most people needed to seal a contract seems to have been abandoned.

Have God's principles changed? Have we become swallowed up in today's dishonest society? Does everything have to be fought out in the law courts?

Do we believe God takes note of our actions, words and motives? Years ago I was offered a large sum of money if I broke a promise to sell my house to buyer A. I chose not to do this. Buyer B could not understand my action. Subsequent blessings have proved God's faithfulness.

Listen carefully to what God says in His Word.

- **"Do not be deceived. God cannot be mocked. A man reaps what he sows."** (Galatians 6:7)
- **"The Lord, the Lord, the compassionate and gracious God, slow to anger, abounding in love and faithfulness, maintaining love to thousands, and forgiving wickedness, rebellion and sin. Yet he does not leave the guilty unpunished."** (Exodus 34:6-7)
- **"Righteousness exalts a nation, but sin is a disgrace to any people."** (Proverbs 14:34)
- **"For the Lord is a God of justice. Blessed are those who wait for him."** (Isaiah 30:18)
- Jesus said, **"If you hold to my teaching, you are really my disciples. Then you will know the truth and the truth will set you free."** (John 8:31-32)

Let us break the mould and live in truth, righteousness and integrity!

Charles

One Year Plan : Psalm 83, Luke 10, Deuteronomy 3 - 4
Two Year Plan : Psalm 46, Romans 6, Exodus 6 (Yr 1)
2 Chronicles 2 (Yr 2)

Urim and Thummim

Part of the equipment of an Old Testament priest were two stones called the Urim and Thummim. He wore them tucked in behind the breastplate over his heart. There is no record of how they were made or how they came into the possession of the High Priest. What we do know is that one meant **"Yes"** and the other **"No"**. They may have glowed like fire because Urim means 'radiant light, aglow' and Thummim means 'truth and integrity'. They were a vital part of the clothing of the High Priest, and these were the instructions given for wearing them: **"Also put the Urim and Thummim in the breastpiece, so they may be over Aaron's heart whenever he enters the presence of the Lord. Thus Aaron will always have the means of making decisions for the Israelites over his heart."** (Exodus 28:30)

Numbers 27:21 tells us how it worked: **"He is to stand before Eleazar the priest, who will obtain decisions for him by inquiring of the Urim before the Lord. At his command he and the entire community of the Israelites will go out, and at his command they will come in."**

Psalm 43:3 says, **"Send forth your light and your truth, let them guide me."** In situations that required an answer, the priest inquired of the Lord using the stones.

As people of the New Covenant, God has given to us not a couple of stones but the inner witness – the glow or presence – of the Holy Spirit. He is the person who communicates: to warn, to encourage, and to direct. He is also positioned near the heart – but internally – and He is never off duty.

Today, purpose to hear what your inner witness has to say to you at every turn and in every situation. Enquire of Him; find out what pleases Him. Ask questions and enjoy the privilege of being led by the Spirit of the living God.

The Holy Spirit wants to give you more than **"Yes"** or **"No"**.

Joyce

One Year Plan : Psalm 84, Luke 11, Deuteronomy 5 - 6
Two Year Plan : Psalm 47, Romans 7, Exodus 7 (Yr 1)
2 Chronicles 3 (Yr 2)

Treasure

Where is your treasure? Jesus wanted to know the answer as He addressed those listening to His famous Sermon on the Mount, recorded in Matthew's Gospel.

Jesus said, **"Do not store up for yourselves treasures on earth, where moth and rust destroy, and where thieves break in and steal. But store up for yourselves treasures in heaven ... For where your treasure is, there your heart will be also."** (Matthew 6:19-21)

You can test out where your treasure is by looking at what you give your time to, what dominates your thinking, and how you respond emotionally.

If your relationship to God is a priority, you will give time to seeking Him – to worship, prayer and reading His Word. You will devote yourself to building a living, vital and personal relationship with God, who will be at the very centre of your life.

Jesus goes on to say that if your treasure is in heaven then you will not worry about everyday things. He says, **"Therefore I tell you, do not worry about your life, what you will eat or drink ... And why do you worry about clothes? See how the lilies of the field grow ... Your heavenly Father knows what you need."**

When we set our hearts on following Jesus, we know we can trust Him to meet our every need. We know He can provide for us, even in the middle of a financial crisis. When our treasure is in heaven, we can live at peace, in total confidence that He is able to do more than we can ask or imagine.

Jesus continues, **"But seek first his kingdom and his righteousness, and all these things will be given to you as well."** (Matthew 6:33)

If your heart is set on seeking God's kingdom, you will be developing and deepening your relationship with Him, but at the same time He has promised to meet all your practical needs.

So, where is your treasure?

Charles

One Year Plan : Psalm 85, Luke 12, Deuteronomy 7 - 8
Two Year Plan : Psalm 48:1-8, Romans 8:1-17, Exodus 8 (Yr 1)
2 Chronicles 4 (Yr 2)

Time to Dream

When God wants to get through to me on a particular subject and I seem to be a bit slow on the uptake, He starts to challenge me from a variety of directions.

A friend was encouraging me to **dream big dreams**, to imagine what I could do to serve my community if I had unlimited resources. Rather than being excited, my somewhat glum response was, **"I don't dream; it's more of an American thing."** I then justified my passivity in rather super-spiritual terms, explaining that I tried to live in very close contact with Jesus and trusted He would lead me – I would just follow!

Next, verses started popping out of my daily Bible readings. Several were about the **desires of the heart**, and I woke up to the fact that God was trying to get my attention and challenging my passivity. Proverbs 10:24 says, **"What the wicked dreads will overtake him; what the righteous desire will be granted."**

I remembered how when we moved from Sussex to Somerset, I had written a list of twelve items that I wanted in our new home. It included a garden that did not grow weeds! When reviewing this list many months after we had moved, I found to my amazement that I was able to tick every point. I had written the list rather casually; God had taken me more seriously.

So why don't we dream or set goals? We have a Father in heaven who is on record as being One for whom nothing is impossible (Luke 1:37). Are we prepared to trust Him with our innermost longings? Or do we not trust our own motives; are we afraid of selfishness?

Proverbs 3:5-6 says, **"Trust in the LORD with all your heart and lean not on your own understanding; in all your ways acknowledge him, and he will make your paths straight."**

Psalm 37:4 says, **"Delight yourself in the Lord and he will give you the desires of your heart."**

Dream with God, seek to co-operate with His view of your future.

Joyce

One Year Plan : Psalm 86, Luke 13, Deuteronomy 9 - 10
Two Year Plan : Psalm 48:9-14, Romans 8:18-39, Exodus 9 (Yr 1)
2 Chronicles 5 (Yr 2)

One Thing – Many Things

Do you find it difficult to set priorities? There are so many demands, it seems time just evaporates, and you arrive at the end of the day without having achieved a fraction of what you intended. Is it a modern-day symptom of the hectic-paced world we live in?

No, it was the same in Jesus' day. When He visited the home of Martha and Mary He noticed their contrasting lifestyles. **"Martha was distracted by all the preparations that had to be made,"** (Luke 10:40) but **"Mary sat at the Lord's feet listening to what he said."** (verse 39)

Martha felt that she had a raw deal as she did all the housework alone and was not slow in voicing her complaint to Jesus. She said, **"Lord, don't you care that my sister has left me to do the work by myself? Tell her to help me!"** (verse 40)

Jesus replied, **"Martha, Martha you are worried and upset about many things, but only one thing is needed. Mary has chosen what is better, and it will not be taken away from her."** (verses 41-42)

There are **many things** that are always screaming out for our attention, but there is only **one thing** that is important. The urgent is always the enemy of the important.

Psalm 27:4 says, **"<u>One thing</u> I ask of the Lord, this is what I seek: that I may dwell in the house of the Lord all the days of my life, to gaze upon the beauty of the Lord, and to seek him in his temple."**

Mark 10:21 says, **"Jesus looked at him and loved him. '<u>One thing</u> you lack,' he said, 'Go sell everything you have and give to the poor, and you will have treasure in heaven. Then come, follow me.'"**

In Philippians 3:13, Paul writes, **"But <u>one thing</u> I do: Forgetting what is behind and straining towards what is ahead."**

In the middle of the demands of **many things**, what is the **one thing** that God is telling you to do today?

Charles

One Year Plan : Psalm 87, Luke 14, Deuteronomy 11 - 12
Two Year Plan : Psalm 49:1-11, Romans 9, Exodus 10 (Yr 1)
2 Chronicles 6 (Yr 2)

The Love Test

The way we treat people is important to God. Numbers 5:5 tells us that if we wrong one another in any way we are unfaithful to the Lord. When Saul was persecuting the Christians and throwing them in prison on account of their faith, Jesus appeared to him asking a question: **"Saul, Saul, why are you persecuting me?"** Jesus was so identified with His people that He counted opposition and persecution of His followers as a direct attack on Him. In Matthew 25:40-46 it says, **"I tell you the truth, whatever you did not do for one of the least of these, you did not do for me."**

I find this greatly challenging; it questions the quality of my love for Jesus. He is easy to love – He loves me so perfectly and completely – but what about other people?

One day I had been particularly gritty towards my husband. I can't remember the details, but I do remember complaining to the Lord, who very gently but firmly rebuked me in this way. He asked me if I loved him. **"Yes,"** I replied, **"you know I do."** There was, however, a sting in the tail! He told me that my love for Him was measured by my love for my husband Charles! This made me look at myself and evaluate my behaviour. In moaning about, and criticising, my husband, I was criticising Jesus in him. In dishonouring him I was dishonouring Jesus in him. It put the spotlight on my behaviour.

The Apostle John has some strong words on this subject in one of his letters: **"The man who says, 'I know him,' but does not do what he commands is a liar."** (1 John 2:4)

"If anyone says, 'I love God,' yet hates his brother, he is a liar. For anyone who does not love his brother, whom he has seen, cannot love God, whom he has not seen." (1 John 4:20)

Today, ask God for His forgiveness, confess your failure to love in this way and ask for heavenly resources.

"Love one another, as I have loved you."

Joyce

One Year Plan : Psalm 88, Luke 15, Deuteronomy 13 - 14
Two Year Plan : Psalm 49:12-20, Romans 10, Exodus 11 (Yr 1)
2 Chronicles 7 (Yr 2)

The Comparison Game

At certain times we all fall into the trap of the **comparison game**. However, it is a completely pointless exercise because there will always be people you consider better, more fortunate and more talented than you and similarly those who are less fortunate and have lesser ability. When you have decided on your place in the pecking order you have achieved nothing!

This thought struck me when reading Galatians 6:4 which says, **"Each one should test his own actions. Then he can take pride in himself, without comparing himself to someone else, for each one should carry his own load."**

The fact is that each one of us is unique, and God has a purpose that He wants to fulfil in you. Someone else cannot achieve your purpose, and you cannot fulfil their destiny. Jesus said, **"You did not choose me, but I chose you and appointed you to go and bear fruit – fruit that will last."** (John 15:16)

So each day, God is calling you to follow Him. That means that you need to listen to His voice and be responsive to His directions. What you achieve may seem small and insignificant in your eyes, but Jesus said, **"I tell you the truth, whatever you did for one of the least of these brothers of mine, you did it for me."** (Matthew 25:40) Do what He tells you, and you will then be bearing the fruit that Jesus is speaking about.

In one of the letters where Paul is sharing his heart, he says, **"I press on to take hold of that for which Christ Jesus took hold of me."** (Philippians 3:12) Today realise that God has a unique call on your life; He is not comparing you with anyone else, and he is delighted when you live for Him with joy and freedom.

Jesus said, **"I won't lay anything heavy or ill-fitting on you. Keep company with me and you'll learn to live freely and lightly."** (Matthew 11:29, The Message)

Charles

One Year Plan : Psalm 89, Luke 16, Deuteronomy 15 - 16
Two Year Plan : Psalm 50:1-15, Romans 11:1-24, Exodus 12 (Yr 1)
2 Chronicles 8 (Yr 2)

See, Hear and Obey

Jesus spoke the **'Parable of the Sower'** to a large crowd, who He said needed this storytelling method because their understanding was limited. Jesus explained that their ears could hardly hear, their eyes were closed and their hearts were calloused – not a pretty picture!

To His disciples, Jesus declared, **"But blessed are your eyes because they see, and your ears because they hear."** (Matthew 13:16)

If you are a child of God, a disciple of Jesus, you can expect to both **see** and **hear** His voice today. Listen to His voice, see what He is doing, enquire of the Lord – He loves to answer questions.

God loves to communicate with His children. Rebekah, Isaac's wife, was wondering why the twins she was carrying in her womb were giving her such a bad time as they jostled each other inside her. So she asked God, **"'Why is this happening to me?' The Lord said to her, 'Two nations are in your womb...'"** (Genesis 25:22-23) Thus, the destiny of Esau and Jacob was revealed to their parents even before birth.

If God were to call out your name would you be listening? Ananias was, and God used him to help launch the Apostle Paul upon his amazing ministry. You can read the full story in Acts 9.

Your ears and eyes are blessed, but you need to use them in co-operation with the Holy Spirit. God wants to speak to you and show you many amazing things.

Don't be blind, deaf or hard-hearted – rather, **see, hear and obey!**

Joyce

One Year Plan : Psalm 90, Luke 17, Deuteronomy 17 - 18
Two Year Plan : Psalm 50:16-23, Romans 11:25-36, Exodus 13 (Yr 1)
2 Chronicles 9 (Yr 2)

Settled

I was reading a verse in Peter's letter which says, **"But may the God of all grace ... perfect, establish, strengthen and settle you,"** (1 Peter 5:10, NKJV) and the word 'settle' jumped off the page.

'Settle' is an old fashioned word, but it is very powerful and succinct. We talk about **settling the children**, which means that they have gone to bed and are peacefully asleep. Then there is **settling an account**, which means that it is paid and the debt has gone. When people move into a new home, we may well ask them the question, **"Have you settled in yet?"** Here again we are speaking about a place of rest, peace and contentment.

The full, complete verse from Peter says, **"But may the God of all grace, who called us to His eternal glory by Christ Jesus, after you have suffered a while, perfect, establish, strengthen and settle you."**

Are you **settled** in mind and heart? It is a promise from God to all His called and chosen people. It does not mean that you are immune from trouble because the verse states, **"...after you have suffered a while."** There are so many things seeking to rob Christians of their peace and strength. I believe that God's word for you today is, **"Be settled."**

In Isaiah 26:3 it says, **"You will keep in perfect peace him whose mind is steadfast [settled] because he trusts in you."**

Psalm 16:8 says, **"I have set the LORD always before me. Because he is at my right hand, I will not be shaken [unsettled]."**

Once again, whatever the circumstances around you, **be settled!**

Charles

One Year Plan : Psalm 91, Luke 18, Deuteronomy 19 - 20
Two Year Plan : Psalm 51:1-12, Romans 12, Exodus 14 (Yr 1)
2 Chronicles 10 (Yr 2)

Remembering: the Key to Hope

Remembering can be a powerful weapon to fight off hopelessness and despair.

So often the Old Testament prophets told the Children of Israel to remember what God had done in their past history. Remembering can bring **hope**. If **hope** is eroded, it's not long before hopelessness turns to fear of the future and opens the door to cynicism and an ever-deepening negative hole.

As Christians we are not immune from attacks, but we do have weapons given by the Holy Spirit to defend ourselves. **Hope** always believes and is confident of good happening because God is for us, with us and in us.

One time we were very short of cash with a pile of bills, all of which needed to be paid. Charles, as he looked at these, was miserable, tired, and weary of living with no resources. Our God had never failed us, yet He seemed to delight in providing at the last minute!

Charles told the Lord how he was feeling, and was prompted by the Holy Spirit to remember God's goodness to us in the past. On his desk was a photo of our children, and so he started to thank God for them, for the way God had blessed them, protected them, provided for them, etc. Soon he was remembering the thousands of ways God had faithfully poured His love upon us. As he did, the despair, sadness and self-pity were replaced by **hope** and joy; and then the phone rang! It was Charles' secretary telling him that we had received a gift a couple of days earlier, but because it had arrived on our free day, she had respected our privacy and had restrained from phoning. The gift more than covered the bills so even the despair proved to be a deception!

Romans 15:13 says, **"May the God of hope fill you with all joy and peace as you trust in him, so that you may overflow with hope by the power of the Holy Spirit."**

Today, bring to mind the good things God has done for you. **Use remembering to attack all that seeks to bind you in helplessness.**

Joyce

One Year Plan : Psalm 92, Luke 19, Deuteronomy 21 - 22
Two Year Plan : Psalm 51:13-19, Romans 13, Exodus 15 (Yr 1)
2 Chronicles 11 (Yr 2)

Rest

When you say, **"I need some rest!"** you might be thinking of spending a little longer in bed or taking a break from certain responsibilities. However, when Jesus spoke about rest He was not thinking of either of these situations.

Jesus said, **"Come to me, all you who are weary and burdened, and I will give you rest. Take my yoke upon you ... for my yoke is easy and my burden is light."** (Matthew 11:28-29) The **rest** Jesus was speaking about was not an absence of activity; it was a deep inner rest that comes from relying on the strength Jesus gives and not on your own ability.

So, are you driven by the tyranny of the urgent or the demands of people around you? Are you working from a place of complete rest, not trusting your own strength or wisdom but drawing your energy and resources from Jesus?

The writer to the Hebrews has a similar message: **"There remains, then, a Sabbath-rest for the people of God; for anyone who enters God's rest also rests from his own work ..."** (Hebrews 4:9-10)

If we will bring our responsibilities and schedules to Jesus each day, He will enable us to fulfil the tasks of the day – not under pressure but from a place of rest. Does this sound impossible?

Jeremiah 6:16 says, **"Stand at the crossroads and look; ask for the ancient paths, ask where the good way is, and walk in it, and you will find rest for your souls."**

Psalm 91:1 says, **"He who dwells in the shelter of the Most High will rest in the shadow of the Almighty."**

In our stress-filled world, there is a place of rest. Live there!

Charles

One Year Plan : Psalm 93, Luke 20, Deuteronomy 23 - 24
Two Year Plan : Psalm 52, Romans 14, Exodus 16 (Yr 1)
2 Chronicles 12 (Yr 2)

Planting Seeds

When I was a little kid I planted a potato in the garden. It had been explained to me that given time and the right conditions it would grow a green top and eventually produce baby potatoes. The green top appeared, grew, and I waited, asking my father whether it had got any babies yet? Impatiently, I scraped a bit of earth away and sought to investigate the crop without disturbing the plant; nothing was happening. Then some weeks later, my patience running out, I again tried to take a look. I fiddled around so much that I managed to uproot the rather unhealthy loose plant and exposed some tiny new potatoes; I was thrilled, but they were hardly a good crop as they had not been given time to mature.

Sometimes you just have to wait! Seeds germinate in different ways and at different speeds; they are living organisms and, as such, beyond our control. I see words and prayers as seeds growing in unseen ways – sometimes forgotten and yet suddenly pushing up through barren ground into visibility.

Once planted, keep watering your seeds, but resist the desire to dig them up to see how they are doing! God is the Master Gardener, and He alone can see into the hearts of men and women. His timing is always perfect, and He lovingly tends His creation.

I remember one week recognising that some of my 'seeds' had germinated and become visible. I was greatly encouraged to see two families back in church after many weeks. Another person who had suffered much pain received the Word with joy and revelation and broke through to hope and healing. Another friend who had been surrounded with a very hard shell saw God work on his behalf, and the shell began to crack.

In 1 Corinthians 3:6 it says, **"I planted the seed, Apollos watered it, but God made it grow."** The seasons are changing; the ground is warming up; keep watering your seeds believing for harvest. **"Let us not become weary ... for at the proper time we will reap a harvest if we do not give up."** (Galatians 6:9)

Joyce

One Year Plan : Psalm 94, Luke 21, Deuteronomy 25 - 27
Two Year Plan : Psalm 53, Romans 15, Exodus 17 (Yr 1)
2 Chronicles 13 (Yr 2)

Protect your Environment

A friend of mine was visiting the home of a member of his church and was amazed to find that Radio 2 played permanently all day from getting up until lights out! A few days later he visited another home later where the television was on whether anyone was watching or not.

Both these scenarios are potentially dangerous. To allow everything and anything to enter our ears and eyes, influence our thinking, or just dull our minds, is not good.

It is not just the radio or TV which is creating the wrong environment; we need to be very careful of what we allow to go on around us.

Paul warns Timothy to **"avoid godless chatter, because those who indulge in it will become more and more ungodly"**. (2 Timothy 2:16) He goes on to say, **"Don't have anything to do with foolish and stupid arguments, because you know they produce quarrels."** (verse 23) When speaking to the church in Ephesus, Paul says, **"Nor should there be any obscenity, foolish talk or coarse joking, which are out of place, but rather thanksgiving."** (Ephesians 5:4)

We are living in a very negative world, where we need to monitor what we allow to go on around us.

After a busy day when Jesus had fed five thousand people and spent time teaching and healing the people, the Bible says, **"After he had dismissed the crowd, he went up on a mountainside by himself to pray. When evening came he was there alone."** (Matthew 14:23) He knew the importance of being quiet and being alone with God.

In Psalm 32, David declares, **"You are my hiding place; you will protect me from trouble and surround me with songs of deliverance."** And in the well-known Psalm 23 we read, **"He leads me beside quiet waters, he restores my soul."**

What is your environment like? Full of noise, strife, arguments, godless chatter and coarse joking? Or is it full of peace, quiet, songs of praise, joy, laughter and happy sounds?

Protect your environment – it is very important.

Charles

One Year Plan : Psalm 95, Luke 22, Deuteronomy 28
Two Year Plan : Psalm 54, Romans 16, Exodus 18 (Yr 1)
2 Chronicles 14 (Yr 2)

Giving Honour

Have you ever reflected on how much you owe to people who have influenced your life at various times and stages? It is not something I often do; life is lived for the most part in the now! However, it is good to remember and to give thanks.

During a short break I read a fictional book called **'Five people you meet in heaven'**. Each of the five people influenced the writer's life – some good, some bad. As the central character in the book meets each in turn he is able to reflect on their part in his life, to gain understanding and to be thankful.

Whilst writing about incidents in my childhood I have been remembering with gratitude people who have influenced me. They probably didn't know it at the time and as far as they were concerned didn't think about what they were doing – they just did it!

There was a neighbour who taught me to do a job properly. **"If it's worth doing, it's worth doing well,"** she said as she made me iron the corners of the handkerchief again!

There was an aunt who had her own daughter and husband to care for as well as a busy social life – but she always welcomed me into her home. Sometimes, I would arrive before her daughter woke up, and yet she always made room for me. Would I have been as welcoming?

I thought about the teacher who saw the hurt inside me rather than my rebellious behaviour and accepted me and made an important contribution towards my ability to change.

Many of the people I found myself remembering have died – but what of those who are still alive; have they ever heard me express my thanks for their friendship, trust, encouragement and many other things?

Let us be of the company of people who encourage and are genuinely thankful for each other. We British so often **think good things** but fail to communicate them. Americans have been taught to speak out their encouragement and appreciation of one another.

So today, a **big thank you** to all of you who have so often encouraged me, believed in me, and expressed it.

Joyce

One Year Plan : Psalm 96, Luke 23, Deuteronomy 29 - 30
Two Year Plan : Psalm 55:1-14, Mark 1:1-20, Exodus 19 (Yr 1)
2 Chronicles 15 (Yr 2)

Freedom

Are you free or are you a slave? It is the birthright of every Christian to live in complete freedom. That means freedom from guilt, shame, fear, worry, doubt, obeying rules and being religious, to name just a few. Jesus said, **"So if the Son sets you free, you will be free indeed."** (John 8:36)

This has been the battleground for believers ever since the church was founded. The central message of Paul's letter to the Galatians is the conflict between bondage and freedom. Paul even needed to confront Peter because of his legalistic behaviour.

This set me thinking about this whole issue of freedom. Paul writes, **"Are you so foolish? After beginning with the Spirit are you now trying to attain your goal by human effort?"** (Galatians 3:3) Many of you will remember the joy of being released into the wonderfully liberating baptism in the Holy Spirit. Are you still enjoying this freedom, or has following Jesus become a bit of a drudge?

The Message translation of Matthew 11:29 says that Jesus will teach us to **"live freely and lightly"**. So that is the challenge; you have been birthed into freedom, but are you living in it?

You may be worrying about financial pressures; the response Jesus gave to this was, **"Therefore I tell you do not worry about what you will eat or drink; or about food and clothes .... your heavenly Father knows what you need."** (Matthew 6)

You may be facing a profound healing need, and rather than being overwhelmed by fear, you need to know that **"nothing is impossible with God"**. (Luke 1:37)

You may be struggling with guilt over a past sin – but the victory of Jesus on the cross has dealt with that: **"He forgave us all our sins having cancelled the written code ... that was against us."** (Colossians 2:14)

That is why Paul reaches a climax in his letter to the Galatians when he says, **"It is for freedom that Christ has set us free. Stand firm, then, and do not let yourselves be burdened again by a yoke of slavery."** (Galatians 5:1)

Live freely and lightly today!

Charles

One Year Plan : Psalm 97, Luke 24, Deuteronomy 31 - 32
Two Year Plan : Psalm 55:15-23, Mark 1:21-45, Exodus 20 (Yr 1)
2 Chronicles 16 (Yr 2)

Reverse Culture Shock

I was told it was probably reverse culture shock... Having just returned to England after six weeks in Central Asia, I was finding life a little unpredictable. I had spent the first weekend in my own home with our youngest son, his wife and four children – they were displaced persons themselves, waiting to return to their work in Chad.

After three days in our own bed, we re-located to the home of our son Daniel and his wife, Tanya, who were in Burundi helping a work among orphan children. We were there to keep the school routine going for their children and be the taxi service to music lessons, dancing, after-school jobs and trips to the skate park.

Nothing was normal; every routine was different. I had to ask where everything lived and that on top of the five hour time change and other adjustments. It was a strange time. I felt disoriented. Had I been praying enough? Had I been reading enough scripture? I was finding it hard to find time to be alone even to think my own thoughts!

Then God spoke two comforting words. He said, **"I am outside of time; I do not evaluate use of time as you do."** There are times when we can beat ourselves up because we haven't been able to spend the time we would like in 'spiritual activity'. But with God a day is like a thousand years, and a thousand years are like a day.

God also said, **"Be aware that I am with you, in you, never leaving you. I am with you, part of you, organically linked to who you are and all you do. We do not need set times to communicate; we are one."** God continued, **"When you start thinking like this you see life as a whole, not in separate compartments. I am with you when you lie down, when you work, rest, sleep."**

So, God's word to me was, **"Relax! My Holy Spirit who indwells you is wisdom and truth and will guide, correct, instruct and lead. Trust me as you let my word be your external source of instruction and my Spirit your internal compass."**

Joyce

One Year Plan : Psalm 98, 1 Corinthians 1, Deuteronomy 33 - 34
Two Year Plan : Psalm 56, Mark 2, Exodus 21 (Yr 1)
2 Chronicles 17 (Yr 2)

Nothing is Impossible

I was reading a prayer letter and came across the statement: **"So often we miss what God has for us because the task seems too impossible."** Immediately the verse came into my mind, **"What is impossible with men is possible with God,"** and with it a memory of a very beautiful little girl called Ruby. She is the daughter of my niece Esther.

Jonny and Esther had been married for thirteen years and longed for a child. Everything humanly had been done, but it appeared that there was no way that they were going to be able to have a child of their own.

When the angel told Mary she was going to conceive, her questioning received the response, **"For nothing is impossible with God."** (Luke 1:37) Jonny and Esther held on to that same promise and made it their own until they proved it true.

Jesus not only declared that nothing was impossible with God; He said something even more amazing: **"I tell you the truth, if you have faith as small as a mustard seed, you can say to this mountain, 'Move from here to there' and it will move. Nothing will be impossible for you."** (Matthew 17:20)

Is there an unattainable task ahead of you? Have you been battling with an impossible situation? Have visions of what you were to become and to achieve been lost through delay and disappointment?

I believe that God wants to restore your hopes and dreams. The Bible is full of people who attempted daunting tasks, for example, childless Abraham who birthed a nation and David who overcame Goliath and numerous enemies who threatened his life.

The writer to the Hebrews said, **"We do not want you to become lazy, but to imitate those who through faith and patience inherit what has been promised."** (Hebrews 6:12)

Charles

One Year Plan : Psalm 99, 1 Corinthians 2, Joshua 1 - 2
Two Year Plan : Psalm 57, Mark 3:1-19, Exodus 22 (Yr 1)
2 Chronicles 18 (Yr 2)

Look and Live

Moses had a crisis: snakes were biting the Israelites and they were dying. He cried out to God, who to his surprise did not produce a serum to cure the snake bites but told Moses to make a brass snake and put it on a pole and to give the command, **"Look and live."** The lifeless snake released life and healing in the people. It sounds too easy.

Jesus recounted this incident as He spoke about His death and the way we are to receive from Him. When you look to Him for your salvation, you see a man dying a death that you should have died, taking punishment that you deserved. Isn't just looking too simple? Surely we need to do something?

Remember the thieves who were hanging alongside Jesus on two other crosses. One railed on Him, but the other looked to Jesus. **"We deserve what we are getting but this man has done nothing wrong!"** He then simply looked at Jesus and said, **"Jesus, remember me when you come into your kingdom."** Immediately Jesus told him, **"...today you will be with me in paradise."** He only looked – was it too easy?

You can also look for healing to Jesus, who spoke to a man who spoiled someone's roof in order to get to Him and said, **"Which is easier to say, 'Your sins are forgiven' or to say, 'Get up, take up your mat and walk'?"** The paralysed man did just that and the watching crowd, filled with awe, said, **"We've seen remarkable things today!"**

You can look to Him who gives wisdom, understanding, strength and patience. He is willing to give you all you need in life. You **look** and receive by believing – it is not rational thinking but rather heart-believing.

So look again to Jesus **"...who has become for us wisdom from God – that is our righteousness, holiness and redemption."** (1 Corinthians 1:30)

It's not too difficult.

Joyce

One Year Plan : Psalm 100, 1 Corinthians 3, Joshua 3 - 4
Two Year Plan : Psalm 58, Mark 3:20-35, Exodus 23 (Yr 1)
2 Chronicles 19 (Yr 2)

Satan Hindered Us

Do you feel that you have a destiny but everything around you is trying to stop it being fulfilled? The Apostle Paul knew how you feel. He had received a word from the Lord who had said to him, **"Take courage! As you have testified about me in Jerusalem, so you must also testify in Rome."** (Acts 27:22)

You might think that having received such a clear word from the Lord it would be plain sailing all the way to Rome. But you would be wrong!

Immediately there is a plot to kill him, which is thwarted by the son of Paul's sister who gets him escorted safely to Caesarea. Then he has to appear before two governors and a king before he boards a ship thinking it will now be an easy passage to Rome.

Wrong! The ship has all kinds of problems, and after incredible delays it runs into a fierce storm which threatens to drown all on board. But God's word will not prove to be untrue, and in the middle of the storm an angel appears before Paul to say, **"Do not be afraid, Paul. You must stand trial before Caesar; and God has graciously given you the lives of all who sail with you."**

It will still take strong faith and determination to reach the goal. For when the boat is shipwrecked, **faith swims!** Now safe on shore, it is cold, miserable, and raining – what does faith **do** now? **Faith lights a fire!** But out of the fire a snake appears and sinks its fangs into Paul. What does faith do when the snake is biting for all it's worth? **Faith shakes it into the fire!**

At last something good happens; Paul is welcomed into the home of Publius the chief official of the island. What does faith do now? **Faith heals his father** and opens the way for an amazing healing meeting for the whole island of Malta.

And three months later Paul sails for Rome, having been supplied with everything he needs to complete his journey and fulfil his destiny.

Don't let satan rob you of your destiny and prevent you reaching your goal. You may have some adventures on the way, but if you have faith you will make it!

Charles

One Year Plan : Psalm 101, 1 Corinthians 4 , Joshua 5 - 6
Two Year Plan : Psalm 59:1-9, Mark 4:1-20, Exodus 24 (Yr 1)
2 Chronicles 20 (Yr 2)

Be United with Me

Modern translations have a way of taking the familiar and using it to both impact and challenge. Here are two examples that have spoken powerfully to me:

Matthew 11:28-30 says, **"Everyone who feels tired and oppressed, come to Me and I will give you rest! Be united with Me and learn from Me, for I have a humble and gentle heart; then you will find peace for your souls. When you are united with Me I make light of your burdens."** (The Truth)

From these verses alone the benefits are obvious – rest, peace, lighter loads – but the access point is the same: **"Be united with Me."** People complain about life being too hectic – no peace – and many are carrying heavy loads. But they want change without following the Master's command, **"Be united with Me."**

The enemy will always try to tell you, "It will take too long to pray, too much time to connect, to be united," and so it becomes a negative cycle. Many are longing for peace, rest, and lifting of load, yet are resisting the means to receive these good things. **"Be united,"** can be a prayer whilst washing the dishes, a song of praise driving to work, a silent glance that says, **"I love you; I need you."**

The second scripture is a paraphrase of Galatians 6:14 where Paul says he has been **"set free from the stifling atmosphere of pleasing others and fitting into the little patterns they dictate"**. (The Message)

Don't let the world around you squeeze you into what it dictates as normal or necessary – when you are united with Jesus, experiencing rest and peace, you will be able to resist unnecessary, time-consuming demands of others which often are introduced with the words **"you ought to"**, **"you must"**, **"everyone does!"**

Today, **connect with Jesus, experience what He promises to give you**, and resist the rat race which is trying to keep you chained to the treadmill.

Joyce

One Year Plan :	Psalm 102, 1 Corinthians 5, Joshua 7 - 8
Two Year Plan :	Psalm 59:10-17, Mark 4:21-41, Exodus 25 (Yr 1) 2 Chronicles 21 (Yr 2)

A Mighty Fortress

I was reading Psalm 46, and when I reached verse 7, **"The Lord Almighty is with us; the God of Jacob is our fortress,"** I realised that this is the verse that inspired the great hymn written by Martin Luther which begins, **"Ein feste Burg ist unser Gott."** in the English language it is translated, **"A mighty fortress is our God, a bulwark never failing."**

There are so many scriptures that speak of God as our help and strength. Nahum 1:7 says, **"The Lord is good, a refuge in times of trouble. He cares for those who trust in him."**

King David had his fair share of trials and tribulations, but in Psalm 18:2 he makes this powerful declaration: **"The Lord is my rock, my fortress, my deliverer; my God is my rock, in whom I take refuge."** It is so easy to sink into self-pity when things go wrong, when it seems that everyone is against you. Anxiety and gloom will not help you in any way – but God will.

Proverbs 18:10 says, **"The name of the Lord is a strong tower, the righteous run into it and they are safe."** It is so possible to run to others, to pour out our woes on whoever is nearby, when to run to the Lord is to go to the only One who can fully meet our needs. James writes, **"If any of you lacks wisdom, he should ask God, who gives generously to all without finding fault, and it will be given to him."** (James 1:5)

I love the verse in Psalm 32:7 where it says, **"You are my hiding place; you will protect me from trouble and surround me with songs of deliverance."**

Go to God today and **let Him be your fortress, your strong tower** – look to Him for wisdom and listen as He sings a song of deliverance over you!

Charles

One Year Plan : Psalm 103, 1 Corinthians 6, Joshua 9 - 10
Two Year Plan : Psalm 60, Mark 5:1-20, Exodus 26 (Yr 1)
2 Chronicles 22 (Yr 2)

Don't Trust in Riches

I have met people who think to be rich would solve all their problems, and I have met rich people who find their riches a responsibility they would rather not have. I have also met others who would gladly exchange their riches for the peace and joy found in people who have so much less.

The Bible speaks a lot about our attitude to money and wealth or lack of it. Whilst reading in 1 Timothy 6, I was marvelling at the practical wisdom that Paul was giving to Timothy. Don't trust in riches which are so uncertain, **"...hope in God, who richly provides us with everything for our enjoyment."** (verse 17)

Proverbs 30:8-9 says, **"...give me neither poverty nor riches, but give me only my daily bread. Otherwise, I may have too much and disown you and say, 'Who is the Lord?' Or I may become poor and steal, and so dishonour the name of God."**

Paul goes beyond the natural when he says, **"...take hold of the life that is truly life."** (1 Timothy 6:19) We must keep our focus beyond the natural; as believers we have the privilege of tapping into supernatural resources. Moses prophesied to the Children of Israel that when they entered the land of plenty, they would forget the God who provided the manna – and they did!

It is good to check your focus – are you trusting in God for provision and help, wisdom and practical directions; or are you trusting in yourself?

We have an African friend who teaches his disciples, **"Our help comes from above, not from abroad."** He teaches his people to look to the Lord and not to the rich western benefactors. God, of course, honours their faith and they see miraculous provision, which enables them to **"take hold of the life that is truly life"** and fulfil God's purpose in their lives.

Bring Jesus into every area of life. He is your provider, but He is so much more than that: your helper, your guide and the One who wants you to enjoy the **"life that is truly life"**.

Joyce

One Year Plan : Psalm 104, 1 Corinthians 7, Joshua 11 - 12
Two Year Plan : Psalm 61, Mark 5:21-43, Exodus 27 (Yr 1)
2 Chronicles 23 (Yr 2)

Do It Now!

Some years ago, a friend of mine bought a very expensive book which promised to help him work more efficiently. When he had finished reading the book he told me that its message could have been given in one sentence: **Do it now!** That book changed his life. He admitted that had the message been written on a postcard he would probably have ignored it. Because it cost so much, he was determined to get his money's worth.

That sentence has also changed my life; I cannot say I always obey it, but I have found it a great help not only in getting things done but also in responding to the voice of God. When God speaks it is important to **do it now!** It could be a prompting to pray, to help someone in need, to make a phone call, to send an email.

I have noticed whilst reading the Gospels that Jesus expected swift obedience when He spoke. When Jesus called Peter and Andrew it says, **"At once they left their nets and followed him."** (Mark 1:18)

When Jesus found Zacchaeus hiding in a tree and asked him to come down, again it says, **"So he came down at once and welcomed him gladly."** (Luke 19:6)

However, it says in Acts 24:25 where Paul was speaking to Felix, that **"as Paul discoursed on righteousness, self-control and the judgement to come, Felix was afraid and said, 'That's enough for now! You may leave. When I find it convenient I will send for you.'"** We never read that Felix ever responded to the challenge to commit his life to Jesus.

The Bible often issues warnings about not acting quickly on God's instructions. Hebrews 3:15 says, **"Today, if you hear his voice do not harden your heart."**

God is prompting many of you to act upon a word He has spoken into your heart and to obey His voice. **Whatever He asks you to do, do it now!**

Charles

One Year Plan : Psalm 105, 1 Corinthians 8, Joshua 13 - 14
Two Year Plan : Psalm 62, Mark 6:1-29, Exodus 28 (Yr 1)
2 Chronicles 24 (Yr 2)

MAY

How Soft is your Heart?

I woke in the night with a question in my heart, an ache that when it formed itself into words sounded like this: **"When are we going to see You move this nation to seek Your help?" "When are we going to see You intervene and reveal Yourself to the helpless and hurting?" "Why do we see more human effort than supernatural intervention?"**

Even as these questions formed in my mind, I found a word forming in my heart which challenged me and which I believe was from God: **"You don't care enough!"** Jesus was constantly moved with compassion for the people He met. He wept over Jerusalem; He saw the people as sheep without shepherds – lost, lonely hurting people. The pain He felt caused Him to draw on supernatural resources received through prayer.

The early Church were convinced that they had answers for the society around them. They also offered the good news of God's love and help. Again their motivation was fuelled by their own experiences of Jesus' love and power, and they were compelled to share the good news of freedom, healing and hope. Peter tells the rulers of his day, **"We can't keep quiet about what we have seen and heard."** (Acts 4:20, The Message)

The prophet Micah lived in similar days to us, at a time when God was mocked or ignored, when foreign gods appeared so attractive. Sex and alcohol numbed the pain as the nation of Israel was attacked by more powerful nations. As you read Micah Chapter 7, it could describe the days in which we now live; Micah, however, refuses to give up. Micah 7:7 in The Message says, **"But me, I'm not giving up. I'm sticking around to see what God will do. I'm waiting for God to make things right. I'm counting on God to listen to me."**

I'm also asking that God's Holy Spirit will touch my heart afresh so that I am delivered from indifference; so that my eyes will see, my ears hear and my heart care; and so that I will cry out for God's mercy on us and our nation.

Joyce

One Year Plan : Psalm 106, 1 Corinthians 9, Joshua 15 - 16
Two Year Plan : Psalm 63, Mark 6:30-56, Exodus 29 (Yr 1)
2 Chronicles 25 (Yr 2)

He Restores my Soul

I had been hearing of many people being overworked, struggling with work/life balance, and trying to cope with stress. While thinking about this the phrase from Psalm 23 came to mind, **"He restores my soul."**

We may think that we are living in the most demanding times and that no-one has ever had to cope with such pressure. But when I began to think about the life of King David, I found the challenges he faced greater than most of our problems.

Having gained honour and acclaim from killing Goliath, he was relentlessly pursued by King Saul who wanted to kill him. During this time he was given the city of Ziklag as a place for his family and followers, and he thought that he now could live in peace. But one day, as he and his men returned to the city, they found it had been attacked, set on fire and all the wives and children had been taken captive – a severe crisis which nearly finished him off. 1 Samuel 30:4-6 says, **"David and his men wept aloud until they had no strength left to weep."** Then it says, **"But David found strength in the Lord his God."** In the moment of extreme trial only God had the resources he needed.

Later, after David became King, his son Absalom tried to usurp his authority and take over the throne. David fled from Jerusalem and eventually arrived at his overnight stopping place where it is recorded, **"The king and all the people with him arrived at their destination exhausted. And there he refreshed himself."** (2 Samuel 16:14)

The Psalm he wrote at that time says, **"My soul finds rest in God alone; my salvation comes from him. He alone is my rock and my salvation; he is my fortress, I will never be shaken."** (Psalm 62:1-2)

The psalms of David show clearly that he had learned how to draw his resources from God. I believe we need to follow his example, so that in our moments of need we can say, **"He restores my soul."**

Charles

One Year Plan : Psalm 107, 1 Corinthians 10, Joshua 17 - 18
Two Year Plan : Psalm 64, Mark 7:1-23, Exodus 30 (Yr 1)
2 Chronicles 26 (Yr 2)

Cursing

Cursing is the opposite of blessing. It uses the power of negative words to release fear, lack, hardship, etc. Jesus said, **"But I tell you who hear me: Love your enemies, do good to those who hate you, bless those who curse you, pray for those who mistreat you."** (Luke 6:27-28)

Words have the power of life and death: words can limit and wither, or words can encourage and build up. We recently watched an amazing YouTube video demonstrating the power of affirming words. It's remarkable how we thrive on affirmation and, equally, how negative statements produce despondency and rob us of self-worth. The video is called 'Validation' – put that word into the search box and watch it for yourself.

Authority figures in your life may have spoken negative words over you which you can easily find yourself repeating. Be careful how you use words; don't curse yourself with statements like **"I'm clumsy"**, **"I'm stupid"**, **"I'm hopeless"**; God calls you the **apple of his eye**. He loves, and delights in you. You can do all things with His help and strength. Jesus lives in you, and He is not stupid or hopeless – and consequently, neither are you. You have been given wisdom, favour, grace and so much more.

If negative words have been spoken over you, ask Jesus to release you from the effect of those words and find a scripture that counteracts them and speaks God's truth and blessing over you. Don't play 'tit for tat' if negative words are directed towards you; neutralise them by speaking the opposite. Always concentrate on building up and not tearing down.

A little girl was being taken out to breakfast by her father. He wanted some quality time with her, and as she ate her food he began to tell her how special she was, how proud he was of her, how she was eating so nicely, and more. When he momentarily stopped so that he could eat his own food, his hand was grabbed before it could reach his mouth and he heard the words, **"More, Daddy, more!"**

Joyce

One Year Plan : Psalm 108, 1 Corinthians 11, Joshua 19 - 20
Two Year Plan : Psalm 65, Mark 7:24-37, Exodus 31 (Yr 1)
2 Chronicles 27 (Yr 2)

Pure Water

A major cause of death throughout the world is the lack of clean water. As we watched the scenes of devastation during the floods in Pakistan, it was hard to grasp that their most urgent need was for pure drinking water.

When Jesus met the woman at the well in Samaria, it was not surprising that the topic of conversation was water. Her reputation made it difficult to be there with everyone else, but she had to visit the well to draw water because her life depended on it.

Jesus began to introduce her to a new source of life and refreshment as He said, **"Everyone who drinks this water will be thirsty again, but whoever drinks the water I give him will never thirst. Indeed the water I give him will become in him a spring of water welling up to eternal life."** (John 4:13)

The Word of God is likened to water in the scriptures and is a vital part of our daily need for cleansing and strength. Paul wrote, **"Christ loved the church and gave himself up for her to make her holy, cleansing her by washing with water through the word."** (Ephesians 5:25-26) The Apostle John said, **"I write to you, young men, because you are strong, and the word of God lives in you, and you have overcome the evil one."** (1 John 2:14)

The world in which we live is full of dirty water. It is very dangerous to drink this water as it can infect us with disease, make us weak and can eventually destroy us. We have a vital need for the pure water of the Word on a daily basis.

When someone first comes to faith there is normally a great hunger for the word: **"Like newborn babies, crave spiritual milk, so that by it you may grow up in your salvation, now that you have tasted that the Lord is good."** (1 Peter 2:2-3)

What are you drinking today?

Charles

One Year Plan : Psalm 109, 1 Corinthians 12, Joshua 21 - 22
Two Year Plan : Psalm 66:1-7, Mark 8:1-21, Exodus 32 (Yr 1)
2 Chronicles 28 (Yr 2)

Will You Swim?

Have you ever watched a young child ready to walk but holding on to the furniture, while the parent is cajoling it to let go and walk on its own? It is a familiar scene. The parent knows the child is steady enough to walk, but fear stops it, and often the parent will stand very close to be ready to reach out a helping hand. When eventually the child succeeds, taking those early independent steps, everyone who is observing the scene shares the joy of success.

In Hosea it is recorded, **"He taught Ephraim to walk taking them by the arms ... drawing them with cords of human kindness."** (Hosea 11:3-4)

Learning to swim is slightly different, but there comes a point where feet come off the bottom and you trust the water to hold you up. Often there is a human hand ready to rescue you at the first sign of sinking – but the aim is to acquire new skills, leading to new experiences and enjoyment.

In the vision that God gave to Ezekiel it says, **"He measured off another thousand, but now it was a river that I could not cross, because the water had risen and was deep enough to swim in."** (Ezekiel 47:5)

Your Heavenly Father knows you are ready to walk and swim. There is a river flowing from the Throne of God – a river that God invites us to swim in. Don't keep your feet on the bottom or remain in the shallows. If God says, **"Swim,"** then He knows you can.

God wants to reveal to you more of His presence, His power, His voice and His heart. Trust Him and experience the new things He has for you. He wants you to flow in the river of His Spirit, to overcome fear, and to adventure with Him as He instructs you.

Joyce

One Year Plan : Psalm 110, 1 Corinthians 13, Joshua 23 - 24
Two Year Plan : Psalm 66:8-15, Mark 8:22-38, Exodus 33 (Yr 1)
2 Chronicles 29 (Yr 2)

Faith is not a Feeling

"Faith is being sure of what we hope for and certain of what we do not see." (Hebrews 11:1)

Faith is not hoping for something; faith is knowing something. Abraham was given a promise from God that he would have a son. He waited twenty-five years for Isaac to be born, and while Isaac was still a child, God gave him an incredible challenge.

"Take your son, go up a mountain and sacrifice him there!" What was he going to do? What was going on in his mind and heart? Can you imagine the emotions that were running riot within him?

Abraham obeyed and set out on that journey to the top of the mountain. He had left the servants, and now he was alone with Isaac, the sticks and the fire, but there was no lamb for sacrifice, a fact that Isaac was not slow to observe.

It was at this point that something happened to Abraham. God had given a promise that through Isaac all people on the earth would be blessed, and yet it seemed that in a very short time he would be dead! Despite his feelings he began to realise that God's promises do not fail and that God is true to His word, a fact recorded in Hebrews 11:19: **"Abraham reasoned that God could raise the dead, and figuratively speaking, he did receive Isaac back from death."**

Despite his feelings, something inside Abraham assured him that whatever happened at the top of the mountain, he would return with Isaac alive! And he did!

Faith is knowing that God is true to His word.

Charles

One Year Plan : Psalm 111, 1 Corinthians 14, Judges 1 - 2
Two Year Plan : Psalm 66:16-20, Mark 9:1-32, Exodus 34 (Yr 1)
2 Chronicles 30 (Yr 2)

Get Ready! Make Room!

We had acquired some new furniture for our lounge. This meant that we needed to get rid of the old in order to accommodate the new. Some things had to be given away; there simply was not room for both the existing and the new.

When Jacob met God at Bethel he received a new revelation of the joy of the Lord's presence and understood the need to walk the rest of his life in step with the living God. However, he had to stop, make room, and prepare for the journey.

In response to God, Jacob spoke to his household and gave them these instructions: **"Get rid of the foreign gods you have with you, and purify yourselves and change your clothes. Then come, let us go up to Bethel, were I will build an altar to God."** (Genesis 35:2-3)

He made room, and immediately God's presence was able to fill him in a new way. God was able to walk and talk with him. He experienced the Lord in an entirely new dimension and was blessed.

A little earlier, Jacob had wrestled all night with God at the brook Jabbok, where God had changed his name to Israel. His old name Jacob was linked to his a life of deception and intrigue. His new name, Israel, and the limp that had resulted from his encounter with God were a constant reminder to him that he could not achieve God's purpose for his life out of his own wisdom and in his own strength.

As you cry out for more of God's presence, power and dynamic, you need to make room for His new activity in your life.

Joyce

One Year Plan : Psalm 112, 1 Corinthians 15, Judges 3 - 4
Two Year Plan : Psalm 67, Mark 9:33-50, Exodus 35 (Yr 1)
2 Chronicles 31 (Yr 2)

Knee-Jerk Reaction

We can probably all think of situations where we were faced with the unexpected and without thinking we spoke or acted rashly and later regretted what we had done.

Mark Chapter 11 begins with Jesus triumphantly entering Jerusalem and the crowds shouting, **"Hosanna! Blessed is he who comes in the name of the Lord!"** However, this moment of joy ends very abruptly as He goes to the temple and sees a very different scene: **"He looked around at everything, but since it was already late, he went out to Bethany with the Twelve."** He observes what is going on but does nothing.

The next day, **"Jesus entered the temple area and began driving out those who were buying and selling there. He overturned the tables of the money changers and the benches of those selling doves ... 'Is it not written: My house will be called a house of prayer for all nations? But you have made it a den of robbers.'"** (verses 15-17) It would have been so easy for Jesus to have had a **knee-jerk reaction**; He could have angrily driven out the money changers the previous evening – but He didn't. Jesus took time to think and pray and then returned with righteous indignation and did what was right.

I had never before noticed this sequence of events, but it has greatly impacted me. I can think of many times when I have acted thoughtlessly and angrily, but I find the way Jesus behaved very impressive. He took time to assess the situation and make a considered decision.

Knee-jerk reaction not only happens in negative situations; it is possible to give something away on the spur of the moment and regret it later, or we can promise to do something for someone else without thinking of the impact it has on our family. We can also lash out with our tongue, when to remain silent would have been better.

After Jesus had given himself time to think and pray, He did the right thing. Let us follow His example - stop the **knee-jerk reactions**, but don't stop confronting wrong or responding to others with love and generosity.

Charles

One Year Plan : Psalm 113, 1 Corinthians 16, Judges 5 - 6
Two Year Plan : Psalm 68:1-6, Mark 10:1-31, Exodus 36 (Yr 1)
2 Chronicles 32 (Yr 2)

Don't Turn a Deaf Ear

Sometimes I don't listen – I may hear spoken words, but I don't take in what is being said. It might be that I am cooking or deeply involved in some other practical task, and even though I may have listened to the information that has been communicated, I have failed to hear it. Later on, when I discover plans that are about to be set in motion, I declare that I knew nothing about them, only to be told, **"I spoke to you about that the other day!"**

I had been informed – but I was not listening! God addresses this same subject in Hebrews 3:7 in the Message: **"Today please listen; don't turn a deaf ear as in 'the bitter uprising'."**

Jeremiah had a similar problem when bringing God's word to the people. In Jeremiah 25:3 he says, **"The word of the Lord has come to me and I have spoken to you again and again, but you have not listened."**

It is possible to read God's Word without listening in your heart. If you receive information but not revelation, it then fails to become a living word and therefore does not bring nourishment or become spiritual food for the day.

Jesus counteracted the devil's temptation in the wilderness by declaring, **"Man does not live on bread alone but by every word that proceeds from the mouth of God."** (Luke 4:4) I want to live on words that come forth from the mouth of God; words that change me; words that give me wisdom and understanding. I want to hear the words that come from heaven.

So my prayer is: **"Open my ears Lord, help me listen, make me sensitive to your voice, so that I can know you better and submit my life to your will and plan for me today."**

Joyce

One Year Plan : Psalm 114, 2 Corinthians 1, Judges 7 - 8
Two Year Plan : Psalm 68:7-14, Mark 10:32-52, Exodus 37 (Yr 1)
2 Chronicles 33 (Yr 2)

24-7 Prayer

Why would anyone want to pray for twenty four hours a day? Why is the 24-7 Prayer movement being such a success? I believe that God is creating a deep desire in people to reach out to Him and to pray. At this moment, there are a large number of 24-7 prayer rooms praying around the world.

In the year 2000, Pete Greig started the 24-7 Prayer movement in direct response to a vision from God, which has now spread around the world. Part of the inspiration came when Pete visited Herrnhut in Germany and heard how the Moravians had prayed non-stop for a hundred years. Surely this is one reason why their influence has had worldwide significance; John Wesley was powerfully affected by his encounter with the Moravians as he crossed the Atlantic Ocean.

We have personally been involved with 24-7 prayer weeks on a number of occasions in our church. We pray because we believe God hears and answers prayer. We have seen people come to faith in the prayer room; others have been healed as they received prayer during these times. God has done many powerful things in answer to prayer

- **"The prayer of a righteous man is powerful and effective."**
- **"Pray without ceasing."**
- **"Then Jesus told his disciples a parable to show that they should always pray and not give up."**
- **"Until now you have not asked for anything in my name. Ask and you will receive, and your joy will be full."**

The International House of Prayer in Kansas City, USA, has been praying continuously for more than ten years. You can participate in their praying by receiving their Live Stream on the internet.

Go to *www.ihop.org/prayerroom*, select the Live Stream, and join in the worship and prayer.

Make a fresh commitment today to pray – go to the IHOP prayer room or seek out a 24-7 prayer room and give it a visit.

Charles

One Year Plan : Psalm 115, 2 Corinthians 2, Judges 9 - 10
Two Year Plan : Psalm 68:15-23, Mark 11, Exodus 38 (Yr 1)
2 Chronicles 34 (Yr 2)

Use Everything You've Got

Jesus is always looking beyond the external. **He is interested in motives and attitudes as well as actions.** At the end of Matthew's gospel, we see Jesus teaching His disciples these important truths. He knows He will be leaving them soon and so wants to impart some vital principles and uses a parable.

Matthew 25:14-30 records the Parable of the Talents. The master is going away and before leaving gives talents to his servants and expects them to use what they have been given. Two servants do this with enthusiasm and a sense of privilege. When the master returns he sees what they have done, praises them and gives them more responsibility. They are commended for their attitude and individual performance.

Servant No. 3 is so different. There is a total absence of thankfulness or privilege; instead there is resentment and fear, blame and accusation of the master and no responsibility for his own actions! He is rebuked.

We had a young man staying with us who was born with cerebral palsy and the prognosis was very poor **but his family, and now he himself, have chosen to live with a 'five talent' attitude.** In spite of severe physical limitations, there is joy and gratitude for being alive as well as a welcoming of new challenges. He has just acquired a dog that helps him undress; it pulls his socks off. It also picks up things he drops and returns them to him. There is no evidence of self-pity or adverse comparison with others who have perfect bodies. He is using all he has to the full and is bringing great pleasure to his master Jesus.

I am personally challenged to use all I have been given to the full – to have an attitude of thanksgiving and privilege. You and I are unique and so are our gifts and talents. Resist the temptation to compare yourself with others; you'll either become proud or discontented. **Just be thankful for who you are, and live today for God's glory and pleasure.**

Joyce

One Year Plan : Psalm 116, 2 Corinthians 3, Judges 11 - 12
Two Year Plan : Psalm 68:24-35, Mark 12:1-27, Exodus 39 (Yr 1)
2 Chronicles 35 (Yr 2)

Wisdom

Wisdom is described as **"having the discipline to prioritise, and the ability to work toward a stated goal"**; also **"wisdom is the art of knowing what to overlook"**.

Proverbs 9:10 says, **"The fear of the Lord is the beginning of wisdom,"** which is to say that wisdom begins by setting your life in a greater context than yourself. To fear the Lord is to live in the understanding of His greatness, knowledge and understanding. He is fully acquainted with your situation at this moment.

A study of the book of Proverbs highlights a number of statements that further expand the meaning of wisdom.

"Wisdom will save you from the ways of wicked men; it will save you also from the adulteress." (Proverbs 2:12,16)

"Do not forsake wisdom, and she will protect you; love her, and she will watch over you." (Proverbs 4:6)

"I guide you in the way of wisdom and lead you along straight paths. When you walk, your steps will not be hampered; when you run, you will not stumble." (Proverbs 4:11-12)

"Pride only breeds quarrels, but wisdom is found in those who take advice." (Proverbs 13:10)

"He who gets wisdom loves his own soul; he who cherishes understanding prospers." (Proverbs 19:8)

"A man's wisdom gives him patience; it is to his glory to overlook an offense." (Proverbs 19:11)

Wisdom is a key quality in the often quoted wife of noble character of Proverbs 31: **"She speaks with wisdom, and faithful instruction is on her tongue."** (Proverbs 31:26)

Finally, James writes, **"If any of you lacks wisdom, he should ask God, who gives generously to all without finding fault, and it will be given to him."** (James 1:5)

Wisdom is available to all who call out to God.

Charles

One Year Plan : Psalm 117, 2 Corinthians 4, Judges 13 - 14
Two Year Plan : Psalm 69:1-12, Mark 12:28-44, Exodus 40 (Yr 1)
2 Chronicles 36 (Yr 2)

Blessings of Obedience

There are blessings associated with obedience. Deuteronomy 6:3 states, **"Hear, O Israel, and be careful to obey, so that it may go well with you and that you may increase greatly in a land flowing with milk and honey."** When the Lord makes a request it is usually because He wants to bless us. When He asks us to do something He gives us everything we need to do it, and always in His heart He wants to do us good.

There are times when we are simply disobedient and forfeit blessing, but there probably are more occasions when we act with partial obedience – **"I'll do it when I choose or when it is more convenient."** – and there are other occasions when we purpose to obey but fail to deliver!

This week I found myself looking back over an old journal, and I was horrified to see how many times the Lord reminded me of things which I hadn't done! I was a bit like the son in the Gospels who said to his father, **"Yes, I'll do it,"** and in reality didn't! I have always sought to be obedient to the Holy Spirit – so it came as a shock to see just how tardy I had been. I needed to repent and do the things I had been asked. I was certainly the one who through partial obedience had forfeited blessing.

How about you? Think back over the last six months – is there any outstanding obedience? If you keep a journal, check it. Put yourself in a position where God can pour out all the blessings He has purposed for you.

Stay tuned to the frequency of the Holy Spirit and you will walk in buoyancy and joy.

Jesus said, **"If you love me you will obey me"**

Joyce

One Year Plan : Psalm 118, 2 Corinthians 5, Judges 15 - 17
Two Year Plan : Psalm 69:13-21, Mark 13, Leviticus 1 - 2 (Yr 1)
Jeremiah 1 (Yr 2)

What Do You Deserve?

I have noticed something in the account of the healing of the centurion's servant I have never seen before. I was reading in Luke 7:3-5: **"The centurion heard of Jesus and sent some of the elders of the Jews to him ... they pleaded earnestly with him, 'This man deserves to have you do this, because he loves our nation and has built our synagogue.'"** These elders believed that Jesus should perform a miracle because the centurion **deserved** it.

However, as Jesus expressed His willingness to respond to their request, the centurion had a completely different reaction. Luke 7:6 says, **"...the centurion sent friends to say to Jesus, 'Lord, don't trouble yourself, for I do not deserve to have you come under my roof.'"** He did not believe that he was worthy of meeting Jesus or that as a Roman citizen he in any way **deserved** to receive from Jesus, yet his attitude opened the way for a miracle.

I meet many people who think their prayers should be answered because they deserve it. They feel because they have sought to live a good life and be faithful in worship and devotion to God, they ought to receive His favour. They live by a gospel of works. On the other hand many people think that their prayers are not being answered because they have failed to live up to God's standards. The fact is, we do not **deserve** anything from God. We receive from God because of His grace.

David understood this; he said, **"The Lord is compassionate and gracious, slow to anger, abounding in love ... he does not treat us as our sins deserve."** (Psalm 103:8-10)

The fact is that Jesus took the punishment for our sins on the cross – that is what we celebrate at Easter. He opened the way for us to receive from him because of His grace. We deserve nothing; He gives us everything. The centurion understood he deserved nothing, but his faith opened the door to a miracle... **and you can receive the same.**

Charles

One Year Plan : Psalm 119:1-56, 2 Corinthians 6, Judges 18 - 19
Two Year Plan : Psalm 69:22-36, Mark 14:1-26, Leviticus 3 (Yr 1)
Jeremiah 2 (Yr 2)

The Most Exalted of Men

Sometimes we forget what a privilege we have to be called **children of God**. As Christians we have been brought into an intimate relationship with God through Jesus. It is good to stop, give thanks and wonder at what God has done for us; we do not want to become casual or over-familiar. We have the honour of an open heaven; we have been welcomed into the presence of Almighty God; we have been given the full rights of sonship and at all times have access to the throne of God. Here we can bring our needs, our praise, our adoration, our heart cry to Him, and receive His full attention – God listening to me!

A prayer of David is recorded in 1 Chronicles 17 which says, **"Who am I, O Lord God, and what is my family, that you have brought me this far? ... You have spoken about the future ... You have looked on me as though I were the most exalted of men."**

As we read this prayer, we see David's heart as he marvels at the privilege of being loved, accepted and provided for by God. So too should we who have been given so much more because of Jesus:

- Our past has been forgiven.
- Our sins and iniquities He remembers no more.
- He doesn't keep a record of our failures.
- He has set His love on us – why? Because He chose to.
- He knows us by name.
- He remembers that we are weak and longs to help us.
- He has given us the Holy Spirit to be our constant companion and helper.
- He has spoken promises about our future, our families and our world.

Wonder and ponder these things today, and thank Him for the amazing privilege of being one **"on whom His favour rests"**. Don't forget there are others who as yet are living without this understanding and for whom our Father is searching, to bring them into His family and bless them.

Live under His blessing today, and don't keep it to yourself!

Joyce

One Year Plan : Psalm 119:57-112, 2 Corinthians 7, Judges 20 – 21
Two Year Plan : Psalm 70, Mark 14:27-52, Leviticus 4 (Yr 1) Jeremiah 3 (Yr 2)

Staying Strong

Our 21st century life seems to do everything it can to undermine strength physically, emotionally, mentally and spiritually. Therefore, it is important to build into your life the things that help keep you strong.

The prophet Isaiah said, **"Those who wait upon the Lord will renew their strength..."** (Isaiah 40:31) What does it mean to **"wait upon the Lord"**? I believe that Isaiah was instructing us to make sure that we give quality time to God each day. It might mean that we need to set the alarm a little earlier and give time to worship, reading the Bible and prayer before the rush of the day propels us into its stress and demands. Perhaps we need to look carefully at how we use our spare time, at midday or in the evening. Protect the spaces in your life, or your enemy, the devil, will fill them up with stress-inducing activity designed to weaken you.

Paul noticed something about the church in Galatia and asked them, **"What has happened to all your joy?"** (Galatians 4:15) He recognised that if the enemy can rob you of joy, he will also be able to rob you of strength. Joy is not the result of good things happening to you – that is happiness. Joy comes from knowing God's goodness and love, and it is released by constantly thanking Him for all the blessings He pours out on your life.

When Nehemiah was addressing his weary wall-builders, he sent them home with these instructions: **"Go and enjoy choice food and sweet drinks, and send some to those who have nothing prepared. This day is sacred to the Lord. Do not grieve, for the joy of the Lord is your strength."** (Nehemiah 8:10)

God has provided all that we need to stay strong. Make sure that you have space to **"wait on the Lord"** and live in the **"joy of the Lord which is your strength"**.

Charles

One Year Plan : Psalm 119:113-176, 2 Corinthians 8, Ruth 1 - 2
Two Year Plan : Psalm 71:1-8, Mark 14:53-72, Leviticus 5 (Yr 1)
Jeremiah 4 (Yr 2)

Obey God; Leave the Practicalities to Him

Whenever God asks you to do something, He already has the practicalities worked out. He knows exactly how it can happen.

In Leviticus, the Children of Israel were asked to rest the land in the seventh year ... and quite naturally they asked, **"What will we eat if we do not plant or harvest our crops?"** Leviticus 25:21-22 states, **"I will send you such a blessing in the sixth year that the land will yield enough for three years. While you plant during the eighth year, you will eat from the old crop and will continue to eat from it until the harvest of the ninth year comes in."**

When the Holy Spirit requires you to **do** a particular thing, He already has His plan to provide in every area. Peter was required to pay the temple tax. How? In Matthew 17:27, Jesus instructs him to, **"Go to the lake and throw out your line. Take the first fish you catch; open its mouth and you will find a four-drachma coin. Take it and give it to them for my tax and yours."**

In Ezekiel 44:30 the people are told, **"The best of all your firstfruits and of all your special gifts will belong to the priests. You are to give them the first portion of your ground meal so that a blessing may rest on your household."**

The Lord always wants to prosper and bless you when He asks you to give. It is never in His mind to rob you but always to position you in order to bless you. So let us continue to be a generous, giving people.

Forgiving so that we can be forgiven.

Giving so that we may be given to.

Refreshing others so that we too may be refreshed.

Obedient so that we may demonstrate our trust in God.

Jesus said, **"If you love me, you will obey what I command..."** (John 14:15) ...and you can leave Him to work out the practicalities!

Joyce

One Year Plan : Psalm 120, 2 Corinthians 9, Ruth 3 - 4
Two Year Plan : Psalm 71:9-18, Mark 15:1-32, Leviticus 6 (Yr 1)
Jeremiah 5 (Yr 2)

On the Victory Side

Many years ago, I helped with a Beach Mission in North Wales, where we used to sing a chorus, *"On the victory side, on the victory side ... with Christ within, the fight we'll win, on the victory side."*

This came to mind while reading Proverbs 2:7 which says, **"He holds victory in store for the upright, he is a shield to those whose walk is blameless."** This promise is for those who are upright – so, **who are they?** The **upright** are all believers, who have been made righteous not by trying to be good but by faith.

Romans 5:17 states that **"...those who receive God's abundant provision of grace and of the gift of righteousness reign in life through the one man, Jesus Christ"**. Righteousness is a gift to all who have faith in Jesus, and because I am righteous, God has given me the right to victory in every circumstance.

Jesus spoke of this victory to His disciples when they had returned from their mission with great joy and excitement. He told them, **"I saw satan fall like lightening from heaven. I have given you authority to trample on snakes and scorpions and to overcome all the power of the enemy; nothing will harm you."** (Luke 10:18-19)

Paul also spoke of the complete victory that Jesus won on the cross: **"And having disarmed the powers and authorities, he made a public spectacle of them, triumphing over them by the cross."** (Colossians 2:15)

The same note of victory is declared again by Paul to the Corinthian Church: **"The weapons we fight with are not the weapons of the world. On the contrary they have divine power to demolish strongholds."** (2 Corinthians 10:4)

We are not living in a bland world; we have an enemy who will try and overwhelm us with fear and defeat. Always remember that when Jesus died and rose again, He won a **complete, eternal and irrevocable** victory over the devil.

You have been given the right to benefit from that great triumph and know that whatever is coming against you, **you are on the victory side!**

Charles

One Year Plan : Psalm 121, 2 Corinthians 10, 1 Samuel 1 - 2
Two Year Plan : Psalm 71:19-24, Mark 15:33-47, Leviticus 7 (Yr 1)
Jeremiah 6 (Yr 2)

Remind yourself you are Valuable

Remind yourself today that you are valuable in God's eyes. You have been chosen to know God intimately, chosen to experience His help and compassion... as you live life.

Peter puts it like this: **"Not one is missing, not one forgotten, God the Father has his eye on each one of you, and has determined by the work of his Spirit to keep you obedient through the sacrifice of Jesus. May everything good from God be yours!"** (1 Peter 1:1-2, The Message)

At all times satan wants to negate this message; he wants to emphasis areas of failure. He lies when he tells you you are valueless or that performance (or lack of it) changes your worth. **Remind yourself** that Calvary proclaims your value to God. Jesus paid the price He considered you were worth. Redeeming love tells you: you're worth it.

Throw off the heaviness of self-effort, and use thanksgiving to bring you back into a place of joy and hope. The same loving Father who helped you, rescued you and enabled you in the past will take care of you today and tomorrow.

Weariness and self-effort can rob you of strength and hope. **Remind yourself** that God is for you and not against you. He is not ticking a to-do list to evaluate your performance; rather, He is holding out loving arms, waiting to comfort and reassure, restore, and help with whatever you are facing today.

Remind yourself: real wisdom comes from Him, as do creative ideas. Today, He is your source of love, joy, peace, hope and everything you need.

Ask for His help **right now** and experience His goodness.

Joyce

One Year Plan : Psalm 122, 2 Corinthians 11, 1 Samuel 3 - 4
Two Year Plan : Psalm 72:1-7, Mark 16, Leviticus 8 (Yr 1)
Jeremiah 7 (Yr 2)

Is Anyone Listening to Me?

I had made one of those infuriating phone calls where I was asked to keep making choices and press all sorts of numbers until eventually I was able to speak to a living person. By the end of the conversation I thought my request had been heard and understood, and I waited to receive the asked-for form in the post.

Days passed and nothing arrived, so I phoned again and ground my way through the process. More time passed; still no result. When I made my third call there seemed to be no record of my earlier requests, but at last I sensed that the person on the other end was really listening and wanted to help. He certainly did - a couple of days passed and the form duly arrived.

In our hectic life, with everyone rushing about preoccupied with their own priorities, we often cry out, **"Is anyone listening to me?"** We may shout it, or it might be just a silent cry from our hearts.

These thoughts were in my mind when I read in Psalm 66:19-20, **"God has surely listened and heard my voice in prayer. Praise be to God, who has not rejected my prayer or withheld his love from me!"**

God is listening to your prayer and the cry of your heart; He not only promises to listen but to act and to do it without delay. As I pondered this I began to think of so many places in scripture where we see God in action, listening and acting.

In Psalm 40:1-2 it says, **"I waited patiently for the Lord; he turned to me and heard my cry. He lifted me out of the slimy pit..."** Psalm 34:4 says, **"I sought the Lord, and he answered me; he delivered me from all my fears."**

We have a God who can hear the faintest whisper of our hearts. He hears and assures us of His love; He hears and lifts us out of our troubles; He hears and delivers us from all our fears.

Is anyone listening to me? Yes!

Charles

One Year Plan : Psalm 123, 2 Corinthians 12, 1 Samuel 5 - 7
Two Year Plan : Psalm 72:8-14, 1 Corinthians 1, Leviticus 9 (Yr 1)
Jeremiah 8 (Yr 2)

A Sowing Project

A friend of ours would not consider himself ready for the day unless he placed some money in his **'sowing pocket'**. He believed God had challenged him to be a radical giver and always to have something in his pocket that could and would meet needs. This is a challenge, but as you cannot out-give God it is not surprising that he prospered.

You and I all have something to give. This time I am not talking about money – but peace! God has given every believer **"peace that passes understanding"**. It is a commodity of such rarity in our society; I want to encourage you to value what you have and to give it away!

Make sure your own peace is a reality. It is Jesus' personal gift to you. "**Peace I leave with you; my peace I give you. I do not give you as the world gives. Do not let your hearts be troubled and do not be afraid."** (John 14:27)

Let this peace rule over anxious thoughts and calm you so you can hear God's wisdom and strategy for your daily life. **"Great peace have they who love your law, and nothing can make them stumble."** (Psalm 119:165) **"Do not be anxious about anything."** (Philippians 4:6)

Sow peace; give it away; take it with you wherever you go; release it to still strife, to calm children, to influence atmospheres. Speak it out into troubled hearts and minds; it is a tangible blessing you have been given to live in but also for you to give away.

Notice the many times Jesus greeted people and situations with, **"Peace be with you."** Don't just use a form of words like **"Shalom"**; give peace and know what you are giving.

In Acts 15:33 the church in Antioch sent the brothers on their way with **"the blessing of peace"**. Jesus told his disciples in Luke 10:5, **"When you enter a house, first say, 'Peace to this house.'"**

Why don't you sow some peace today?

Joyce

One Year Plan : Psalm 124, 2 Corinthians 13, 1 Samuel 8 - 9
Two Year Plan : Psalm 72:15-20, 1 Corinthians 2, Leviticus 10 (Yr 1) Jeremiah 9 (Yr 2)

Look After your Bones

If you have you ever described yourself as being **'bone tired'**, I believe what you are describing is beyond tiredness, physical fatigue or lack of sleep. It comes from what is going on deep inside.

In Proverbs 3:8 it says, **"Do not be wise in your own eyes; fear the Lord and shun evil. This will bring health to your body and nourishment to your bones."** The writer of the Proverbs has a very perceptive understanding of how our relationship to God and our lifestyle affects our health. There are other places bones are mentioned which expand this insight.

When we live in an atmosphere of love and affirmation there is a real flow of strength. Proverbs 15:30 says, **"A cheerful look brings joy to the heart, and good news gives health to the bones."** Proverbs 16:24 says, **"Pleasant words are a honeycomb, sweet to the soul and healing to the bones."** Our homes should be havens of peace and joy. We should always look for ways of building one another up, of expressing thanks to those who care for us and gratefulness for those who keep us well fed.

When we live with constant criticism, complaining, backbiting and strife, there are very real consequences. We may think our words and attitudes don't matter, but that is tragically wrong. Once again Proverbs has some very insightful words: **"A cheerful heart is good medicine, but a crushed spirit dries up the bones."** (Proverbs 17:22)

The writer of Proverbs even comments on the quality of our marriages: **"A wife of noble character is her husband's crown, but a disgraceful wife is like decay in his bones."** (Proverbs 12:4)

Remember, the fatigue you are feeling may not need a visit to the doctor but time meditating on God's words and changing the way you live.

Do yourself a favour: **look after your bones!**

Charles

One Year Plan : Psalm 125, John 1, 1 Samuel 10 - 11
Two Year Plan : Proverbs 9:1-9, 1 Corinthians 3, Leviticus 11 (Yr 1)
Jeremiah 10 (Yr 2)

God is Pleased with You!

Perhaps you need to personalise this statement so that it becomes reality for you. God is pleased to see that you have received His Son.

Pleased to call you His child.

Pleased to communicate with you through His Holy Spirit.

Pleased to use you in extending His kingdom.

Pleased to explain His Word and His ways to those who seek understanding – pleased, pleased, pleased.

He is pleased to hear your voice in prayer and praise.

Pleased to solve your problems by giving insight and wisdom.

Pleased when you obey Him.

Pleased when you show mercy and compassion.

Why do so many Christians fear that they can never gain God's approval and pleasure? Why do they feel that God will always major on their mistakes and faults?

God gave you a Saviour because you needed one – but He has also given you peace, pardon and freedom of access into His presence. He has given Jesus to live inside of you; when He looks at you He sees Jesus, and Jesus always carries the stamp of God's approval. My sins have been, are being, and will be taken care of by the sacrifice of Calvary – so God's favour towards me because of Jesus' death is constant for all eternity.

That doesn't mean I don't need to be changed, to put to death certain aspects of my life. God's Holy Spirit challenges me to change – dying daily but living with the knowledge that God loves me, saves me, lives in me, delights in me.

It is God's pleasure to give us His Son and His Kingdom – **so rejoice!**

Joyce

One Year Plan : Psalm 126, John 2, 1 Samuel 12 - 13
Two Year Plan : Proverbs 9:10-18, 1 Corinthians 4, Leviticus 12 (Yr 1) Jeremiah 11 (Yr 2)

Him or Things?

Genesis 15 records a conversation between God and Abram: **"After this, the word of the Lord came to Abram in a vision: 'Do not be afraid, Abram. I am your shield, your very great reward.' But Abram said, 'O Sovereign Lord, what can you give me since I remain childless...'"**

Here God is offering **Himself** to Abram, who is unable to receive it because of his childlessness. All he can think about is the fact that he and Sarah have no children. He is consumed with **things** when God wants to give him something far greater. The process of getting **Isaac** spanned twenty-five years, led to poor decisions and great heartache. What would have happened if Abram had accepted the offer God was making? The word given was, **"I am your shield, your very great reward."** God was saying, **"I want to give you Myself; I know you have needs, but if you have Me you have everything."** But all Abram could think of was **things**.

What about us? Are we so focussed on **things** that we cannot receive **Him**? It may be healing. Perhaps we are going through great difficulties in our family. We may be facing great financial need. What is dominating your thoughts at this time?

If Abram had received the word from God, would he have had to wait so long for God's promise to be fulfilled? Would there have been so much heartache? I don't think so.

Romans 8:32 says, **"He who did not spare his own Son, but gave him up for us all – will he not also, along with him, graciously give us all things?"**

When our hearts are set on seeking **Him** we will discover that the **things** we so desire are given so much more readily and spontaneously.

Today, turn your eyes to **Him** and watch Him deal with the **things**.

Key Verse – Psalm 37:4: **"Delight yourself in the Lord and he will give you the desires of your heart."**

Charles

One Year Plan : Psalm 127, John 3, 1 Samuel 14 - 15
Two Year Plan : Proverbs 10:1-10, 1 Corinthians 5, Leviticus 13 (Yr 1)
Jeremiah 12 (Yr 2)

Give Him Away

You've got so much to give away!
Who, me?
Yes, you!

Peter met a beggar and was asked for money. He didn't have money, but he did have something better that ultimately would transform this man's situation. He was healed and now would be able to work, earn money, care for his family – because healing had removed his limitations.

You and I are containers of a priceless treasure named **Jesus**. He has answers for each situation you meet: wisdom, truth, healing, love, joy, peace, understanding, counsel and hope, to name just a few.

You can't give away what you don't have so you need to be filled to overflowing with the Spirit of Jesus – ready for anything.

Check what you are giving away; it could be misery, criticism, negativity in many forms, or perhaps unbelief, doubt or fear.

Stop! No one wants that junk, including you and those who are looking to you for positive input.

Seek to always leave others better than you find them. Always aim to speak something positive into every situation, but also pray and ask Jesus to help them and give them what they need. As you do that you will find your own needs being met. **"Give and it will be given unto you"** and **"a man reaps what he sows"** are spiritual laws, so check what you are giving and sowing. Jesus is what everyone needs – in Him are the resources to mend broken hearts and bodies.

Give Him away today and see Him change lives.

Joyce

One Year Plan : Psalm 128, John 4, 1 Samuel 16 - 17
Two Year Plan : Proverbs 10:11-21, 1 Corinthians 6, Leviticus 14 (Yr 1)
Jeremiah 13 (Yr 2)

Always

Those involved in marriage counselling will tell couples that there are two words that must be eradicated from all conversation: **"always"** and **"never"**. However, the Bible uses those words quite regularly.

Almost the last words Jesus speaks to His disciples are, **"And surely I am with you always, to the very end of the age."** (Matthew 28:20) On another occasion Jesus tells a parable about prayer and says **"...that they should always pray and not give up."** (Luke 18:1)

In 2 Corinthians 1:18-20, Paul speaks about God's faithfulness to His promises: **"But as surely as God is faithful, our message to you is not 'Yes' and 'No' ... but in him it has always been 'Yes.' For no matter how many promises God has made they are "Yes" in Christ."**

The writer to the Hebrews tells of what Jesus is doing in heaven right now. He says, **"Therefore he is able to save completely those who come to God through him, because he always lives to intercede for them."** (Hebrews 7:25)

Once again Paul has another **"always"** to say to the believers at Philippi: **"Rejoice in the Lord always. I will say it again: Rejoice!"** (Philippians 4:4)

Put the **"always"** back into your life today:

- Jesus is with you **always**.
- **Always** pray and don't give up.
- God-promises are **always** "Yes".
- Jesus is interceding for you **always**.
- And don't forget to **"Rejoice in the Lord always"**.

And here is a **"never"** to finish off with:

- God has said, **"Never will I leave you; never will I forsake you."** (Hebrews 13:5)

Encourage someone today with an **"always"** or a **"never"**.

Charles

One Year Plan : Psalm 129, John 5, 1 Samuel 18 - 19
Two Year Plan : Proverbs 10:22-32, 1 Corinthians 7, Leviticus 15 (Yr 1)
Jeremiah 14 (Yr 2)

Conform

There are certain words that fall out of general usage; we know what they mean, but they are not part of our everyday vocabulary. **'Conform'** is one such word.

I probably am a non-conformist in the widest sense of the word. I resist being moulded by other people's expectations or ideas of what I should be or what I ought to do.

'Conform' in the dictionary is defined as **"Adapted to be like"** or **"made to become as"**. However, conform can be used both negatively and positively.

Paul uses the word **'conform'** in Romans 12:2 where he says, **"Do not conform any longer to the pattern of this world, but be transformed by the renewing of your mind."**

In Romans 8:29, this word is used in quite the opposite way when Paul says, **"For those who God foreknew he also predestined to be conformed to the likeness of his Son."**

I need adapting, to be made anew to become like Jesus. I want to be conformed to His image and have my thinking and actions changed to be like His. I want His mercy and compassion for people; His authority when I teach; His power when I pray; His faith in God. I want to be like Jesus. I want people who meet me... to meet Him.

My prayer for myself is, **"Conform me; adapt me; change me; remake me in the likeness of Jesus!"** It is also my prayer for you.

Joyce

One Year Plan : Psalm 130, John 6, 1 Samuel 20 - 21
Two Year Plan : Proverbs 11:1-10, 1 Corinthians 8, Leviticus 16 (Yr 1)
Jeremiah 15 (Yr 2)

Being Changed

You need to change! Do you find that statement threatening? The fact is that change is here to stay!

My son Daniel, who now leads Living Waters Church, made this statement in a message he preached: **"One reason we come to church is so that God can change our thinking and in the process change us."** Does that make you want to go to church or stay home?

God chose us and saved us with the intent of changing us into the likeness of Jesus. So if we are not acting, thinking and behaving like Jesus we need to change.

In Isaiah 55:8-9 we read, **"'For my thoughts are not your thoughts, neither are your ways my ways,' declares the Lord. 'As the heavens are higher than the earth, so are my ways higher than your ways and my thoughts than your thoughts.'"**

Paul tells us that our thinking needs to change: **"Do not conform any longer to the pattern of this world, but be transformed by the renewing of your mind."** (Romans 12:2) Too much of our thinking is conditioned by the world around us; we need to start thinking like God.

2 Corinthians 3:18 states, **"And we, who with open faces behold the glory of the Lord are being changed into his likeness."** So often our faces are so fully occupied with our problems that we fail to look to the One who has the answers and can transform our situation.

The facts are: the devil is a defeated foe; fear was conquered by Jesus on the cross; and by the stripes of Jesus we are healed.

So if you think the devil is giving you a hard time, you are full of fear and are sick, something needs to change. **When you let God change you within, your circumstances outside will be transformed.**

Charles

One Year Plan : Psalm 131, John 7, 1 Samuel 22 – 23
Two Year Plan : Proverbs 11:11-20, 1 Corinthians 9, Leviticus 17 (Yr 1)
Jeremiah 16 (Yr 2)

A Force to Be Reckoned With!

When David confronted Goliath, he was seen by the Philistine as a mere boy, a pushover, 'wet behind the ears', and he despised him. 1 Samuel 17:42-45 says, **"Am I a dog, that you come out to me with sticks? ... Come here, and I'll give your flesh to the birds of the air and the beasts of the field."** David's reply shows where his resources are coming from: **"You come against me with sword and spear and javelin, but I come against you in the name of the Lord Almighty, the God of the armies of Israel, whom you have defied."**

You may feel like **little David fighting a giant Goliath**. It might be false accusations in the workplace or intimidation and bullying at school. Remember David, and be aware that you are not alone; you have the resources of heaven behind you. God is for you and will expose every lie and false accusation.

The film **'The Bear'** illustrates this principle. A small bear, raised by its father after the death of its mother, is confronting a pack of snarling wolves. The little bear is standing and roaring as he has seen his father do. To his surprise the wolves retreat and flee. The camera then pans out, and you see right behind the little bear, looming large, the father bear also roaring. The wolves were no match for the father who stood behind the small animal.

The Roman Centurion who met Jesus (see Matthew 8:5-13) understood that when he gave orders the full might of Rome was behind him. He described himself as a man under authority who knew that Caesar stood behind his every command.

Use the authority of Jesus today. Rebuke the enemy using the Name of Jesus. Get on the offensive, and resist things that are seeking to destroy you. Take the battle to the things that are attacking you. The battle is the Lord's, and God will help you.

Deuteronomy 3:22 says, **"Don't be afraid of them; the Lord your God himself will fight for you."**

Joyce

One Year Plan : Psalm 132, John 8, 1 Samuel 24 - 25
Two Year Plan : Proverbs 11:21-31, 1 Corinthians 10, Leviticus 18 (Yr 1) Jeremiah 17 (Yr 2)

Indignation

Indignation is a powerful emotion which stirs action and reaction. It is the opposite of passivity. In Mark 10:13-14, **"People were bringing little children to Jesus for him to place his hands on them, but the disciples rebuked them. When Jesus saw this he was indignant. He said to them, 'Let the little children come to me and do not hinder them...'"** Jesus was not prepared to see the weak and vulnerable pushed aside; He saw what was happening, let it touch His emotions, indignation rose within and it spurred Him to action.

Paul, when writing to the church at Corinth, says, **"Who is weak, and I am not weak? Who is made to stumble, and I do not burn with indignation?"** (2 Corinthians 11:29) Paul's heart was always towards those who were struggling; he wanted to lift them up and not put them down. He used his indignation creatively.

Indignation is not always used in a good way. The disciples watched a woman anoint Jesus with very expensive perfume and were indignant because they considered it a waste (Mark 14:3-4). Ten of the disciples were indignant that James and John should want the best seats in heaven, perhaps because they wanted them for themselves (Mark 10:41). The high priest and the Sadducees saw the disciples healing people and setting them free in the name of Jesus, and they were filled with such indignation that they put the apostles in prison (Acts 5:17-18).

We were speaking with a lady who works in a refuge with vulnerable women battered by domestic abuse. We listened to her heart of love for these sad and hurting people and the stories of those who have been rescued and healed. However, another person in the conversation showed no compassion, declaring that these women had been the cause of their own problems. Both were indignant – for one it led to compassion and mercy, for another to judgment and criticism.

God's heart is always for those who cannot help themselves, for the weak and down-trodden. There is indignation in His heart when He sees people being abused, and He longs for His people to take action, to reach out with love and compassion.

Charles

One Year Plan : Psalm 133, John 9, 1 Samuel 26 - 27
Two Year Plan : Proverbs 12:1-9, 1 Corinthians 11, Leviticus 19 (Yr 1)
Jeremiah 18 (Yr 2)

Self-Effort or Help from Heaven?

Some people like to keep rules; they experience satisfaction as they perform well and love the sense of control that success brings. The **rich young ruler** who came to talk with Jesus was possibly such a type. He'd keep the Ten Commandments and was looking for external security through the means of performance. So his question to Jesus was, **"What must I do to inherit eternal life?"** Jesus' reply was, **"If you want to give it all you've got, go sell your possessions; give everything to the poor. All your wealth will be in heaven. Then come follow me."** (Matthew 19:21, The Message)

This was the last thing the young man expected to hear, and crestfallen he walked away. He was holding tight to a lot of things and couldn't bear to let go. Jesus wasn't against riches or rule-keeping – but this man was trusting in his own ability, thinking somehow he could achieve an entrance into God's approval by self-effort.

The disciples were astounded with the whole situation, and they too asked questions. If the rich and nearly perfect can't make it, who can? Jesus has a clear and simple answer: **"No chance at all if you think you can pull it off yourself. Every chance in the world if you trust God to do it."** (Matthew 19:26, The Message)

None of us deserve God's grace and favour; none of us can achieve entrance into heaven by performance. We need God's help, His mercy, compassion and all He promises to give when we ask Him. It was easier for the 'sinners' (i.e. prostitutes, tax gatherers, criminals, etc.) to receive this good news – they knew their need. The self-righteous couldn't admit their own inadequacy so struggled on in self-effort.

We need to respond in the words of a well-known hymn:

Nothing in my hand I bring,
Simply to the cross I cling
Naked, come to Thee for dress,
Helpless, look to Thee for grace
Foul, I to the fountain fly:
Wash me, (Help me) Saviour, or I die!

Joyce

One Year Plan : Psalm 134, John 10, 1 Samuel 28 - 29
Two Year Plan : Proverbs 12:10-18, 1 Corinthians 12, Leviticus 20 (Yr 1)
Jeremiah 19 (Yr 2)

JUNE

Spread It Out Before the Lord

King Hezekiah was a good leader, who loved God and sought to live right, but that did not prevent threats from his enemies to defeat and destroy him. His chief enemy, Sennacherib, King of Assyria, was a dominant force at the time and had already captured fortified cities in Judah.

In great distress, Hezekiah went into the temple to pray, and he also sent a messenger to the prophet Isaiah, who was quick to send back a word from God that all would be well and the enemy would be defeated. Sennacherib was still on the warpath and now sent a letter to Hezekiah repeating his threats.

In Isaiah 37:14 it records, **"Hezekiah received the letter from the messengers and read it. Then he went up to the temple of the Lord and spread it out before the Lord."** In his prayer, he declared the greatness of God, acknowledged the real threat posed by the enemy, and cried out to God for deliverance.

Isaiah was sent to bring God's answer: **"Because you have prayed to me concerning Sennacherib, this is the word the Lord has spoken..."** (Isaiah 37:21) The word clearly laid out what was to happen to the enemy; it spoke blessings on Hezekiah and his people and promised that God would defend and save the city. In due time this prophecy was fulfilled and Hezekiah and his people were saved.

I believe this has a modern-day parallel. Life with all its demands wants to defeat us and render us powerless and full of fear. The circumstances of life gang up to overwhelm us; letters arrive in the post, bills that we find difficult to pay. We want to tell everyone around how badly life is treating us; however, that is not the solution.

Do as Hezekiah did: take your situation – that threatening letter or email – and **spread it out before the Lord.** As you do, your peace will be restored, you will receive wisdom from above, and God will answer your prayer.

Charles

One Year Plan : Psalm 135, John 11, 1 Samuel 30 - 31
Two Year Plan : Proverbs 12:19-28, 1 Corinthians 13, Leviticus 21 (Yr 1)
Jeremiah 20 (Yr 2)

Quiet Authority

Paul speaks of Jesus in 1 Corinthians 15:45 as the **last Adam**: the perfect man and all that God had in mind when He created the **first Adam**. Jesus was, as Adam had been, in perfect connection with His Father and therefore could exercise the original authority given to the first Adam who was told to rule over the created world. (Genesis 1:26)

I had these thoughts in mind as I was walking along the river near where I live. To continue on my walk and go to the next field I needed to cross a stile... but there was a problem! A group of young frisky horses had decided to gather around the stile, and in order to proceed, I had to break up the 'horsey meeting' or land in the middle of them – not something I wanted to do. I shouted, clapped my hands and waved my coat, and they did not budge. Intimidated, I considered retracing my steps, and then I remembered that Calvary had provided the reconnection with the living God. Was it possible that authority over animals had also been restored? Was I to let horses, or fear, prevent me from continuing my journey? What would Jesus have done?

So, I spoke in this manner: **"Horses you must move; you are hindering me, so in the Name of Jesus, go now!"** I didn't shout but simply commanded in a reasonable tone (feeling, I must say, a little foolish), and to my amazement they, to a horse, walked off – allowing me to continue my journey.

Matthew 9 tells of the healing of a paralysed man, to whom Jesus had said, **"Son, your sins are forgiven,"** followed by, **"Rise, pick up your bed and go home."** The reaction of the crowd as stated in The Message (Matthew 9:8) was, **"The crowd were awestruck, amazed and pleased that God had authorised Jesus to work among them in this way."**

You and I have been authorised by Jesus to use His Name, to take authority over all the works of the enemy, to rule using delegated authority, but are we doing this?

I'm challenged when I see so many bruised lives, so much disease and fear, and I pray, **"Lord help me understand and exercise the authority you have given me."**

Joyce

One Year Plan : Psalm 136, John 12, 2 Samuel 1 - 2
Two Year Plan : Proverbs 13:1-8, 1 Corinthians 14, Leviticus 22 (Yr 1)
Jeremiah 21 (Yr 2)

Words that Transform

In Isaiah 50:4 it says that I can **"...know the word that sustains the weary"**. I find this challenging and inspiring. What words will I say to those weary folk around me that will help and sustain?

Glib cliches like **"Cheer up!"** or **"Pull yourself together!"** are not helpful, nor is a lecture on how you never feel weary and work much harder than your worn out friend. The beginning part of this verse indicates that this word which will **sustain** will come from God. He knows each one of us, loves us and wants to make His resources available to us.

The **words** that He gives are not necessarily Bible verses, but they will be creative and dynamic. A few weeks ago we had some folk from our church for lunch in our house, and as I was in conversation with one couple, I found myself saying how much I appreciated them being in our church and that their quiet love and faithfulness was such a blessing. The lady turned to me surprised, almost in tears, and said, **"I really needed to hear that. I have been feeling very discouraged over the past few weeks; all our plans seem to be getting nowhere, and it has made me feel almost useless."** That encouraged me too; God had spoken a **word that sustains** through me.

We were watching the Olympics as a British swimmer, trained by her father, was just about to start her race. One of the commentators said, **"I wonder what motivational words her father says to her just before a race."** The other replied, **"I know what he says because I asked her. He just says, 'I love you!'"** What words to encourage her to perform to her highest potential!

When Paul was battling with persecution, fatigue and fear, God said to him, **"My grace is sufficient for you, for my power is made perfect in weakness."** (2 Corinthians 12:9)

God has a strengthening **word** to speak through you to those around you who are weary.

Charles

One Year Plan : Psalm 137, John 13, 2 Samuel 3 - 4
Two Year Plan : Proverbs 13:9-16, 1 Corinthians 15:1-34, Leviticus 23 (Yr 1)
Jeremiah 22 (Yr 2)

God has No Grandchildren

God wants our relationship with Him to be first-hand, real and experiential. He wants **sons** who know Him, walk with Him and find the more they trust Him, the more real and relevant He is in their lives.

David had just such a relationship. He never stopped responding to God; his greatest fear was that God would remove His presence. David knew that his achievements counted for nothing if he was out of relationship with God.

Solomon was David's son, who had been blessed with wisdom and manifestations of God's glory, but sadly wealth, fame, women, and horses took God's place, and he had little first-hand experience to impart to his son Rehoboam.

Rehoboam grew up with wealth and acquired the same taste for women as his father, having eighteen wives and sixty concubines. He had little time for seeking God, and his strategy for his own sons was to **"keep them happy with much food and many wives"**. (2 Chronicles 11:23, The Message)

Here was a grandson of a great God-lover, the son of one who knew God, but he chose to fill his life with material rather than spiritual riches: **"But the final verdict on Rehoboam was that he was a bad king – God was not important to him; his heart neither cared for nor sought after God."** (2 Chronicles 12:14, The Message) I'm so glad David didn't live to see the end of Solomon's life or the spiritual poverty of his grandson.

The greatest gift you can give your children is to demonstrate that you live as a **son**, totally dependent on your Father God. Tell them of the reality of your relationship, the ups and downs, the failures and successes. Speak of how God delights to pour out His blessings on His children. God is not against material success but **"when riches increase, set not your heart upon them"**. (Psalm 62:10)

So the challenge for us today is to live in a present, real and vital relationship with God but also to believe that the generation after us will discover for themselves how great is their God and develop their own living and essential relationship with Him.

Joyce

One Year Plan : Psalm 138, John 14, 2 Samuel 5 - 6
Two Year Plan : Proverbs 13:17-25, 1 Corinthians 15:35-58, Leviticus 24 (Yr 1) Jeremiah 23 (Yr 2)

Being Zealous

The book of Nehemiah tells of the rebuilding of the walls of Jerusalem, and in Chapter 3 verse 20 it says, **"Next to him, Baruch son of Zabbai zealously repaired another section..."** Building walls was not a particularly glamorous task, and the attitude of the workers varied. It says of the nobles of Tekoa that **"they would not put their shoulders to the work"** – perhaps they thought wall-building was beneath them – and yet Hananiah, **"one of the perfume makers, made repairs"**, so he was out of his comfort zone.

Why was Baruch noticed as one who built zealously? I do not know, but God spoke to me as I read these verses. He said, **"There are a lot of folk out there who are seeking to follow God with all their hearts, and yet they wonder whether it ever does any good."**

Jesus was zealous; in John 2:17 it says, **"His disciples remembered that it is written, 'Zeal for your house will consume me.'"** When I was growing up and asked to do some rather unglamorous task and not looking too cheerful about it, my father would quote to me from Ecclesiastes 9:10: **"Whatever your hand finds to do, do it with all your might."** I did not appreciate it at the time, but I value those words now.

In Nehemiah 6:15-16 it says, **"So the wall was completed on the twenty-fifth of Elul, in fifty-two days. When all our enemies heard about this, all the surrounding nations were afraid and lost their self-confidence, because they realised that this work had been done with the help of our God."**

An amazing task had been completed and there is no mention of Baruch, but his part had been of the greatest importance. There are some of you who are zealous for God in your prayer and in obedience to His call on your life, and you are wondering whether it has any effect. **God sees your heart – being zealous is always effective.**

Charles

One Year Plan : Psalm 139, John 15, 2 Samuel 7 - 8
Two Year Plan : Proverbs 14:1-9, 1 Corinthians 16, Leviticus 25 (Yr 1)
Jeremiah 24 (Yr 2)

Singing Yourself to Wholeness

The Fayu Tribe in Papua New Guinea do not seem to suffer from depression or other psychological disorders. Feelings are immediately expressed and times set aside for the release of emotions. When a person experiences a traumatic event, they might lie for weeks in their hut – not talking but singing for hours at a time. Their friends and loved ones will provide food and meet their practical needs until the person emerges, trauma behind them, cleansed from pain and able to resume everyday life.

These songs are words sung to a three-note tune, expressing anguish and grief, **singing it as it is** and letting it go! In Isaiah 41:1, The Message, God says, **"Quiet down, far-flung ocean islands. Listen! Sit down and rest, everyone. Recover your strength. Gather around me. Say what's on your heart. Together let's decide what's right."**

Maybe today you need to tell God all that is on your heart; **pour it out before Him**, take time, be honest; get the emotion out and then listen and let Him speak words of comfort and peace into your innermost being.

Bottling up painful emotions and thoughts, or even trying to push them down and pretend they don't hurt, is not the answer.

God wants you to pour out your heart before Him; **try singing and keep it up until you break through.**

Psalm 62:8 says, **"Trust in him at all times, you people; pour out your hearts to him, for God is our refuge."**

Joyce

One Year Plan : Psalm 140, John 16, 2 Samuel 9 - 10
Two Year Plan : Proverbs 14:10-18, 2 Corinthians 1, Leviticus 26 (Yr 1)
Jeremiah 25 (Yr 2)

Energy

"You both seem to have a lot of energy" is a comment that Joyce and I often receive. We do eat healthily, sleep well and do some exercise (probably not enough), but that is not the secret of having energy.

As believers we have a heavenly power source that is ours to tap into. Paul said in Romans 8:11, **"And if the Spirit of him who raised Christ from the dead is living in you, he who raised Christ from the dead will also give life to your mortal bodies through his Spirit, who lives in you."** Being filled with the Holy Spirit is not only to give us power in our spiritual life, but this verse declares that we will also receive strength in our physical bodies. Learn to draw upon this power when your natural strength is waning; look to the One who has supernatural strength and resources for you.

Philippians 2:12-13 in The Message says, **"Be energetic in your life of salvation ... that energy is God's energy, an energy deep within you, God himself willing and working at what will give him the most pleasure."** When we tap into God's energy we find that we are alive, alert and full of purpose in a unique way. This is not just for specially favoured believers; it is available to us all.

There is another key to having this kind of energy, which Paul spoke about in Philippians 3:12: **"Not that I have already obtained all this, or have already been made perfect, but I press onto take hold of that for which Christ Jesus took hold of me."** In all Paul's writings we find dynamic purpose in everything he did.

There is no retirement in the kingdom of God because we never lose our usefulness to God or the sense of purpose that we receive from Him. We keep living with joy and focus, not because we are superhuman but because we have a supernatural power source that is constantly available to us all.

Get an **energy boost** today as you draw from the Holy Spirit's power, and receive renewed vision and purpose for the days ahead.

Charles

One Year Plan : Psalm 141, John 17, 2 Samuel 11 - 12
Two Year Plan : Proverbs 14:19-27, 2 Corinthians 2, Leviticus 27 (Yr 1)
Jeremiah 26 (Yr 2)

Disappointment – A Deadly Enemy

We all have to face times of disappointment: times when what we thought would happen, didn't; people who we expected to behave in a particular way, didn't; promises that we thought would have been fulfilled very quickly have yet to be fulfilled!

In situations like these the enemy has a heyday, and as he did in the Garden of Eden, he whispers doubt, **"Did God really say?"** Don't give in to it; it is called temptation and Jesus faced it all the time. Did He expect such things when, full of the Holy Spirit, He was thrust into a time of **aloneness** in the desert? Did He expect He would have quality time fellowshipping with His Father, when constantly interrupted? Were the attacks unexpected?

They certainly seemed to be 'below the belt' – questioning God's love, God's Word and His purpose. What do you think Jesus felt when John the Baptist questioned Him asking, **"Are you really the Messiah?"** He would have thought that John, who was a prophet, had understood. Was it a disappointment to find the religious leaders of the day opposing Him?

Can you understand what was going on in the heart of Jesus? People following Him and then turning away, attracted by the miracles but not really prepared to face the challenge of discipleship?

Disappointment – Jesus kept His peace by constantly going back to the Father and His Word; countering the lies of satan with, **"It is written…"**; keeping His heart right by worshipping the Father; and declaring, **"Hallowed be your name."**

We have the same resources – when circumstances don't work out, when people let us down and even betray us, when there is no understanding from those we expect to 'see'.

The antidote to **disappointment** is to constantly go back to the Father, pour out your heart before Him, go back to the Word, steady yourself, fill up with God's Spirit, feel His love again, and keep going.

Psalm 22:31 in The Message says, **"God always does what he says."**

Joyce

One Year Plan : Psalm 142, John 18, 2 Samuel 13 - 14
Two Year Plan : Proverbs 14:28-35, 2 Corinthians 3, Numbers 1 (Yr 1)
Jeremiah 27 (Yr 2)

Faith is a Lifestyle

When we hear of those who have experienced profound healing, great deliverance from danger or miraculous financial provision, we often feel that these are people who have real faith. Yes, they are people of faith, but faith is not judged by miraculous events because first and foremost faith is a lifestyle.

Enoch was called a man of faith because he **"walked with God"**. Hebrews 11:5-6 says, **"He was commended as one who pleased God. And without faith it is impossible to please God..."**

Abraham is described as the father of those who have faith, and yet he had to wait years to receive what God had promised. But it says of him, **"Yet he did not waver through unbelief regarding the promise of God, but was strengthened in his faith and gave glory to God, being fully persuaded that God had the power to do what he had promised."** (Romans 4:20-21)

Joseph was a man of faith, but he had to endure great hardship for thirteen years before he was vindicated and promoted to be the Prime Minister of Egypt. He had been treated very badly by his brothers, who thought that he would eventually take revenge. Joseph's response was, **"You intended to harm me, but God intended it for good to accomplish what is now being done, the saving of many lives."** (Genesis 50:20)

Moses left a life of privilege in the palace in Egypt to become the one who lead God's people out of bondage. Hebrews 11:27 says, **"By faith he left Egypt, not fearing the king's anger; he persevered because he saw him who is invisible."**

All these people of faith had a relationship with God that was the foundation of their lives. They all proved that God was faithful and powerful. Such people, who live a life of faith, constantly receive healing, know divine protection and prove that, **"My God will meet all your needs according to his glorious riches in Christ Jesus."** (Philippians 4:19)

You may be waiting for the answer to your prayer. **Be encouraged and just keep on living the life of faith.**

Charles

One Year Plan : Psalm 143, John 19, 2 Samuel 15 - 16
Two Year Plan : Proverbs 15:1-8, 2 Corinthians 4, Numbers 2 (Yr 1)
Jeremiah 28 (Yr 2)

Will your Anchor Hold?

A cousin had described a tricky sailing situation; he had been trying to enter a small Greek harbour with no engine, and a fairly strong wind was blowing. He attempted to use his anchor whilst manoeuvring, but it wouldn't hold. The seabed was soft and sandy and the anchor kept dragging. He persisted and eventually found rock; it held firm and the boat was safely negotiated onto a mooring.

Shortly after this conversation, I was reading in Hebrews 6:19, **"We have this hope as an anchor for the soul, firm and secure."** When God wants to assure us of the certainty of His promises, He gives us His Word as a rock solid guarantee.

It is impossible for God to lie, He cannot break His Word, and His promises are likewise unchangeable – an anchor that holds whatever is buffeting us. His Word is our spiritual lifeline keeping us steady, reaching into the very presence of God.

Rely on your anchor today. Whatever storms of life rage around you, do not be afraid. You are held firm by God Himself – safe and secure, anchored to the God who loves you and whose name is 'The Rock'.

Some of you will know this old and well-loved hymn:

Will your anchor hold in the storms of life,
When the clouds unfold their
wings of strife?
When the strong tides lift
and the cables strain,
Will your anchor drift, or firm remain?

We have an anchor that keeps the soul
Steadfast and sure while the billows roll,
Fastened to the Rock which cannot move,
Grounded firm and deep
in the Saviour's love.

Joyce

One Year Plan : Psalm 144, John 20, 2 Samuel 17 - 18
Two Year Plan : Proverbs 15:9-16, 2 Corinthians 5, Numbers 3 (Yr 1)
Jeremiah 29 (Yr 2)

Influence

I had been reading a new biography of Dietrich Bonhoeffer and was amazed at the powerful effect that his mother had upon his life. There is no doubt in my mind that her influence was pivotal to him becoming such an amazing man.

I then began to think about particular people who would have never been the people they were without the influence of others. Would John Wesley ever have been the man he was without the great influence of his mother Suzannah?

Hannah agonised over her childlessness for many years, and once her prayer was granted and Samuel was born, she made this declaration: **"The Lord has granted me what I asked of him. So now I give him to the Lord for the whole of his life."** She prepared him in those early years, so much so that he is one of the greatest prophets in the Bible.

As a young man I worked on a Beach Mission in North Wales and was eager and willing to do whatever was asked of me but shy and lacking in confidence. The leader of the mission will never know the effect of the words he spoke at a preparation meeting, when he announced, **"Charles, you will lead the Holiday Club."** His confidence in me did something that I value and appreciate to this day.

I was speaking to a minister who many years ago had attended a Hyde Leaders Week, which I led during the time I worked with Colin Urquhart. Referring to that week he said, **"That was the most life-changing week of my life."**

Colossians 4:6 says, **"Let your conversation be always full of grace, seasoned with salt..."** Everything we say and do is influencing those around us – our children, family, friends, work colleagues etc. We have the possibility of making a creative, powerful, and life-changing difference.

Who will you influence for good today?

Charles

One Year Plan : Psalm 145, John 21, 2 Samuel 19 - 20
Two Year Plan : Proverbs 15:17-25, 2 Corinthians 6, Numbers 4 (Yr 1) Jeremiah 30 (Yr 2)

Rest and Refreshment

I had been awake for a considerable time, lying in bed, praying, hoping sleep would come. It didn't, so I descended the stairs, to my warm kitchen. The command **"Be still and know that I am God"** was very much in my mind, and I began to explore with the Lord Jesus what 'being still' means. 'Be still' in the Hebrew literally means 'enough' – the same word Jesus used to quiet the storm on the Sea of Galilee. (Mark 4:39)

As we quiet ourselves before the Lord, by simply 'being' instead of 'doing', His Spirit will literally pour over us bringing a deep level of unspoken communication – a knowing that brings peace, refreshment and physical strength. A short time in this kind of quietness can be more refreshing than hours in bed!

How do we get quiet and still?

- Concentrate on Jesus.
- Remember what His presence feels like.
- Bring to mind special times of nearness.
- Exclude the thoughts and demands of the moment.

Most of us find it hard to be quiet; our thoughts dart here and there, and we have to learn to take them captive and refuse to be diverted. Keep at it and you will come through.

Look at these scriptures and let them help and encourage you:

Isaiah 30:15: **"This is what the Sovereign LORD, the Holy One of Israel, says: 'In repentance and rest is your salvation, in quietness and trust is your strength.'"**

Zechariah 2:13: **"Be still before the LORD, all mankind, because he has roused himself from his holy dwelling."**

Exodus 14:14: **"The LORD will fight for you; you need only to be still."**

Psalm 37:7: **"Be still before the LORD and wait patiently for him."**

Psalm 116:7: **"Be at rest once more, O my soul, for the LORD has been good to you."**

Joyce

One Year Plan : Psalm 146, Galatians 1, 2 Samuel 21 - 22
Two Year Plan : Proverbs 15:26-33, 2 Corinthians 7, Numbers 5 (Yr 1)
Jeremiah 31 (Yr 2)

Gaining Perspective

It had been an exceptionally busy time; during the preceding few weeks we had entertained twenty eight people in our home. Most had stayed, some had just come for meals; children had been constantly bouncing on the trampoline; and we had talked and talked. We had been dealing with the sadness of death and the joys of spending time with family, friends and our grandchildren.

It had been physically and emotionally demanding; there had been little time for quietness or time to read and pray... but God is good.

In all the busyness, I had on most days managed to read a psalm, and it had constantly struck me that David's life seemed even more stressed than ours. His enemies were constantly attacking, he was battling with sickness and fatigue, and yet the greatness of God shines through.

Here are a few quotations that helped to give me perspective on all that had been going on around us:

"The Lord is a refuge for the oppressed, a stronghold in times of trouble. Those who know your name will trust in you, for you, Lord have never forsaken those who seek you." (Psalm 9:9-10)

"I love you, O Lord, my strength. The Lord is my rock, my fortress and my deliverer." (Psalm 18:1-2)

"Some trust in chariots and some in horses, but we trust in the name of the Lord our God. They are brought to their knees and fall, but we rise up and stand firm." (Psalm 20:7-8)

"Surely goodness and mercy shall follow (pursue) me all the days of my life." (Psalm 23:6)

"I am still confident of this: I will see the goodness of the Lord in the land of the living. Wait for the Lord; be strong and take heart and wait for the Lord." (Psalm 27:13-14)

Step back from the demands of today and gain a fresh perspective on life.

Charles

One Year Plan : Psalm 147, Galatians 2, 2 Samuel 23 - 24
Two Year Plan : Proverbs 16:1-8, 2 Corinthians 8, Numbers 6 (Yr 1)
Jeremiah 32 (Yr 2)

Powerful Words, Powerful Deeds

In 1 Kings 8:15 Solomon, the new King, is thanking God for enabling him to finish building the temple, and he says, **"Praise be to the Lord, the God of Israel, who with his own hand has fulfilled what he promised with his own mouth to my father David."**

I find those words so encouraging; God with His mouth made a promise, and with His own hand He fulfilled it. Paul declares, **"It is God who works in you to will and to act according to his good pleasure."** (Philippians 2:13)

So what is my part? To believe.

The disciples asked Jesus, **"What must we do to do the works God requires?"** The reply they received was, **"The work of God is this: to believe in the one he has sent."** (John 6:29)

So simple and yet so difficult – I need to receive faith from God.

Remember, you first received from God simply by believing and receiving what He promised.

- Romans 6:23: **"...the gift of God is eternal life."**
- Galatians 3:2: **"Did you receive the Spirit by observing the law or by believing what you heard?"**

The principle remains the same whenever you want to see God at work in your life. You need to receive a word from Him that is specific to your need. Then you must place your faith behind that promise and word. God will willingly speak His promises over your life and wants to act according to His word; you simply need to add your faith.

Keep believing the promises you have received from God for your own life; however long it takes to happen, God will fulfil His promises.

By his **own hand** He will **fulfil** what He has spoken with His **own mouth**.

Joyce

One Year Plan : Psalm 148, Galatians 3, 1 Kings 1 - 2
Two Year Plan : Proverbs 16:9-16, 2 Corinthians 9, Numbers 7 (Yr 1)
Jeremiah 33 (Yr 2)

Sunflowers

During a time of prayer God began to speak to me about **sunflowers**. They have some unique qualities. Firstly, they always face the sun, which means the flower moves as the sun traces its path through the sky from east to west. Secondly, as they mature, sunflowers not only produce beautiful blooms but seeds which produce oil, and they can also be roasted and used as a garnish or a snack.

God was saying to me, **"I want you to learn from the sunflower. It always faces the sun, and I want you to be constantly gazing at Me. The result of that gaze will create My beauty in you and provide a reservoir of oil which will bring My resources into your life as well as to pour out to others."**

Paul said in 2 Corinthians 3:18, **"And we, who with unveiled faces all reflect the Lord's glory, are being transformed into his likeness with ever-increasing glory, which comes from the Lord, who is the Spirit."**

Isaiah 40:31 says, **"But those who wait upon the Lord will renew their strength. They will soar on wings like eagles; they will run and not grow weary, they will walk and not be faint."**

We need strength and resources for every day. How are we to obtain them? We need to look at the sunflower and seek to imitate it. A face constantly gazing at the Son will live out of resources that can only come from God.

Then our lives will be radiant, full of blessing – and like the roasted, salted, sunflower seeds, they will bring a good taste into the mouths of others!

Charles

One Year Plan : Psalm 149, Galatians 4, 1 Kings 3 - 4
Two Year Plan : Proverbs 16:17-25, 2 Corinthians 10, Numbers 8 (Yr 1)
Jeremiah 34 (Yr 2)

What do you see?

When you look at someone, what do you see? You may simply see the external – the clothes, the complexion – or you can look again and see beyond the superficial. You can see facial expressions, body language, eyes that express a whole range of emotions.

What you see will depend on how you look. Are you just observing what is on the surface or are you looking with deeper intent? Someone may comment to you that 'such and such' is not well; this will prompt you to look at that person in a different way. How do they look to you? Do you see weight loss? Do you see pain or sadness? Looking with intent causes you to see more than just an impression.

Take another step and expect to see through the lens of God's vision – what do you see? If you look with the intention of seeing what God sees, you will see beyond the natural – and what you see may surprise you.

When Jesus first met Peter He not only told Him his name but He spoke out what He would become: **"You are ... you will be..."** John 1:42: **"You will be a rock, called Cephas – the pillar of the Church."** The Peter who was impulsive, unstable, headstrong, under the transforming grace of Jesus would become a constant, strong, godly and effective leader. Jesus saw beyond the present and created an environment of hope that enabled Peter to walk into his destiny.

If you were to look at the needlepoint hanging in my home, you may see strange hieroglyphics or you may see a word you recognise. You are meant to be able to see the word 'Jesus' but many have real difficulty getting the right focus – until eventually you say, **"I see it!"**

Look at yourself today through God's eyes. He loves you, sees not only what you are now but what He wants you to become. Rejoice! He believes in you. As you look at others, take your eyes off the natural – the imperfections, and the limitations. Look beyond that, and speak out what you see they will become.

Joyce

One Year Plan : Psalm 150, Galatians 5, 1 Kings 5 - 6
Two Year Plan : Proverbs 16:26-33, 2 Corinthians 11, Numbers 9 (Yr 1)
Jeremiah 35 (Yr 2)

Wisdom or Good Advice

James writes in his letter, **"If any of you lacks wisdom, he should ask of God, who gives generously to all without finding fault, and it will be given to him."** (James 1:5) If we ask of God concerning any issue in our life, He has promised to give us the wisdom to know how to deal with it.

This verse contains the phrase **"without finding fault"** – which is significant. Many times we ask others for their wisdom and all we receive is good advice (or sometimes bad advice). **"If you hadn't done this, all would be well." "If you had acted this way, you would not be in such trouble."**

God's wisdom does not blame you for your foolishness or criticise you for your poor judgement; it shows you the way out. In Isaiah 11:2 there is a prophetic word that points forward to Jesus: **"The Spirit of the Lord will rest on him – the Spirit of wisdom and of understanding, the Spirit of counsel and of power, the Spirit of knowledge and of the fear of the Lord."** The Holy Spirit fills you with those same attributes, if you seek God and constantly ask to be filled.

God's wisdom is available for every situation and every crisis. Jesus said, **"Whenever you are arrested and brought to trial, don't worry beforehand about what to say. Just say whatever is given you at the time, for it is not you speaking, but the Holy Spirit."** (Mark 13:11)

I am not expecting that you are going to be arrested and brought to trial! Whilst driving in Central Asia, I was aware of the possibility of being stopped by the police to examine my documents and probably to try and solicit a bribe. I decided beforehand that I would not be gripped by fear because of this possibility but put what Jesus said to the test. I was stopped three times, and God's wisdom prevailed; I was not asked for a bribe.

On one occasion Joyce asked God for wisdom to remove crayon marks from our bedroom wall and was told, **"Use Methylated Spirits."** It may be something intensely practical or something more profound.

God's wisdom is available for you today – use it.

Charles

One Year Plan : Proverbs 16, Galatians 6, 1 Kings 7 - 8
Two Year Plan : Psalm 73:1-12, 2 Corinthians 12, Numbers 10 (Yr 1)
Jeremiah 36 (Yr 2)

Victory

Whatever battle you are involved in, God has promised **victory**. When all you can think about is survival, remember God promises triumph over the circumstances you are facing.

"But thanks be to God! He gives us the victory through our Lord Jesus Christ" is the promise given to all who are **"in Christ Jesus"** (1 Corinthians 15:57). It does not mean we escape the circumstances of life; rather we have been given that internal winning attitude and know ultimately that we will triumph over all our enemies.

David had this assurance in his heart as he faced Goliath; he knew he was going to be victorious. Later, he battled for a very long time with King Saul's jealousy, rage and life threatening attacks – but ultimately he experienced victory.

You may have experienced the death of a loved one and yet know victory over grief. A young widower told me, **"Yes, I experienced grief, but I learned to rule over it. I continue to live in victory, because I know death has been defeated in Jesus."**

Psalm 129:1-2 speak of the nation of Israel being greatly oppressed from her youth, but it then declares, **"...but they have not gained the victory over me."** The key to this victory is God's presence with an individual or a nation. King Saul could not gain the victory over David. 1 Samuel 18:12 says, **"Saul was afraid of David, because the Lord was with David but had left Saul."**

Proverbs 2:7 says, **"He holds victory in store for the upright..."** You qualify because you have been made righteous in Jesus. Be encouraged, and take comfort; you know the end of the story. Take heart; the Lord God Almighty is with you, He is in you and wants you to approach life with a certainty of victory – **whatever comes against you.**

Joyce

One Year Plan : Proverbs 17, Ephesians 1, 1 Kings 9 - 10
Two Year Plan : Psalm 73:13-28, 2 Corinthians 13, Numbers 11 (Yr 1)
Jeremiah 37 (Yr 2)

We Need Each Other

Some people going through difficult times isolate themselves from their friends and stop worshipping with others at church. The fact that they may have 'missed church' is not the issue – it is that they are cutting themselves off from those who love them and are the most committed to them.

This is why the writer to the Hebrews says, **"Let us not give up meeting together, as some are in the habit of doing, but let us encourage one another..."** (Hebrews 10:25) We need to meet together so that we can encourage one another.

When Jesus was speaking to His disciples at the last supper, He knew how much they would need each other once He was gone, and so He gave them a new directive: **"A new command I give you: Love one another. As I have loved you, so you must love one another. By this will all men know that you are my disciples, if you love one another."** (John 13:34-35)

Psalm 55:22 says, **"Cast your cares on the Lord and he will sustain you."** But Paul adds, **"Carry each other's burdens, and in this way you will fulfil the law of Christ."** (Galatians 6:2) We do need to cast our cares on God, but we also need our brothers and sisters to support us.

The tactic of the devil is always to separate us from each other. He lies to us suggesting that our problem or challenge is unique and no-one else could possibly understand or even want to help – **that is not true**.

Have you been cutting yourself off from those who love you and really want to support you in your time of trial? You need to allow your friends to 'pour the oil and wine' into your wounds **and to pray for a breakthrough.**

Can you think of someone who has been getting isolated and you know is really struggling? Give them a phone call today; send them a text message to cheer them up; go around and see them and **don't leave without praying for them.**

You need me, and I need you.

Charles

One Year Plan : Proverbs 18, Ephesians 2, Ecclesiastes 1 - 2
Two Year Plan : Psalm 74:1-11, Galatians 1, Numbers 12 (Yr 1)
Jeremiah 38 (Yr 2)

Keep Shining

Jesus described his cousin, John the Baptist, as **"a lamp that burned and gave light"**. John 5:35 in the Message reads, **"John was a torch, blazing and bright."** I'm challenged by that statement and ask myself how much light is shining out of me.

If you have ever been out in the country searching for a house, you will instinctively look for lights. Even at a far distance, you will notice them and be drawn to their brightness.

Crowds were drawn to John – he had **'something'** or rather **'someone'** – he was in touch with God and spoke from God. His words were always challenging but they were full of hope.

What did the crowds go out to see? A strange prophet who had a message of a coming King, and a new Kingdom; a man who told them they could make a new start in life, that sin could be washed away. If they confessed, they could receive cleansing; the light would transform them and connect them to God.

People from Jerusalem and Judea flocked to hear what he had to say. He challenged empty religion, calling for faith to be expressed in life. He told soldiers to be content with their pay and not to extort money or make false accusations. Tax collectors were challenged to take no more than was due by law, and those who had a surfeit of clothing and money were to share with others.

This was a radical and fearless message, constantly challenging without compromise even King Herod himself. However uncomfortable, he told people the truth because ultimately it produced changed lives. He let light shine through him and not only exposed darkness but brought hope. He consistently pointed to Jesus, the Light who was coming into the world. We are called to do the same.

Are you full of light? Are you shining? Does your light point to Jesus? Is that light dictating how you live each day? Shining light expels darkness, is clearly visible, and can speak louder than words.

Keep shining.

Joyce

One Year Plan : Proverbs 19, Ephesians 3, Ecclesiastes 3 - 5
Two Year Plan : Psalm 74:12-23, Galatians 2, Numbers 13 (Yr 1)
Jeremiah 39 (Yr 2)

Shut the Door

There are times when other people's advice and opinions are not helpful, when we need heavenly and not human solutions.

Two incidents recorded in 2 Kings 4 struck me. First, there was a widow who was destitute and, with her sons, about to be sold into slavery. She cried out to Elisha who asked, **"How can I help you? Tell me, what do you have in your house?" "Your servant has nothing there at all,"** she said, **"except a little oil."**

Elisha instructed her to borrow empty vessels, as many as she could find, and to go into her house and **shut the door**. She was then to pour oil into the jars from her little cruise of oil. It sounded crazy and an unlikely solution.

Verses 5 and 6 say, **"She left him and afterwards shut the door behind her and her sons. They brought the jars to her and she kept pouring. When all the jars were full, she said to her son, 'Bring me another one.' But he replied, 'There is not a jar left.' Then the oil stopped flowing."**

She sold the oil, paid her debts and was able to live on the rest of the money. When human answers have failed and our own resources have run out, it is time to **shut the door** and watch God act on our behalf.

Later in Chapter 4, the child of the Shunammite woman had died, and the dead body had been laid on the bed in the prophet's room. Verses 32 and 33 say, **"When Elisha reached the house, there was the boy lying dead on the couch. He went in, shut the door on the two of them and prayed to the Lord."** God answered Elisha's prayer: the boy was raised to life and restored to his mother.

Human reasoning destroys faith. **Shut the door** and pray, and see how God steps into your place of need today.

Charles

One Year Plan : Proverbs 20, Ephesians 4, Ecclesiastes 6 - 7
Two Year Plan : Psalm 75, Galatians 3, Numbers 14 (Yr 1)
Jeremiah 40 (Yr 2)

Thankfulness

Many years ago we were a small link in a long chain of people who were instrumental in a godless seasoned fisherman receiving Jesus. Years later we caught up with him. He was fishing off the Outer Hebrides, Scotland; lived in a caravan, with his boat moored nearby – totally isolated with only his Bible, the Holy Spirit and some teaching tapes to nourish him.

We were holidaying nearby, went to search him out, and eventually found him. Our children have never forgotten the feast of lobster and cocoa! I have never forgotten the questions he asked, nor the joy he radiated as he described how he was getting to know God better. One of his questions went something like this: **"Tell me, what has God been doing in your life?"** At that moment I couldn't think of a single thing!

He began to recount a whole array of small ways in which the Lord had been protecting him and guiding him; it was wonderfully uplifting and very challenging. I realised that he was a man with a thankful heart who was living in praise and thanksgiving, and it simply flowed out of him and was contagious.

I had to **make myself** think of something to be thankful for; he was living with a **thankful mindset.**

I recalled this as everyone was miserable because of a cold, wet, stormy, UK summer and decided that thanksgiving was a weapon against impending misery and that I would use it! I also encouraged the folk at our church to speak out their praise and thankfulness to God, and once again a heavy spirit was dismissed and perspective restored.

"In everything give thanks" (1 Thessalonians 5:18) is not simply a command or just good advice; it's a weapon to use against misery, depression and heaviness. Use it today!

Hold out your hands in front of you; look at your fingers; start with ten things to thank the Lord for – and I guarantee you'll feel brighter and blessed.

Joyce

One Year Plan : Proverbs 21, Ephesians 5, Ecclesiastes 8 – 9
Two Year Plan : Psalm 76, Galatians 4, Numbers 15 (Yr 1)
Jeremiah 41 (Yr 2)

Stop Paddling – Start Swimming

Can you remember the moment you started to swim? Did it seem amazing to you that having taken your feet off the bottom, you did not sink? When you swim you have to trust yourself to the buoyancy of the water. To start to swim is an act of faith.

In a well-known prophetic vision, Ezekiel was shown a river that was flowing out from the temple. It started off ankle deep and finally became water deep enough to swim in.

I have been pondering this story and asking myself, **"Am I a paddler or a swimmer?"** We have all been for a paddle at the seaside; it is gentle, safe and predictable, with our feet firmly on the ground. Are you like that in daily life, always living within your experience, in a place of safety and predictability? Or are you a swimmer, in water out of your depth, needing to swim to remain afloat?

I believe that God wants us to live our Christian lives **out of our depth** – where we take risks and live on the edge. He wants us to do things we have never done before, say things that we have never said before, and pray things we have never prayed before.

Jesus said these amazing words to His disciples even after they had spent three years working alongside Him: **"Until now you have not asked for anything in my name. Ask and you will receive, and your joy will be complete."** (John 16:24)

It was too easy to watch Jesus doing the stuff, preaching radical truth, healing the sick and doing miracles. Now it was their turn – **"Ask and you will receive…"** Jesus said, **"Anyone who has faith in me will do what I have been doing."** (John 14:12)

It is time to stop paddling and dive into the deep end and swim!

Charles

One Year Plan : Proverbs 22, Ephesians 6, Ecclesiastes 10 - 12
Two Year Plan : Psalm 77:1-9, Galatians 5, Numbers 16 (Yr 1)
Jeremiah 42 (Yr 2)

Make it Visible

You are never too young to see God at work. Encourage children to ask for God's help in the practical issues that affect their lives. He always loves to help.

We were on holiday with our son and his family. Olivia, their four-year-old, had been given a small doll which could be dressed and undressed. She spent hours playing with it; the shoes were pink and girly, and it was fun putting them on and off. One evening, as she was getting ready for bed, she noticed one of the shoes was missing! We searched the holiday house, all to no avail – and there were tears. I then explained how I pray when I have lost something. I ask God to shine a light on the missing object and make it visible. I asked her if she wanted to pray and ask God to help her find the shoe; she agreed, so we prayed.

Very early the next morning there was a knock on the door of our bedroom as three of our grandchildren stood outside chanting, **"Little pig, little pig, let me come it!"** We shouted back, **"Not by the hair of my chinny, chin, chin – you can't come in!"** The morning game continued for some time, when up piped Olivia saying, **"I must come in; I've got something to show you."** In her hand she held two minuscule pink shoes and with a beaming face told me she 'saw' the shoe in the dirt outside the kitchen door; we agreed that Jesus had made it visible and we needed to thank Him – which we did.

The lady who had been cleaning the house had swept everything on the floor out of the kitchen door. However, Olivia had discovered her shoe in the dirt, had her prayer answered and seen her personal understanding of God's love and care grow.

God is interested in every detail of our lives; James 4:2 says, **"You do not have, because you do not ask God."**

Joyce

One Year Plan : Proverbs 23, Philippians 1, Song of Songs 1 - 3
Two Year Plan : Psalm 77:10-20, Galatians 6, Numbers 17 (Yr 1)
Jeremiah 43 (Yr 2)

Rock of Ages

We live about five miles from **'The Rock of Ages'**, which is situated in Burrington Coombe, Somerset. This is where, in 1763, Rev Augustus Toplady sheltered with his horse, having been caught in a violent storm. When the crisis had passed and he was safe and dry back at home in Blagdon, he penned one of the best loved and most famous hymns in the English language.

Rock of Ages, cleft for me,
Let me hide myself in Thee;
Let the water and the blood,
From Thy riven side which flowed,
Be of sin the double cure;
Save me from its guilt and power.

We often take friends for a drive to the Rock of Ages, stand in the cleft of the rock, take some photos, and remind ourselves of the amazing truths of that hymn.

A recent visit there reminded me of our constant need for a rock and shelter in these times of uncertainty. Psalm 61:2 says, **"I call as my heart grows faint; lead me to the rock that is higher than I."**

Again, in Psalm 40:2 it says, **"He lifted me out of the slimy pit, out of the mud and the mire; he set my feet upon a rock and gave me a firm place to stand."**

Psalm 62:1-2 says, **"My soul finds rest in God alone; my salvation comes from him. He alone is my rock and my salvation; he is my fortress, I will never be shaken."**

Jesus spoke about our lives being founded on the rock of His word so that the storms cannot undermine us and knock us down. Matthew 7:24-25 says, **"Therefore everyone who hears these words of mine and puts them into practice is like a wise man who built his house on the rock. The rains came down, the streams rose, and the winds blew and beat upon against that house; yet it did not fall because it had its foundation on the rock."**

Keep your feet on the Rock today.

Charles

One Year Plan : Proverbs 24, Philippians 2, Song of Songs 4 - 6
Two Year Plan : Psalm 78:1-16, Ephesians 1, Numbers 18 (Yr 1)
Jeremiah 44 (Yr 2)

Fear or Faith?

It is not every morning you wake up with the phone ringing and the news that one of your children and their family are being evacuated from the country where they live and work, due to potential war and violence. But when it happens you can have one of two reactions, and you must choose which to live with – **fear or faith?**

Fear is very natural. Five people you love are in a very vulnerable and dangerous situation. They are sitting in an airport hangar; Mirage jets are taking off and landing; rumours abound of rebel troops advancing on the capital city where they are living.

But faith says in Psalm 91, **"He who dwells in the shelter of the Most High will rest in the shadow of the Almighty."** And as the Message expresses it, **"His huge outstretched arms protect you – under them you are perfectly safe, his arms fend off all harm."**

I chose to trust in God's ability to protect my children and keep them under His Almighty wings. Shortly after the phone call they were in the air flying to a safe place in an adjoining country.

We may not be living with such political uncertainty, but we constantly face situations where we have to make the same choice: **fear or faith?** To resist images of disaster and destruction and to confess our faith and trust in the one who not only loves but has the ability to meet every need.

Today, take a faith look and see yourself and those you love under the shadow of Almighty God, our Refuge and our Fortress, our God who is utterly trustworthy.

Joyce

One Year Plan : Proverbs 25, Philippians 3, Song of Songs 7 - 8
Two Year Plan : Psalm 78:17-31, Ephesians 2, Numbers 19 (Yr 1)
Jeremiah 45 (Yr 2)

It's Raining Again!

Why is it that, after weeks of dry sunny weather, the moment they take the covers off the courts at Wimbledon it rains? I don't know the answer to that question. This country is blessed to have so much rain. It is described as **"a green and pleasant land"**. For those of us living in this country rain is an inconvenience, particularly during the summer; but for the vast majority of the world, rain is a friend, it is a blessing.

We live in a world where there is famine, parched ground, crops that do not grow, and people dying through lack of rain. Providing the Third World with clean drinking water is a major challenge to the prosperous developed nations.

God spoke about rain in the similar way when He was telling His people about the Promised Land they were to inherit:

"The land you are entering to take over is not like the land of Egypt, from which you have come, where you planted your seed and irrigated it by foot as in a vegetable garden. But the land you are crossing the Jordan to take possession of is a land of mountains and valleys that drinks rain from heaven. It is a land the LORD your God cares for; the eyes of the LORD your God are continually on it from the beginning of the year to its end." (Deuteronomy 11:11-12)

If we choose to live out of our own resources, strength and ingenuity, it is like irrigating the land by foot. When we live with heaven's resources, God promises His people lives lived under the **rain of His blessing**. When we commit our lives to Jesus we come under His blessing and leave our striving and struggling.

Today, stand under the downpour of God's rain from heaven, and leave a life that is dry and full of toil.

God's rain is a blessing.

Charles

One Year Plan : Proverbs 26, Philippians 4, Isaiah 1 - 2
Two Year Plan : Psalm 78:32-55, Ephesians 3, Numbers 20 (Yr 1)
Jeremiah 46 (Yr 2)

Big or Small – It's All the Same to God

It's possible to live with the attitude that I can manage small problems myself. Big ones, those beyond me, I'll ask for help from above! However, the things we consider small enough to be able to handle alone often remain unresolved and can grow imperceptibly until they become too big to handle.

This is what happened to me. For a long time I recognised that I didn't like coming back home from holidays or ministry trips. I love my home, my family and friends, but returning to base was always tinged with a small but very definite negative emotion. I tried to shrug it off but in reality failed to face up to it. Once settled back home and getting along with life, I seldom thought about it – that is until recently.

A friend was recounting how much she liked to get home after being away, which made me realise how different I felt, and it prompted me to speak out my feelings. The small, fleeting, undealt-with emotion had grown – and was becoming too big for me to handle.

My friend started to ask the 'why' questions, and I realised that it wasn't small at all. There were associated issues of finding it difficult to relax at home, viewing the telephone as demanding, rather than a joy, to answer. I now saw that I needed to bring this whole area of my life to the Lord; it was bigger than I had thought, and I needed God's help to give me understanding and to release me from a false sense of responsibility into peace and rest.

It only took a short time to bring my 'problem' to the Lord and an even shorter time for Him to release me from false pressure and wrong thinking – but the effect has been enormous. I am now happy to answer the phone; I'm enjoying a new level of internal peace and rest.

Let us bring everything, however small or insignificant, to our heavenly Father, who has the patience to listen and the power to act in every situation small or great.

Joyce

One Year Plan : Proverbs 27, Colossians 1, Isaiah 3 - 4
Two Year Plan : Psalm 78:56-72, Ephesians 4, Numbers 21 (Yr 1)
Jeremiah 47 (Yr 2)

A Spacious Place

While reading in the Psalms, I was struck by the phrase **"a spacious place"**; this set me thinking. We all need **a spacious place**; life has a habit of trying to hem us in, to confine and diminish.

I love the west coast of Scotland. For seven years we took our holidays in Applecross where we stayed in a very remote croft, one and a half miles' walk from where we left our car; it was more accessible by sea. But to stand on the shore and look out towards Syke and Raasay was wonderful; you couldn't see anything man-made, only God's creation. It was truly **a spacious place**, and it gave you perspective; you saw how big God is and how small you are, and you began to realise that His great power was not only for creating the world but also available to you.

David spoke about how God had helped him: **"He brought me out into a spacious place; he rescued me because he delighted in me."** (Psalm 18:19) David was under pressure, he had enemies on every side, but when he cried out to God he was rescued. God wants to bring you into **a spacious place** of victory over circumstances and pressures that are trying to crush you.

Isaac re-opened the wells that had been dug in the time of his father Abraham. He first dug at Gerar, but there was quarrelling, then at Esek, but there was a dispute. When he came to Rehoboth, he opened the well and there was peace and no quarrelling, and he said, **"Now the Lord has given us room and we will flourish in the land."** (Genesis 26:17-22)

We all need space, not just physically but deep inside. This does not mean we have to travel to Scotland, but we **all need to cry out to God**, and He will bring us into **a spacious place**.

Charles

One Year Plan : Proverbs 28, Colossians 2, Isaiah 5 - 6
Two Year Plan : Psalm 79, Ephesians 5, Numbers 22 (Yr 1)
Jeremiah 48 (Yr 2)

When did you last have a Sabbath?

Sabbath could be defined as 'a rest from every day activities; a time to be quiet; a time to recharge the batteries, to do something different in order to be refreshed'.

A lot of you may say, impossible, can't even think about it, the kids, the pressure of work, the house, the decorating, the garden, the in-laws! What's that? Meetings and more meetings! I can hear the frustration, and I've been in that place so many times, and yet Jesus says, **"Come apart and rest a while."** God initiates Sabbath because He made us and knows our needs better than we do.

Is it not a period of inactivity or a day of prayer and fasting but rather a time to 'be', to relax, to stop and stare, to enjoy God's creation. A day off from shopping! A day off from cooking if you find that a chore!

Plan Sabbath. The Israelites in the wilderness had to gather twice the quantity of manna; none was provided on the Sabbath. Make preparation for a different day; dedicate it to God as a family; ask for His refreshment and perspective. Talk. Communicate from your hearts. It won't just happen; you will have to make it happen.

Men: don't leave your wives to plan it! You prepare **Sabbath** one week; let the family do it another week; involve your older children; choose special food; do things that involve the whole family.

Such a day will bring refreshment and perspective. If you can't manage it every week, try taking a monthly **Sabbath**. Chill out. Be a Mary and not a Martha. Just do it for one day and notice the difference.

If you had lived in Egypt and now were being given a day off, you would rejoice in **Sabbath**.

Joyce

One Year Plan : Proverbs 29, Colossians 3, Isaiah 7 - 8
Two Year Plan : Psalm 80:1-7, Ephesians 6, Numbers 23 (Yr 1)
Jeremiah 49 (Yr 2)

JULY

Being Generous

I was reading a devotional book by Harry Westcott, a good friend who lives in Australia. In it he recounts a situation where he was in sharp disagreement with a colleague and was seeking to convince his boss how this colleague should be put in his place. He tells how the response he received has remained with him ever since: **"Harry, in every situation we do the generous thing!"**

There are times when we are mistreated and feel that we should repay ungenerous behaviour by acting meanly. This is not the way God wants us to live.

In Acts 2:46 we read of the lifestyle of the new believers: **"They worshipped together at the Temple each day, met in homes for the Lord's Supper, and shared their meals with great joy and generosity."** I love the way it declares that their lives were marked by **"joy and generosity"**.

Paul tells how the Macedonian believers were well known for their generosity. He says, **"Out of the most severe trial, their overflowing joy and their extreme poverty welled up in rich generosity. For I testify that they gave as much as they were able, and even beyond their ability."** (2 Corinthians 8:2-3) It should be the trademark of all believers that they will be givers and not just takers.

In Proverbs 11:25 it says, **"A generous man will prosper; he who refreshes others will himself be refreshed."** There is a blessing in being generous; when we are prepared to overlook areas of irritation and disagreement and respond with love and giving, we will ultimately be the ones who benefit.

In Corinthians when Paul is teaching about giving, he concludes, **"You will be made rich in every way so that you can be generous on every occasion, and through us your generosity will result in thanksgiving to God."** (2 Corinthians 9:11)

Generosity is not simply about giving money; it is showing kindness; it is being thoughtful and taking an interest in others; it is overlooking how we are being treated and... **in every situation doing the generous thing.**

Charles

One Year Plan : Proverbs 30, Colossians 4, Isaiah 9 - 10
Two Year Plan : Psalm 80:8-19, Luke 1:1-25, Numbers 24 (Yr 1)
Jeremiah 50 (Yr 2)

Where God is at Home

In Deuteronomy 33, God speaks prophetically through Moses over each of the twelve tribes of Israel. **"About Benjamin he says, 'God's beloved; God's permanent residence. Encircled by God all day long, within whom God is at home.'"** (Deuteronomy 33:12, The Message)

You also are God's beloved child on whom the Father has lavished His love; so put your name in that verse in place of 'Benjamin' and see how it reads! Now feel it! You already know this in your head, but you need to feel the love, acceptance and honour that are poured out on every child of God. Isn't it amazing?!

No wonder John exclaims, **"How great is the love the Father has lavished on us, that we should be called children of God! And that is what we are!"** (1 John 3:1) Consider the love you have for your children; do they have to perform to earn your love? They are part of you – in a sense, created by you. It isn't hard to love your own flesh and blood, and as **children of God** you are His own flesh and blood!

Parents delight in each new development of their children: the first smile, the first step, the triumph when hand-eye co-ordination is achieved and the spoon and food reach the right spot. Others might not notice, but you see the development.

Bask in God's acceptance and love today; He's feeling at home with you. He watches every step and picks you up when you stumble. See yourself encircled by His presence. Ask Him to reveal afresh **the marvel of His love**, not based upon performance but lavished on you because God has created you, chosen you, likes you. Why?

He made you, you are His and He is love. **Wow!**

Joyce

One Year Plan : Proverbs 31, Matthew 1, Isaiah 11 - 12
Two Year Plan : Psalm 81, Luke 1:26-56, Numbers 25 (Yr 1)
Jeremiah 51 (Yr 2)

You are Blessed

I was reading about Balaam in the book of Numbers. What a remarkable story it is! Balak is trying his hardest to get Balaam to curse God's people, but he can't do it. Balaam desperately wants to pronounce a curse and get his money, but God says, **"You must not put a curse on these people, because they are blessed."** (Numbers 22:12)

The Children of Israel have been moaning and complaining, they have been giving their leader Moses a hard time, and still God says, **"...they are blessed."** The reason for this goes back to the time God called Abraham and promised blessing, which is not only for the nation of Israel but for all those who have put their faith in Him.

Galatians 3:14 makes it very clear that when Jesus triumphed on the cross, **"He redeemed us in order that the blessing given to Abraham might come to the Gentiles through Christ Jesus."**

Blessing does not mean that life is always going to be plain sailing and that there will be no problems or challenges; it means that God is right there seeking to bring His presence, power and destiny into every situation.

Aaron is commanded to pronounce a blessing over the Israelites: **"The Lord bless you and keep you; the Lord make his face to shine upon you..."**

In Proverbs 10:22 it says, **"The blessing of the Lord makes rich and he adds no sorrow with it."**

In the Sermon on the Mount, the first thing Jesus speaks about is blessing, not only for the successful but also for those in need.

Peter in his letter continues this theme: **"Not one is missing, not one forgotten, God the Father has his eye on each one of you, and has determined by the work of his Spirit to keep you obedient through the sacrifice of Jesus. May everything good from God be yours!"** (1 Peter 1:1-2, The Message)

You are blessed because you belong to God; you are blessed because He is always on your side; you are blessed because He gives you a hope and a future.

Joyce and I often say to each other, **"We are blessed."** Say it today, and know that God is with you in every detail of life.

Charles

One Year Plan : Psalm 1, Matthew 2, Isaiah 13 - 14
Two Year Plan : Psalm 82, Luke 1:57-80, Numbers 26 (Yr 1)
Jeremiah 52 (Yr 2)

Using your Authority

Have you ever wondered how the animals in Noah's day came into the Ark? There is no evidence of sweat and toil, of rounding them up; it appears they just came. Could it be that they had come under the authority given to Noah by God? Did he speak and say, **"Come!"** and they had to respond? Adam had been granted authority over every living creature and understood the power of the spoken word of command. (Genesis 1:26)

In Mark 11:23 Jesus illustrates this principle: **"I tell you the truth, if anyone says to this mountain, 'Go, throw yourself into the sea,' and does not doubt in his heart but believes what he says will happen, it will be done for him."**

You and I are called to rule over our circumstances and change them. We often allow all sorts of things to bog us down and waste our time. Choose to rule and use the authority you have been given. It may seem a little strange to command winds and tell fruit trees to wither and die, but it is the lifestyle of Jesus we are called to follow.

A friend in Sweden had a large unfruitful cherry tree in her garden; she spoke to it in the name of Jesus saying, **"I will give you one more year and if you fail to produce fruit you will be cut down."** I was there the summer after the tree responded to her word of command, and I have never seen such an abundant harvest – the tree still stands!

Our cat went missing, and after much searching, tears and concern, I told the children, **"We are going to command it to come home now!"** I did also ask for a few angels to chase it home! Less than ten minutes later a very out of breath cat appeared; it had heard the voice of authority.

Don't allow circumstances to dominate; change them by using the power and authority given to you.

Joyce

One Year Plan : Psalm 2, Matthew 3, Isaiah 15 - 16
Two Year Plan : Psalm 83, Luke 2:1-20, Numbers 27 (Yr 1)
Lamentations 1 (Yr 2)

Walk with the Wise

Some years ago we were at a crossroads; we knew it was right to move on to a new chapter in our lives. As we were praying about this with some friends, a new plan emerged which seemed right, challenging and exciting. The new venture began to develop and was moving forward with speed and confidence.

A pause then occurred as I left with a small team to go to East Germany. It was still the days of the communist era, the iron curtain and the Berlin Wall, so that when we entered the country we deliberately cut communications with home.

As our team gathered to prepare for the ministry ahead, I told them all about our new venture and the vision that we were pursuing. They listened carefully, were very kind and gracious, but I could sense they had genuine reservations. This caused me to go back to the Lord and to seek to listen afresh to His voice.

At the same time Joyce was at home and during a power cut began chatting to one of our daughters about our future plans. She said, **"Do you want to hear what God has been saying to me?"** then fetched her journal and began to share that God had also been warning her that this was not the right way forward.

When we were back together, we set aside time and were clearly shown that we had, in our enthusiasm, got ahead of God. Proverbs 13:20 says, **"He who walks with the wise grows wise,"** and another of the proverbs says, **"Plans fail for lack of counsel."** (15:22) I am so thankful for wise and mature friends who could signal danger. I also praise God for a daughter who could hear from God and help us find the right way.

I am hearing of many folk making poor and independent decisions. Let us be sufficiently humble to receive wisdom from both old and young. **"Rebuke a wise man and he will love you."** (Proverbs 9:8)

Charles

One Year Plan : Psalm 3, Matthew 4, Isaiah 17 - 18
Two Year Plan : Psalm 84, Luke 2:21-52, Numbers 28 (Yr 1)
Lamentations 2 (Yr 2)

When Hurting, Find Someone to Give to

You may find that a strange statement, but it's what Jesus did when He was faced with the brutal death of His cousin, John the Baptist. He tried to get alone to process the news and pray, but the crowd followed Him and He put the God-principle into practice: **"Give, and it will be given to you."** He chose to turn from His own sorrows and give healing to those who clamoured for His touch!

It was late in the day and the crowd was hungry; He chose to feed them, meeting their physical need for bread. The disciples wanted to send the multitude away, but Jesus was willing to go beyond what could have been expected of Him. His giving is endless, His compassion beyond expectation.

Jesus still needed to find a place of prayer where He could be alone with God, so He climbed a mountain at night. The disciples set off in a boat to the other side of the lake. At last He was able to receive what He needed from His Father. We can only imagine the love and comfort that flowed out from heaven to Jesus, the approval of the Father, and encouragement to press on with the appointed task. The choice of giving away from yourself, letting love flow, focussing on others rather than yourself, will always be there – it's a challenge. His obedience led to an increase in power: **"All who touched him were healed!"**

Think of what could have happened! Jesus could have been fearful: **"Will they get me?"** He could have been full of self-pity and self-protection. He could have stopped ministering and laid low. He could have been defensive and sought time out.

He went on giving, taking the offensive, destroying the work of the devil – and as He gave, so He received all He needed personally – **and more to give away.**

Joyce

One Year Plan : Psalm 4, Matthew 5, Isaiah 19 - 20
Two Year Plan : Psalm 85, Luke 3, Numbers 29 (Yr 1)
Lamentations 3 (Yr 2)

Where are you Planted?

The UK was experiencing a drought, there were hosepipe bans in many areas, and we were told that this was likely to last until Christmas. Those who were keen on gardening and growing things were making sure that plants were placed where they could flourish.

Psalm 92 tells us that the righteous are like a palm tree planted in the house of the Lord and that they will flourish. The conditions for this are: praising the Lord, proclaiming His love in the morning and faithfulness at night, and singing for joy at the works of His hand. This would indicate that **in order to flourish, we need to make sure we plant ourselves in an environment of praise, love and faithfulness.**

Psalm 1 also speaks about being like a tree planted by streams of water. Here the conditions for blessing are that we **"delight in the law of the Lord and on his law meditate day and night."** The result of all that is that we are like that tree **"which yields its fruit in season and whose leaf does not wither"**. I like the phrase **"whose leaf does not wither"** which indicates freshness and energy. I hear so many people these days complain of fatigue and weariness. Does not this psalm give us a key to remaining fresh?

In Jeremiah 17 we again find a tree planted by the water; it says, **"Blessed is the man who trusts in the Lord, whose confidence is in him. He will be like a tree planted by the water..."** Here the key is trusting in the Lord, living with a faith and confidence that God is more powerful than the circumstances around us. The promised result is, **"It does not fear when the heat comes; its leaves are always green. It has no worries in the year of drought..."**

So let's be people of praise and thankfulness, who love God's word and live by faith. We will then know that we are like a tree that is planted in the right place!

Charles

One Year Plan : Psalm 5, Matthew 6, Isaiah 21 - 22
Two Year Plan : Psalm 86:1-10, Luke 4:1-30, Numbers 30 (Yr 1)
Lamentations 4 (Yr 2)

Rahab

It's always good to be reminded that God knows the heart of every human being. He knows those who are seeking Him and responding internally, even when they are as yet outside the family of God. God reminded Elijah that He had seven thousand people in Israel who didn't worship Baal. Elijah couldn't see them, but God could.

Consider Rahab – an unlikely believer in God; a prostitute and, in Israel, therefore an outcast. She is, however, a believer in the God of Israel even though she doesn't know Him personally.

She says to the spies sent by Joshua, **"I know God has given you the land. We're all afraid. Everyone in the country feels hopeless. We heard how God dried up the Red Sea before you left Egypt, and what He did to the two Amorite kings east of Jordan etc. etc."** (Joshua 2:9-11, The Message)

She is collecting data about this great God, the God of the heavens above and the earth below. She wants His help and is prepared to risk her life aiding the spies. God sees this and delights in rescuing her and her family.

Today, there are many who really want to know God; they are waiting for someone to tell them about Jesus and what He has done to make it possible for them to enter into personal knowledge, relationship and connection.

Ask God to send you to someone today **prepared by God** – already aware of spiritual realities but ignorant of the wonderful riches of having a personal friendship with God and salvation through Jesus.

Rahab was rescued from Jericho, married into an Israelite family, became the great great grandmother of King David and part of the lineage of Jesus! God was on her case; even when she was without hope and without God, He saw her and reached out to her in mercy and love.

This is God's heart for His world. Make it ours, Lord Jesus.

Joyce

One Year Plan : Psalm 6, Matthew 7, Isaiah 23 - 24
Two Year Plan : Psalm 86:11-17, Luke 4:31-44, Numbers 31 (Yr 1)
Lamentations 5 (Yr 2)

Stay on Course

I had been reading reading 'Amazing Grace' by Eric Metaxas – a remarkable biography of William Wilberforce, telling of his heroic campaign to end slavery. His determination, against all odds, to achieve his goal, is a triumph of faith.

For more than twenty years he brought bills to Parliament and was defeated time and time again, but he did not give up. After committing his life to Jesus, he wanted to live the gospel in every area of life and so devoted himself to changing the society of his day.

One fact fascinated me: Wilberforce wanted to live nearer to Parliament so that he didn't have to keep two residences, so he bought a house at Kensington Gore, close to the location where the Royal Albert Hall now is. It was quite rural but still near enough to Parliament that he could walk home from work. If he was alone, he would sometimes **recite the 119th Psalm out loud as he walked.**

I found that amazing – not only that he had committed the 119th Psalm to memory but also that he should feel the need to regularly recite it at the end of a busy day. What sort of impact did this have? At the time of reading the book, we were having a 24-7 Prayer week at Living Waters Church, so on my next visit to the prayer room, I sat and slowly read through the 119th Psalm. I was trying to imagine the effect on Wilberforce as he spoke out these words – it is powerful.

Verse 2-3: **"Blessed are they who keep his statutes and seek him with all their heart. They do nothing wrong; they walk in his ways."**

Verse 23: **"Though rulers sit together and slander me, your servant will meditate on your decrees."**

Verse 28: **"My soul is weary with sorrow; strengthen me according to your word."**

Verse 165: **"Great peace have they who love your law, and nothing can make them stumble."**

That is just a small selection, but it gives you an indication of how Wilberforce was able to **stay on course** and change the world. Try it for yourself; get somewhere quiet and read through Psalm 119.

Charles

One Year Plan : Psalm 7, Matthew 8, Isaiah 25 - 26
Two Year Plan : Psalm 87, Luke 5:1-16, Numbers 32 (Yr 1)
1 Kings 1 (Yr 2)

A Useful Container

It's a good feeling when you find a container where you expected to find it – and better still if it's clean and ready for use. The same with tools; it's great when the screwdriver, scissors or needle are in the right place but totally frustrating when you want to use something and it's missing or in an unusable state.

Many times I have people staying in our home. They help clear the kitchen and then I can't find a thing; I later marvel at the strange places I discover them!

2 Timothy 2:21 says in the Message, **"Become the container God can use to present any and every kind of gift to his guests for their blessing."**

Be ready – clean and available. Every day God has purpose for your life. You carry Jesus with you at work, at school, whether you talk about Him or not; His presence is with you and you make a difference. Jesus wants you to keep short accounts; the moment you fail, confess, receive forgiveness and make sure you are ready, so you can be filled with blessing and be a blessing.

Peter was ready and alert when he passed the lame man outside the temple. He was listening to the prompting of the Holy Spirit, gave what he had and the man was healed. What if Peter had just been quarrelling with his wife and was feeling guilty and a total failure? I don't think the result would have been the same.

During a mission in London, Arthur Blessitt asked each person on his team to go out on the streets and be ready for God to use them in whatever way He chose. One lady was extremely reluctant to do this. It wasn't her style – she felt nervous and totally inadequate – so she simply went to the park, sat on a bench next to a man, said hello and commented about the weather. To her surprise, he said to her, **"I had decided to end my life today but came to this park and sat on this bench to see whether anyone would notice me and speak to me; if not I would do what I had planned!"** An amazing conversation resulted in that man meeting Jesus and finding a whole new life.

Joyce

One Year Plan : Psalm 8, Matthew 9, Isaiah 27 - 28
Two Year Plan : Psalm 88:1-9a, Luke 5:17-39, Numbers 33 (Yr 1)
1 Kings 2 (Yr 2)

Smile... That's Better!

I heard the other day that laughter is good for you and that it takes less energy to smile than it does to frown. Someone also told me that if I smile before I answer the phone, my voice will sound better!

It is amazing how modern research so often confirms what was written in the Bible many years before; it could have saved some folk a lot of money!

Proverbs 17:22 says, **"A cheerful heart is good medicine, but a crushed spirit dries up the bones."**

There are other verses from the Bible which say similar things; for example, **"The joy of the Lord is your strength."** In Peter's letter, he says, **"...you believe in him and are filled with inexpressible and glorious joy."** It says of Jesus that He was **"anointed with the oil of joy"**.

What is your joy level? Some of you by now may be saying, **"If you knew my situation you would understand why I never smile."**

That is where God can step into your situation: **"He heals the broken hearted and binds up their wounds."** (Psalm 147:3)

When Jesus was explaining God's purpose for sending Him to earth, He said, **"He has sent me to proclaim freedom for the prisoners and recovery of sight for the blind, to release the oppressed, to proclaim the year of the Lord's favour."** (Luke 4:18-19)

God is able to come into your situation today and bring His love and healing power. He is committed to putting joy into your life; He can heal you, He can restore you, and replace your sadness with His joy.

Don't stay crushed and broken; God can transform your situation.

Charles

One Year Plan : Psalm 9, Matthew 10, Isaiah 29 - 30
Two Year Plan : Psalm 88:9b-18, Luke 6:1-26, Numbers 34 (Yr 1)
1 Kings 3 (Yr 2)

Panning for Gold

We had spent a holiday with my brother and sister-in-law in New Zealand. Apart from viewing the wonderful scenery, Phil had another goal: to find gold! It needed preparation and it cost him time and money:

- He had researched carefully.
- He knew where to do his panning.
- He had bought and made the necessary equipment.
- He prioritised his time in order to seek out the gold.
- He was prepared for the discomfort of standing in cold water in order to find what he had set his heart upon.

So it was with this in mind that I read these words from Proverbs 2:2-5 in The Message: **"Tune your ears to the world of wisdom; set your heart on a life of understanding. That's right – if you make insight your priority, and won't take no for an answer, searching for it like a prospector panning for gold, like an adventurer on a treasure hunt, believe me, before you know it fear-of-God will be yours; you'll have come upon the knowledge of God."**

I found myself asking: how much do I want wisdom and insight? Do I have the same desire to find God's mind and ways? Although my priority was not panning for gold, I was fascinated when shown a few flakes of gold. Phil was thrilled with what he found, which gave him an appetite to search for more.

I am challenged; do I want to find wisdom and insight? Am I prepared to focus on them at the expense of time spent on other things? Will I pay the cost of searching for this spiritual gold and treasure? Will you?

Our wisdom is found in Jesus, who is wiser than Solomon who wrote the Proverbs. 1 Corinthians 1:30 speaks of Jesus, **"...who has become for us wisdom from God – that is, our righteousness, holiness and redemption."**

Joyce

One Year Plan : Psalm 10, Matthew 11, Isaiah 31 - 32
Two Year Plan : Psalm 89:1-13, Luke 6:27-49, Numbers 35 (Yr 1)
1 Kings 4 (Yr 2)

The Love Bank

We had been speaking at a day for married couples, and as part of the teaching we introduced the concept of **the love bank**. We learned this from a very experienced marriage counsellor who had been an expert in teaching couples how to resolve conflict and to improve their ability to communicate, but was devastated to discover that all these skills had done very little to stop marriage breakdown. However, when he began to teach **the love bank**, the results were amazing.

Within our own finances, we may have a number of bank accounts, and it is a great blessing when they are all in the **BLACK**. We also have many different love accounts: our marriages, children, family, friends, church and work.

The key factor is to make more deposits than withdrawals.

We make deposits by...

- Attention
- Affection
- Acceptance
- Approval
- Fun
- Surprise

We make withdrawals by...

- Criticism
- Arguing
- Indifference

When we love, accept, give to, and bless others, we deposit something very rich in their **love bank**. If we are always criticising, spreading negativity and ignoring the needs of those we ought to be loving, we are emptying their **love bank**, which under-mines them and will also hurt us.

Loving, accepting and forgiving will always be a blessing both for the one who gives and the one who receives. God's principle is, **"Give and it will be given to you."** We never give away from ourselves without receiving. A full **love bank** makes it easier to handle offences, as another verse says, **"Love covers over a multitude of sins."**

It is time to review your love bank accounts – are they in the **BLACK** or in the **RED**? If you find them in the **RED** you need to make some deposits!

Charles

One Year Plan : Psalm 11, Matthew 12, Isaiah 33 - 34
Two Year Plan : Psalm 89:14-29, Luke 7:1-23, Numbers 36 (Yr 1)
1 Kings 5 (Yr 2)

What's your Password?

Whenever you are using the internet to access various websites or to register for information, you will usually be asked for a password. This means remembering the one you have chosen to use – although many of us tend to use the same password on multiple sites.

I was reading Psalm 100 in The Message. Verse 1 encourages us to **"sing ourselves into his presence,"** and verse 4 gives us the command to **"enter with the password 'Thank you!'"** On the internet, if you can't remember the correct password, you have to ask for a reminder of your original password or choose a new one – all time-consuming operations!

Our heavenly access code is officially **"thank you"**. We don't have to guard it against information theft; we simply have to use it. I had a quiet chuckle as I thought about this – but as I came to prayer sometime later I thought, **"Password!"** and I immediately began to thank God for a number of things before I started to offload.

I am sure our Heavenly Father will listen however we come to Him. Hebrews 4:16 tells us **"to come boldly to the throne of grace, so that we may receive mercy and find grace to help us in our time of need"**.

For me this was a good reminder to not only make requests but to come into His presence with thanksgiving and into His courts with praise.

Our heavenly access code is **"thank you"**. As you enter your password today, use your fingers to say thank you for ten things that are a blessing in your life.

Joyce

One Year Plan : Psalm 12, Matthew 13, Isaiah 35 - 36
Two Year Plan : Psalm 89:30-52, Luke 7:24-50, Deuteronomy 1 (Yr 1)
1 Kings 6 (Yr 2)

Urgent or Important?

We all know what it is to be a victim of the **'tyranny of the urgent'**. The phone rings, and we interrupt what we are doing to respond to the strident ring tone. How long after the **'beep beep'** can you wait to read the text message that has arrived on your mobile phone?

When national or international crises occur, it is right that we respond quickly and generously and that we don't give up caring as soon as the images leave our television screens. Tragically, disasters happen every week in Africa as tens of thousands die of disease, starvation, through genocide, and lack of clean water – and the world looks on and does very little.

Paul says to the Christians living in the Rome of his day, **"Let no debt remain outstanding, except the continuing debt to love one another, for he who loves his fellow man has fulfilled the law."** (Romans 13:8)

There is a massive challenge being delivered to the rich and developed countries of the world. **Are we going to pour out our lives and our resources to tackle world-wide disease, war and hunger? Or will we just be those who respond financially to the 'tyranny of the urgent'?**

History tells of God's people who risked their lives, who were the pioneers in feeding the hungry, in healing the sick and bringing the good news of the gospel to a dying world. Let us again be at the forefront of not only helping with a present crisis but giving ourselves no rest until we see the love and compassion of Jesus reach our dying world.

Need on a global level can leave us bemused and unable to know exactly how to respond, but there are things happening right where we live. Jesus said, **"I tell you the truth, whatever you did for one of the least of these brothers of mine, you did for me."** (Matthew 25:40)

Charles

One Year Plan : Psalm 13, Matthew 14, Isaiah 37 - 38
Two Year Plan : Psalm 90:1-10, Luke 8:1-25, Deuteronomy 2 (Yr 1)
1 Kings 7 (Yr 2)

Wisdom, Worth its Weight in Gold

I long for wisdom. In Proverbs it declares, **"Blessed is the man who finds wisdom, the man who gains understanding, for she is more profitable than silver and yields better returns than gold."** (Proverbs 3:13-14)

I love watching craftsmen at work; they make what they are doing look so simple. But don't be fooled; you are looking at years of experience and love applied to a task, and you rightly marvel at the result.

Watch Jesus operate in wisdom. Where did He get it? It came from heaven by the presence and anointing of the Holy Spirit.

In the early hours of the morning as dawn was breaking, Jesus had made His way to the temple expecting to teach those who came to Him. But today was different. A young woman was being dragged through the temple courts by a group of Pharisees and made to stand in the middle of the crowd. She was terrified, embarrassed, and cowered before them all. She had been caught in the act of adultery, and they waited to hear what Jesus would have to say after reminding Him that the law required stoning.

A catch-22 situation: the law was unequivocal, and yet Jesus saw her desperate need and wanted to give love and forgiveness. It was a trap: fail to uphold the Law of Moses and He would have no credibility with the Jews; advise stoning and He would fall foul of the Roman law which denied the Jews the right to carry out death sentences.

Jesus writes on the ground. At the same time He is seeking wisdom from His Father. He straightens up and says, **"If any one of you is without sin, let him be the first to throw a stone at her."** From the oldest to the youngest they slink away. Finally Jesus looks at her and asks, **"Has no one condemned you?" "No one, sir,"** she says. **"Then neither do I condemn you. Go now and leave your life of sin."** (John 8:1-11)

He does not condone her action, but I believe His command released her to live a new kind of life.

Isn't He brilliant? What would you have done? Seek His wisdom in every detail of life; nothing is too trivial.

Joyce

One Year Plan : Psalm 14, Matthew 15, Isaiah 39 - 40
Two Year Plan : Psalm 90:11-17, Luke 8:26-56, Deuteronomy 3 (Yr 1)
1 Kings 8 (Yr 2)

Truth and Lies

A few weeks ago, a friend of ours who is a school teacher was asked to sign a document which was to help another member of staff get an advancement in her job. However, before signing she read what was contained in the statement and was alarmed to discover it contained blatant untruths - and refused to sign. The reaction of her work colleagues caused her further distress, as she realised they were victimising her for her action. So it seemed lies are okay if it helps someone get along in their career!

Truth seems to have become optional in our society today. This is not new because in Jeremiah 7:28 it says, **"Truth has perished, it has vanished from their lips."** This friend was shocked that a group of professional people could be so unconcerned with truth that they could tell lies if it suited their cause.

I have heard of folk who say, **"I think I'll take a 'sickie' tomorrow,"** because they want a day off work to do something more pleasurable. The phone call made to the employer will say that one of his employees is sick and not able to come to work – it is a lie.

We use words like **'telling fibs'** and **'it's only a white lie'** to try to make lying respectable and acceptable. Paul spoke to the new believers in Colossae and said, **"Do not lie to each other, since you have taken off your old self with its practices."** (Colossians 3:9)

Psalm 51:6 says, **"Surely you desire truth in the inner parts."** David's adulterous relationship had been discovered, and he was not going to lie to try to get away with it.

Jesus said to his disciples, **"Then you will know the truth and the truth will set you free."** (John 8:32)

When Jesus met Nathaniel he declared, **"Here is a genuine son of Israel – a man of complete integrity."** (John 1:47)

Would we be worthy of such an accolade? Are we completely and utterly committed to telling the truth whatever the circumstances?

Charles

One Year Plan : Psalm 15, Matthew 16, Isaiah 41 - 42
Two Year Plan : Psalm 91:1-8, Luke 9:1-36, Deuteronomy 4 (Yr 1)
1 Kings 9 (Yr 2)

Who are you Feeding?

The story is told of a man involved in cock fighting. He owned two cockerels – one black and one white, both similar in size and strength. Those who gambled on them were constantly wondering which one would win the fight and how they should place their bets.

A friend asked, **"Which one do you think will win tonight?"** The cock owner answered very definitely, **"The white one."** And it won! Each time he was asked he confidently predicted the one which would win – sometimes it was the white one at other times the black one – and he was always right. Eventually the friend asked, **"How do you always know which one will win?"**

"That's easy," the man replied. **"The one I want to lose I stop feeding two days before the fight, and the one I want to win I give extra food. Whichever one I want to win I feed, and the one I want to lose I starve!"**

It's easy when you see the big picture. In your life which part are you feeding? The flesh or the spirit? Which one is uppermost and dominating your life?

If you feed the spirit with God's Word, with worship and fellowship with Jesus, your spirit will be fat and strong and able to overcome the flesh and the devil.

Similarly, if you feed the flesh in any area, it seeks more and more satisfaction and will dominate your life.

"The fruit of the Spirit is love, joy peace, patience, kindness, goodness, gentleness, faithfulness and self-control." (Galatians 5:22)

The works of the flesh include **"sexual immorality, impurity, hatred, discord, jealousy, fits of rage, selfish ambition, envy and drunkenness"**. (Galatians 5:19)

Which do you see the most of? Who is winning?

Decide today to feed your spirit, and you will not gratify the flesh. But remember, you are not under law or condemnation. If you are **in Christ** you are forgiven, being forgiven and will go on being forgiven.

So just have a spiritual feast and get strong.

Joyce

One Year Plan : Psalm 16, Matthew 17, Isaiah 43 - 44
Two Year Plan : Psalm 91:9-16, Luke 9:37-62, Deuteronomy 5 (Yr 1)
1 Kings 10 (Yr 2)

The Old Leather Chair

When my mother decided that it was time to give up the family home, she moved to my sister's house, where a bed sitting room and en-suite bathroom had been constructed to make it ideal for her needs.

My mother was decisive and non-sentimental, so the old home was quickly put on the market and the contents divided among her four children. Choices were made by each one, and we were all happy with what we were getting. That left the things that no one wanted, and among those items was an old and faded leather chair.

When purchased it had been my father's favourite chair. You know the kind: leather, reclining, with a footstool to match. The adverts said it was **"the most comfortable chair in the world"**. My father never told my mother how much it cost because it was the most expensive piece of furniture he had ever purchased!

"What should we do?" we wondered. **"Throw it away? Send it to the charity shop?"** However, my wife Joyce had her eye on the chair. **"If no one wants that chair, I would love it. It only needs to be recovered and it will be as good as new."**

And that was what happened. It was removed from the house, taken straight to the upholsterer, and blue leather chosen. Soon it was finished; I collected it and took it home. It is splendid, like new, wonderfully comfortable. (The advert was right!)

This morning as I looked at the chair taking pride of place in the living room, I thought, **"This chair is a parable. It is like so many lives – tired, faded, springs broken and without any hope for the future."**

Then I remembered the words in Revelation, **"I am making everything new!"** (Revelation 21:5). That's fantastic; God wants to take hold of those who are tired, jaded and have lost all hope, and his promise is to make it all new.

I can think of many people who were like the faded chair; they met Jesus and he has made them brand new!

Charles

One Year Plan : Psalm 17, Matthew 18, Isaiah 45 - 46
Two Year Plan : Psalm 92, Luke 10:1-24, Deuteronomy 6 (Yr 1)
1 Kings 11 (Yr 2)

Asking or Receiving

"He who did spare his own Son, but gave him up for us all – how will he not also, along with him graciously give us all things?" (Romans 8:32)

I prayed for years to be filled with God's Holy Spirit, and then one day a moment of revelation came. I realised I had been filled when I first prayed but had not believed. Luke 11:10 says, **"For everyone who asks receives; he who seeks finds; and to him who knocks the door will be opened."** My continued asking merely demonstrated my unbelief. At that moment of understanding, I started to thank God for his precious Holy Spirit, dwelling within me and empowering me; I then became aware of His presence.

We already have been given everything. Jesus said that in John 16:15, **"All that belongs to the Father is mine. That is why I said the Spirit will take from what is mine and make it known to you."**

Ask for what you desire, and believe the Holy Spirit will take what belongs to Jesus and God and **"make it known to you"**.

Do you seek to understand what is happening in our world? Do you want a more intimate relationship with Father God and his Son Jesus? Do you want to live in heaven whilst here on earth? Perhaps you are looking for practical needs to be met.

Revelation 22:17 says, **"Whoever is thirsty, let him come; and whoever wishes, let him take the free gift of the water of life."**

- Stop begging and start receiving.
- Believing is the activity that brings all that God is into our lives today.

Joyce

One Year Plan : Psalm 18, Matthew 19, Isaiah 47 - 48
Two Year Plan : Psalm 93, Luke 10:25-42, Deuteronomy 7 (Yr 1)
1 Kings 12 (Yr 2)

What are Gracious Words?

Reading Psalm 45:2 I found myself fascinated by the phrase, **"Your lips have been anointed with grace."** The psalm is a wedding song, which may well have been used at the coronation of King Solomon. What did he say to deserve this accolade?

Luke 4:22 tells us that those listening to Jesus **"were amazed at the gracious word that came from his lips"**. There was something about the way he spoke that caused surprise in his listeners, so much so that they felt the need to comment and draw attention to it.

Isaiah gave this testimony of the way God had influenced his speech: **"The Sovereign Lord has given me an instructed tongue to know the word that will sustain the weary."** (Isaiah 50:4)

Could the phrase **'gracious words'** be the headline over the way you speak to others? What are gracious words? I have been looking at a number of scripture verses that quite clearly show the effect of **gracious words.**

The centurion said to Jesus, **"Just say the word and my servant will be healed."** (Matthew 8:8) He had total faith that the words Jesus spoke would bring healing.

Hebrews 10:24-25 says, **"And let us consider how we may spur one another on toward love and good deeds ... let us encourage one another..."**

Colossians 4:6 says, **"Let your conversation be always full of grace, seasoned with salt, so that you may know how to answer everyone."**

Lips anointed with grace do not just speak sentimental phrases; they strengthen, bring healing, comfort, build up and encourage. How will others describe the words that you speak today? Will they be **gracious words**?

Charles

One Year Plan : Psalm 19, Matthew 20, Isaiah 49 - 50
Two Year Plan : Psalm 94:1-11, Luke 11:1-28, Deuteronomy 8 (Yr 1)
1 Kings 13 (Yr 2)

Wake Up

Have you ever noticed that Peter had a sleep problem? There is a natural tiredness that causes sleep through which your body is refreshed and sustained. However, there is another form of sleep that is not because of natural tiredness but prevents you from remaining alert. This sleepiness has more to do with the spiritual realm than the physical.

Jesus chose to take Peter, John and James up on a mountain to pray. We don't know if the climb had been strenuous; however, the account of this story in Luke tells us they were very sleepy and almost missed seeing Jesus in his glorious splendour. They needed to be fully awake to experience these events.

Peter struggled with sleep in the Garden of Gethsemane when he had been commanded to watch and pray! He knew danger was lurking and that Jesus' captors were on the prowl. Even the adrenaline rush could not keep him awake! Jesus discovers him and asks, **"Why are you sleeping? Watch and pray so that you will not fall into temptation."**

I believe the church in this land is being lulled into sleepy complacency, when we should be on guard. This is not natural sleep, but I believe the enemy is seeking to dull our spirits to the dangers that surround us.

Peter eventually got the message because in his first letter he says, **"Be self controlled and alert. Your enemy the devil prowls around like a roaring lion looking for someone to devour. Resist him standing firm in the faith..."** (1 Peter 5:8-9)

It is possible to be physically awake but so spiritually sleepy that even when Jesus is speaking you fail to recognise what he is saying. You need to be alert to heavenly instructions and earthly danger. Do not be like those who have eyes and ears but fail to use them.

The heavenly call to all of us is, "Wake up."

Joyce

One Year Plan : Psalm 20, Matthew 21, Isaiah 51 - 52
Two Year Plan : Psalm 94:12-23, Luke 11:29-54, Deuteronomy 9 (Yr 1)
1 Kings 14 (Yr 2)

Strong in Spirit

How much nourishment is being given to your spirit? You may be watching carefully to see that your diet is good (your food may be 100% organic and bursting with healthy vitamins); you may be taking good exercise and have even signed up for a gym membership; but what are you doing to exercise your spirit?

Luke's Gospel tells us that both John the Baptist and Jesus, as they were growing, became **"strong in spirit"**. (Luke 1:80, 2:40) It is of real significance that this is recorded for us in scripture – so how do we strengthen our spirits?

First of all we need to be filled with the Holy Spirit. Jesus made it very clear that His disciples were not to start working for Him until they had been filled with His Spirit. Luke 24:49 states, **"I am going to send you what my Father promised; but stay in the city until you have been clothed with power from on high."**

Paul speaks of being **filled with the Spirit** as a constant need: **"Be [continuously and daily] filled with the Spirit. Speak to one another with psalms, hymns and spiritual songs. Sing and make music in your heart to the Lord."** (Ephesians 5:18-19) This indicates that worship, fellowship and thanksgiving are all part of making your spirit strong.

The Word of God is also vital to building up your spirit. Job said, **"I have treasured the words of his mouth more than my daily bread."** (Job 23:12)

So then, what will be the result of being **strong in spirit**?

Proverbs 18:14 says, **"A man's spirit sustains him in sickness."** Paul states it even more strongly in Romans 8:11, which says, **"And if the Spirit of him who raised Christ from the dead is living in you, he who raised Christ from the dead will also give life to your mortal bodies through his Spirit, who lives in you."**

Charles

One Year Plan : Psalm 21, Matthew 22, Isaiah 53 - 54
Two Year Plan : Psalm 95, Luke 12:1-34, Deuteronomy 10 (Yr 1)
1 Kings 15 (Yr 2)

How Transparent are you?

Is it easy for others to read you?

Have you got anything to hide?

When we come to the Cross and ask to be forgiven, we become recipients of God's grace. Acts 15:11 says, **"We believe it is through the grace of our Lord Jesus that we are saved."** We get mercy and forgiveness, cleansing and freedom from guilt and accusation. Our past record is cancelled out; the old man dies, and we are resurrected – born again – a new creation.

"If God kept a record of wrongs, who could stand?" (Psalm 130:3) Thank God He chooses to wipe out our sins and remember them no more! Jeremiah 31:34 says, **"For I will forgive their wickedness and will remember their sins no more."**

Transparent people can stand before God clean because of faith in Jesus. They have nothing to hide – and equally nothing to be proud of, for God has made them what they are.

Revival has been pictured in the form of someone living in a house. The roof needs to come off so that we are open and transparent towards God, and the walls need to come down so that we can be open (**'on view'**) to our fellow men. They can see our weakness but also Jesus' strength; our struggles but also Jesus' victories in us; our pain but also how we process it, letting Jesus heal us and set us free.

Transparency is so attractive and brings glory to Jesus.

Matthew 5:16 says, **"Let your light so shine before men, that they may see your good deeds and praise you Father in heaven."**

Joyce

One Year Plan : Psalm 22, Matthew 23, Isaiah 55 - 56
Two Year Plan : Psalm 96, Luke 12:35-59, Deuteronomy 11 (Yr 1)
1 Kings 16 (Yr 2)

How is your Singing?

The ability to sing is a unique gift of God to humankind. The birds can make music and many other animals make interesting sounds, but God sings and so do people made in his image.

God sings over His children. In Zephaniah 3:17 it says, **"The Lord your God is with you, he is mighty to save. He will take great delight in you, he will quiet you with his love, he will rejoice over you with singing."** You may be going through a difficult time. Your emotions may be in turmoil; you may even feel lonely and abandoned. But God is rejoicing over you with singing. He wants to tell you how valuable you are to Him and to restore your peace and joy. Listen for the song from heaven.

Job 38:4-7, which gives the account of when God was creating the world, says, **"Where were you when I laid the earth's foundation? ... while the morning stars sang together and the angels shouted for joy?"** God's activity and creativity always lead to an outburst of song and joy.

In Psalm 40:1-3 at a time of great distress, David says, **"I waited patiently for the Lord; he turned to me and heard my cry. He lifted me out of the slimy pit ... He set my feet on a rock ... He put a new song in my mouth, a hymn of praise to our God."** His immediate response to God's deliverance is to sing.

God gave us song so that we can sing praises to Him. In Psalm 104:33-34 the psalmist bursts forth, **"I will sing to the LORD all my life; I will sing praise to my God as long as I live. May my meditation be pleasing to him, as I rejoice in the LORD."** What a way to live!

Ethan the Ezrathite said, **"I will sing of the Lord's great love forever; with my mouth I will make you faithfulness known through all generations."** (Psalm 89:1)

Don't neglect singing your praises to God; **it's life-changing!**

Charles

One Year Plan : Psalm 23, Matthew 24, Isaiah 57 - 58
Two Year Plan : Psalm 97, Luke 13:1-17, Deuteronomy 12 (Yr 1)
1 Kings 17 (Yr 2)

Do You Know What you are Worth?

Charles had been bidding on eBay for a familiar CD recorded by Andrae Crouch. We already had the tape but needed a CD for better sound quality. He kept bidding and the price kept rising. He put in what he thought was a winning bid... He lost. When he looked on the internet, he discovered it would cost $65 to purchase the CD elsewhere. Suddenly, our nearly worn out cassette became instantly more valuable! It was retrieved from the tape rack and put into the cassette player in the car. We now listened to this wonderfully valuable recording!

Graham Kendrick wrote a song entitled **'How much do you think you are worth?'** *(Graham Kendrick © 1974 Make Way Music, www.grahamkendrick.co.uk)*

Is a rich man worth more than a poor man?
A stranger worth less than a friend?
Is a baby worth more than an old man?
Your beginning worth more than your end?

Is a president worth more than his assassin?
Does your value decrease with your crime?
Like when Christ took
the place of Barabbas?
Do you think he was wasting his time?

Well, how much do you think
you are worth, boy?
Will anyone stand up and say?
Would you say that a man is worth nothing
Until someone is willing to pay?

I suppose that you think you matter
Well, how much do you matter to whom?
It's much easier at night when
with friends and bright lights
Than much later alone in your room.

Do you think they'll miss one in a billion
When you finish this old human race?
Does it really make much of a difference
When your friends have
forgotten your face?

If you heard that your life had been valued
That a price had been paid on the nail
Would you ask what was traded,
How much and who paid it
Who was He and what was His name?

If you heard that His name was called Jesus
Would you say that the price was too dear?
Held to the cross not by nails but by love
It was you broke His heart, not the spear!
Would you say you are worth
what it cost Him?
You say 'no', but the price stays the same.
If it don't make you cry,
laugh it off, pass Him by.
But just remember the day
when you throw it away
That He paid what He thought
you were worth.

God values you as priceless. Jesus paid the price for you... because you are worth it!

Joyce

One Year Plan : Psalm 24, Matthew 25, Isaiah 59 - 60
Two Year Plan : Psalm 98, Luke 13:18-35, Deuteronomy 13 (Yr 1)
1 Kings 18 (Yr 2)

How to Love Life and See Good Days

I was reading a book by Kenneth Hagin, who recounts a wonderful testimony. At the end of a meeting where Kenneth had been preaching, a Brother Smith, who was in remarkably good shape, came out to speak with him.

"Brother Kenneth, I'll be ninety years old in three weeks, and you know, I'm just as strong and healthy as I was as a young man. God has kept me, and you know I haven't been sick in forty years."

He went on to say that he had trusted God to keep his hair from turning grey and enable him to keep all his own teeth. It was very evident that this man believed that God would act according to His word, for the Bible says, **"According to your faith be it unto you."** (Matthew 9:29)

He then started to walk away but turned back and continued the conversation. **"Brother Kenneth, I'll tell you the secret of the whole thing. You already know it, but I'll tell you anyway. I asked God to help me keep this – to help me keep my tongue."** And he stuck his tongue out.

You see, the Bible says, **"Whoever would love life and see good days must keep his tongue from evil and his lips from deceitful speech."** (1 Peter 3:10)

This testimony is very powerful. We live at a time where there is an epidemic of negative speech. People are constantly undermining each other with their words.

Do you realise that you could be damaging your health and shortening your life by your careless speech?

King David prayed, **"Set a guard over my mouth, O Lord; keep watch over the door of my lips."** (Psalm 141:3)

Charles

One Year Plan : Psalm 25, Matthew 26, Isaiah 61 - 62
Two Year Plan : Psalm 99, Luke 14:1-14, Deuteronomy 14 (Yr 1)
1 Kings 19 (Yr 2)

Performance? Or Acceptance?

The Bible clearly tells us that while we were helpless, God sent Jesus to rescue us and make us His own.

Romans 5:6-7 in The Message puts it like this: **"Christ arrives right on time to make this happen. He didn't, and doesn't, wait for us to get ready. He presented himself for this sacrificial death when we were far too weak and rebellious to do anything to get ourselves ready. And even if we hadn't been so weak, we wouldn't have known what to do anyway."**

We sing, **"Love reached down and rescued me."** So why are so many people still performing in order to be acceptable? God knows us completely and isn't impressed by performance, however good or bad! He is looking for relationship and those who will depend on His resources. Our **performance** is then simply to be a conduit to bring His divine resources where they are needed. We do not need to perform in order to be acceptable to God.

It is only because of His wonderful love and grace that we can know forgiveness, cleansing and acceptance, which produces in us peace, security and the certainty that what God has graciously given to us, He also wants to give to others we know and love.

However much dirt or tar covers you, the blood of Jesus washes completely and His fire burns up without destruction everything that has tried to destroy you. Stop trying to make yourself acceptable to God; instead receive what He has freely made available – and rejoice!

Paul was a driven performer until he received the grace of God; he then willingly devoted his life to tell others that same good news.

Acceptance leading to spontaneous action... NOT performance trying to gain acceptance.

Joyce

One Year Plan : Psalm 26, Matthew 27, Isaiah 63 – 64
Two Year Plan : Psalm 100, Luke 14:15-35, Deuteronomy 15 (Yr 1)
1 Kings 20 (Yr 2)

Coming Home

How do you feel about coming home? Is it a place of love, warmth and safety? To have a home is a great blessing, as there are vast numbers of folk around the world who are homeless.

Home is not so much about bricks and mortar as about the people who live there. To come home should be to join your family and loved ones; however, the place where you live could have a threatening and fearsome environment if those who live there are at enmity with you and with each other.

Jesus invited His disciples to make Him their home. **"But if you make yourselves at home with me and my words at home in you, you can be sure that whatever you ask will be listened to and acted upon."** And also, **"Make yourselves at home in my love."** (John 15:7,9, The Message)

Jesus is extending an amazing invitation! It does not matter what kind of earthly home you have; it could be wonderful or dreadful, but you can have a home with Jesus. When you invite Jesus to become the Lord of your life, to live in you, and you welcome His words into your heart, He promises to make a home within your heart. He also promises to make His home your home.

The promise doesn't end there because Jesus says that if we make ourselves at home with Him, whatever we ask will be heard and acted upon.

You may have been a believer for a long time, but are you at home in His love? Do you feel safe and supported in His presence? Does His Word find a home in your heart?

Come Home and end loneliness and isolation forever!

Charles

One Year Plan : Psalm 27, Matthew 28, Isaiah 65 - 66
Two Year Plan : Psalm 101, Luke 15:1-10, Deuteronomy 16 (Yr 1)
1 Kings 21 (Yr 2)

Bring Heaven to Earth

Jesus often talked about the Kingdom of God (or the Kingdom of heaven) which prompted the Pharisees to ask him, **"Where is it?"** Jesus astonished them with his reply: **"The kingdom of God is within you."**

The Pharisees didn't understand this; neither did Pilate, although he recognised that Jesus was different and enquired, **"Are you a king?"** Jesus' answer was, **"My kingdom is not of this world."** He was telling Pilate that He had not come to establish an earthy kingdom but a heavenly one, which one day will be established **"on earth, as it is in heaven"**.

We need to understand that Jesus is seeking a people who will live in two worlds simultaneously. Physically we live **on earth**, but at the same time it is possible to live **in heaven**, intimately walking and talking with Jesus by His Spirit.

Many things that surround us would not be allowed in heaven, and God is looking for those who will bring heaven down to earth. As you look at the things that are going on around you, ask yourself, **"Would this be tolerated in heaven?"**

One day a prominent Pharisee invited Jesus into his house, and he was being carefully watched as a sick man lay in front of him. Jesus saw something that would not be allowed in heaven – a swollen sick man. Jesus asked, **"Is it lawful to heal on the Sabbath or not?"** Once He had silenced their religious legalism He brought heaven to bear upon the situation and the man was healed.

Jesus wants a people who will know they have authority to bring heaven to earth. We often pray, **"Your kingdom come on earth as it is in heaven."** Jesus both demonstrated and testified to the power of another kingdom and has commissioned us to do the same.

Today, bring the King and His rule into your everyday life and into the needs you see around you. Ask Jesus, **"What does heaven require here?"** Then just do it.

Joyce

One Year Plan : Psalm 28, 1 Thessalonians 1, 1 Chronicles 1 - 2
Two Year Plan : Psalm 102:1-11, Luke 15:11-32, Deuteronomy 17 (Yr 1)
1 Kings 22 (Yr 2)

Protecting Your Children

To keep our children safe and know they are in the best environment possible is a challenge to every parent. When they are young and with us at home, this task fills our lives daily. It brings us joy as we see good things happening but also can cause anxiety and fear as we see things that concern us. They do become adults and 'fly the nest' but are never out of the minds of their parents.

So how do we sustain this love and care for our children? I came across this verse in Proverbs 14:26 which both challenged and encouraged me:

"He who fears the Lord has a secure fortress, and for his children it will be a refuge."

This proverb places the focus of our children's protection on us rather than on them! So now we need to discover what it means to **'fear the Lord'**.

To fear the Lord is not to be afraid of Him, but it is to live in living and loving relationship with Him. When I know that God is all-powerful, all-loving, all-forgiving, all-understanding, and that I can live in vital connection with Him on a daily basis, my life changes:

- I do not live for myself but to serve others, including my children.
- I live knowing that God loves me unconditionally which means He makes it possible to love others in the same way.
- I live with the knowledge that I am always forgiven by God and so can extend forgiveness to others, especially my children.
- Because I can connect with God constantly and in every situation, I can model this for my family.
- Because God is all-powerful, there is nothing that is impossible for Him; I can then live in faith, a faith that others can see and imitate.

Psalm 112:1-2 says, **"Blessed is the man who fears the Lord, who finds great delight in his commands. His children will be mighty in the land; the generation of the upright will be blessed."**

Very encouraging and very challenging!

Charles

One Year Plan : Psalm 29, 1 Thessalonians 2, 1 Chronicles 3 - 4
Two Year Plan : Psalm 102:12-22, Luke 16:1-18, Deuteronomy 18 (Yr 1)
2 Kings 1 (Yr 2)

August

Be Blessed and Ready to Bless

Years ago I attended a Youth Pentecost Praise at Wells Cathedral, and I was thrilled to see a vast cathedral packed with young people. However, the feature that remains in my memory and impacted me so strongly was how the service finished.

The Bishop told us that he had been given authority from God to bless us. He spoke very seriously about the reality of what we were about to receive. He then asked those who wanted to receive this blessing to stand while he prayed. To this day I remember the authority with which he spoke out God's blessing; the power of God's Spirit was tangible and I certainly received a blessing but also a revelation of how much God wanted to protect me and make my path smooth.

The words of the blessing came from Numbers 6:24-26: **"The Lord bless you and keep you; the Lord make his face to shine upon you and be gracious to you; the Lord turn his face toward you and give you peace."**

It is not only bishops who can pronounce blessing – you can. Bless your family. Parents, send your children to school under a blessing. Pastors, bless your congregations as you send them out into the workplace. Husbands, bless your wives as you leave for work. Practise this in every situation of life, and I am sure you will see results.

Blessing can release favour even outside of a Christian context. An African friend of mine told me this story. His mother had gone to market to sell meat, but she had left home in a mood, taking him with her, after having had a strong disagreement with her husband. She sold no meat so returned home to be reconciled with her husband and to ask him to bless her in her work. She immediately returned to the market, and her supply of meat rapidly sold. As this young child watched this scene he became convinced of the power of blessing.

Joyce

One Year Plan : Psalm 30, 1 Thessalonians 3, 1 Chronicles 5 - 6
Two Year Plan : Psalm 102:23-28, Luke 16:19-31, Deuteronomy 19 (Yr 1) 2 Kings 2 (Yr 2)

Celebrate

"Be who God meant you to be and you will set the world on fire" is how the Bishop of London began his sermon at the wedding of William and Catherine in April 2011. It was a wonderful day and a great time of celebration.

Celebration is a time when we look back with thanksgiving and look forward with faith, anticipation and joy. We chose to make it a great day for our family; in the morning most of our children and grandchildren came to our house to watch the wedding together, and later in the afternoon more of our family joined us to celebrate two significant birthdays. I don't think we have enough of these great times of rejoicing.

God constantly called His people to celebrate; the Passover and other feasts were declared to be times for celebration. But you may ask: what is the point of celebrating? A wedding is an obvious time for celebration, but other occasions like birthdays and anniversaries can pass almost unnoticed.

As Richard Chartres gave his message to the royal couple, he spoke of hope and joy; he told them they had so many possibilities ahead of them, if they would embrace the principles that God gives to enable them to fulfil their destiny, starting with that great quote from St Catherine of Siena.

God told His people to celebrate the Passover because they were never to forget the miraculous way in which they had been rescued from Egypt. Every time we take the bread and wine at the Communion, we are celebrating the victory of Jesus and the way He has rescued us from sin and meaninglessness. We are not only to look back, but we are to reach out and take hold of all that God has for us in the future.

Let's Celebrate! **"Be who God meant you to be and you will set the world on fire."**

Charles

One Year Plan : Psalm 31, 1 Thessalonians 4, 1 Chronicles 7 - 8
Two Year Plan : Psalm 103:1-12, Luke 17:1-19, Deuteronomy 20 (Yr 1)
2 Kings 3 (Yr 2)

Help... Where do I Go?

When **'all hell breaks loose'** and you see no way out of the situation that confronts you, when fear and hopelessness come knocking on your door, there is a place to go! There is someone on your side who will give comfort, peace, wisdom and direction – **"...it's the Lord!"**

Sometimes we rely on our own ideas and endlessly look for solutions, but when all fails there is still a place to go: **"...to the Lord!"**

King Hezekiah had plenty of trouble; the Assyrian army had conquered the countries surrounding Israel and advanced on Israel. The envoys came to ask for surrender; they mocked God, told lies, threatened and intimidated the people and ridiculed the reigning King. Hezekiah had to make a choice, and he used it. He went to the Lord and laid the whole situation before Him.

God's answer was, **"O people of Zion, who live in Jerusalem, you will weep no more. How gracious he will be when he hears your cry for help! ... your ears will hear a voice behind you, saying, 'This is the way; walk in it.'"** (Isaiah 30:19,21)

God heard Hezekiah's heart cry and spoke through Isaiah telling him not to be afraid, that God had heard the blasphemous words of the Assyrians. God would deal with the whole situation; the enemy King would hear a rumour of impending attack, would return to his own country and there lose his life. You can read the whole account in Isaiah.

God is longing to be gracious to you, but He doesn't force Himself on you; He waits for you to ask for His help, to lay out your situation, pain and despair before Him. When He hears you ask for help, He will tell you not to be afraid and show you the way ahead.

Human resources run out; circumstances get beyond our control. Where can you go? Nahum 1:7 in The Living Bible says, **"When trouble comes – He is the place to go!"**

Joyce

One Year Plan : Psalm 32, 1 Thessalonians 5, 1 Chronicles 9 -10
Two Year Plan : Psalm 103:13-22, Luke 17:20-37, Deuteronomy 21 (Yr 1)
2 Kings 4 (Yr 2)

Gatekeepers

In the past I don't think I really took any notice of the role of gatekeepers in the workings of the tabernacle in the Old Testament. But as I read in 1 Chronicles 9, I saw for the first time how important these people were.

Gatekeepers **"were responsible for guarding the thresholds of the Tent"**; **"they were assigned to their positions of trust by David and Samuel"**; **"they would spend the night stationed around the house of God, because they had to guard it; they had the key for opening it each morning."**

As I was reading this, God spoke to me and challenged me as to how well I was doing as the gatekeeper of my life, home and family. Just as my last task at night is to check the doors of my house and make sure they are locked, I need to make sure I have locked out all the negative influences that could be attacking.

Proverbs 4:23 says, **"Above all else, guard your heart, for everything you do flows from it."** David prayed in Psalm 141:3, **"Set a guard over my mouth, O Lord; keep watch over the door of my lips."** Job declared in Job 31:1, **"I made a covenant with my eyes not to look lustfully at a girl."**

As gatekeeper over my home and family, what do I allow to come into my house? Do I tolerate anger and strife? Is criticism of others part of everyday conversation? Is all that I say positive and up-building?

What do my family watch on television? Do I know the internet sites that my children are looking at? What books, newspapers and magazines are being read?

Paul said in Philippians 4:8, **"Finally brothers, whatever is true, whatever is noble, whatever is right, whatever is pure, whatever is lovely, whatever is admirable – if anything is excellent and praiseworthy – think about such things."**

You are the gatekeeper of your life and family. How are you doing?

Charles

One Year Plan : Psalm 33, 2 Thessalonians 1, 1 Chronicles 11 - 12
Two Year Plan : Psalm 104:1-9, Luke 18:1-17, Deuteronomy 22 (Yr 1)
2 Kings 5 (Yr 2)

He Touched Me

The disciples were on the Mount of Transfiguration, cowering and out of their depth with what was happening, when **"Jesus came and touched them. He said, 'Get up, don't be afraid.'"** (Matthew 17:7) He could have simply used words, but He chose also to touch.

We are all human, tactile creatures, and often need physical touch to settle us. The disciples had seen heavenly things which unsettled them and needed that physical arm around them. When we are afraid we often shut our eyes to blot out the source of fear. Notice that when the disciples opened their eyes, Jesus filled their picture.

Many years ago, a friend of mine, whose young wife had died shortly after the birth of their first child, told me about his experience. Heartbroken and fearful for himself and his new daughter – life having crumbled into pieces – he stood at the graveside and felt a hand on his shoulder. As he looked around to see who was standing with him, he saw the impression of a hand on his jacket. The hand was holding him steady, but no-one was there. It wasn't a human hand; it was the touch of Jesus who also whispered inside him, **"I'm here, and I will never leave you."**

We do need to have the knowledge of the Godhead as we read and know God's Word, but we also need a tangible experience. Jesus knows just how to touch you and comfort you. You may be longing for the touch of a past loved one, which you know is an impossibility. But you can ask Jesus for His touch, His hug, His presence, His re-assurance, His hand to bring stability, to combat fear and loneliness.

"His touch has still its ancient power."

- You may feel dead. He'll raise you, as with Jairus' daughter in Luke 8:54.
- You may be sick. He'll heal you, as with Peter's mother-in-law in Mark 1:31.
- You may feel leprous and unclean. He'll cleanse you and receive you, as with the leper in Luke 5:13.
- All who touched Him (and consequently were touched by Him) were healed; read Matthew 14:36.

Joyce

One Year Plan : Psalm 34, 2 Thessalonians 2, 1 Chronicles 13 - 15
Two Year Plan : Psalm 104:10-18, Luke 18:18-43,
Deuteronomy 23 (Yr 1)
2 Kings 6 (Yr 2)

Two Grandmothers

The Bible says that when Ruth had given birth to Obed, **"Naomi took the child, laid him in her lap and cared for him. The women living there said, 'Naomi has a son.'"** (Ruth 4:16-17) This is the end of a well-known story. Naomi leaves Bethlehem at a time of famine to go to Moab with her husband and two sons. But it all ends in tragedy; her husband and sons die, leaving Naomi, Orpah and Ruth widows. Naomi returns to Bethlehem bereft, with only her daughter-in-law Ruth, who believes her future is with God's people.

But God! The story of redemption unfolds. Ruth gleans in the field of Boaz, who shows favour to this Moabite lady. Under Naomi's guidance the pathway to marriage is made, and a wedding takes place between Ruth and Boaz. They conceive a child, and suddenly all the tragedy and pain of the past move towards a wonderful healing by God's grace and His good plans for their lives. God is always the great redeemer, who delights to turn tragedy to triumph!

Who then is the other grandmother? Her name is Rahab; she is trapped in a destructive and unhealthy lifestyle until she becomes the rescuer of spies sent by Joshua to Jericho. This act of bravery and kindness not only saves her life and that of her family but enables her to become part of Israel, marry Salmon, and become the mother of Boaz and grandmother of Obed. We do not know whether she too was able to hold this precious grandchild on her knee, but these two grandmothers set me thinking.

God is always seeking to bring good out of evil, triumph out of tragedy, healing out of brokenness; He is the great Redeemer! Naomi and Ruth could have remained trapped in their grief in Moab; Rahab could have lost her life as Jericho was destroyed; but God had other plans.

Revelation 21:4-5 says, **"He will wipe every tear from their eyes ... he who was seated on the throne said, 'I am making everything new!'"**

That's our God; He takes what looks like disaster and turns it into destiny!

Charles

One Year Plan : Psalm 35, 2 Thessalonians 3, 1 Chronicles 16 - 17
Two Year Plan : Psalm 104:19-26, Luke 19:1-27, Deuteronomy 24 (Yr 1)
2 Kings 7 (Yr 2)

Greater Things

Many times in John's gospel, Jesus tries to explain how He has no power of His own, how He is limited by His human form and can do nothing without the Father's instructions and activity through Him. The disciples see the miracles and authority, but they can't quite work it out.

Peter has the revelation of, **"You are the Christ the Son of the living God,"** and yet Philip and Thomas can't quite get it. In John 14 Philip is still asking Jesus to show him the Father and Thomas has no idea what Jesus is saying or where He is going when He speaks about preparing a place in the Father's house.

Jesus comments on the fact that even though **they have been with Him so long, yet they still do not understand.** (John 14:9) Are we any different? Perhaps like me, you have been with Jesus 'a long time'. How much understanding do we have of total reliance on God within us? Can you really do nothing without His power? How clearly do you hear His voice?

It is so easy to think that by knowledge of someone we can become different people, but it is only by the One who lives in us, and to the extent that He is able to demonstrate His love and power through us, that we will be made like Jesus, like God.

Many years ago I saw a powerful drama about a young man with a French girlfriend. Her father refused to allow his daughter to marry him because he was English! This young Englishman learned the French language, immersed himself in the culture; he tried so hard to become 'French'. The father could not be convinced to part with his daughter; the reason given: **"You are not French."** In frustration the young man angrily said, **"What more do you want me to do – be born again?!"**

Yes – being supernaturally birthed by the Spirit of God, like Jesus, we have within us the nature of God and, because of that, the ability to do what Jesus did and greater things.

Read John 14:12 again: **"Anyone who has faith in me will do what I have been doing and greater things will he do because I am going to my Father."** It is mind-blowing.

Joyce

One Year Plan : Psalm 36, 1 Timothy 1, 1 Chronicles 18 - 19
Two Year Plan : Psalm 104:27-35, Luke 19:28-48, Deuteronomy 25 (Yr 1)
2 Kings 8 (Yr 2)

Stop Trusting in Man

Have you ever listened to one of those radio programmes where a group of experts discuss some topic or other? How did you feel as the programme finished? My experience has usually been a mixture of frustration and weariness.

Have you had an issue in your own life and found yourself sharing it with various friends and family? Were the answers helpful or did everyone have something different to say? On many occasions the avalanche of opinions only leaves me confused.

I am not saying that the counsel of a friend or wise family member is not good. Proverbs 22:17 says, **"Pay attention and listen to the sayings of the wise..."**

However, when I came across the words, **"Stop trusting in man..."** whilst reading in Isaiah, I immediately thought of the verses in Jeremiah 17:5-8:

"Cursed is the one who trusts in man, who depends upon flesh for his strength and whose heart turns away from the Lord. He will be like a bush in the wastelands..."

This is then contrasted with the benefits of trusting God:

"But blessed is the man who trusts in the Lord, whose confidence is in him. He will be like a tree planted by the water..."

We are bombarded on every side by the opinions of people; every one we talk to wants to have their say; everyone has a piece of advice.

I believe we need to draw aside and listen to the voice from heaven. God is vitally interested and wants to be fully involved in helping you in the challenges of life.

James 1:5 says, **"If any of you lacks wisdom, he should ask God, who gives generously without finding fault, and it will be given him."**

When we turn away from human wisdom and listen to God, we stop feeling like a bush in the wastelands, and start becoming ...

"...like a tree planted by the water that sends out its roots by the stream. It does not fear when heat comes; its leaves are always green. It has no worries in a year of drought and never fails to bear fruit."

Charles

One Year Plan : Psalm 37, 1 Timothy 2, 1 Chronicles 20 - 22
Two Year Plan : Psalm 105:1-11, Luke 20:1-19, Deuteronomy 26 (Yr 1)
2 Kings 9 (Yr 2)

Don't Put Yourself in Unnecessary Danger

Jesus didn't put Himself in unnecessary danger. He knew the Jews in Judea were looking for opportunities to kill Him, and he could have ignored that knowledge and travelled through Judea to the feast in Jerusalem; however, **"Jesus went around Galilee purposely staying away from Judea because the Jews there were waiting to take his life."** (John 7:1)

Jesus did not take a gung-ho attitude of **"God will protect me; I've got a job to do and it isn't accomplished yet."** He had already experienced God's protection when the whole family were sent to Egypt at the time of His birth. He had also known God's deliverance when they drove Him out of Nazareth and wanted to throw Him over the cliff.

To me there is no conflict between faith and common sense. God has promised His divine protection to those who put themselves in His hands, but that does not give us the right to act with stupidity – and claim Psalm 91 as our right, our insurance policy.

We have faith for God's protection as we travel on the roads, but we keep our car serviced and in good order. We avoid putting ourselves in dangerous situations and use our common sense when in crowds or in vulnerable places, while still believing for God's protection and peace.

Jesus knew God's promises both generally and specifically but still chose to avoid danger. When challenged in the wilderness to throw Himself from the temple, the devil even quoted scripture to show that the angels would catch Him, but Jesus replied, **"Do not put the Lord your God to the test."** (Luke 4:12)

We are promised that if we listen to God's voice and live carefully and watchfully, He will protect us and give us peace. Proverbs 1:33 says, **"Whoever listens to me will live in safety and be at ease, without fear of harm."**

Real faith is never fearful – nor foolish – but wise.

Joyce

One Year Plan : Psalm 38, 1 Timothy 3, 1 Chronicles 23 - 24
Two Year Plan : Psalm 105:12-22, Luke 20:20-47, Deuteronomy 27 (Yr 1)
2 Kings 10 (Yr 2)

Given a Second Chance

The story of Jonah really fires the imagination:

- God's instructions ignored;
- Running away to sea;
- A violent storm;
- Thrown overboard;
- Swallowed by a whale;
- After prayer vomited onto the shore – but in total despair.

What do you do when everything has gone wrong and you can see no possibility of any hope for your future?

Some years ago, Joyce and I were in Hungary; we had just finished speaking at a Leaders Conference and were feeling quite tired, when our hosts announced that a very desperate pastor was on his way to see us.

We summoned up our energies and sat down to listen to his story. He had been ministering in a church out in a rural area but felt that all his endeavours had been a total failure. He, like Jonah, had even run away to a foreign land, his house had been broken into and all his theological and ordination documents had been stolen. He believed that this was a divine message informing him that his time as a pastor was over and that God was putting him on the scrapheap.

We tried to tell him that this was not true and that God would never do such a thing. All our words failed to give him any comfort or encouragement. So we turned to prayer. After a few moments God spoke and directed me to the book of Jonah, Chapter 3 verse 1: **"Then the word of the Lord came to Jonah a second time: Go to that great city of Nineveh and proclaim to it the message I give you."**

Those words hit him like a bolt of lightning, totally transforming his attitude. In that moment he realised that God was ready to give him another chance. His future was not ruined – God was speaking again – and he left with joy and relief to begin the next chapter of his life.

Do you need a second chance? God is ready to speak to you again – just listen.

Charles

One Year Plan : Psalm 39, 1 Timothy 4, 1 Chronicles 25 – 26
Two Year Plan : Psalm 105:23-36, Luke 21:1-19, Deuteronomy 28 (Yr 1)
2 Kings 11 (Yr 2)

If... Then!

Deuteronomy Chapter 30 sets out instructions, given by God, in order that life will be joyful, protected, and things will go well for you. **"If you obey the Lord your God ... the Lord will delight in you and make you prosperous."** (Deuteronomy 30:8-10)

God wants you to enjoy an all-round good life. He wants you to succeed, to see you enjoy what He has made and what He is doing, and as you give thanks, recognising His generosity and kindness, it gives Him pleasure. Parents love to see their children delight and marvel at some new experience, and so does our Heavenly Father.

We marvelled at His creation as we toured New Zealand – rejoicing to see Mount Cook bathed in sunshine, the west coast wild with crashing seas and blowholes sending spray way into the air, amazing rock formations and vegetation so diverse in form and colour. We also received such love and care from family and friends reflecting a God who wants to bless and is so creative in the way He demonstrates His love.

In Deuteronomy, God expresses His great desire that His people will make the right choices. He does, however, set out consequences of making wrong choices – but the cry of His heart comes through so strongly: **"Now choose life so that you and your children may live ... for the Lord is your life."** (Deuteronomy 30:19-20)

Joshua knew that to walk in God's ways was best as he challenged the people, **"Choose for yourselves this day whom you will serve ... but as for me and my house-hold, we will serve the Lord."** (Joshua 24:15)

David made good choices, and he declared, **"Surely goodness and mercy shall follow me all the days of my life and I will dwell in the house of the Lord forever."** (Psalm 23:6)

The **'if'** relates to choice, but the outcome God desires **'then'** is blessing, as we follow His ways and allow Him to demonstrate His love to us.

Joyce

One Year Plan : Psalm 40, 1 Timothy 5, 1 Chronicles 27 - 29
Two Year Plan : Psalm 105:37-45, Luke 21:20-38, Deuteronomy 29 (Yr 1)
2 Kings 12 (Yr 2)

What Are You Expecting?

Children generally live with expectancy. They usually know what they are longing for and they expect their parents to provide it. They rarely forget the promised ice cream or the trip to the 'Wacky Warehouse'. It is hard to get past McDonald's without your offspring expressing their longing for the latest 'Kid's Meal' free toy, however many times you have said no.

As adults, many of us have lost the freshness and excitement of expectancy. So many disappointments have dragged us down that now we always fear the worst rather than believe for the best.

We can even believe that God is a disappointment and does not want to fulfil our needs or wants. Isaiah 30:18 says, **"Yet the LORD longs to be gracious to you; he rises to show you compassion. For the LORD is a God of justice. Blessed are all who wait for him!"**

I wonder how much disappointment and rejection there was in the heart of the leper when he said to Jesus, **"Lord if you are willing, you can make me clean."** (Matthew 8:3) Can you imagine his joy and relief as Jesus reached out and said, **"I am willing. Be clean!"**

When Jesus spoke to His disciples just before He went to the cross, He recognized their lack of expectancy and fear of the future and said to them, **"Until now you have not asked for anything in my name. Ask and you will receive that your joy may be full."** (John 16:24)

God is for you, He longs to be gracious to you, He wants to answer your prayers, and He seeks to bless you.

Start expecting and stop doubting!

Charles

One Year Plan : Psalm 41, 1 Timothy 6, 2 Chronicles 1 - 3
Two Year Plan : Psalm 106:1-12, Luke 22:1-38, Deuteronomy 30 (Yr 1)
2 Kings 13 (Yr 2)

The Power of Joy

I was talking to a friend about the power of joy. This amazing dynamic had come alive to me, particularly through reading a biography of the Cornish miner, Billy Bray. *(Billy Bray of Cornwall – Cornish Miner, Dancing Preacher; by Chris Wright; published by Highland Books.)*

It contains the incredibly challenging account of this old saint who tapped into the **river of joy** and found that the promise of supernatural strength is a reality. He certainly knew the power of joy released through praise, which consistently gave him amazing physical strength and stamina!

He had a revelation of his need for supernatural resources and knew he could not function unless he kept himself full of joy. I too have discovered the link between joy and physical strength.

The following article was then brought to my attention: **"Abraham Lincoln was once going to hire a man for a high-level position in his cabinet. He took the man with him for three weeks, checking him out. Finally, Lincoln told the man, 'You are very qualified, but I can't hire you.' 'Why not?' the man asked. Lincoln answered, 'Because for the last three weeks, you have not smiled one time. As President of the United States, I live with intense situations every day. I have to have people around me who can help me and lift me up.'"**

Proverbs 12:25 (AMP) says, **"Anxiety in a man's heart weighs it down, but an encouraging word makes it glad."**

In the days of Nehemiah the people were weeping and discouraged and needed to hear, **"Go and enjoy choice food and sweets drinks ... this day is sacred to the Lord. Do not grieve, for the joy of the Lord is your strength."** (Nehemiah 8:10)

Your smile and words of encouragement can lift someone's heavy load today.

Joyce

One Year Plan : Psalm 42, 2 Timothy 1, 2 Chronicles 4 - 5
Two Year Plan : Psalm 106:13-23, Luke 22:39-71, Deuteronomy 31 (Yr 1)
2 Kings 14 (Yr 2)

High Calling

Paul speaks of the focus and ambition of his life when he says, **"I press toward the mark for the prize of the high calling of God in Christ Jesus."** (Philippians 3:14) This set me thinking: what is a **high calling**? I don't think it is trying to become a great evangelist like Billy Graham or missionary like Amy Carmichael. I believe it is being true to God's call on your life.

There was a particular time in my life when I had come to the end of The Leaders' Week ministry at The Hyde in Sussex, was looking forward to the next thing that God was going to lead me into, and was at peace with things, but various folk kept asking me, **"What are you going to do now that the Leaders' Weeks have finished?"** An uncertainty crept in, until one morning I was reading Ephesians 2:10 which says, **"For we are God's workmanship, created in Christ Jesus to do good works, which God prepared in advance for us to do."**

This verse set me free from any fear regarding the future. From that moment I knew that all I wanted to do were the **good works which God had prepared for me to do.** As the weeks and months rolled by, God opened up a new and fulfilling phase of ministry; it was my **high calling**.

Other verses which have been key in seeking to fulfil my **high calling** are John 15:16 **"You did not choose me, but I chose you and appointed you to go and bear fruit – fruit that will last."** and John 3:27 where John the Baptist refuses to compete with Jesus and says, **"A man can receive only that which is given him from heaven."**

So what then is a **high calling**? It is not striving to do something spectacular that will make you famous; it is receiving from heaven the unique role assigned to you, doing the works that God has prepared for you, and bearing fruit that will last!

It is a **high calling** because of the One who calls; it may be unseen by others but it is valued by God.

Charles

One Year Plan : Psalm 43, 2 Timothy 2, 2 Chronicles 6 - 7
Two Year Plan : Psalm 106:24-33, Luke 23:1-25,
Deuteronomy 32 (Yr 1)
2 Kings 15 (Yr 2)

Grace is Not Cheap

I believe in the grace of God – His total forgiveness and cleansing from every sin and, whenever we turn to Jesus in repentance, His restoration from our sinful past.

However, grace is not cheap. It cost the lifeblood of Jesus. He took your place and mine on the cross. We deserved to die; we are the ones who have sinned, and if God was to punish us because of our sin, we would have no excuse. Psalm 130:3 says, **"If you, O Lord, kept a record of sins, O Lord, who could stand?"**

Thank God we received pardon because of the sacrifice of Jesus. It is so easy to forget, to become complacent. Paul writes to the new churches, **"We urge you not to receive the grace of God in vain."** (2 Corinthians 6:1) He tells the believers at Corinth, **"You are saved, if you hold firmly to the word preached to you. Otherwise, you have believed in vain."** (1 Corinthians 15:2)

He tells them, **"Jesus died for all, that those who live should no longer live for themselves but for him who died for them and was raised again."** (2 Corinthians 5:15)

Living in grace is a daily reality. I can look back to a point in time when I realised that Jesus took my place and gave me the gift of salvation, but unless I live today acknowledging that reality, it's possible for this wonderful provision that keeps us in contact with God to be **in vain** – wasted and in reality not operating in our lives.

Ezekiel 33:10–20 contains both sobering and hopeful news: **"The righteousness of the righteous man will not save him when he disobeys, and the wickedness of the wicked man will not cause him to fall when he turns from it."** Read the whole passage and thank God for Jesus, but pray for those who seem to have forgotten; **grace** is not an historic gift but something we need to live by on a daily basis.

Joyce

One Year Plan : Psalm 44, 2 Timothy 3, 2 Chronicles 8 - 9
Two Year Plan : Psalm 106:34-48, Luke 23:26-56, Deuteronomy 33 (Yr 1)
2 Kings 16 (Yr 2)

Words from Heaven

Are you ever stuck for words? Have you found your faith being challenged and did not know how to answer? Have you ever been asked a tricky question and been speechless?

Jesus knew this would happen to His disciples and so instructed them, **"When you are brought before synagogues, rulers and authorities, do not worry about how you will defend yourself or what you will say, for the Holy Spirit will teach you at that time what you should say."** (Luke 12:11-12)

We find Peter putting this into practice in the early days of the church. He and John had been arrested and dragged in front of the Sanhedrin because they had healed the man at the Gate Beautiful. The questioning was aggressive: **"By what power or what name did you do this?"**

Peter remembered what Jesus had said and did not retaliate angrily or try to produce a clever answer. The scripture says, **"Then Peter, filled with the Holy Spirit, said to them: 'Rulers and elders of the people! If we are being called to account today for an act of kindness shown to a cripple and are asked how he was healed, then know this, you and all the people of Israel: It is by the name of Jesus Christ of Nazareth, whom you crucified but whom God raised from the dead that this man stands before you healed.'"** (Acts 4:8-10)

This answer astonished the rulers, and they immediately recognised their connection with Jesus. They did not continue with their threats of punishment but released Peter and John, who returned to the rest of the disciples for a meeting of praise.

This same provision is available for all believers, and I am personally challenged to rely completely on the Holy Spirit when confronted with difficult situations. I can think of many times when I have given a reactive reply with all its consequences, when the Holy Spirit was waiting to give me **words from heaven** that would have brought resolution and peace.

Charles

One Year Plan : Psalm 45, 2 Timothy 4, 2 Chronicles 10 - 11
Two Year Plan : Proverbs 17:1-9, Luke 24:1-35, Deuteronomy 34 (Yr 1)
2 Kings 17 (Yr 2)

Shining Like Stars

A lot of media attention had been focussed on an employee of British Airways who had been suspended because she insisted on wearing a small cross around her neck. While being interviewed on Radio 4, the presenter asked some penetrating questions: **"Do you need to wear a cross to show you are a Christian?" "Would people be aware of your faith simply by the way they relate to you and you to them?"** His questions were very perceptive, and in her answers she spoke of truthfulness, integrity, and kindness in action, whilst maintaining her right to wear the cross as a symbol of her faith.

Whatever we might choose to wear, you and I are billboards advertising God's grace to a lost world. We are supposed to make Him visible, displaying His glory, His presence, and His actions. He has entrusted His public image to us! We are ambassadors, constantly on the job, and the way people see Jesus is our responsibility.

In The Message it says, **"Go out into the world uncorrupted, a breath of fresh air in this squalid and polluted society. Provide people with a glimpse of good living and of the living God."** (Philippians 2:14-15)

The same passage in the NIV says, **"...become blameless and pure, children without fault in a crooked and depraved generation, in which you shine like stars in the universe."**

As Christians, we need to be indelibly branded with the Cross of Jesus. To display the nature of Jesus in every facet of life. This is 'jewellery' which can never be removed and is what the world around us needs to see.

Jesus said to His disciples, **"If you have seen me, you have seen the Father."** Can you and I say, **"If you have seen me, you have seen Jesus?"**

Joyce

One Year Plan : Psalm 46, Titus 1, 2 Chronicles 12 - 13
Two Year Plan : Proverbs 17:10-19, Luke 24:36-53, Joshua 1 (Yr 1)
2 Kings 18 (Yr 2)

Stress or Peace?

Stress is one of today's major problems. It is the principal cause of illness in our nation and the loss of more man-hours in the workplace than any other factor. It costs the Health Service billions of pounds and is undermining families and destroying lives.

One of the chief reasons that Jesus came was to bring peace. He not only came to give us peace with God through the forgiveness of sins but to give us a peace that drives away all anxiety and stress.

Jesus said, **"Peace I leave with you; my peace I give to you. I do not give to you as the world gives. Do not let your hearts be troubled and do not be afraid."** (John 14:27)

Paul told the Christians at Philippi, **"Do not be anxious about anything, but in everything, by prayer and petition, with thanksgiving, present your requests to God. And the peace of God, which transcends all understanding, will guard your hearts and minds in Christ Jesus."** (Philippians 4:6-7)

And if our lives are producing the fruit of the Spirit it will include **peace** in addition to love, joy, patience, kindness, goodness, faithfulness, gentleness and self-control. (See Galatians 5:22-23.)

Reading and meditating on God's Word is also a source of peace. Psalm 119:165 says, **"Great peace have those who love your law, and nothing can make them stumble."**

You do not have to live with stress! God has provided everything you need to live in total peace and without stress. Does it sound too simple? A friend once said to me, **"You can pray or you can worry – you can't do both!"**

This peace is beyond understanding; it is available to you today and is received by faith.

Charles

One Year Plan : Psalm 47, Titus 2, 2 Chronicles 14 - 15
Two Year Plan : Proverbs 17:20-28, Philippians 1, Joshua 2 (Yr 1)
2 Kings 19 (Yr 2)

Rejoice Greatly

"Rejoice greatly, O Daughter of Zion! Shout, Daughter of Jerusalem! See, your king comes to you..." (Zechariah 9:9)

Originally these words were addressed to a crushed people returning from exile in Babylon, trying to rebuild their temple and capital city. They were facing much opposition and weariness and wondered if there would ever be an end to conflict. God spoke these words through His prophet and He goes on to say what He is going to do: **"...I will take away conflict ... I will proclaim peace ... I will free your prisoners ... I will make you like a warrior's sword ... I will restore"**.

Today, hear these words again: **Rejoice greatly;** your King has come and is coming again. He has recorded for us what He will do, and we know the outcome of world history. We too are commanded in the New Testament, **"Rejoice in the Lord always. I will say it again: Rejoice!"** (Philippians 4:4)

Rejoice as you remember what He has done. Rejoice; sing a new song.

Once unloved – now loved.

Once a slave to sin – now set free.

Once helpless – now filled with hope.

Once in darkness – now in light.

Once alone – now indwelt by Jesus, who will never leave you nor forsake you.

Rejoice in His goodness, His kindness, His faithfulness, His provision, His protection, His mercy, His forgiveness... and remember that He watches over you; He never slumbers nor sleeps. He goes ahead of you into every new day, and He stands behind you watching your back. What a Saviour!

Rejoice as you speak out the promises God has given to you personally; speak out blessing over your family, over the nation, over the nations.

Rejoice greatly; it will lift your spirit and cause strength to flow into your whole being.

Joyce

One Year Plan : Psalm 48, Titus 3, 2 Chronicles 16 - 17
Two Year Plan : Proverbs 18:1-8, Philippians 2, Joshua 3 (Yr 1)
2 Kings 20 (Yr 2)

Seasoned with Salt

I love my food well-seasoned with salt. I know there is a lot written these days about the harmful effect of too much salt in our diet, but I have enjoyed my food well-seasoned all my life and enjoy extremely good health so I am not changing now!

I was struck by the verse in Paul's letter to the Colossians which says, **"Let your conversation be always full of grace, seasoned with salt, so that you may know how to answer everyone."** (Colossians 4:6)

As I meditated on these words, God began to speak clearly to me. Our speech and words spoken to others need always to be full of grace; which means that they will bring healing, forgiveness and love. However, they also need to be seasoned with salt; which means we will not avoid the truth but will point to a new way of living.

When they brought Jesus a woman who had been caught in the very act of adultery, He spoke words of grace to her, and as her accusers left the scene, His parting words were, **"Then neither do I condemn you, go now and leave your life of sin."**

Down through the centuries religious people have been known for being quick to pass judgement and to condemn. Today's believers need to change that image by being people who are quick to forgive, who seek to restore and who are always looking to bring healing. However, that does not mean we are soft on sin.

During the 'Sermon on the Mount' Jesus said, **"You are the salt of the earth. But if the salt loses its saltiness, how can it be made salty again? It is no longer good for anything, except to be thrown out and trampled by men."**

We do need to be those who reach out to others with love, healing, forgiveness and hope, but at the same time we need to speak truth and be open and forthright as we not only seek to restore but also point people to a new and better way of living. Jesus said, **"You will know the truth and the truth will set you free."** (John 8:32)

Speak today with grace, seasoned with salt.

Charles

One Year Plan : Psalm 49, Philemon 1, 2 Chronicles 18 - 19
Two Year Plan : Proverbs 18:9-16, Philippians 3, Joshua 4 (Yr 1)
2 Kings 21 (Yr 2)

On Whom Are You Relying?

After the healing of the crippled man (in Acts 3), Peter addressed the crowd that had gathered and said, **"Why does this surprise you? Why do you stare at us as if by our own power or godliness we made this man walk?"** He went on to explain that the miracle was done by Jesus in order to bring Him glory. Peter personally knew he had no **power or godliness**; the only value or power was not in Peter but came from **'Jesus in Peter'**.

What about you and me – on whom are we relying? Do you acknowledge that you have **no power or godliness** or have you subtly started to think you have answers for the needs around you? It is possible to think you know a lot, have experience, or expertise, having been to all the important conferences and read the right books.

This shift in thinking can be gradual, but it is rooted in deception. We are intended to be vessels to carry the presence of God into every part of life, but we ourselves have nothing to give except Jesus. He is the answer; He alone has the love both to see and meet the need we encounter; and He alone has the resources and power to bring a miracle into every situation.

If you believe you have to do the work, you will be bound by your own limitation.

Step aside today and let Jesus be seen. Relax, live lightly; it is not your power or godliness that brings a miracle – it is Jesus who does it, and He needs to take all the glory, not you or I. It all starts with Jesus; miracles happen when He acts and ends up with both you and the person who has received the miracle worshipping Him.

Have you been relying on yourself? **Acknowledge it now; confess it and start trusting in Jesus to live out His life in you today.**

Joyce

One Year Plan : Psalm 50, Mark 1, 2 Chronicles 20 - 21
Two Year Plan : Proverbs 18:17-24, Philippians 4, Joshua 5 (Yr 1)
2 Kings 22 (Yr 2)

Pray with Joy

In the opening verses of his letter to the Philippians, Paul says, **"I always pray with joy."** This challenged me, and I pondered whether that would be the way I could always describe my praying. However, I do believe it is a vital key to effective praying.

So often I find people pray only when they are desperate; I see others who pray only as a last-gasp attempt to pull things back from the brink of disaster. For others it is a time of pouring out pain and anguish, without any expectancy of change.

That is not the way Paul prayed; he declares that he **prays with joy** because he is confident that God who has begun a good work will complete it. When we **pray with joy** we are praying with faith. When we **pray with joy** we are declaring that God is good and that we can trust Him to work powerfully in our moment of need.

We should always **pray with joy** because it shows that we are not gripped by fear; it demonstrates that we believe that God is on our side; it declares to all around that we are confident in God and trust Him to act on our behalf; it fills our hearts with thanksgiving and praise and causes us to speak out God's faithfulness to those who know our situation.

Later on in the same letter Paul writes, **"Rejoice in the Lord always, I will say it again rejoice! ... Do not be anxious about anything, but in everything, by prayer and petition with thanksgiving, present your requests to God."** (Philippians 4:4-6) Here again the key principles are joy and thanksgiving.

Let me encourage you: as you reach out to God in prayer today, whatever circumstances you face, **pray with joy.**

Charles

One Year Plan : Psalm 51, Mark 2, 2 Chronicles 22 - 23
Two Year Plan : Proverbs 19:1-9, Colossians 1, Joshua 6 (Yr 1)
2 Kings 23 (Yr 2)

Let the Worker do his Work

When you are asked to do something, is your first reaction to think, **"I can't"**? And, your second, to think of a dozen people who could do it better? This reaction is fairly typical but poses a bigger question: **who is doing the work?** God's word clearly states that it is **"Christ in you who is at work both to will and to act according to his good purpose"**. (Philippians 2:13)

In Ephesians 1:8, it says, **"...he has lavished on us all wisdom and understanding."** Because the One who has all knowledge, all wisdom, all experience, and all ability is resident in you and is the One who is at work, you can relax and simply let Him do what He pleases to do.

A friend of mine was invited to pray for a young woman who was suffering epileptic seizures. She lived in an African village and came to town to see her brother and seek medical treatment. He asked my friend to pray, but the girl reacted strongly: **"Not prayer again; it doesn't work."** My friend, conscious that he was carrying **'Jesus the worker'** simply listened for instructions from the Spirit within, who said, **"Don't pray; tell her the work is done – then leave."**

The girl was shocked and was intent on proving that she was not healed. In fact, she stayed with her brother two months before returning home, but there were no further attacks. Her village elders said, **"Why are you keeping this secret remedy to yourself? Come let us all receive."** Later a team of young men, each carrying **'the worker Jesus'**, visited that village, and many were healed, delivered and saved. Not experienced, not highly trained, not great evangelists – they were simply letting **the worker** do His work.

May God help you today to accept that you are to be a vessel carrying the person of Jesus into whatever situation He wants to work.

Joyce

One Year Plan : Psalm 52, Mark 3, 2 Chronicles 24 - 25
Two Year Plan : Proverbs 19:10-20, Colossians 2, Joshua 7 (Yr 1)
2 Kings 24 (Yr 2)

How's Your Body Armour?

"Put on faith and love as a breastplate." (Words of Paul to the Christians at Thessalonika.) This set me thinking about body armour; we have heard a great deal of discussion about this during the conflict in Afghanistan, but what does it mean for us in our everyday life?

A breastplate is to guard our heart from attack; in Proverbs 4:23 it says, **"Above all else, guard your heart for it is the wellspring of life."** In the verse above, Paul was in effect saying that faith and love will protect your heart as life comes against you and seeks to defeat and overwhelm.

So how does faith work? Well, faith is always looking to God for strength, protection and wisdom. Ephesians 6:16 says, **"Take up the shield of faith with which you can extinguish all the flaming arrows of the evil one."**

One time when the Israelites were being attacked, King Jehoshaphat gathered all the people together, told them to fast and pray and to seek the Lord. He then said these amazing words: **"For we have no power to face this vast army that is attacking us. We do not know what to do, but our eyes are on you."** (2 Chronicles 20:12) Faith keeps us looking to God, not to our own resources. They trusted God and He delivered them.

And, how does love work? Love focuses on others; John wrote, **"Dear friends, since God so loved us, we also ought to love one another."** (1 John 4:11) Other qualities of love are that **"love covers a multitude of sins ... love is patient, love is kind, it always protects, always trusts, always hopes, always perseveres"**.

Self-pity, self-reliance and self-centeredness make you vulnerable and unprotected. Faith focuses on God, who is longing to help and to be gracious to you. Love focuses on others because when you seek to meet the needs of others, when you involve yourself in their lives, you get your own life in perspective.

So protect your heart today, God's way: **put on faith and love as your body armour.**

Charles

One Year Plan : Psalm 53, Mark 4, 2 Chronicles 26 - 27
Two Year Plan : Proverbs 19:21-29, Colossians 3, Joshua 8 (Yr 1)
2 Kings 25 (Yr 2)

God Keeps His Word

When God announces He is going to do a thing, **it is already done** – it will certainly happen at the appointed time.

This truth was underlined to me when reading in Jeremiah how the leaders of Israel ask him to enquire of God where they should go and what they should do. (Jeremiah 42:3-4) The answer given to them is unacceptable, and they reject it. They completely disobey Jeremiah's instructions and flee to Egypt.

Jeremiah, who reluctantly goes with them, finds himself at Tahpanhes where, while the Jews are watching, he takes some large stones and buries them in the brick pavement at the entrance to Pharaoh's palace and then prophecies this word from the Lord: **"I will send my servant Nebuchadnezzar ... he will come and attack Egypt, bringing death, captivity and the sword."** (Jeremiah 43:10-13)

As I was reading this using my NIV Study Bible, my eyes caught a note on 43:11, stating that a fragment of text owned by the British Museum records that Nebuchadnezzar carried out a punitive raid against Egypt in his 37th year 568-567 BC during the reign of Pharaoh Amasis. In Ezekiel 29:17-20, **God tells the prophet he is going to give Egypt to Nebuchadnezzar, and history tells us it happened.**

When God says that something will happen, be assured it will. As I pondered this, I found myself actively remembering words of promise yet to be fulfilled – words spoken over my life, over my nation and the nations. Some of those things seem as impossible as the prophesied attack on Egypt, but just as surely as that word was fulfilled, so will every promise and prophecy uttered by God be fulfilled. Isaiah 44:26 assures us that **"the Lord will carry out the words of his servants and fulfil the predictions of his messengers."**

Today, keep your faith behind every word the Lord has spoken to you personally, as well as the many as yet unfulfilled promises concerning the nations in these last days.

Joyce

One Year Plan : Psalm 54, Mark 5, 2 Chronicles 28 - 29
Two Year Plan : Proverbs 20:1-7, Colossians 4, Joshua 9 (Yr 1)
Ezekiel 1 (Yr 2)

Dying to Live

A number of years ago, I was with Colin Urquhart when he spoke at the Sunday Service at Strangeways Jail in Manchester. He was given a ten-minute slot to speak to five hundred prisoners, and as the men restlessly and noisily assembled, I wondered how Colin would handle this challenge. **"I have good news for you,"** he began. **"God does not want to reform you!"** A cheer rang out, followed by hushed silence as they waited for what was to follow. **"He wants you to die,"** Colin continued. Everyone listened intently as Colin explained that the message of the Cross was death to the old life and the gift of brand new resurrection life in Jesus.

One time, when speaking at a conference on 'Christ in You', we asked, **"How many of you, when you became believers, understood that it meant death to the flesh and being given a completely new life in Christ?"** Only one in ten answered yes to this question.

Paul preached Jesus and the resurrection; he knew that the Cross had dealt with his past and had set him free from the power of sin. He did not try to improve his old life; he knew that new life in Christ is the only good news.

Are you battling with the flesh, your old human self? Trying harder and self-improvement will not work. Paul clearly expressed his gospel when he preached, **"We died to sin; how can we live in it any longer?"** (Romans 6:2)

In another letter Paul explains that the work of the Cross in our lives is the key to releasing the life of Jesus in our bodies. **"We always carry around in our body the death of Jesus, so that the life of Jesus may also be revealed in our body."** (2 Corinthians 4:10)

Paul's own testimony is this: **"I have been crucified with Christ; I no longer live, but Christ lives in me."** (Galatians 2:20)

We don't need more trying; we need more dying!

Charles

One Year Plan : Psalm 55, Mark 6, 2 Chronicles 30 - 31
Two Year Plan : Proverbs 20:8-15, 1 Thessalonians 1, Joshua 10 (Yr 1)
Ezekiel 2 (Yr 2)

Don't Play Mind Games

Satan is a master of innuendo; he loves to attack by planting half-truths in our minds. Words are so subtle; they raise questions that we have not asked and yet appear to have come from our own minds! He attacked Eve in the Garden of Eden with the doubt question, **"Did God really say?"** He tempted Jesus with mind games, with illusions of victory, but without pain – just compromise. He planted evil ideas in Judas Iscariot's mind, deceiving him into valuing money above the life of Jesus.

Your mind is a battlefield. You need to win the thought encounter by concentrating on truth – the truth of God's word – and not accepting deception. Don't get side-tracked trying to fight the devil; he thrives on attention and is very theatrical. Concentrate of God's written word and use the technique Jesus employed in the desert: **"It is written..."**

2 Corinthians 10:4 says, **"We use God's mighty weapons to knock down the strongholds of human reasoning and to destroy false arguments."** Don't allow negative thoughts to settle and build a stronghold in your mind; keep believing the truth God has spoken. The truth will not only **set** you free but **keep** you free.

If you are experiencing an attack in a particular area of life, ask God for a specific scripture to meditate on; it is your antidote so use it.

When our son Ben lived and worked in Chad, he and his wife Anne visited a nomad's settlement in the desert. As they entered a tent they were aware of an unusually heavy atmosphere. The reason soon became apparent as they discovered a young girl near to death; she had been bitten by a snake named 'the death snake'. These people were completely ignorant of the fact that there was an antidote readily available in the city. Ben and Anne quickly gathered up the child and parents, rushed them to the hospital in N'Djamena where the serum was administered, and the child recovered.

Satan's venom is just as dangerous. **Make sure you carry the antidote of God's word today.**

Joyce

One Year Plan : Psalm 56, Mark 7, 2 Chronicles 32 - 33
Two Year Plan : Proverbs 20:16-23, 1 Thessalonians 2, Joshua 11 (Yr 1) Ezekiel 3 (Yr 2)

The Email Culture

Two of my granddaughters had come from Bulgaria to stay with us for a few weeks. One of the first requests from Gillian was, **"Grandpa, can I check my emails?" "Yes,"** I responded and later asked whether there were any messages in her inbox, to which the reply was, **"No." "Have you sent any emails lately?"** I continued, and again the answer was, **"No."**

Emails, apart from the spam with which we all battle, work on the principle of **sowing and reaping** – you send emails to your friends and you get replies.

Sowing and reaping is a universal principle; you sow love and you will reap love. You sow care and concern for your friends and family and you will reap their gratitude and appreciation.

On the other hand, if you sow hatred and unforgiveness, you will reap rejection and bitterness.

In Galatians 6:7-10 it says, **"Do not be deceived: God cannot be mocked. A man reaps what he sows. The one who sows to please his sinful nature, from that nature will reap destruction; the one who sows to please the Spirit, from the Spirit will reap eternal life. Let us not become weary in doing good, for at the proper time we will reap a harvest if we do not give up. Therefore, as we have opportunity, let us do good to all people, especially to those who belong to the family of believers."**

Do some sowing today. Sow an email to a friend; sow some love to your family; sow a phone call to someone who is lonely; sow a kindness to someone in need;

...and you will reap a good harvest!

Charles

One Year Plan : Psalm 57, Mark 8, 2 Chronicles 34 - 35
Two Year Plan : Proverbs 20:24-30, 1 Thessalonians 3, Joshua 12 (Yr 1)
Ezekiel 4 (Yr 2)

Access

Most of us use a **PIN number** to access our bank account, check data and withdraw money. You and I have been given such a **PIN number** to access the resources of heaven.

However, it is not a series of numbers but a person – **Jesus** – and it is by believing in what He has done for us, what He has promised us, and **using His Name**, that we have the possibility to access all of heaven's grace in whatever form we need.

Romans 5:2 says, **"Jesus Christ, through whom we have gained access by faith into this grace in which we now stand."** Paul is referring here to the work of Jesus on the cross, which gives us peace with God and justifies us from everything that has to do with sin, failure, guilt and shame.

Many people want to **feel** salvation, **feel** they are baptised in the Spirit, before receiving it by faith. I prayed for years, asking God to fill me with His Holy Spirit, but because I didn't instantly speak in tongues, experience great feelings or other manifestations, I reasoned I had not received. But my job was to receive and say thank you by faith before there were any manifestations. I repented, believed and very soon had plenty of evidence.

Faith in the promises written in the Word of God, made personal by His Holy Spirit and accessed by **the Name of Jesus**, is what opens the door to all of heaven's resources. Jesus said, **"And I will do whatever you ask in my name, so that the Son may bring glory to the Father. You may ask me for anything in my name, and I will do it."** (John 14:13-14)

We want to see more miracles, healing, more manifestations of God's power and ability to do the impossible. However, there is a battleground – rational thinking that opposes faith in God's promises.

I can see the problem; I can see the solution. I have chosen to set a course to be one who will battle against unbelief and enter my **PIN number** to acquire what only heaven can provide.

Joyce

One Year Plan : Psalm 58, Mark 9, 2 Chronicles 36
Two Year Plan : Proverbs 21:1-8, 1 Thessalonians 4, Joshua 13 (Yr 1)
Ezekiel 5 (Yr 2)

Harvest Times

Even during rainy summers the harvest still ripens and is gathered in. Each year churches celebrate their Harvest Festivals. However, the most important harvest comes from spiritual seeds that have been planted in people's hearts.

I had recently received an email prayer letter from Don Double. I quote: **"The visit to Grapevine was amazing, some ten thousand people present, great worship and preaching. I was introduced from the platform, which resulted in several people coming to me saying how they had been saved through our ministry; others told how they had been healed, baptised in the Spirit and in water. They certainly were telling of their changed lives, it was quite humbling especially when one international minister came and hugged me and said he wanted to thank me for all my preaching of the gospel, because as he travels around he meets so many who testify to having met the Lord and been blessed through the ministry. Now I want to give God all the praise and glory as it is His doing."**

At that time Joyce and I had also received an email from Swedish friends: **"I'm busy training pastors and missionaries at Livets Ord University. We see the equipping of the next generation of leaders as the most important question for the Body of Christ ... We think of you, our dear friends, as key tools for our development during a very important time!"**

Nothing thrills me more than to hear that seeds planted many years ago have ripened into a harvest.

Colin Urquhart once had a dream in which he saw himself queuing at the gate of heaven. As each person passed St. Peter they were being asked only one question: **"Who have you brought with you?"**

The most significant harvest is that of lives transformed by the message of the Cross and eventually gathered into God's heavenly barn.

"Let us not become weary in sowing seeds, for at the proper time we will reap a harvest if we do not give up." (Galatians 6:9)

Charles

One Year Plan : Psalm 59, Mark 10, Jeremiah 1 - 2
Two Year Plan : Proverbs 21:9-16, 1 Thessalonians 5, Joshua 14 (Yr 1)
Ezekiel 6 (Yr 2)

Find God's Perspective

Isaiah Chapter 11 describes how it is possible to minister as Jesus did whilst here on earth. Verse 3 tells us the Messiah will not judge situations using natural means; He will receive knowledge from a far more accurate source – from the Spirit of God – **spiritual knowledge, which includes wisdom, understanding and counsel.** Spiritual knowledge sees beyond the immediate and obvious and results in an understanding of God's heart regarding the situation or person you are engaging with.

In John 7:24, Jesus tells His disciples to stop judging by mere appearances and make right judgements. Here are two good questions to ask yourself if you choose to work with the Spirit rather than natural knowledge: **"Lord, what do you see in this situation?"** and, **"Lord, what do you feel about this situation?"** What He tells you may surprise you!

I remember being present in a large meeting where a woman began to cry out in agony; she was screaming with intense emotion, and the pain of listening to her was excruciating and disturbing. The meeting was being led by John Wimber, who took the microphone and spoke: **"What you are listening to is grief, raw exposed agony; it has been stored for years and is now leaving our dear sister."** He was listening to the voice of the Spirit, and as he spoke the atmosphere in the meeting changed from tension and annoyance to compassion, mercy and prayer.

Today our God is reaching out in mercy, offering healing to a very wounded generation. In the natural, flesh wounds are not pretty, and if not cleansed quickly stink. Ask the Lord for understanding. So often angry people are wounded, hurting, and are waiting for the next rejection. Seductive people are looking for real love. Those who mock and bully, being so inadequate inside, present themselves big for their own protection.

"Dear friends, let us love one another, for love comes from God." (1 John 4:7) Choose to listen to the voice of His Spirit today as you let His love flow in and out of you.

Joyce

One Year Plan : Psalm 60, Mark 11, Jeremiah 3 - 4
Two Year Plan : Proverbs 21:17-24, 2 Thessalonians 1, Joshua 15 (Yr 1)
Ezekiel 7 (Yr 2)

SEPTEMBER

Free from Guilt

Are you the kind of person who gets things out or bottles things up? I was struck when reading Psalm 32:3 with these words: **"When I kept silent my bones wasted away through my groaning all day long."**

It is a known fact that unexpressed anger, unforgiveness and resentment can be very damaging to health; they are some of the causes of depression and other stress-related illnesses. The psalm continues, **"...my strength was sapped as in the heat of summer."** Now comes the good news: **"Then I acknowledged my sin to you and did not cover up my iniquity. I said, 'I will confess my transgressions to the Lord' – and you forgave the guilt of my sin."**

When we confess our sins, forgive those who have offended us and release our anger to God, we open the way for God to forgive, heal and release us from pain and guilt.

Unforgiveness does not punish the offender; it damages the person who withholds forgiveness. Resentment does not vindicate your behaviour; it cuts you off from friends and family. Unexpressed anger does not justify your feelings of injustice; it only builds stress within you.

Proverbs 28:13 says, **"He who conceals his sins does not prosper, but whoever confesses and renounces them finds mercy."**

I know that when I let anger and resentment find a lodging place in me, I am robbed of strength and joy. I know that getting it all out in the open, admitting my faults, confessing my failures, giving forgiveness, and releasing those who have offended me is a wonderfully liberating exercise.

It opens to door to freedom: free from guilt; free from condemnation; free from anger; free to live in joyful abandonment; **free to enjoy God's favour and blessing; and free to be a blessing to others.**

Charles

One Year Plan : Psalm 61, Mark 12, Jeremiah 5 - 6
Two Year Plan : Proverbs 21:25-31, 2 Thessalonians 2, Joshua 16-17 (Yr 1)
Ezekiel 8 (Yr 2)

God's Kind of Peace

Many of us are returning from holidays, getting ready for school to start or going back to work. Some have been fortunate to holiday in idyllic resorts with everything you could wish for – every form of luxury and pampering!

Did you find what you were looking for? Do you feel refreshed and renewed? Has it restored your strength and given you peace?

Or, you may have been very busy during this holiday period, been inundated with visitors, serving others, stretching your resources of time and energy – but been surprised at how fulfilled you have felt!

So what is the factor that enables us to enjoy whatever situation we find ourselves in? Peace – it is **God's Kind of Peace** that makes all the difference and causes deep refreshment which is more to do with internal than external circumstances. Without it, the most luxurious holiday can leave you with a feeling of emptiness.

Jesus said, **"Peace I leave with you; my peace I give you. I do not give to you as the world gives. Do not let your hearts be troubled and do not be afraid."** (John 14:27)

Proverbs 17:1 says, **"Better a dry crust of bread with peace and quiet than a house full of feasting with strife."**

God's peace is a gift; freely available on request; bought at a price we could never afford to pay but free to His children.

Ask Jesus for His peace today –

- Peace as you return to work or school
- Peace as you face new challenges
- Peace in the mundane and the extraordinary

It is part of your promised inheritance.

Joyce

One Year Plan : Psalm 62, Mark 13, Jeremiah 7 - 8
Two Year Plan : Proverbs 22:1-9, 2 Thessalonians 3, Joshua 18 (Yr 1)
Ezekiel 9 (Yr 2)

God is For You!

"Does the devil make things more difficult when you have decided to be totally committed to following Jesus?" was the question I was asked. **"Not especially,"** was my reply. The fact is that the devil is against all of God's people, all of the time, but the good news is **"God is for you."**

When we experience challenges and difficulties in life it is all too easy to try and find someone to blame. **"It's the devil's fault; he is focussing his venom on me!" "It's my mother's fault; she brought me up wrong!"** or **"It's God's fault; he is punishing me for what I have done wrong!"**

No, it is not God's fault! God is always on your side; He wants the best for you; He wants to help you. Romans 8:31 says, **"If God is for us, who can be against us?"** We need to understand that as believers in Jesus we have supernatural resources available for every situation of life.

Jesus' victory on the cross has delivered an eternal, irrevocable and complete defeat to the devil. In his letter to the church at Rome, Paul makes it clear. He declares that Jesus is at the right hand of God interceding for us. When satan is accusing you, Jesus is in the presence of God taking your side against him.

He continues, **"Who shall separate us from the love of Christ? Shall trouble or hardship or persecution or famine or nakedness or danger or sword? NO! In all these things we are more than conquerors through him who loved us."** (Romans 8:35-37)

If you are in the habit of writing things down, do this. On the top of the next clear page write, **"GOD IS FOR ME!"** and underneath write, **"IT IS NOT GOD'S FAULT."** Write these statements in big letters and in bold, for those two counteract the most common lies of the enemy.

Finally in the words of Paul, **"I am convinced that neither death nor life, neither angels nor demons, neither the present nor the future, nor any powers, neither height nor depth, nor anything else in all creation, will be able to separate us from the love of God that is in Christ Jesus our Lord."** (Romans 8:38-39)

Charles

One Year Plan : Psalm 63, Mark 14, Jeremiah 9 - 10
Two Year Plan : Proverbs 22:10-16, 1 Timothy 1, Joshua 19 (Yr 1)
Ezekiel 10 (Yr 2)

Be Happy

Over and over God commands His people to rejoice, to be glad, thankful – **"Happy"**. The benefits are declared in such verses as **"The joy of the Lord is your strength"** and **"A cheerful heart is good medicine."** Our bodies respond to what is going on in our souls. Heavy and depressed hearts soon result in physical symptoms, weakness and sickness.

Peace and joy seem to go hand in hand, so everything that disturbs your peace or causes anxiety will be a potential happiness drain. Actively bring the Holy Spirit into every aspect of life, including the difficulties, and know that He has answers to every dilemma, understands the emotions you are experiencing, cares deeply and wants to bring you peace as you talk through each situation with Him.

There are times when I know I need to address my soul and command myself to cheer up, to stop being heavy or anxious, and to choose to focus on what God has promised to do because I've committed my way to Him, and to thank Him in advance for His action on my behalf.

I find that rejoicing becomes a possibility when I look at the Father's greatness and ability rather than my problems and limitations. Psalm 16:7-11 flows out of the heart of David, a man in touch with God, who says, **"I will praise the Lord who counsels me; even at night my heart instructs me. I have set the Lord always before me. Because he is at my right hand, I will not be shaken. Therefore my heart is glad and my tongue rejoices ... you fill me with joy in your presence."**

Jesus lived in joy – **"he was anointed with the oil of joy, set above his companions."** Let your joy be the evidence that Jesus is alive in you today.

Joyce

One Year Plan : Psalm 64, Mark 15, Jeremiah 11 - 12
Two Year Plan : Proverbs 22:17-29, 1 Timothy 2, Joshua 20 (Yr 1)
Ezekiel 11 (Yr 2)

The Hand of God

Many years ago my grandfather was standing on the kerbside waiting to cross the road. He saw a lorry approaching, and after that it looked as if the road was clear so he was getting ready to step out. The lorry came past, and just as my grandfather was about to walk into the road, he felt a strong hand grip his shoulder and pull him back onto the pavement. At that moment, he saw that the lorry was towing a trailer, and he had been about to step into the gap, with potentially fatal consequences. He immediately looked around to see who had saved his life, and no-one was there. A supernatural hand had held him back.

When God rescued His people from Egypt it says, **"He brought Israel out from among them with a mighty hand and outstretched arm."** (Psalm 136:11-12)

David describes the way God takes infinite care over each of His children: **"If I rise on the wings of the dawn, if I settle on the far side of the sea, even there your hand will guide me, your right hand will hold me fast."** (Psalm 139:9-10)

Isaiah declares, **"Surely the arm of the Lord is not too short to save, nor his ear too dull to hear."** (Isaiah 59:1)

Jesus said, **"My sheep listen to my voice; I know them, and they follow me. I give them eternal life, and they shall never perish; no one can snatch them out of my hand."** (John 10:27-28)

When we place our lives into the hand of God, we are in the safest place. Not only do we receive His forgiveness and new life, but we are under the protection, guidance, and care of a God who has a Mighty Hand and an Outstretched Arm.

Nothing is beyond His Strength, and nothing is beyond His Reach.

Charles

One Year Plan : Psalm 65, Mark 16, Jeremiah 13 - 14
Two Year Plan : Proverbs 23:1-9, 1 Timothy 3, Joshua 21 (Yr 1)
Ezekiel 12 (Yr 2)

Win your Battles

The book of Joshua records the campaign to take over the land of Canaan in order to establish God's rule and drive out powerful enemies. God's instructions were to utterly destroy, to make no alliances – no compromise. The people failed to do it, and the mandate is repeated in Judges 2: **"But you haven't obeyed me! ... if you won't drive them out before you, they will trip you up and their gods will become a trap."** (The Message)

The rest of the book of Judges records a grim tale of domination by hostile nations they failed to remove. There were periods when brave warriors like Gideon drove back the enemies of God and for a season peace prevailed. But time and again those they failed to eradicate, regrouped and continued their attacks.

Pondering spiritual battles, I'm challenged to pursue and put to death all that opposes the kingdom of God in my life, knowing that there is no lasting peace without victory and without death to self.

Self in all its forms is not a playmate; rather an enemy that seeks to rule and, given the chance, leaves destruction in its wake. It is so easy to accommodate and excuse selfish behaviour until it reveals its true colours and has you trapped. **Self** destroys and will dominate wherever it is allowed to reign.

Paul instructions are, **"Put to death the sinful, earthly things lurking within you."** When the Israelites were being crushed and oppressed by their enemies they cried out to the Lord for help. He heard them, took their troubles to heart and sent warriors to help them in battle.

Today you may feel **self** is dominating and you are overwhelmed by trouble. You may blame yourself for letting situations get so out of hand. Call out for help, deliverance and reinforcements. Ask the Holy Spirit to enforce the victory of Jesus in your life and over **self** and your circumstances.

Choose today to keep advancing; God is for you and knows exactly how to win your battles and come alongside to help. Jesus said, **"In this world you will have trouble. But take heart! I have overcome the world."** (John 16:33)

Joyce

One Year Plan : Psalm 66, Hebrews 1, Jeremiah 15 - 16
Two Year Plan : Proverbs 23:10-18, 1 Timothy 4, Joshua 22 (Yr 1)
Ezekiel 13 (Yr 2)

Winning and Losing

Each year we enter the annual summer drama of Wimbledon, English Cricket, and sometimes European or World Cup Football to add to the equation. Our emotions are raw, our nerves are on edge; we desperately want to be winners. Not that it demands too much effort on our part – a little energy expended pressing the remote control, some shouting and perhaps leaping into the air when that smash wins the point or a magical goal is scored.

Why are we so concerned? It's only a game! But is it revealing something much deeper? We want to identify with the winners because in so many other areas of life we are losers.

Jesus said, **"What good is it for a man to gain the whole world, yet forfeit his soul?"** (Mark 8:36)

Jesus came to this earth not to applaud winners but to rescue losers. He wants us to be successful but not by our own efforts. He said, **"I didn't come to call the righteous – but sinners."** In other words, **"Give me the failures; give me those who have messed up; give me those who have lost hope."**

What is going on inside of you today? How do you feel about your own life and future? Are you buoyant and confident, or discouraged and looking at potential failure on every side?

You may have made a mess of everything so far, but this is what God says to you: **"He who was seated on the throne said, 'I am making everything new!' Then he said, 'Write this down, for these words are trustworthy and true.'"** (Revelation 21:5)

In Philippians 2:13, Paul says, **"...for it is God who works in you, both to will and to act according to his good pleasure."**

God is always the winner; let Him work out His victories in your life!

Charles

One Year Plan : Psalm 67, Hebrews 2, Jeremiah 17 - 18
Two Year Plan : Proverbs 23:19-28, 1 Timothy 5, Joshua 23 (Yr 1)
Ezekiel 14 (Yr 2)

You've got a Wonderful Son!

We have noticed a striking difference between Americans and us British. Those from the States are spontaneous in their praise of people and are ready to speak positive and affirming words. We often think them but find it hard to verbalise them. Challenged by this, I engaged in conversation with a lady whose son had been a great help to me.

"Betty," I said, **"You've got a wonderful son; he's so kind, so considerate, always going the extra mile."** She was encouraged and blessed to hear these truths. It was important; they needed to be spoken out, and the more I said, the more she glowed and grew!

Later God spoke to me and said, **"Tell me what you think of <u>my</u> Son."** And so I found myself speaking about Jesus, telling the Father how unique, wonderful, and amazing His Son Jesus is; how kind He has been to me, how understanding, how faithful.

I sensed God's pleasure as I honoured His Son – just as Betty basked in the warmth of my praise of a human son.

Matthew records that when Jesus was about to begin His ministry here on earth and was baptised, **"he went up out of the water. At that moment heaven was opened, and he saw the Spirit descending like a dove and lighting on him. And a voice from heaven said, 'This is my Son whom I love; with him I am well pleased.'"** (Matthew 3:16-17)

The Father knew it was important to speak out His approval, love and pleasure over Jesus, and that was before He had accomplished anything. Affirming people and expressing our love and honour is very important.

Spend time today telling Father how wonderful His Son is.

Joyce

One Year Plan : Psalm 68, Hebrews 3, Jeremiah 19 – 20
Two Year Plan : Proverbs 23:29-35, 1 Timothy 6, Joshua 24 (Yr 1)
Ezekiel 15 (Yr 2)

Grow Grass – Don't Just Kill Weeds

A friend was visiting our home, and we were in the garden enjoying the surprisingly warm, sunny day. We were looking at my moss and weed ridden lawn when he said, **"Don't bother about the weeds and the moss, just give it a good feed of nitrogen and the vigorous growth of the grass will drive out the weeds!"**

That set me thinking about how we tackle problems, attacks and weaknesses in our lives. Do we try to defeat temptation, rebuke the devil, try to overcome some besetting sin – or do we focus on building our faith and seeking to be strong in the Lord?

Jude 1:20 says, **"But you, dear friends, build yourselves up in your most holy faith and pray in the Holy Spirit. Keep yourselves in God's love..."**

Paul's prayer for the Ephesians is, **"I pray that out of his glorious riches he may strengthen you with power through his Spirit in your inner being, so that Christ may dwell in your hearts by faith."** (Ephesians 3:16-17)

Paul says something similar to the Colossians: **"We pray ... that you may please him in every way ... growing in the knowledge of God, being strengthened with all power according to his glorious might so that you may have great endurance and patience."** (Colossians 1:10-11)

To live under condemnation, constantly occupied with weakness and failure, is a ploy of the devil; he wants us to be occupied with our shortcomings, constantly thinking of how we fail. God, on the other hand, always wants to pour out His grace and forgiveness and seeks to build us up and affirm His love for us.

A chorus we used to sing many years ago says:

Turn your eyes upon Jesus,
Look full in His wonderful face,
And the things of earth
Will grow strangely dim,
In the light of His glory and grace.

Let's get our focus right, and put some spiritual **nitrogen** into our lives today.

Charles

One Year Plan : Psalm 69, Hebrews 4, Jeremiah 21 - 22
Two Year Plan : Proverbs 24:1-7, 2 Timothy 1, Obadiah 1 (Yr 1)
Ezekiel 16 (Yr 2)

My Dad!

Have you ever heard young children boasting about their **superhero dads**?!

The conversation goes something like this: **"Well, my Dad can do..."** (all sorts of extraordinary feats), and inevitably the next one who chips in has a dad even bigger and better!

It's time for us to recall who our Dad is and what He can do:

My Dad... never sleeps; He is always awake, watching out for me. (Psalm 121:3-4)

My Dad... will warn me of danger if I keep listening to His voice. (Proverbs 1:33)

My Dad... tells me what's best for me. (Isaiah 48:17)

My Dad... never lets go of my hand. (Isaiah 41:10)

My Dad... is still caring for me when I'm old and have grey hair! (Isaiah 46:4)

My Dad... made the universe. (Isaiah 48:13)

My Dad... commands angel armies. (Psalm 91:11, Psalm 34:7)

My Dad... reigns over the nations. (Psalm 47:7-8)

My Dad... is the Father of our Lord Jesus Christ, King of Kings and Lord of Lords, Supreme Ruler of this World, the Only Wise God.

Isn't it time for us to declare His Greatness and worship afresh with awe and wonder?

Joyce

One Year Plan : Psalm 70, Hebrews 5, Jeremiah 23 - 24
Two Year Plan : Proverbs 24:8-16, 2 Timothy 2, Jonah 1-2 (Yr 1)
Ezekiel 17 (Yr 2)

Hope and Future

Joyce and I had been visiting a country in Central Asia where the annual per capita income is $200. With that level of poverty, you are surrounded with a great deal of hopelessness and despair.

As we returned home the morning news was dominated by two suicide bomb explosions in Turkey which devastated the British Consulate and the HSBC Bank. The loss of life and personal tragedy were terrible.

How are we to live in such a world? The psalmist says in Psalm 42:5, **"Why are you downcast, O my soul? Why so disturbed within me? Put your hope in God, for I will yet praise him, my Saviour and my God."**

We met young people in Central Asia whose lives had been scarred by great trauma and tragedy. One girl had witnessed her mother cutting her father's throat; and yet we were now looking at a young life that had been redeemed and healed by the power of Jesus.

Despite tragedy, loss and devastation, in Jesus there is always hope of restoration and a new future. Jesus said, **"I have come that you might have life, and have it to the full."** (John 10:10)

When we commit our lives fully to Jesus He promises us a life of abundance here and now. He also is interested in our future and wants to guide us every day, and the life that Jesus gives lasts forever.

1 Corinthians 15:19 says, **"If only for this life we have hope in Christ, we are to be pitied more than all men."**

In such a troubled and uncertain world, be glad that your life and future are in the hands of a living and powerful Jesus.

Charles

One Year Plan : Psalm 71, Hebrews 6, Jeremiah 25 - 26
Two Year Plan : Proverbs 24:17-26, 2 Timothy 3, Jonah 3-4 (Yr 1)
Ezekiel 18 (Yr 2)

Could it get any Worse?

A fierce battle is about to be fought – against enormous odds. The army deserts because of fear and frustration in the ranks. They only have two swords in serviceable condition! Their leader is incompetent! Could it get any worse?

In these situations that seem impossible, God shows His mighty hand and gains glory. He loves to turn the impossible into victory.

Samuel had reminded Israel that they had been in impossible situations many times in the nation's history, and when they had come to the end of their human resources and had cried out for God's intervention, He had answered them and given supernatural help.

Now under the leadership of their new King Saul they find themselves in such a predicament – it is recorded in 1 Samuel Chapter 14. What are they to do?

1. Jonathan, Saul's son, decides to rely on God's help. Verse 6 says, **"Nothing can hinder the Lord from saving, whether by many or by few."**

2. He advances against the enemy accompanied by his armour bearer; there are two who are in agreement (perhaps he remembers the promise of Deuteronomy 32:30: **"one can chase a thousand, but two can put ten thousand to flight!"**)

3. They listen to God through the circumstances they face. Verse 10 says, **"If they say, 'Come up to us,' we will climb up, because that will be the sign that the Lord has given them into our hands."**

4. Faith is in operation. They are in a vulnerable situation, totally outnumbered and mocked, but God is with them and acting on their behalf.

5. Jonathan gives his human weapon to his armour bearer. He climbs a cliff on his hands and knees and **supernaturally** the Philistines fall before Jonathan – and his armour bearer finishes them off. What caused this fear? It was God's presence – possibly His glory. Certainly Jonathan believed God was with him, acting on his behalf. (verse 13)

6. Panic strikes the enemy camp and total confusion leads to mass destruction among the Philistine ranks. (verse 15)

7. **"So the Lord rescued Israel that day."** (verse 23)

Impossible – Yes!
Outnumbered – Yes!
Victorious – Yes!

Joyce

One Year Plan : Psalm 72, Hebrews 7, Jeremiah 27 - 28
Two Year Plan : Proverbs 24:27-34, 2 Timothy 4, Amos 1 (Yr 1)
Ezekiel 19 (Yr 2)

The Fourth Man

As my mother aged and her short-term memory waned, sometimes conversation became difficult and could easily dry up. However, she loved to hear me read the Bible and clearly recalled many events from scripture. One time whilst visiting her, she suddenly said, **"I do love the story of the fourth man in the fiery furnace with Shadrach, Meshach and Abednego."** So I turned it up and read out the account of the amazing deliverance of these three stalwarts. This then led to a great conversation about the way God can come into the most extreme situations.

I have been meditating further about this – thinking of these three men who loved God and were not willing to compromise their faith. They held to their beliefs, would not bow to the golden statue of King Nebuchadnezzar and found themselves being thrown into the blazing furnace. But God stepped in and joined them in the middle of the fire.

Are you in the middle of a furnace because of your stand for righteousness and unwillingness to compromise? Well, God is still in the business of walking into blazing furnaces and rescuing His people.

When the disciples were in a dilemma because they could not deliver the demon-possessed boy who had been brought to them, Jesus came down from the mountain, walked into the middle and rescued them from their plight. The distraught father turned to Jesus and said, **"If you can do anything, take pity on us and help us." "If you can?"** said Jesus, **"Everything is possible for him who believes."** At the moment of despair Jesus stepped into the middle and dealt with the predicament. Are you in crisis? Let Jesus step into the middle and resolve your crisis.

After the resurrection the disciples were in turmoil; some of them had seen Jesus, but most of them were fearful and doubting. The account in Luke's Gospel says, **"While they were still talking about this, Jesus himself stood among them and said to them, 'Peace be with you.'"** Are you in a place of fear and turmoil? Let Jesus come into your dilemma and bring you His peace.

Charles

One Year Plan :	Proverbs 1, Hebrews 8, Jeremiah 29 - 30
Two Year Plan :	Psalm 107:1-9, Titus 1, Amos 2 (Yr 1)
	Ezekiel 20 (Yr 2)

The Big Picture

God alone sees **the big picture** in each of our lives. He, being outside of time, sees the end as well as the beginning – and all the bits in between.

In Psalm 22, prophetically speaking of Jesus' death on the cross, verse 24 states, **"He [God] has not hidden his face from him but has listened to his cry for help."**

Two thousand years later we understand the supreme purpose in Jesus' death. We know about the wonder of resurrection and how essential that death was for our salvation. Hebrews 5:7 also states that **"Jesus cried ... to the one who could save him from death, and he was heard..."** The death was not averted, but Jesus is alive today. Hallelujah! We can now see **the big picture**, and it all makes sense.

As I have looked again at the story of Joseph, there are many incidents that are tragic, unjust and painful, but when looking back Joseph was able to see **the big picture** and was able to tell his brothers not to be angry with themselves. **"It was to save lives that God sent me ahead of you, so it was not you but God!"**

As he experienced each detail of the story, Joseph could not see **the big picture** and that is the same for you and me. I hear many people ask, **"Why? Why isn't God answering? Why isn't He healing? Why is this happening to me? Why has He allowed that?"**

I don't know – we do not have **the big picture** until God reveals it to us. Today, you need to know He hears your cry, sees your tears, loves you as He has loved Jesus, will never leave you, will keep His word, watches over you, and is intimately concerned about your present circumstances.

He is your Strong Tower, your Place of Refuge, and your help in time of trouble. Don't try to make sense of the now; just trust your Father who loves you, has your life in His hands and knows... **the big picture.**

Joyce

One Year Plan : Proverbs 2, Hebrews 9, Jeremiah 31 - 32
Two Year Plan : Psalm 107:10-22, Titus 2, Amos 3 (Yr 1)
Ezekiel 21 (Yr 2)

Whinging – or Crying Out for Help?

When our children were small, we learned to interpret what was happening when they were crying. There were times when their discontented whinging clearly showed that they were unhappy, but it did not indicate what they really wanted. Ignoring this was often the best remedy. However, when they were in crisis their strong and insistent cries drew an instant and active response.

I believe our prayers are often like that. We know we are unhappy and we would like things to change, but we are not desperate enough to really cry out to God with specific and faith-filled cries.

In Psalm 86:6-7, David cries out, **"Hear my prayer, O Lord; listen to my cry for mercy. In the day of trouble I will call to you, for you will answer me."**

Are there things that you have been moaning about, but nothing is changing? Are you just whining like a small child without being specific about what you want to happen?

Jesus said, **"Ask and it will be given to you; seek and you will find; knock and the door will be opened to you."** (Luke 11:9)

Peter told the crowd on the day of Pentecost, **"And everyone who calls on the name of the Lord will be saved."** (Acts 2:21)

James wrote, **"You do not have, because you do not ask God."** (James 4:3)

I do believe that we endure many things and do not see breakthrough because all we do is complain about the problem rather than cry out to God for the answer.

Stop whinging and start crying out to God today.

Charles

One Year Plan : Proverbs 3, Hebrews 10, Jeremiah 33 - 34
Two Year Plan : Psalm 107:23-32, Titus 3, Amos 4 (Yr 1)
Ezekiel 22 (Yr 2)

Destiny

In a particular African tribe, when a woman becomes pregnant, she is given space to hear **a song for her unborn child**. In fact, she is not allowed to re-join the village community until she has heard the song and sung it over and over to her unseen child. On returning to her people, she teaches the new song to those among whom the child, once born, will grow and develop.

At the point of birth, the women sit outside her hut and **sing the destiny of the child** who is in the very process of birth. It is the child's special song and becomes synonymous with his or her destiny. When correction is needed, the song is used to remind the child of who they are to become – the implication being that they are not behaving in line with their destiny!

You and I are not part of this tribe, but we are part of the Kingdom of God, and God has spoken both life and destiny into us. When Samson's birth was announced by the angel, the question was asked, **"What do you have to tell us about this boy and his work?"** (Judges 13:12) It is a good question to ask, especially if you are pregnant. John the Baptist's destiny was proclaimed by the angel to Zechariah and Elizabeth.

It is never too late to ask the question about destiny – for yourself and those you love and care for. All the promises of God are **"Yes and Amen in Christ Jesus"** so everything promised to God's children is part of your inheritance. Ask God to tell you what special purpose He had in mind when He created you. Ask Him to tell you about the unique things about you that He delights in.

God the Father went to such lengths to re-establish relationship with you. He values you, and He has parts of His plan for mankind that require your co-operation. As you understand what He has called you to be, you will be delighted to know that **He has marked out His special path** for your journey.

Joyce

One Year Plan : Proverbs 4, Hebrews 11, Jeremiah 35 - 36
Two Year Plan : Psalm 107:33-43, Philemon 1, Amos 5 (Yr 1)
Ezekiel 23 (Yr 2)

Songs of Joy

Whilst reading Psalm 126, I was struck by the phrase **"songs of joy"** which appears three times. God's people had just returned from the captivity in Babylon after years of being enslaved in a foreign land, and their joy was amazing. It says in verse 2, **"Our mouths were filled with laughter, our tongues with songs of joy."**

In Isaiah 52:9 it says, **"Burst into songs of joy you ruins of Jerusalem, for the Lord has comforted his people, he has redeemed Jerusalem."**

I have been looking at all the scriptures that include this phrase, and it seems to me that **"songs of joy"** are a response to the victory that comes after experiencing extreme trials.

In Psalm 137, God's people couldn't sing such songs: **"Our captors asked us for songs, our tormentors demanded songs of joy; they said, 'Sing us one of the songs of Zion!'"** To which they replied, **"How can we sing the songs of the Lord while in a foreign land?"**

Psalm 126:5-6 says, **"Those who sow in tears will reap with songs of joy. He who goes out weeping carrying seed to sow will return with songs of joy, carrying sheaves with him."**

If you have been sowing with tears, praying into seemingly impossible situations, the promise is that you will reap with **"songs of joy"**. If it seems that you have been living in captivity, feeling trapped by your situation, you are promised freedom when there will be laughter and **"songs of joy"**.

Don't remain a captive or think that all the seeds you have sown will never result in a harvest. **Wait and expect that your sorrow will turn into "songs of joy"**.

Charles

One Year Plan : Proverbs 5, Hebrews 12, Jeremiah 37 - 38
Two Year Plan : Psalm 108, Hebrews 1, Amos 6 (Yr 1)
Ezekiel 24 (Yr 2)

Kindness

Kindness makes headlines in today's society because of its rarity. God loves kindness and He himself is kind. Solomon made many of his subjects little more than slaves, labourers, conscripts in his building programme. When Rehoboam, his son, came to the throne, a large delegation came to him to beg a re-negotiation of their working conditions; they sought a lightening of the load and in return promised to serve the new king faithfully.

The older counsellors advised, **"Be kind, give them a favourable answer and they will always be your servants."** His power-conscious peers, lacking in experience and wisdom, advised even harsher conditions: **"Tell them, my father punished you with whips, I'll use scorpions."** His choice to be harsh rather than kind was not good and resulted in further division and hatred.

Do you value kindness? When given a choice, do you act wisely? – or do you harshly exercise your authority, when a kind word would get you a lot further than insisting or demanding what you feel is your right?

"Be kind and compassionate to one another, forgiving each other, just as in Christ God forgave you." (Ephesians 4:32)

"A kind-hearted woman gains respect, but ruthless men gain only wealth. A kind man benefits himself, but a cruel man brings trouble on himself." (Proverbs 11:16-17)

"Make sure that nobody pays back wrong for wrong, but always try to be kind to each other and to everyone else." (1 Thessalonians 5:15)

"Love is patient, love is kind, It does not envy, it does not boast, it is not proud ... It always protects, always trusts, always hopes, always perseveres." (1 Corinthians 13:4)

There is someone out there who needs to be shown kindness by you today.

Joyce

One Year Plan : Proverbs 6, Hebrews 13, Jeremiah 39 - 40
Two Year Plan : Psalm 109:1-15, Hebrews 2, Amos 7 (Yr 1)
Ezekiel 25 (Yr 2)

Peace is a Gift

We so often think of peace as the absence of conflict or the feeling we have when all the noise has stopped, everyone has gone to bed, and we can enjoy a few minutes of peace and quiet at the end of the day.

Jesus spoke of giving us a **gift of peace**, He said, **"Peace I leave with you; my peace I give you. I do not give you as the world gives. Do not let your hearts be troubled and do not be afraid."** (John 14:27) Jesus gives us peace because when we have placed our trust in Him we can have complete confidence that He will give us all that we need to handle our everyday lives.

Peter said, **"Cast all your cares on him for he cares for you."** (1 Peter 5:7) If Jesus is carrying all your cares and burdens, you can rest in peace. It seems illogical but it works. Worrying never solved anything; it only robs you of peace and drains you of strength.

When Paul was writing to the Philippians he said, **"Do not be anxious about anything, but in everything, by prayer and petition, with thanksgiving, present your requests to God. And the peace of God which transcends all understanding will guard your hearts and your minds in Christ Jesus."** (Philippians 4:6-7) Notice in these verses, that Paul does not say anything about the answer to your prayer and petition; he simply says that having given your problem to Jesus, **you will be given peace** for both heart and mind.

When your heart is at peace, knowing that your life situation has been placed into the hands of Jesus, faith rises and you know that God is in control and will meet you at your point of need.

John expressed it this way: **"This is the confidence we have in approaching God: that if we ask anything according to his will, he hears us. And if we know that he hears us – whatever we ask – we know that we have what we asked of him."** (1 John 5:14-15)

Receive this gift of peace today – and enter a new way of living.

Charles

One Year Plan : Proverbs 7, Luke 1, Jeremiah 41 - 42
Two Year Plan : Psalm 109:16-31, Hebrews 3, Amos 8 (Yr 1)
Ezekiel 26 (Yr 2)

It's Harvest Time!

I went to bed, woke sometime in the small hours and spent time downstairs with the Lord, praying and reading. I follow the Bible Reading Plan included in this book. As I began reading I was thinking, **"I'm sure I've read this recently."** It then dawned on me... It was a new day; I was reading what I had read twenty four hours earlier. Then the Lord said to me, **"It is a new day, a new season for reaping. <u>It's harvest time</u>! It's not yesterday; it's not familiar; it's new!"**

I began to read what Jesus says about **harvest time**.

- He says, **"Look the harvest is white, it's ready, it's there; ask for eyes to see it."**
- He says, **"The people are lost sheep, no shepherd to protect, lead and provide for them; they wander aimlessly into danger."**

Ask for a compassionate heart. If you have ever been lost, remember the helplessness and the longing you had for someone to help.

- He says, **"Pray the Lord of the harvest to send reapers."** I want to be part of a **combine harvester** working with others to love and reach out to all those we come into contact with.
- You are part of the reaping; others may have sown the seed many years ago. Maybe it has lain dormant, but in this present climate of uncertainty and need it has germinated and is ripening.
- He says, **"Don't worry about what to say or how to say it – you will not be speaking, but it will be the Spirit of the Father speaking through you."**
- Keep believing; if God declares it is **harvest time** He can see the whole world, He can hear the cry of every human heart and intends to make Himself known.

Pray: Let me be part of this <u>harvest time</u>.

Joyce

One Year Plan : Proverbs 8, Luke 2, Jeremiah 43 - 44
Two Year Plan : Psalm 110, Hebrews 4, Amos 9 (Yr 1)
Ezekiel 27 (Yr 2)

A Spring of Water

How would you describe what happened to you when you came to personal faith in Jesus?

Perhaps you might say, **"My sins were forgiven,"** or, **"When I gave my life to Jesus, He gave me peace."** Some might add, **"I knew that God was my Father and that I was safe in His care and love."** For others it may have been, **"My guilt was gone, and I felt really clean for the first time in my life."**

All those statements are wonderful and true, and if they describe your own experience, that's fantastic. However, looking at the account in John 4 when Jesus had that remarkable encounter with a woman at a well, another quality of God's salvation appears.

Jesus, who sat beside the well with no visible means of drawing water declared, **"If you knew the gift of God and who it is that asks you for a drink, you would have asked him and he would have given you living water."**

An amazing conversation follows in which Jesus reveals the life secrets of this very sinful and disreputable woman. The intention is not to condemn but to forgive and to introduce her to a supernatural resource.

Jesus continues, **"Everyone who drinks this water will be thirsty again, but whoever drinks the water I give him will never thirst, indeed, the water I give him will become in him a spring of water welling up to eternal life."**

If you have come to a living faith in Jesus and received His salvation, you have a spring of water inside of you.

It's a spring of cleansing; it's a spring of healing; it's a spring of supernatural strength; it's a spring that will never run dry and will supply your needs on a daily basis. Your coming to faith in Jesus is not merely an historic event; it is the opening up of a fountain within.

So today draw refreshment and resources from that spring of living water.

Charles

One Year Plan : Proverbs 9, Luke 3, Jeremiah 45 - 46
Two Year Plan : Psalm 111, Hebrews 5, Hosea 1 (Yr 1)
Ezekiel 28 (Yr 2)

How do we treat Jesus?

When Saul encountered Jesus on the Damascus Road, he was asked a question – **"Why are you persecuting me?"** – to which he replied, **"Who are you Lord?"** The answer that came was **"I am Jesus."**

Saul thought he was persecuting men and women but they were containers of the risen Christ, and when Jesus appeared to Saul, He was making it very clear that He lived in each of these believers. Therefore, the way Saul treated them, in reality, was the way he was treating Jesus.

Suddenly the scales were taken off his eyes and understanding came, his life was transformed, and from that time on he preached the resurrected Christ living in men and women.

So, how do I treat Jesus? How do I speak to fellow believers? How do I serve them? Support them? Honour them? Help them? How can we say we love God whom we have not seen unless we love the brother/sister who we have seen – and in whom Jesus lives.

1 John 4:19-20 in the Message says, **"If anyone boasts, 'I love God,' and goes right on hating his brother or sister, thinking nothing of it, he is a liar. If he won't love the person he can see, how can he love the God he can't see?"**

A minister friend of ours was at one time seeking to share this lesson. One Sunday he arrived in church dressed like a tramp – unshaven, in filthy clothes – and sat in the front pew munching sandwiches. No one in this fairly respectable congregation knew what to do so they ignored him and watched from a distance. Imagine their horror and surprise when he got up, climbed into the pulpit and began to address them. They instantly recognised the voice of their own pastor, and as he removed the heavy coat and hat, they saw who it was. They had ignored him, distancing themselves through fear and the outward packaging – **and in so doing had in reality done the same to Jesus.**

Joyce

One Year Plan : Proverbs 10, Luke 4, Jeremiah 47 - 48
Two Year Plan : Psalm 112, Hebrews 6, Hosea 2 (Yr 1)
Ezekiel 29 (Yr 2)

Hungry and Thirsty

There is a striking sentence in Mary's song in Luke 1:53 which says, **"He has filled the hungry with good things but has sent the rich away empty."** These words came to me strongly as Joyce and I were driving home after having spent a morning praying with folk in a nearby village.

Over several weeks we had been teaching about the gifts of the Spirit and the power of God. At the end of this series of meetings it was suggested that we made a time available on a future Saturday morning for personal prayer. When we gathered, there was a real sense of peace and anticipation. A steady stream of people came to receive prayer. It was wonderful. Many were filled with the Holy Spirit and released into speaking in tongues; others received healing and freedom; and God also spoke words of wisdom into many hearts. They came hungry and thirsty and left satisfied.

Jesus said to the crowds on that last day of the feast: **"If anyone is thirsty, let him come to me and drink. Whoever believes in me, as the Scripture has said, streams of living water will flow from within him."** (John 7:37-38) I do believe that our lack of receiving often happens because we lack hunger and thirst. On that Saturday morning we were amazed at such openness and longing to receive all the good things that God has in store for His people.

In the Sermon on the Mount Jesus said, **"Blessed are those who hunger and thirst for righteousness for they shall be filled."** (Matthew 5:6) It is so easy to become passive, to accept circumstances which surround our lives and undermine our strength, without going to God who longs to be gracious to us.

Are you hungry for more of God? Are you thirsty for more of His power?

He will meet your need for **"He satisfies the thirsty and fills the hungry with good things."** (Psalm 107:9)

Charles

One Year Plan : Proverbs 11, Luke 5, Jeremiah 49 - 50
Two Year Plan : Psalm 113, Hebrews 7, Hosea 3-4 (Yr 1)
Ezekiel 30 (Yr 2)

God Wants to Serve You!

What is your reaction if I suggest that God wants to serve you? To some people the suggestion is almost akin to blasphemy – repugnant and to be rejected!

Certainly that is how Peter responded when Jesus wanted to wash his feet. He could not conceive of the Christ, the Messiah, God in human form, serving him in such a way – and said so. Jesus, however, insisted that He must do this for Peter: **"Unless I wash you, you have no part with me."** (John 13:8) Peter had to learn to receive in order to be part of Jesus. Even after he had agreed he still wanted to dictate the terms: **"Wash all of me!"**

Jesus knows what to do; we simply need to let Him. The Apostle Paul had to be rendered blind and helpless in order to receive from Jesus but later wrote in Romans 5:6, **"You see, at just the right time, when we were still powerless, Christ died for the ungodly."**

God the Father saw our condition and sent a Saviour whose work becomes personally effective only when we receive Him: **God serving mankind.** Without Him you and I can do nothing; the Holy Spirit always comes alongside to help. God is a present help in times of trouble.

If you cannot receive His help and resources then you are operating out of self-effort, which is not only futile and achieves nothing but you are also in danger of missing a blessing! Jeremiah writes that **the man who trusts in himself is cursed, but the man who trusts God is blessed.** (Jeremiah 17:5-8)

If you have ever tried to dress a struggling, wilful child, you'll know how exhausting it can be and in contrast what a pleasure it is to change a child who lets you serve him!

Jesus, who served a wedding by providing the guests with wine, loves to serve his children and turn sorrow into joy!

Be childlike today, and ask for God to serve you in your time of need!

Joyce

One Year Plan : Proverbs 12, Luke 6, Jeremiah 51 - 52
Two Year Plan : Psalm 114, Hebrews 8, Hosea 5 (Yr 1)
Ezekiel 31 (Yr 2)

Headspace

The term **headspace** has become a very familiar expression. There are times when our lives seem so full of stuff that when someone comes along with something else to tell us, we exclaim, **"Don't tell me another thing; I don't have any more headspace!"**

The Bible is full of references to the things that can fill our minds, both negative and positive. Jesus said, **"Take no thought for your life, what you shall eat or what you shall drink, or what you shall put on..."** (Matthew 6:25) Our lives can be so full of thinking of how to make ends meet that we lose sight of God who has promised to provide for us.

Paul says, **"Get rid of all bitterness, rage and anger..."** because he knows that if your head is filled with these things they will not only damage you but leave no room for what God intends.

In Philippians 4:8 we read, **"Whatever is true, whatever is noble, whatever is right, whatever is pure, whatever is lovely, whatever is admirable, excellent or praiseworthy – think about such things."** What a challenge to us when the media fills our minds daily with such negativity, uncleanness and things that exalt decadence.

Exodus 23:25-26 says, **"Worship the Lord your God, and his blessing will be on your food and water. I will take away sickness from among you, and none will miscarry or be barren in your land. I will give you a full life span."** What an amazing set of promises for the person who gives **headspace** to worshipping God.

Paul says, **"Don't let the world around you squeeze you into its mould, but let God remould your minds from within."** (Romans 12:2, J B Phillips)

Make sure that your **headspace** is filled with the right stuff.

Charles

One Year Plan : Proverbs 13, Luke 7, Lamentations 1 - 2
Two Year Plan : Psalm 115:1-11, Hebrews 9, Hosea 6 (Yr 1)
Ezekiel 32 (Yr 2)

From Sorrow to Joy

There are times when sorrow and pain threaten to overwhelm. Death, separation, and broken relationships all cause an inner pain, an agony intensified by loneliness and the sense that no-one understands.

Today, reflect on a loving Father God who has experienced all that you are going through and who understands. When Jesus took upon Himself the sin of the whole world, the unity of the Godhead was broken. Jesus' agonising cry, **"My God my God, why have you forsaken me,"** reflects an inner anguish which seems greater than physical pain. For the first time the unity of the Godhead is broken, and Father, Son and Holy Spirit grieve at a depth we can only imagine. No wonder darkness covered the land as sin was atoned for.

However, this is not the end of the story but the beginning! This is the price paid so that we may have joy: a joy no-one can take away; a joy of connection with the Father, Son and Holy Spirit; a joy unspeakable and full of glory. This joy is supernatural and comes from connection with the Godhead. This joy can be experienced in the most desperate situations we face. We place ourselves in the arms of One who knows and understands, who promises to heal broken hearts, to walk us through the valley of the shadow of death, and who gives resources that comfort and strengthen, whilst we walk out of whatever has tried to overwhelm and destroy.

Jesus spoke to His disciples just before He went to the cross and said, **"Now is your time of grief, but I will see you again and you will rejoice, and no one will take away your joy."** (John 16:22)

If you are hurting today, ask for supernatural joy to give you strength. He has promised **never to leave you nor forsake you.**

If you have come through to joy, ponder the enormity of the price paid by Jesus and the Godhead to make this joy available to you.

Joyce

One Year Plan : Proverbs 14, Luke 8, Lamentations 3
Two Year Plan : Psalm 115:12-18, Hebrews 10, Hosea 7 (Yr 1)
Ezekiel 33 (Yr 2)

Flood Protection

There seem to be increasing incidents of devastating floods, killing and displacing whole communities. Our hearts go out to all who have been flooded. We who are dry and secure would all want to give practical help to those who are suffering.

As I was thinking about this and praying for those who are suffering, I thought about the other kinds of floods that can overwhelm our lives. Floods of fear, anxiety and discouragement are just as real as the wet stuff, but they may well be unseen.

However, God is well able to handle floods. King David, who had his fair share of 'floods' wrote these words: **"Therefore let everyone who is godly pray to you while you may be found; surely when the mighty waters rise, they will not reach him. You are my hiding place; you will protect me from trouble and surround me with songs of deliverance."** (Psalm 32:6-7)

Are the flood waters rising in your life today? There is a hiding place where the mighty waters will not reach you. The instructions given are for you to pray to God who will prevent the waters rising so high that they overwhelm you, and you also will be surrounded with songs of deliverance.

I have found that in times of need, when the flood waters have been rising in my life, God brings a song to mind that exactly fits the circumstances. It could be a contemporary song such as **'Mighty is our God'** or an old favourite like **'Great is Thy faithfulness'**. I am amazed at the songs of deliverance that God brings to mind in times of need, often 'golden oldies' or a song from a brand new album. They are God's way of lifting the load and stopping the flood.

God knows your need, and as you pray He will protect you, prevent the floods overwhelming you, **and give you a "song of deliverance."**

Charles

One Year Plan : Proverbs 15, Luke 9, Lamentations 4 - 5
Two Year Plan : Psalm 116:1-11, Hebrews 11, Hosea 8 (Yr 1)
Ezekiel 34 (Yr 2)

What is Overflowing?

I woke up very early and took my MP3 Player to check some recordings I had made during our stay in Central Asia. Whilst there, we had produced weekly reports, recording incidents and impressions. At the beginning of the first recording I had pressed the record button without realising it; Charles had been trying to explain a technical point to me to which I responded very sharply – and it was all recorded! I quickly repented and asked him to forgive me for the times when I have been quick to react to correction. I am glad to report that I was immediately and unreservedly forgiven! Phew!

However, this led me to think about a verse in Luke 6:45 which states that **"out of the overflow of the heart the mouth speaks."** I then began to think about overflow.

There are many verses that speak about this:

Psalm 119:171 speaks of **overflowing with praise**.

Romans 15:13 speaks of **overflowing with hope**.

2 Corinthians 4:15 speaks of **overflowing with thanksgiving**.

1 Thessalonians 3:12 speaks of **overflowing with love**.

The verse that challenged me the most was Romans 5:15: **"...how much more did God's grace and the gift that came by the grace of the one man, Jesus Christ, overflow to the many!"**

I want to be so full of Jesus, that the overflow is **Jesus Himself** meeting whatever need presents itself. Isn't that what Jesus was like – so full of His Father God that He overflowed with heavenly life and resources in every encounter?

When Paul says, **"Be filled with the Spirit,"** his intention is that we will be filled and filled and continually filled so that we can at all times **overflow.**

Joyce

One Year Plan : Psalm 73, Luke 10, 1 Kings 11 - 12
Two Year Plan : Psalm 116:12-19, Hebrews 12, Hosea 9 (Yr 1)
Ezekiel 35 (Yr 2)

Choosing the Right Name

Did you know that names have meanings and can affect destiny? One woman in the Bible had such a difficult experience in childbirth that she named the baby Jabez which means pain!

Joseph, on the other hand, knew the power of giving his children the right names. He had spent thirteen years in Egypt, separated from his family and under great pressure and hardship. But now, having interpreted Pharaoh's dream, life had changed dramatically and he had been promoted to become Prime Minister of Egypt. Sometimes it is easier to maintain faith in God under pressure than when things are going well.

Joseph had that challenge. After all the years of hardship, he was now in a place of privilege and power. When Pharaoh gave him a wife and an Egyptian name, Zathenath-Paneah, he could so easily have been absorbed into Egyptian society. However, he knew his roots, his heritage and his destiny. When two sons were born to Joseph by Asenath he gave them Hebrew names that were full of meaning and helped to keep his heart and vision focussed.

Genesis 41:51-52 says, **"Joseph named his firstborn Manasseh and said, "It is because God has made me forget all my trouble and my father's household." The second son he named Ephraim and said, "It is because God has made me fruitful in the land of my suffering."**

In order to go forward with purpose and energy, Joseph needed to deliberately have forgiven his brothers (who had sold him into slavery), Potiphar's wife (who had wrongly accused him and had had him thrown in jail), and the butler (who had forgotten to recommend his early release and had left him languishing in the prison for another two years). Every time he looked at Manasseh he knew his spirit was free of past hurts. When he looked at Ephraim he was filled with thankfulness for God's blessing and the way his life had so dramatically changed.

Surround your life with things that strengthen faith and keep you focussed on your destiny.

Charles

One Year Plan : Psalm 74, Luke 11, 1 Kings 13 - 14
Two Year Plan : Psalm 117, Hebrews 13, Hosea 10 (Yr 1)
Ezekiel 36 (Yr 2)

Baby Christians?

At a Conference we had been taking, we were singing an old hymn: *"Immortal, invisible, God only wise..."* – great words. The theme of our teaching had been about "Christ in you – the hope of glory", and as the young pastor turned and looked in my direction, I mouthed, **"This is who lives in you: the Son of the living God, the One who is 'Almighty, Victorious, whose Great Name we praise.'"**

It almost seemed blasphemous – but that is what the New Testament teaches: God himself lives in me. **"I no longer live, but Christ lives in me. The life I live in the body, I live by faith in the Son of God, who loved me and gave himself for me."** Wow! Wow! Wow! (Galatians 2:20)

I've often wondered why some believers seem to have the label **"baby Christian"** when they have been born again for years. Others seem to have matured quickly like Paul: saved, baptised, preaching Jesus within such a short space of time. I believe is has to do with understanding who came to live inside of you when you received new birth. It wasn't **Baby Jesus** who had to grow inside you – rather you received the resurrected **Lord of glory!**

However, if you have not truly died and been resurrected into the new life Jesus spoke about to Nicodemus, it is possible that there is so much of you still in action and so little of Jesus to be seen that people can still call you a **baby Christian.**

The **Jesus** who lived in Paul lives in you. The **Jesus** who lived in Stephen, in Dorcas, in Aquila and Priscilla, lives in you and me! Not just some half-hearted influence for good, but a living person – **Jesus** – the resurrected God-Man of the Trinity. It is beyond our understanding, but it needs to be revealed **and then we will let Him live and be glad to die daily.**

Joyce

One Year Plan : Psalm 75, Luke 12, 1 Kings 15 - 16
Two Year Plan : Psalm 118:1-14, John 1:1-28, Hosea 11-12 (Yr 1)
Ezekiel 37 (Yr 2)

OCTOBER

Fathers and Sons

Despite having read the book of Proverbs many times, it is only recently that I have noticed that the first eight chapters are almost entirely spoken by a father giving instruction to his sons.

God has given fathers a particular responsibility in giving instruction and training to their sons; they have a unique influence in the lives of their sons, and it does not end when they leave home. I have three sons, they are all married and two of them live abroad; however I consider my father/son chats to be very important. I also count it a privilege when they contact me to ask for advice and wisdom.

So start reading these chapters in Proverbs in their right context – fathers speaking to their sons:

- **Proverbs 1:10-19** gives warning against getting into bad company and becoming involved in poor financial arrangements.
- **Proverbs 1:20-23** speaks of the importance of being able to respond to a rebuke and being able to receive words of wisdom.
- **Proverbs 2:1-8** tells of the power of integrity and the blessings of living an upright life.
- **Proverbs 2:9-22** speaks of the power of wisdom to keep you from being influenced by wicked people and protected from immorality
- **Proverbs 3** contains two of the most well-known verses in the Bible: **"Trust in the Lord with all your heart and lean not on your own understanding; in all your ways acknowledge him and he will make your paths straight."** Words that are directing sons to trust God in all circumstances so that they can walk on a straight path.
- **Proverbs 4** extols the supreme value of words of wisdom: **"...for they are life to those who find them and health to a man's whole body"**.
- **Proverbs 5** warns against adultery. Fathers, you have the ability to warn your sons about the dangers and stupidity of a promiscuous life and the blessings of faithfulness to their wives.
- **Proverbs 6 & 7** warn against folly and getting trapped by foolish words and agreements, and again against adultery.
- **Proverbs 8** speaks again of wisdom and concludes with these words: **"For whoever finds me [that is, wisdom] finds life and receives favour from the Lord. But whoever fails to find me harms himself; and all who hate me love death."**

Charles

One Year Plan : Psalm 76, Luke 13, 1 Kings 17 - 18
Two Year Plan : Psalm 118:15-29, John 1:29-51, Hosea 13 (Yr 1) Ezekiel 38 (Yr 2)

Ash Heap

The Bible uses the words **'ash heap'** to symbolise a place of utter despair and helplessness; a place where there seems no solution, no hope, only a sense of desolation and abandonment. This was the place Hannah found herself in; unable to bear children, mocked and taunted by her husband's other wife, unable to eat because of sadness and anguish. Even the love of her husband and his gentleness towards her couldn't comfort or bring relief.

Hannah did something that scripture also encourages us to do: she ran to God, poured out her anguish and cried until she had no tears left. It was at this point that Eli the high priest observed her distress but mistakenly thought she was drunk and was about ready to rebuke her and expel her from the sanctuary. However, once Eli had listened to her plight, he proclaimed that God had heard her cry, would grant her request and would change her situation.

God answered Hannah's prayer, and her song of thankfulness and rejoicing is recorded for us in 1 Samuel 2:8 where she declares, **"...he lifts the needy from the ash heap."**

Paul comments on those who run to God when they are in the place of distress and despair, rather than run away. In 2 Corinthians 7:10 in the Message it says, **"Distress that drives us to God turns us around. It gets us back in the way of salvation. We never regret that kind of pain. But those who let distress drive them away from God are full of regrets, end up on a deathbed of regrets."**

Today, if you are hurting and are sitting on an **ash heap**, go before God, pour out your heart, tell Him everything and hide nothing. Let Him give you peace, then direction and hope. Don't let distress drive you away from God... There is no way you want to end up on a **"deathbed of regrets"** and bitterness.

Joyce

One Year Plan : Psalm 77, Luke 14, 1 Kings 19 – 20
Two Year Plan : Psalm 119:1-8, John 2, Hosea 14 (Yr 1)
Ezekiel 39 (Yr 2)

Overflowing with Thankfulness

Paul used a phrase **"overflowing with thankfulness"** when he was giving words of encouragement and instruction to the believers in Colossae. (Colossians 2:7)

We all know that it is good to be **thankful**, but what is all this about **overflowing**? Overflowing can be good and bad. When the washing machine overflows and deposits all its contents on the floor, that is bad. However, when we see a fruit bowl which is so full that the grapes are hanging over the side, we like that kind of **overflowing**. It speaks of abundance and generosity.

God's love and His blessings on our lives are generous and more than we deserve. David writes in Psalm 23:5-6: **"You anoint my head with oil; my cup overflows. Surely goodness and mercy will follow me all the days of my life."** It was not that everything in David's life had been smooth and plain sailing, but he recognised that in all of life God had been more than generous to him, so he could boldly say, **"My cup overflows."**

Because God has been so loving and generous to me, I want to live a life that overflows. Today I am thanking Him for all His blessings on my life. He is my provider, my strength, my wisdom, and my healer, which means I can **overflow with thankfulness.**

In Psalm 119:171 it says, **"May my lips overflow with praise, for you teach me your decrees."** When we live overflowing, it impacts every area of life and all the words that we speak.

There is an amazing verse in 2 Corinthians 8:2: **"In the midst of a very severe trial, their overflowing joy and their extreme poverty welled up in rich generosity."**

Whatever is going on in your life today, be an overflowing person – overflow with thankfulness, praise and joy.

Charles

One Year Plan : Psalm 78, Luke 15, 1 Kings 21 – 22
Two Year Plan : Psalm 119:9-16, John 3:1-21, Judges 1 (Yr 1)
Ezekiel 40 (Yr 2)

Prayer Works

I love Paul's prayers as recorded in his letters to the Thessalonians and Timothy. It makes an interesting Bible Study to search them out and meditate on their content. Here are some of them:

2 Thessalonians 1:11-12 (The Message) says, **"We pray for you all the time - pray that our God will make you fit for what he's called you to be, pray that he will fill your good ideas and acts of faith with his own energy so that it all amounts to something."**

2 Thessalonians 2:15-17 (The Message) says, **"May Jesus himself and God our Father, who reached out in love and surprised you with gifts of unending help and confidence, put a fresh heart in you, invigorate your work, enliven your speech."**

2 Timothy 2:21 (The Message) says, **"Become the kind of container God can use to present any and every kind of gift to his guests for their blessing."**

I marvel at Paul's creativity as he prays for fresh heart, invigoration, energy and divine help. This is prayer that calls down heavenly resources to give us all we need to become all that He designed us to be; not self-effort but rather God-reliance.

Today as I echo these prayers for you, take time to pray fresh heart, God's energy, fitness, and lively speech for those you love and care for, and pray for yourself that all these things will be happening in you too!

Joyce

One Year Plan : Psalm 79, Luke 16, 2 Kings 1 - 2
Two Year Plan : Psalm 119:17-24, John 3:22-36, Judges 2 (Yr 1)
Ezekiel 41 (Yr 2)

The Fruit of the Spirit

When in Italy on a ministry trip, I was given a book **'The Paraclete'** by W. R. Thomas. The author was a pioneer sent from Wales in the 1930's to evangelise and plant Apostolic Churches all over Italy. He died many years ago, but we have come to know some of his children – Andrew, Beryl and Joan – who are still actively involved in the work. The book was written around 1960 in Italian, and only in recent years, through the dedicated work of another daughter, Violetta, has this book been available in English.

The Paraclete is an old-fashioned word for The Holy Spirit as Comforter, Counsellor, Friend and Helper. This book shows that W.R. Thomas had a great depth of insight into the work and the power of the Spirit.

In the chapter on the **Fruit of the Spirit** he has a very interesting understanding. He writes:*

Love, Joy and Peace speak of our relationship with God.

Patience, Kindness and Goodness speak of our relationship to the people around us.

Faithfulness, Gentleness and Self-control speak of our relationship to ourselves.

I have found this to be very challenging.

When the fruit of the Holy Spirit is being seen in me, my heart will be filled with love towards God and people, I will carry around an atmosphere of joy, God's peace will fill my heart, and others will be conscious of that peace.

In my relationship with people, they will see that I act towards them with patience, kindness, and that I can be relied upon to make good decisions and always seek their good.

God's Spirit flowing into my life will build character in me, so that I am known for my faithfulness and gentleness, and even when I am in stressful situations the Holy Spirit will enable me to have self-control.

I do not claim to always act in the way I have just suggested! However, I am challenged and stirred as I have meditated upon this insight.

Fruit is always for others to pick. The apple tree does not consume its own fruit.

What fruit is being picked from your life?

Charles

One Year Plan : Psalm 80, Luke 17, 2 Kings 3 - 4
Two Year Plan : Psalm 119:25-32, John 4:1-26, Judges 3 (Yr 1)
Ezekiel 42 (Yr 2)

Jesus... at the Wheel

Jesus doesn't want back seat drivers – He wants to lead. Luke 9:23-24 in The Message says, **"Anyone who intends to come with me has to let me lead. You're not in the driving seat – I am."** He continues, **"Self-help is no help at all. Self-sacrifice is the way, my way, to finding your true self."**

Are you ready to let Jesus control the direction of your life? If not, why not? Don't you believe He has your best interests in His heart, or are you expecting Him to make life difficult?

I talk to people who have heard what Jesus is offering them – forgiveness for the past, a new beginning, a unique friendship with the Godhead, and so much more – yet they fail to enter into the family of God, the Kingdom ruled by Jesus, because they fear losing control of their own sovereignty.

God's word says, **"If God is for us, who can be against us?" "He longs to be gracious to you."** He neither treats us as our sins deserve, nor how we would treat ourselves. He is love and always desires the best for each individual. Yes, He corrects and trains us, but He is not into recrimination and fault-finding. He wants us to live a life of joy and freedom in fellowship with Him and set us on a journey that will last forever – moving eventually from earth to heaven.

Who makes you afraid? Who distorts God's image and motives? Who keeps you from experiencing all the joy God has planned for you? It is our enemy the devil, the deceiver who is still at work – his tactics haven't changed. He deceived Eve into doubting God's intentions towards her, tricking her out of her wonderful intimacy and trust in God, and he is trying to do the same to you and me. We were designed for connection with God, and without Him we do not function well.

So today, move over and let Him take control. He knows the way, and your journey will be unique, amazing – just what you have always longed for!

Joyce

One Year Plan : Psalm 81, Luke 18, 2 Kings 5 - 6
Two Year Plan : Psalm 119:33-40, John 4:27-54, Judges 4 (Yr 1)
Ezekiel 43 (Yr 2)

The Moment you Begin to Pray

Daniel was living in Babylon, in a pagan society, and he was deeply concerned about the situation of God's people who were living in exile. He was crying out to God on their behalf and confessing his sins and those of the nation. In response God sent the angel Gabriel with a message for him.

This is what he said: **"The moment you began praying, a command was given. I am here to tell you what it was, for God loves you very much."** (Daniel 9:23, New Living Translation)

As I read this, I realised that there is a vital principle contained in these words. It is so possible when we are under pressure, to only worry and fret; perhaps we will tell our woes to a friend, or we might even have a complaining session with the Almighty.

Something powerful happens **the moment you begin to pray**. This verse states that at that **moment** a command was given. When you pray, a command is given in heaven concerning your situation. You may not receive your answer immediately, but the command has been given. You may not immediately know what that command is, but it means that God is on your case – for good and not for evil – because He loves you very much.

Paul says the same thing: **"Don't worry about anything; instead, pray about everything."** (Philippians 4:6)

What are you doing about your situation at this moment? Are you worrying; are you fretting; are you stressed?

Paul goes on to say, **"Tell God what you need, and thank him for all he has done. If you do this you will experience God's peace, which is far more wonderful than the human mind can understand."** (Philippians 4:6-7, NLT)

Never forget that something amazing happens **the moment you begin to pray.**

Charles

One Year Plan : Psalm 82, Luke 19, 2 Kings 7 - 8
Two Year Plan : Psalm 119:41-48, John 5:1-23, Judges 5 (Yr 1)
Ezekiel 44 (Yr 2)

Life-Giving Words

Deuteronomy 8:3 declares, **"Man shall not live by bread alone, but by every word that proceeds from the mouth of God."** Bread sustains but does not give life. Living Words from God release life and shape all we do and are.

Jesus lived and modelled abundant life, fullness of joy and stress-free living, and dealt with individuals and crowds with love and compassion. He confronted sinful attitudes and actions with straight-forwardness, saying what was needed to bring correction but also showing the way forward. I constantly marvel at His wisdom and composure. He reveals the secret as He declares, **"I and the Father are one"; "I only do what the Father tells me to do"; "I only say what the Father has told me to say."** Even **how** He says what the Father has revealed is crafted by divine instruction. Words have the power to build up or destroy; the tone is important so that the hearer can receive what is being said.

If you have travelled by air, you will be familiar with the safety instructions given each time; they go something like this: **"In the event of a loss of cabin pressure, oxygen masks will be released. Put your own on first before helping others with theirs."** Obedience to these words will ensure you are kept alive in an alien atmosphere.

Our natural world is an alien atmosphere spiritually – but we have access to words which are life-giving. In 1 Samuel 3:21 it says, **"The Lord continued to appear at Shiloh, and there he revealed himself to Samuel through his word."** When Samuel was very young he had learned how to tune into God's voice, and it remained a key principle of his life. He may have had access to the Books of Moses, but it is more than possible that he learned to hear from God **"face to face"** as Moses had – **"as a man speaks with his friend."** (Exodus 33:11)

Are you expecting to receive **life-giving words**? Do you need practical wisdom? Do you expect to receive instructions for your own life? When was the last time God spoke to you specifically? Are you listening or have you given up?

Joyce

One Year Plan : Psalm 83, Luke 20, 2 Kings 9 - 10
Two Year Plan : Psalm 119:49-56, John 5:24-47, Judges 6 (Yr 1)
Ezekiel 45 (Yr 2)

The God of All Comfort

There is great sadness and finality in death. I had recently been closely involved with two deaths. My aunt, who was 85 years old, died in California, and I was privileged to be able to go and love and support my family. Upon my return from the States, I attended the funeral service of a six-year-old who died in tragic circumstances. I went to support the family and the grandmother in particular, who is a member of our church.

As I was pondering these two events, the words written by St. Paul came strongly to mind: **"...the God of all comfort who comforts us in all our troubles..."** (2 Corinthians 1:3-4)

The word **'all'** was what struck me: the God of **all** comfort – who comforts us in **all** our troubles.

The circumstances of these two deaths was very different. For one it was the end of a long life; for the other, a life prematurely brought to an end. In both situations the families and friends are grieving.

For each of these families there are those who are being sustained and strengthened by **the God of all comfort**. How does this happen?

In 1 Thessalonians 4:13, Paul writes, **"Brothers, we do not want you to be ignorant about those who fall asleep [die], or to grieve like the rest of men who have no hope."** Those who have a living faith in Jesus know that death is not the end but that we will be reunited with our loved ones in heaven.

In Isaiah 53:4 it says, **"Surely he has born our griefs, and carried our sorrows."** When Jesus died on the cross He not only paid the price for our sins, He broke the power of grief.

There are many situations which will bring sadness and grief into our lives. However, those who know and love Jesus can experience the reality today of receiving comfort from **the God of all comfort.**

Charles

One Year Plan : Psalm 84, Luke 21, 2 Kings 11 - 12
Two Year Plan : Psalm 119:57-64, John 6:1-24, Judges 7 (Yr 1) Ezekiel 46 (Yr 2)

Stress or Rest?

You couldn't have two more extremes – let me define them:

Stress – is a mental or physical reaction to threats and the pressure of life, with assaults on mind and emotions. It will leave you drained of energy and with a sense of purposelessness.

Rest – is to be surrounded by peace, without fear of external threat or pressure, with an internal harmony and freedom from strife or foreboding.

God promised His Old Testament people **"a place of rest"** which encompassed the external and internal – a land of their own characterised as **"flowing with milk and honey"** and internal peace as they walked with Him. Rest and wellbeing came and went in direct proportion to their willingness to obey and follow God.

Ultimately Jesus brings true rest, through salvation which leads to forgiveness and peace – a knowledge that living in you, loving and caring for you at all times, is the One who knows everything about the now and the future. Because He is **peace** you too can **rest**.

Tell Jesus you want to know what **rest** is and that you do not want to be squeezed into today's **stress**-filled culture.

Hebrews 4:9 says, **"There remains, then a Sabbath-rest for the people of God; for anyone who enters God's rest also rests from his own work, just as God did from his."**

Rest is possible; it's wonderful and a rare commodity in our society. All those who walk with Jesus have been promised this **rest**.

Charles

One Year Plan : Psalm 85, Luke 22, 2 Kings 13 - 14
Two Year Plan : Psalm 119:65-72, John 6:25-59, Judges 8 (Yr 1)
Ezekiel 47 (Yr 2)

Catch the Wind

Some years ago we met a wonderful elderly couple. Both of them had previously been widowed, but they had met each other and decided to marry. They were in their late seventies and flew off to Mauritius for their honeymoon. The hotel owned a fleet of catamarans and one of the highlights of the week was a sailing race.

The husband of our elderly couple was an expert sailor, although his best sailing days had long gone, and his new wife had never sailed! The rest of the competitors were bronzed youths who were relishing the contest.

While the youthful competitors muscled their boats into the water and headed towards the first marker buoy, our couple quietly eased their craft into the sea. Everyone thought they were just going to calmly follow the flotilla of boats, but the experience of years was put into action, and little by little they overhauled the whole fleet and were back on the beach a full ten minutes before the first of the 'young bloods' breathlessly arrived.

"How did you do it?" was the question on everyone's lips. **"Well, it is very simple,"** came the reply. **"You have to learn how to catch the wind."**

Jesus said, **"The wind blows wherever it pleases. You hear its sound, but you cannot tell where it comes from or where it is going. So it is with everyone who is born of the Spirit."** (John 3:8)

The wind of the Holy Spirit is always blowing, providing power and direction for every situation of life. If we will tap into God's power source we can **catch the wind** and let it be the power source of our lives. Or, like the bronzed youths in our story did, we can rely on our own strength and wisdom, wear ourselves out and still **lose the race**.

Charles

One Year Plan : Psalm 86, Luke 23, 2 Kings 15 - 16
Two Year Plan : Psalm 119:73-80, John 6:60-71, Judges 9 (Yr 1) Ezekiel 48 (Yr 2)

Focussed or Frazzled?

Being a practical, hardworking person, I've always had a great deal of sympathy for Martha and wondered if Mary was not a bit work-shy. In His teaching Jesus emphasised the need for us to serve each other and that **"whosoever would be first among you, shall be servant of all."** So He must have been addressing a deeper issue when He visited the home of Mary and Martha – an issue of the heart.

Martha was hassled, distracted and frazzled – not knowing where she was or what she wanted. I once heard someone comment that Martha was making sandwiches Jesus hadn't ordered! Mary was focussed – with a single purpose and aim. She had picked up on Jesus' heart's desire which was to have her company. It is this focus, I believe, that Jesus is addressing when He says, **"Martha, Martha, you are worried and upset about many things, but only one thing is needed. Mary has chosen what is better, and it will not be taken away from her."** (Luke 10:41-42)

Mark 3:14 tells of how Jesus appointed the twelve **"to be with him."** He also said that eternal life is **"...that they may know you, the only true God and Jesus Christ whom you have sent."** (John 17:3) Mary chose to give priority to focussing on Jesus, and for this He commends her.

Upon what are you focussed? Is it success? Reputation? Building popularity? Perfection?

Focus on Jesus, the Light of the World, and He will draw you into hidden dimensions of the Spirit, satisfy you and give you peace.

This is not a passive spirituality that is divorced from life issues; it is drawing Jesus into every part of life and into everything you are doing.

Joyce

One Year Plan : Psalm 87, Luke 24, 2 Kings 17
Two Year Plan : Psalm 119:81-88, John 7:1-24, Judges 10 (Yr 1)
Daniel 1 (Yr 2)

Dependant Faith

The Bible records accounts of both success and failure, strengths and weaknesses. I had been reading about King Joash and was greatly saddened as I read these words: **"Joash did what was right in the eyes of the Lord all the years of Jehoiada the priest."** (2 Chronicles 24:2) – but after Jehoiada died, his life went completely off track!

What kind of faith do you have? Is it a personal relationship with a God who is a friend, confidant and source of your strength? Or, are you living as a Christian only because of influence of others or peer pressure?

Dependant faith is very unreliable; your friends can let you down, your mentors can lose their focus. Even your church is not perfect, nor are its leaders. Each one of us needs a personal faith which is vitally connected to God.

The psalmist David writes, **"My soul finds rest in God alone; my salvation comes from him. He alone is my rock and my salvation; he is my fortress, I will never be shaken."** (Psalm 62:1-2)

Test yourself: can you say confidently and without hesitation, **"He is my fortress, I will never be shaken?"** If not, you need to spend time talking to God and asking Him to reveal Himself to you in a new, personal and powerful way.

Building a strong personal faith is one of the most important things you can do. A well-respected man of God, E. Stanley Jones, spoke these words as he was coming to the end of his life: **"The innermost strands are the strongest. I need no outer props to hold up my faith, for my faith holds me."** *

Take time today to build up your personal faith through reading the Bible, speaking to God and listening to Him, and also simply spending time quietly in His presence.

Charles

One Year Plan : Psalm 88, James 1, 2 Kings 18 - 19
Two Year Plan : Psalm 119:89-96, John 7:25-52, Judges 11 (Yr 1)
Daniel 2 (Yr 2)

Just Hold Me

Our granddaughter Alice was three years old, highly independent, wanting to do everything herself, and managing to hold her own with her older cousins... most of the time! As she was playing with the others outside, something happened, and Alice was upset and in tears. Her mum rescued her, checked for cuts and bruises, at the same time asking, **"What's the matter Alice? Why are you crying? What happened?"** Alice responded, **"Just hold me, Mummy."**

There are times when it's too complicated to say what's happened – times when we ourselves don't really know **what's going on**. We would do well at such times to say to our heavenly Father, **"Just hold me."** He has promised to be there for us especially in times of need, but most of us are too grown-up to receive His comfort as directly as little Alice received hers. God our Father has arms to hold us, knows how to comfort us, and always has time to listen when we are upset. More than that, He corrects us firmly and lovingly and promises us wisdom to find the way out of trouble and conflict.

As I observed this situation, I found myself thinking about my own reactions when I am hurting and upset. Often I try to work it all out in my head, going round and round, getting nowhere. Sometimes I want to accuse someone else, but that seldom makes the situation better.

I found myself asking the Lord Jesus to make me childlike – to help me to say what I really need; and then receive quickly and get on with the action.

Are we weak and heavy laden,
Cumbered with a load of care?
Precious Saviour, still our refuge
Take it to the Lord in prayer!
In his arms He'll take and shield us
We will find our solace there.

Joyce

One Year Plan : Psalm 89, James 2, 2 Kings 20 - 21
Two Year Plan : Psalm 119:97-104, John 8:1-30, Judges 12 (Yr 1)
Daniel 3 (Yr 2)

Risk Assessment

We had recently learned of the tragic death of Russian ex-spy Alexander Litvinenko through poisoning by radioactivity, which had shocked us all. It had brought the intrigue of sinister death plots out of fiction into the reality of our everyday lives. It had clearly shown us that life is fragile and vulnerable.

Risk assessments are part of our lives these days as we weigh up the risks and dangers of given situations and clearly lay out the steps that we need to take to protect us against them.

Those of us who know Jesus and have committed our lives to Him will find that the Bible is a wonderful Health & Safety Manual.

It protects us from the burden of guilt and shame, because Psalm 130:3-4 says, **"If you, O Lord, kept a record of sins, O Lord who could stand? But with you there is forgiveness..."**

It enables us to enjoy deep peaceful sleep, because Psalm 127:2 declares, **"In vain you rise up early and stay up late, toiling for food to eat – for he grants sleep to those he loves."**

It enables us to tap into daily supernatural power, as we are filled with God's Holy Spirit: **"But you will receive power when the Holy Spirit comes on you; and you will be my witnesses in Jerusalem, and in all Judea and Samaria, and to the ends of the earth."** (Acts 1:8)

It provides us with daily promises of safety as we step out into a world of violence and terrorism. Psalm 91:9-10 says, **"If you make the Most High your dwelling – even the Lord, who is my refuge – then no harm will befall you, no disaster will come near your tent."**

Even when we are in vulnerable situations God will warn us of danger because Proverbs 1:33 says, **"But whoever listens to me will dwell in safety and be at ease, without fear of harm."**

Charles

One Year Plan : Psalm 90, James 3, 2 Kings 22 - 23
Two Year Plan : Psalm 119:105-112, John 8:31-59, Judges 13 (Yr 1)
Daniel 4 (Yr 2)

Keep Limber

We have all seen marathon runners reaching out for a drink whilst still continuing to run towards the finishing post. At that point, their whole being is craving an energy boost. Similarly, there are times when we need refreshing in our battle of faith. When we do not receive an instant answer to prayer and realise we are in for the long haul, we can feel very weary.

Take a refreshing drink from God's word. Genesis 49:23-25 says, **"With bitterness archers attacked him; they shot at him with hostility. But his bow remained steady, his strong arms stayed limber, because of the hand of the Mighty One of Jacob, because of the Shepherd, the Rock of Israel, because of your father's God, who helps you, because of the Almighty, who blesses you..."**

These words were spoken over Joseph by his father Jacob. You can take these promises for yourself today – Let your hands hold steady, because **"the hand of the Mighty One"** holds you.

Receive the personal blessing: wellbeing, renewed hope, all you need to keep your arms limber.

You may feel battle weary, but **"The God of all grace ... will himself restore you and make you strong, firm and steadfast."** (1 Peter 5:10)

Keep your eyes on the goal of your faith. The devil wants you to focus on how you feel, your lack, your physical symptoms, your exhaustion and spent energy.

If you are engaged in a healing battle, hold on to the promises God has given to you. If you are waiting for financial provision, stand firm and resist doubt and unbelief.

Keep limber – pliant, supple, lithe and nimble.

Joyce

One Year Plan : Psalm 91, James 4, 2 Kings 24 - 25
Two Year Plan : Psalm 119:113-120, John 9:1-34, Judges 14 (Yr 1)
Daniel 5 (Yr 2)

What is God Saying?

It is very easy to use logic and reason to make decisions in everyday life, but it limits us to our own knowledge and analysis. It is so much better when seeking to make decisions, to ask ourselves, **"What is God saying about this?"**

Joshua landed himself in a wrong alliance when he listened to the lies of the Gibeonites and did not ask God for wisdom. They made a treaty with enemies and suffered for it. Joshua 9:14 says, **"The men of Israel sampled their provisions but did not inquire of the Lord."**

God is so willing to speak to us if we will only ask. James 1:5 says, **"If any of you lacks wisdom, he should ask God, who gives generously to all without finding fault, and it will be given to him."** We need great wisdom in all the details of daily life; don't make reactive and impulsive decisions – ask God.

I met a lady who, when she prays for her family and those she is helping and encouraging, first asks God what to pray for – **"Does she need courage today?" "Does he need patience?" "Do they need to be encouraged?"** There are times when God tells her that they are going through difficult times, and then she can pray for wisdom, solutions and steadfastness. I found this very helpful, as it is so easy just to say vague prayers for those we have committed to pray for and not be specific.

Jesus himself assured His disciples that they could hear God when He told them, **"He who belongs to God hears what God says."** (John 8:47) If you belong to God, He is committed to speak to you and answer your questions. **"My sheep listen to my voice; I know them, and they follow me."** (John 10:27) We need to hear what God is saying about every area of life.

Don't just make random decisions – **what is God saying?**

Charles

One Year Plan : Psalm 92, James 5, Ezekiel 1 - 3
Two Year Plan : Psalm 119:121-128, John 9:35-41, Judges 15 (Yr 1)
Daniel 6 (Yr 2)

"Wake Up" – "Watch" – "Be Alert"

Those are all words Jesus spoke to His close friends in the hours before His arrest and death. He knew what lay ahead and He needed their support and prayer – not in order to prevent the crucifixion but to support Him, to strengthen Him. Sadly, they slept, both physically and spiritually.

I believe these words are being spoken to the living church in the UK at this present time. **"Wake up!"** – **"Be on your guard!"** – **"Watch!"** The clash of the kingdoms of darkness and light is a present day reality. You and I are part of God's victorious army, enforcing the victory that Jesus has already won. We are not fighting to win but to implement the victory that has already been won at Calvary and to conquer every area of satan's activity in and around us.

You cannot do this **sleepwalking** or **sleep-talking**; you need to be on your guard and alert at all times. You are a **special agent** – not trained to kill a physical enemy, but you have been enrolled in the army to fight a cosmic battle and there is no retirement. You can be called upon at any time and in any place to pray and to do what the Holy Spirit commands you.

To this end you need to look after your physical body. Don't abuse it by over or underuse. Get enough sleep, exercise and food. Do the same with your spiritual body. Wake up to danger; stir yourself; be ready for action. Listen to the Holy Spirit and heed the words of Luke 12:35: **"Be dressed ready for service and keep your lamps burning."**

You can be alert and at rest at the same time. This is how Jesus lived this out: always alert; never hassled.

Joyce

One Year Plan : Psalm 93, 1 Peter 1, Ezekiel 4 - 6
Two Year Plan : Psalm 119:129-136, John 10:1-21, Judges 16 (Yr 1)
Daniel 7 (Yr 2)

Refreshed in Spirit

If I say the names Stephanas, Fortunatus and Achaicus, what springs to your mind? Probably nothing – which is what I would have said until a few days ago when I read the words of 1 Corinthians 16:18: **"For they refreshed my spirit and yours also. Such men deserve recognition."**

Whenever we meet another believer we should seek to refresh them in spirit. Physical tiredness is often the result of discouragement and weariness of spirit. We may take time out to rest our bodies yet can still feel tired after extra sleep and days off. Perhaps we have failed to recognise the vital importance of strengthening our spirit.

Paul said, **"And if the Spirit who raised Jesus from the dead is living in you, he who raised Christ from the dead will also give life to your mortal bodies through his Spirit who lives in you."** (Romans 8:11) Our spirits, made strong and given life by the Holy Spirit, enable us to live at a different level to unbelievers!

Being refreshed also involves giving rather than always wanting others to give to us. Proverbs 11:25 says, **"...he who refreshes others will himself be refreshed."** In 2 Corinthians 7:13, Paul commends the believers because they brought this refreshment of spirit to Titus: **"In addition to our own encouragement, we were especially delighted to see how happy Titus was, because his spirit has been refreshed by all of you."**

When Paul wrote his very short letter to Philemon asking that he show clemency and grace to Onesimus, the runaway slave, he speaks of this same quality in Philemon: **"Your love has given me great joy and encouragement, because you, brother, have refreshed the hearts of the saints."** (Philemon 1:7) Here 'hearts' can be synonymous with 'spirits'.

It is in God's character to bring refreshment to others; Psalm 68:9 says, **"You gave abundant showers, O God; you refreshed your weary inheritance."**

Whose spirit are you going to refresh today?

Charles

One Year Plan : Psalm 94, 1 Peter 2, Ezekiel 7 - 8
Two Year Plan : Psalm 119:137-144, John 10:22-42, Judges 17 (Yr 1)
Daniel 8 (Yr 2)

Know where you are heading

"Jesus never lost sight of where he was heading..." (Hebrews 12:2, The Message)

Recently I have been bombarded with accounts of human failure, gross sin, deception, etc. I have felt a great weight of sadness, particularly for those who are left to **pick up the pieces.** It is hard not to feel very disappointed.

I was helped by reading Hebrews 12:3 in The Message: **"When you find yourselves flagging in your faith, go over that story again, item by item, the long litany of hostility he ploughed through. That will shoot adrenaline into your souls!"**

While Jesus was here on earth, He constantly encountered those who let Him down, failed, and messed up:

- His own family lacked understanding.
- His disciples had little knowledge of what He was really here to do and what load He was carrying.
- His closest friends understood more but failed to stand by Him when He most needed them.
- Some betrayed and others denied him; self-preservation caused some to run away

And Jesus did not stand in judgement on any of them – that's amazing!

The crowds were fickle, cheering one minute and baying for blood the next. The religious people were jealous and vindictive – even Pilate could see that.

What was the effect of all this? The loneliness inside pushed Him into the presence of the only One who fully understood, could comfort, strengthen and encourage: His Father, gracious and merciful, who will never abandon and in whose presence perspective returns as He repeats His promises to us and encourages us to press on.

Heaven is urging you on; crowds of witnesses are shouting, **"Keep going, keep believing, and keep proclaiming. Jesus is the only answer, the Saviour, Healer, Deliverer, Strong Tower."**

We have an appointed task: **"Go – don't lose sight of where you are heading!"**

Joyce

One Year Plan : Psalm 95, 1 Peter 3, Ezekiel 9 - 10
Two Year Plan : Psalm 119:145-152, John 11:1-27, Judges 18 (Yr 1)
Daniel 9 (Yr 2)

Out of the Mouths of Babes

There is a Junior School in our area that has a box in which children can post their prayers. It has been placed there by a group of Christian parents who regularly pray for the school and seek to support the teaching staff in helping meet the real needs of the children.

They receive some heartrending cries but also prayers that demonstrate a great sense of love and thankfulness. I have been shown some of these prayers.

"Dear Lord, Please make the poor rich and make the rich share and the middle be middles. Armen."

"Dear Lord, I am happy, but not everyone else is so please may you make everyone happy! Armen."

"Dear Lord, Thank you for everything we have in our world. I think you have a busy life and you should have a break. Armen."

"Dear God, I love you and fank you for everyfink."

What is God saying to you as you read these prayers? The simplicity of children is very powerful.

I am challenged by the generosity of the prayer about rich and poor. Do we have loving, giving and generous hearts?

I find the prayer about happiness very profound. In our prosperous Western world there is so little happiness, and yet the Bible has so much to say about joy: **"The joy of the Lord is your strength."**

So often we hear complaints about what God has seemingly failed to do, and yet here is a young child telling God that he needs a holiday!

May the inspiration of these prayers cause us to have more generous, loving, joyful and grateful hearts.

Charles

One Year Plan : Psalm 96, 1 Peter 4, Ezekiel 11 - 12
Two Year Plan : Psalm 119:153-160, John 11:28-57, Judges 19 (Yr 1)
Daniel 10 (Yr 2)

A Thirst for the Living God

I have been reading my Bible in two translations – the NIV and the Message. I find the Message jolts me into reading with greater understanding. The more familiar NIV sometimes flows over me, and I find I am reading without taking in the enormity of what is being said.

Ephesians 1:17 in the Message says, **"I ask the God of our Master, Jesus Christ, the God of glory – to make you intelligent and discerning in knowing him personally, your eyes focussed and clear, so that you can see exactly what he is calling you to do, grasp the immensity of this glorious way of life he has for us Christians, oh, the utter extra-vagance of his work in us who trust in him – endless energy, boundless strength!"** Paul, who had such a life-changing encounter when he was taken out of the kingdom of darkness and made alive in the kingdom of God, wants more of this experiential knowing for himself and for all those to whom he is talking.

Later in his letter to the Philippian church he says, **"I gave up all that inferior stuff so I could know Christ personally, experience his resurrection power, be a partner in his suffering, and go all the way with him to death itself. If there was any way to get in on the resurrection from the dead, I wanted to do it."** (Philippians 3:10-11, The Message)

Do you hear in Paul the longing for more knowledge, for more intimacy? All those who have truly met God in Jesus long for more; there is a divine dissatisfaction. Moses had intimate encounters with the God of glory, but his heart cry was, **"Teach me your ways so that I might know you ... show me your glory."** (Exodus 33:13,18)

I pray that your heart would thirst for the living God and, having slaked that thirst, your thirst would remain, still needing to be satisfied. **There is no end to knowing and being known**; the amazing God of glory is inviting you and me to draw near and to know Him personally. **Isn't that astounding?!**

Joyce

One Year Plan : Psalm 97, 1 Peter 5, Ezekiel 13 - 14
Two Year Plan : Psalm 119:161-168, John 12:1-19, Judges 20 (Yr 1)
Daniel 11 (Yr 2)

Don't Lose your Place of Faith

Most believers have their own testimonies of God's faithfulness. They love telling their **faith stories** demonstrating how God has acted on their behalf by doing amazing things: protecting, healing, or providing miraculously in a crisis.

However, have you noticed how despite all that God has done for you, each life challenge you face demands a fresh act of faith? Even though you have seen God's faithfulness and mighty acts, it is all too easy to be gripped by fear or look for some human resolution to your problem.

This was King Asa's weakness. When he came to the throne he destroyed the heathen altars, removed the idols and led the people in seeking and worshipping God. When faced by an enemy, he prayed, **"Lord there is no one like you to help the powerless against the mighty. Help us, O Lord our God, for we rely on you..."** (2 Chronicles 14:11-12) And the Lord gave him a great victory.

The whole nation entered into a covenant to seek the Lord with all their heart and soul. **"They sought the Lord eagerly, and he was found by them. So the Lord gave them rest on every side."** (2 Chronicles 15:15)

After many years of peace and rest, another enemy came against King Asa, and rather than continue to place his faith in God, he turned to a human king and made a treaty with him. This was complete foolishness; his loss of faith led to defeat and a decline that ultimately ended his life.

God sent a prophet to him who said, **"Were not the Cushites and Libyans a mighty army with great numbers of chariots and horseman? Yet when you relied on the Lord, he delivered them into your hand."** (2 Chronicles 16:8) Now comes a very famous verse: **"For the eyes of the Lord range throughout the earth to strengthen those whose hearts are fully committed to him."** God is saying that He is looking for those who will stay in a place of faith whatever the circumstances because He wants to strengthen them, to give them victory, and to answer their prayers.

Joyce

One Year Plan : Psalm 98, 2 Peter 1, Ezekiel 15 - 16
Two Year Plan : Psalm 119:169-176, John 12:20-50, Judges 21 (Yr 1) Daniel 12 (Yr 2)

Honey, We're Killing the Kids

Romans 11:22 tells us to **"consider therefore the kindness and sternness of God."** If we take away His sternness, He can be perceived as a doting father, but if we remove His kindness, as a ruthless tyrant. God is neither of these; kindness and sternness must be held in tension – not biased one way or the other.

Jeremiah 9:24 tells us that God **"delights in kindness, justice and righteousness."** He loves to be kind to us; He understands us and yet He does not want us to destroy ourselves – He steps in because He cares. Sometimes that kind of caring can be perceived as sternness, especially when we want to have or do something, and God says, **"No!"**

In Britain we have a problem with over-indulgence in the area of eating – childhood obesity is a national issue. Parents think they are being kind and give in to all the demands for sweets, crisps, soft drinks, etc., when it would be much kinder to say, **"No."** Your child may perceive you as stern, not kind, but you have a better picture of the long term health issues.

It is God's kindness and immense love that has provided Jesus our Saviour, the one who took all the punishment that we really deserved for our sin, failure and rebellion.

It is His kindness that warns of danger, keeps us prayerful, guides us and gives wisdom. His kindness gives us **"all things"** richly to enjoy. He wants the best for you and me; He wants us to live full and fruitful lives.

I once had to tell a young girl that the way of life she was pursuing was not the way of blessing, only sorrow. She could choose to have what she wanted, but it would bring **"leanness of soul"** – destruction and not blessing.

The words I spoke came out of the kindness in my heart, but they were warning her of danger. She probably thought I was being stern – I was, but only because I love her. I wanted to warn her of danger and at the same time encourage right choices.

Be ready to receive God's correction as well as His encouragement.

Joyce

One Year Plan : Psalm 99, 2 Peter 2, Ezekiel 17 - 18
Two Year Plan : Psalm 120, John 13:1-17, Isaiah 1 (Yr 1)
Micah 1 (Yr 2)

I will give you Rest

Jesus said, **"Come to me, all you who are weary and burdened, and I will give you rest."** (Matthew 11:28) Jesus was not referring to the way we might feel after a good day's work. To feel tired after having worked hard is natural and is in many ways very satisfying. This is different.

I believe the **"weary"** Jesus is talking about is the way we feel when drained because of disappointment, failure, unfulfilled dreams and things that bring discouragement. In the Proverbs we read, **"...a crushed spirit dries up the bones."** (Proverbs 17:22). Isaiah refers to **"a spirit of despair"**. Elijah said, **"I have had enough Lord."** Are any of those emotions familiar? – That's why Jesus said, **"I will give you rest."**

I believe the **"burdened"** Jesus is referring to is when we are carrying loads greater than we should. Moses knew this feeling when he said, **"But how can I carry your burdens ... all by myself?"** Do you feel a weight on your shoulders that is beyond your ability to carry? That's why Jesus said, **"I will give you rest."**

The solution that Jesus gave was, **"Take my yoke upon you and learn from me."** A yoke is the wooden device that joins two animals so that they can work in harmony and greatly increase their effectiveness. Jesus is saying, **"Yoke yourself to me. When you allow me to share your life situation you will discover something wonderful and powerful."**

The result is this: **"You will find rest for your souls. For my yoke is easy and my burden is light."**

God has always had a way for those who turn to Him. The psalmist says, **"Cast your burden on the Lord for he will sustain you; he will never let the righteous fall."** (Psalm 55:22). Isaiah says that God wants to give you **"...the oil of gladness instead of mourning, and a garment of praise instead of a spirit of despair"**. (Isaiah 61:3)

Jesus understands your situation perfectly, and still says, **"I will give you rest."**

Charles

One Year Plan : Psalm 100, 2 Peter 3, Ezekiel 19 - 20
Two Year Plan : Psalm 121, John 13:18-38, Isaiah 2 (Yr 1)
Micah 2 (Yr 2)

When the Going gets Tough

To whom shall we go? To the One who knows the whole situation and has the ability to act on our behalf. To the One who loves us and wants the best for His children. To God of the angel armies who has all power and authority in heaven and on earth.

This is what King Jehoshaphat did when faced with a vast army, rapidly approaching. Although shaken by the news, he immediately went to God, called on others to join him, including the children. The reality of the situation couldn't have been worse. **"O dear God, won't you take care of them? We're helpless ... we don't know what to do; we're looking to you,"** was how he prayed, and having put the whole situation into God's hands, he had to believe that God would answer – and He did. (2 Chronicles 20:12, The Message)

The prophetic instruction from God to Jehoshaphat was:

1. Don't be afraid.
2. Don't do anything; stand firm believing that God will do what you have asked.
3. Watch God act on your behalf. As you face them, God is with you.

It takes a great deal of trust and courage to act on a word like this. We somehow feel irresponsible if we do nothing. Worry and anxiety can make us feel we are involved but cannot change the situation.

We need to trust God and His ability to act on our behalf, to give instructions and peace in place of panic. We also have been given authority to bind and loose, to rebuke, and to proclaim, using the Name of Jesus. I am not advocating passivity in the face of trauma – quite the reverse – we need to be tough but not with human aggression, rather with spiritual strength that turns to God and stands firm.

From the outside this may look like weakness and inactivity; but viewed from heaven's perspective, refusing to be afraid, standing firm and trusting God, is spiritual strength which will open the door for God to act on our behalf.

Joyce

One Year Plan : Psalm 101, 1 John 1, Ezekiel 21 - 22
Two Year Plan : Psalm 122, John 14:1-14, Isaiah 3-4 (Yr 1)
Micah 3 (Yr 2)

He's My Rock

We have a good friend who experienced terrible abuse and mental torment which resulted in her having to spend four years in a mental hospital restrained by a straightjacket! I have never heard a more heartrending life story. But when she met Jesus, a healing process began which has completely restored her. She is now leading people to receive total freedom and release as she shares her own pathway to freedom, and the principles that God taught her.

God told her:

- **When your mind is troubling you, read My Word.**
- **When your emotions are out of control, worship Me.**

And so the process of healing began. The tangled thoughts of her mind and the memories of the past began to come under the transforming power of God's Word, and truly the words of Jesus were fulfilled: **"And you will know the truth, and the truth will set you free."**

When her emotions became disturbed she would sing a popular worship song: **'Praise the Name of Jesus'**. *

Praise the Name of Jesus
He's my Rock, He's my fortress
He's my deliverer in Him will I trust
Praise the Name of Jesus

She followed the instructions given to her by the Lord, and step by step, slowly yet surely, the healing and restoring power of God transformed her life.

Her testimony came into my mind as I was reading Isaiah 26:4: **"Trust in the Lord forever, for the Lord, the Lord, is the Rock eternal."** Most of us have experienced disturbed emotions and the feeling that our foundations are being shaken. God's answer remains the same: **"I am your Rock."**

King David understood this and declares in Psalm 18:2, **"The Lord is my rock, my fortress and my deliverer; my God is my rock, in whom I take refuge."**

Are your thoughts troubling you?
Let His truth set you free!
Are your emotions in turmoil?
Worship Him; He is your Rock!

Charles

* Roy Hicks Jnr. © 1976 Latter Rain Music/EMI CMP/Small Stone Media BV, Holland (Adm. By Song Solutions www.songsolutions.org)

One Year Plan : Psalm 102, 1 John 2, Ezekiel 23 - 24
Two Year Plan : Psalm 123, John 14:15-31, Isaiah 5 (Yr 1) Micah 4 (Yr 2)

Follow Heaven's Instructions

What do you do when someone says, **"Please help me; pray for me"**? Be honest - it's easy to think we know what to do, how to pray; however, we don't unless we find out what God wants in this situation.

Moses was surrounded by rebellious hurting people, dying from snake bites, and they were desperate for Moses' help. They cried out, **"We have sinned … pray that the Lord will take the snakes away from us."** (Numbers 21:7) It would have been very easy for Moses to think he knew what to do – command the snakes to go, hold out his rod of authority, or any number of things that had worked for him in the past. He did pray for the people, but first he listened for instructions from heaven. The unique direction he received was, **"Make a snake and put it on a pole; anyone who is bitten can look at it and live."** Those who looked at the bronze snake were healed!

If you try to analyse this there is nothing logical about it, no reason why it should work – except that God said that it should be done. They believed and experienced an amazing deliverance.

Peter found himself in a similar crisis. He was asked to come to the home of a lady who had just died. Peter entered the room, knelt down beside the bed and received instructions. We don't hear the download from heaven, but we see the results. **He did what he was told to do and Tabitha was raised from the dead**! (Acts 9:36-43)

We have no expertise, no power of our own; but we do have the ability to hear what the Holy Spirit is saying – and to obey. This is how Jesus ministered: **"For I did not speak on my own accord, but the Father who sent me commanded me what to say and how to say it."** (John 12:49) Not only what, but how and when – and the results? Miracles and the glory of God.

Joyce

One Year Plan : Psalm 103, 1 John 3, Ezekiel 25 - 26
Two Year Plan : Psalm 124, John 15:1-17, Isaiah 6 (Yr 1)
Micah 5 (Yr 2)

Enough!

Whilst reading Psalm 46, **"Be still, and know that I am God,"** I discovered that the Hebrew for **'Be still'** probably means **'Enough!'** This put an entirely new slant on this verse. Many of you will know the song based on the words from this psalm. It is quiet and meditative and can be inspiring and uplifting. However, there are many situations when the phrase **'Be still'** sounds weak and pathetic.

You may be facing a situation that is robbing you of peace and creating mayhem all around. It is time for you to say, **"Enough! Know that I am God!"** It is possible to let the circumstances around you so overwhelm you that you feel powerless to do anything about it. It is time to say, **"Enough!"**

Think of those times when your children have all their things strewn around the room, there is mess everywhere and you walk through the door. You don't quietly say, **"Be still; will you please listen to me?"** You say, **"That's enough children; pick up those toys, tidy this room and get up those stairs, brush your teeth and be ready for bed in five minutes!"** The voice of command demands immediate action.

When we say **"Enough!"** we declare that God is bigger than the problem we are facing. We are saying, **"Know that God is great and powerful, and for Him nothing is impossible!"**

We may have a crisis in our families where we need to say, **"Enough devil, you are not having my children; they belong to God."** It could be any number of things that are robbing you.

What is it in your life situation today to which you need to say, **"Enough! Know that I am God, I will be exalted among the nations, I will be exalted in the earth. The Lord Almighty is with us; the God of Jacob is our fortress."**? (Psalm 46:10-11)

Charles

One Year Plan : Psalm 104, 1 John 4, Ezekiel 27 - 28
Two Year Plan : Psalm 125, John 15:18-27, Isaiah 7 (Yr 1)
Micah 6 (Yr 2)

Connection, Connection, Connection

If you are thinking of purchasing a house, the words you will hear ringing in your ears are **"location, location, location"**.

When I think about my life as a believer, the words that I hear in my heart are **"connection, connection, connection"**. Jesus paid the ultimate price to connect fallen man back to His Father. He made the connection – as an old song says, *"There was no other good enough to pay the price of sin. He only could unlock the gate of heaven and let us in."*

Do you value connection? Do you run to the Father only when you are in trouble or when your resources have failed? Do you value His wisdom, advice, help, friendship, companionship on a moment by moment basis? We have access to the supreme ruler of the universe yet so often fail to connect, rather trusting in our own resources – so fragile and limited by comparison.

How do you keep connected? In human relationships, connection means being with a person, talking, listening, enjoying their presence; interacting, asking questions, sharing events you've recently been involved in; speaking about sorrows and blunders, as well as rejoicing over the good things you've been experiencing.

The enemy of our souls, the devil, the accuser, the liar, has one aim, which is to keep believers from being in intimate contact with the living God. He doesn't mind religious activity; it is intimacy that he attacks. **So ask yourself: what is my connection like?**

Some time ago, I had a loose connection on my vacuum cleaner. When I fully extended the lead, the power went off. I had known about it for a long time, but because it would take time to fix, I vacuumed with uncertainty, frustration and intermittent power. **"How foolish!"** I hear you exclaim. But how much more foolish to have a loose connection with our Father?

Check your connection with Him today. He loves you; you are the apple of His eye. Your sins have been covered by the blood of Jesus. You can approach the throne clothed with the righteousness of Jesus – and the Father is longing to enjoy you. **He paid the ultimate price to bring you into connection.**

Joyce

One Year Plan : Psalm 105, 1 John 5, Ezekiel 29 - 30
Two Year Plan : Psalm 126, John 16:1-16, Isaiah 8 (Yr 1) Micah 7 (Yr 2)

Blessing and Cursing

I received a report from a friend, who had been teaching a group of students in Moscow which said, **"We prayed the Aaronic blessing over them at the end of the course and so many were very touched; some shed a few tears and one girl was completely overcome with emotion. When I spoke with her afterwards she said that no-one had ever prayed a blessing over her before."**

We are surrounded by such negativity in today's world that we can easily forget that words have tremendous power. Proverbs 18:21 says, **"The tongue has the power of life and death."**

"You'll never learn to read," were words spoken to one of our children by an exasperated school teacher, which had a powerfully negative effect and took years to reverse.

I have prayed with many people whose lives have been blighted by parents who constantly undermined them with words such as, **"You'll never be any good; you're going to be a failure."** Such words become a curse and can affect people for their whole life.

First, reject any curse that has been spoken over you because in Proverbs 26:2 it says, **"Like a fluttering sparrow or a darting swallow, an undeserved curse does not come to rest**." God's purpose for the lives of His children is that they will be blessed. When God declared the future of Abraham he said, **"I will bless you ... you will be a blessing ... and all peoples will be blessed through you."** (Genesis 12:2-3)

When Mary the mother of Jesus sang out her song of thanksgiving, she said, **"From now on all generations will call me blessed."** (Luke 1:48)

On Mother's Day I prayed Aaron's blessing over all the ladies in our church – it was powerful. Since then I heard testimonies of people who have been saved, healed and set free as this prayer was prayed over them.

"The Lord bless you and keep you;
The Lord make his face shine upon you and be gracious to you;
The Lord turn his face toward you and give you peace."
(Numbers 6:24-26)

Charles

One Year Plan : Psalm 106, 2 John 1, Ezekiel 31 - 32
Two Year Plan : Psalm 127, John 16:17-33, Isaiah 9 (Yr 1)
Nahum 1 (Yr 2)

NOVEMBER

Please Lord, Clear the Way!

A small phrase caught my attention as I was reading 1 Thessalonians 3:11: **"clear the way."** Paul was praying that he might be able to come and visit a group of believers in Thessaloniki. The verse says, **"Now may our God and Father himself and our Lord Jesus clear the way for us to come to you."** There must have been something that was trying to get in the way of Paul's intended journey.

Imagine cutting a path through brambles on an overgrown pathway to remove the obstacles, making a clear route to your destination. Paul is asking the Godhead to do this for him, so that he may reconnect with these folk.

My response to this verse was to start praying for a number of situations: **"Lord, clear the way for this and this and this to happen!"** For me the picture is so vivid; I've walked many overgrown tracks, been snagged by brambles and stung by nettles. I have also followed someone who has been clearing the way ahead of me so that I have a clear path to walk.

Ask the Father to **clear the way** for you in your situation today and expect that He will.

"<u>Clear the way</u> for this house to sell."

"<u>Clear the way</u> so that I can receive revelation from heaven to know what I should do."

"<u>Clear the way</u> for circumstances to change."

Believe that God is acting on your behalf to grant the requests you are making in Jesus' Name! God wants you to trust Him, to expect His help, and to overflow with thanksgiving as you receive His help to **clear the way** in every area of your life.

God wants to make a pathway and give you everything you need, so that you can become everything you are meant to be!

Joyce

One Year Plan : Psalm 107, 3 John 1, Ezekiel 33 - 34
Two Year Plan : Psalm 128, John 17, Isaiah 10 (Yr 1)
Nahum 2 (Yr 2)

Faith is a Lifestyle

Whilst reading Hebrews chapter 11, I realised that the heroes of faith mentioned there had chosen **faith as a lifestyle**. We may think only of exercising faith when facing a crisis. We may have a healing need or a financial challenge; we may be threatened with redundancy, or our family may be going through a tough time. We know that trusting in our own resources has failed, so in our moment of need we feel now we should exercise our faith. There is a better way: **choose to live by faith every day, at all times and in every situation.**

Enoch was a man of faith who pleased God. There does not seem to have been anything spectacular about his life except that he walked with God and of him it says, **"And without faith it is impossible to please God, because anyone who comes to him must believe that 'he is' and that he rewards those who earnestly seek him."** (verse 6)

Moses chose to leave the safety and privilege of Egypt to be God's instrument of deliverance for the Children of Israel, and of him it says, **"He persevered because he saw him who is invisible."** (verse 27) Earlier in the chapter it says, **"All these people were still living by faith when they died."** (verse 12)

Here are people who had chosen to place their confidence and faith in God, not to let the challenges and circumstances of life dominate, and they saw God's mighty acts of power at work on their behalf. God has not changed.

Hebrews 12:1 states, **"Therefore since we are surrounded by such a cloud of witnesses, let us throw off everything that hinders ... and run with per-severance the race marked out for us ... Let us fix our eyes on Jesus ... Consider him who endured such opposition from sinful men, so that you will not grow weary and lose heart."**

Let us refuse to let circumstances and difficulties dominate our lives; let us choose to make **'living by faith'** our lifestyle, and the miracles will follow!

Charles

One Year Plan : Psalm 108, Jude 1, Ezekiel 35 - 36
Two Year Plan : Psalm 129, John 18:1-18, Isaiah 11 (Yr 1)
Nahum 3 (Yr 2)

Being Friends

Tanya, our daughter-in-law, was leading the Easter Celebration at Living Waters Church. It's a demanding role which was new to her, and it's quite a task to be sensitive to the Holy Spirit and what He wants to do; time needs to be given to worship, preaching, notices; everyone needs to be welcomed, etc. She was great but Daniel, her husband/our son, became aware of some tension; he stood beside her and said, **"Tanya is a little nervous, but I have told her, 'It's OK – you're among friends!'"**

It was this statement that lodged in my mind, and I began to think about **being among friends**. You can relax when you don't feel judged; real friends understand and don't criticise. They may ask questions to find out where you are coming from – but we trust them to listen, understand and want the best for us.

I have a friend who, by her own admission, makes choices based on keeping other people happy – not always good choices (they often seem random and chaotic) but I understand the 'why behind the what', and because I don't judge her she is able to share honestly with me and ask for my help and advice. That is another facet of friendship and intimacy.

You and I have been called to **be friends of God**. Although God knows everything about me, He doesn't judge me. He has assigned that role to Jesus who knows me inside out but also doesn't condemn me when I do wrong. He will take the time to reason with me, and I am able to be totally honest and vulnerable because I know He is my friend who will never reject me. I want to change, and with His help I know I can.

The acceptance and value we give to others enables them to be fully themselves. Most of us are only too aware of our inadequacies and weaknesses, and true friends meet us where we are and walk with us to where we want to be.

Jesus said, **"I no longer call you servants … I have called you friends."** (John 15:15)

Joyce

One Year Plan : Psalm 109, John 1, Ezekiel 37 - 38
Two Year Plan : Psalm 130, John 18:19-40, Isaiah 12 (Yr 1)
Habakkuk 1 (Yr 2)

The Last Days

Over recent years we have witnessed some devastating events – the Tsunami, New Orleans Hurricane, Earthquake in Haiti, Pakistan floods and the Japanese Tsunami – events that shocked us all. As the latest horror is played out hour by hour on our television screens we feel helpless and yet are moved to respond. We can give money; we could even travel to one of the stricken countries – but what should be our long-term response?

I have been asked, **"Is this a sign of <u>the last days</u>?"** I find my response in words from the Bible. In Matthew's gospel, the words of Jesus describe the last days: **"Nation will rise against nation, and kingdom against kingdom. There will be famines and earthquakes in various places."** (Matthew 24:7)

Peter says, **"You must understand that in <u>the last days</u> scoffers will come, scoffing and following their evil desires."** (2 Peter 3:3) That seems a fair description of present day society.

When Peter is reflecting on this situation he asks, **"What kind of people ought you to be? You ought to live holy and godly lives as you look forward to the day of God and speed its coming."** (2 Peter 3:11-12)

Beyond our immediate response to the latest crisis is a bigger question: how should it change the way we live? It is not simply how much money we can give or how much aid we can send.

What does it mean to live holy and godly lives? It means generosity and compassion. It means laying down our lives for one another. It means having a passion to share the gospel of Jesus Christ with as many people as possible. It means loving one another. It means living to please God and not to please ourselves.

Let us reach out in these **last days** and make a vital and dynamic contribution.

Charles

One Year Plan : Psalm 110, John 2, Ezekiel 39 - 40
Two Year Plan : Psalm 131, John 19:1-27, Isaiah 13 (Yr 1)
Habakkuk 2 (Yr 2)

Alabaster Box

Luke writes of an incident when Jesus is invited into a Pharisee's home. While He is there a woman of 'questionable repute' washes Jesus' feet with her tears and dries them with her hair, then anoints them with precious and costly perfume. (Luke 7:36-50)

The host, Simon, is highly critical, expecting Jesus to 'suss out' what kind of woman is doing this and to reject her. Jesus rather commends her and says that what she has done will never be forgotten.

Jesus now comments on Simon's hospitality: **"You didn't give me water to wash, or greet me with a kiss nor put oil on my head!"** She did all these acts of love and kindness, treating me as an honoured guest – you did not even give me the minimum of hospitality! Whoops!

It is easy to feel negatively towards Simon as you read this account – but what about me? Do I have an agenda when I come to Jesus? Do I launch right in to my latest need or prayer request? Do I fail to honour Jesus, to kiss Him, to give Him thanks?

As I pondered my own behaviour, I saw how casually I treat Jesus, so often failing to be thankful – expecting Him to listen to me but often in too much of hurry to wait to hear what He is saying.

It is a privilege to be a child of God; don't take it for granted. Today, come and worship, come and love Him, come and pour out your thanksgiving and praise.

"For You are Alpha and Omega, we worship you O Lord, You are worthy of our praise!"

CeCe Winans sings a song 'Alabaster Box' inspired by this incident in the life of Jesus. You can listen to it on YouTube and be encouraged.

Joyce

One Year Plan : Psalm 111, John 3, Ezekiel 41 - 42
Two Year Plan : Psalm 132:1-9, John 19:28-42, Isaiah 14 (Yr 1)
Habakkuk 3 (Yr 2)

Reading Hearts

John the Baptist was living in the desert, eating locusts and wild honey and doing what God had assigned to him: to baptise people in the Jordan and to prepare for the coming ministry of Jesus. But John was also learning to read the hearts of those who came to him.

A group came from Jerusalem, Judea and the region of the Jordan, and it says, **"Confessing their sins they were baptised by him in the Jordan River."** (Matthew 3:6) John was able to read their hearts and see that they had come because they needed cleansing and they wanted to enter into a new relationship with God.

In the very next verse we read, **"...Many of the Pharisees and Sadducees were coming to where he was baptising."** Here we find a completely different reaction as John read their hearts. **"You brood of vipers! Who warned you to flee from the coming wrath? Produce fruit in keeping with repentance."** John saw their pride, self-righteousness and religious legalism and reacted accordingly.

Then Jesus came from Galilee to the Jordan to be baptised by John. Again here is another totally different response from John. As he was able to read Jesus' heart of purity and love he said, **"I need to be baptised by you."** Jesus then said, **"It is proper for us to do this to fulfil all righteousness. Then John consented."**

As Jesus humbled Himself, submitted to the baptism of John, something amazing happened:

- Heaven was opened
- The Spirit of God descended like a dove
- A voice from heaven said, **"This is my Son, whom I love; with him I am well pleased."**

God can read our hearts, and when we come to Him in humility and faith and submit our lives to His will, heaven opens, the Spirit of God fills us, and God says, **"You are my child with whom I am well pleased."**

What does God see when He reads your heart?

Charles

One Year Plan : Psalm 112, John 4, Ezekiel 43 - 44
Two Year Plan : Psalm 132:10-18, John 20:1-18, Isaiah 15 (Yr 1)
Zephaniah 1 (Yr 2)

The God of Elijah

Psalm 146:3 says, **"Do not put your trust in princes or mortal men who cannot save."** Instead put your hope in God and know His power and blessing.

Elisha had seen the reality of God working through his master Elijah; he wanted more of the same power and set out to shadow Elijah until he was taken to heaven. He then took hold of Elijah's cloak, symbolising the authority and anointing he sought, but he first took off his own clothes and tore them apart, in recognition of his own limitation. He knew that human resources could never be compared with divine power.

Moses too came to this point; after trusting himself and failing, God was now asking him to deliver His people from their captivity. His response was, **"Who am I that I should go to Pharaoh and bring the Israelites out of Egypt?"** To which God replied, **"I will be with you."** (Exodus 3:11-12) Later on, when he was in the desert struggling and again acknowledged his inadequacy, God said, **"My presence will go with you, and I will give you rest."** (Exodus 33:14)

David conquered Goliath with that same sense of personal inadequacy. He knew that humanly speaking he was facing an impossible situation, but declared, **"I come against you in the name of the Lord Almighty ... this day the Lord will hand you over to me..."** (1 Samuel 17:45-46)

Peter and John also acknowledged their human weakness as they declared, **"Why do you stare at us as if by our own power or godliness we had made this man walk? ... By faith in the name of Jesus this man whom you see and know was made strong."** (Acts 3:12,16)

Take your example from Elisha who stripped of his own human resources, took hold of Elijah's cloak, struck the water of the Jordan and said, **"Where now is the Lord, the God of Elijah?"** God showed up, the waters divided, and Elisha walked through into a new life of faith and trusting in God.

So, who do you trust today?

Joyce

One Year Plan : Psalm 113, John 5, Ezekiel 45 - 46
Two Year Plan : Psalm 133, John 20:19-31, Isaiah 16 (Yr 1)
Zephaniah 2 (Yr 2)

Say, "No"

'No' is a simple word that can be used in many creative ways. When raising our children we found a clearly spoken and strongly directed **'No'** to have a powerful effect. Today, sadly, I observe too much of what I would describe as **'discipline by negotiation'**. When I am in the supermarket, I often see parents trying to stop their children taking the sweets off the shelves by seeking to reason with them and persuade them to return the packet to its rightful place! Saying, **"No!"** is quicker and more effective; when you start negotiating you can so easily lose the argument and spoil the child.

Titus 2:11-12 says, **"For the grace of God that brings salvation has appeared to all men. It teaches us to say 'No' to ungodliness and worldly passions, and to live self-controlled, upright and godly lives in this present age."** That is an amazing statement; God's grace gives us the power to say, **"No!"** to sin. God knows that once we start have an internal discussion about whether or not to sin, we are much more likely to fall. Just say, **"No!"** to sin.

When the devil tempted Jesus in the wilderness, He did not enter into a discussion with him; He refused to be drawn, spoke words of scripture and ended the argument swiftly. The devil tried to make Him turn stones into bread, and Jesus replied, **"Man does not live by bread alone but by every word that proceeds from the mouth of God."** (Luke 4:4) Just say, **"No!"** to temptation.

Jesus said, **"Who of you by worrying can add a single hour to his life?"** (Matthew 6:27) Worry is a fruitless and energy-sapping exercise. Paul takes up the same theme when he says, **"Do not be anxious about anything but in everything by prayer and petition with thanksgiving make your requests known to God."** (Philippians 4:6) The clear instruction is to pray and not to worry. Just say, **"No!"** to worry.

Let us recapture the power of saying, **"No!"**

Charles

One Year Plan : Psalm 114, John 6, Ezekiel 47 - 48
Two Year Plan : Psalm 134, John 21:1-14, Isaiah 17 (Yr 1)
Zephaniah 3 (Yr 2)

Be Alert Today!

"So, if you think you are standing firm, be careful that you don't fall!" (1 Corinthians 10:12) The Message says it this way: **"Don't be so naïve and self-confident ... you could fall flat on your face as easily as anyone else. Forget about self-confidence; it's useless. Cultivate God-confidence."**

Jesus constantly warned the disciples to be alert, on their guard, to stay awake and to be vigilant. It's a good warning. I find that there are times when I am very aware of needing and asking for heavenly resources, and then at other times I catch myself doing 'my own thing' using human experience rather than asking what the Holy Spirit is saying. In 2 Peter 1:3 we are promised **"everything we need for life and godliness."**

While thinking about such things, I read a story of an Old Testament prophet who started by listening and then moved into human wisdom with **grave consequences**. 1 Kings 13 tells this amazing story. A man of God was directed to speak and prophesy against pagan worship. King Jeroboam, who was actively involved in such practices, tried to seize him, but in so doing his hand shrivelled up. The prophet prayed for him and the arm was restored. The king was thrilled and asked the prophet to eat with him, but the prophet revealed that he was under orders to eat nothing and to go home by another route. Awesome stuff!

Having accomplished his mission, he let down his guard and was totally deceived when an old man claiming to be a prophet with a contrary word, supposedly from God, persuaded him to eat with him. The consequences were disastrous: **he was killed by a lion!**

He started alert but died because he failed to remain on duty. It is a strange incident but one we need to take note of – at all times we need to be listening to the voice of the Holy Spirit.

Be alert today – stay on duty!

Joyce

One Year Plan : Psalm 115, John 7, Daniel 1 - 2
Two Year Plan : Psalm 135:1-12, John 21:15-25, Isaiah 18 (Yr 1)
Ezra 1 (Yr 2)

The Holy Scissors

During some days of Prayer and Fasting, a prophetic word came in which God said, **"I want you to be a holy people, fully set apart for my purposes."** This reminded me of an incident that happened when our children were in their teens and the challenge of getting five children out of the house in time to catch the school bus was considerable.

One morning in the middle of the melee, Joyce was preparing for a day of dressmaking, when the cry went out, **"Has anyone seen my dressmaking scissors?"** These were not **any old scissors** but a very expensive instrument, which was normally very carefully stored with the rest of the dressmaking equipment.

This galvanised the whole household; a rapid search ensued, with an eye on the clock as the time of the impending departure of the school bus drew ever nearer. It was clear to all when the question rang out that no-one would be leaving the house until the scissors were found – bus or no bus.

In a very short time one of our sons came down the stairs clutching the item in question. Joyce looked relieved but then asked, **"What on earth were you doing with my scissors?"** The reply came, **"I was cutting my toe nails!"** There was a minor explosion: **"These scissors must not be used for anything except my dressmaking; to use them for something else will blunt the blade and render them useless. Don't you ever cut your toe nails with them again!"**

Peace was soon restored, forgiveness given and the bus caught, but as I reflected on this incident, I realised that these were **holy scissors**: they had one dedicated purpose. When God says to us, **"Be holy, for I the Lord am holy,"** He means that He wants us fully dedicated to Him and His purpose for our lives and not used in any other way.

Charles

One Year Plan : Psalm 116, John 8, Daniel 3 - 4
Two Year Plan : Psalm 135:13-21, James 1, Isaiah 19 (Yr 1)
Ezra 2 (Yr 2)

Something Special

What was it about Jesus that caused the gospel writers to record that **"He grew in favour with God and men"** and that when **"He taught in their synagogues, everyone praised him"**? Children were drawn to Him; His reputation as a teacher, healer, and deliverer soon began to influence the masses. Something drew the people to Him; there was a grace and a favour, something special, a kind of perfume, a mystery quality that was magnetic.

Psalm 67:1 says, **"May God be gracious to us and bless us and make his face to shine upon us, that your ways may be known on earth, and your salvation among the nations."**

The writer of this psalm is asking personally for this blessing in order to reflect God to those around him. Jesus demonstrated this, and the individuals and crowds He met marvelled at Him – and knew it was God at work.

How about you and I? Do we attract in the same way? I believe we should and that as God's blessing and favour rests on us it should be visible. Our countenance should reflect inner peace and joy. The way we act should be motivated by love and compassion, rather than by selfishness.

We have a responsibility to give **'good press'** to our Saviour and to attract people as He did. Often Christians are portrayed as miserable, long-faced and sober – their chief colour, black, and their favourite word, 'No'.

This was not how Jesus lived and acted, and it must not be how we are seen.

Psalm 67:1 in the Message is a prayer: **"God, mark us with grace and blessing! Smile! The whole country will see how you work, all the godless nations see how you save."**

Joyce

One Year Plan : Psalm 117, John 9, Daniel 5 - 6
Two Year Plan : Psalm 136, James 2, Isaiah 20 (Yr 1)
Ezra 3 (Yr 2)

What Hymn did They Sing?

At the end of the account of the Last Supper in Matthew's Gospel it says, **"When they had sung a hymn, they went out to the Mount of Olives."** (Matthew 26:30) Every time I read those words I thought, **"What hymn did they sing?"** It obviously did not come from 'Hymns Ancient & Modern' or even from 'Songs of Fellowship'! But one day, as I was reading Psalm 118 in my NIV Study Bible, I referred to the notes and read concerning this psalm that **"...it may have been sung by Jesus and His disciples at the conclusion of the Last Supper."** I read the psalm again with fresh eyes. These may have been the words that were sung by Jesus as He was facing the greatest trial of His life and by His disciples as they stepped into unknown territory. Would this hymn have given them strength in their time of need? Would it have encouraged their faith?

Here are some extracts from the Psalm:

"Give thanks to the Lord, for he is good; His love endures forever."

"The Lord is with me; I will not be afraid. What can man do to me?"

**"I was pushed back and about to fall,
But the Lord helped me.
The Lord is my strength and my song;
He has become my salvation."**

"Shouts of joy and victory resound in the tents of the righteous."

"This is the day that the Lord has made; Let us rejoice and be glad in it."

**"You are my God,
And I will give you thanks;
You are my God and I will exalt you.
Give thanks to the Lord for he is good;
His love endures forever."**

Hymns can provide tremendous comfort and give strength when we are facing difficulties, challenges and the unknown.

If you are facing trials and difficulties today, what hymn will you sing?

Charles

One Year Plan : Psalm 118, John 10, Daniel 7 - 8
Two Year Plan : Psalm 137, James 3, Isaiah 21 (Yr 1)
Ezra 4 (Yr 2)

Watching your Patch

Are you **watching** over **your patch**? In Mark 13:32-36 Jesus uses such words as **"Be on guard!" "Be alert!" "Keep Watch!"** and **"Watch!"** As I was thinking about this, I was reminded of the story of how Nehemiah rebuilt the walls of Jerusalem and positioned guards on duty outside their houses, who worked with swords in one hand and trowels in the other! Nehemiah 4:17-18 says, **"Those who carried materials did their work with one hand and held a weapon in the other, and each of the builders wore his sword at his side as he worked."**

Everyone was involved: goldsmiths, perfumers, local mayors, as well as Levites and temple servants. Residents of Jerusalem were appointed as guards, some at their posts and some near their own houses.

It is our job to **watch our patch**: our family, our dwelling, city, land, and nation. Watching has an active sense of being on the offensive, looking out for trouble in order to avert it, taking the initiative, listening with intent.

Peter gives these instructions: **"Be self-controlled and alert. Your enemy the devil prowls around like a roaring lion looking for someone to devour. Resist him, standing firm in the faith..."** (1 Peter 5:8-9)

Remember the words of Jesus: **"You know that if the homeowner had known what time of night the burglar would arrive, he would have been there with his dogs to prevent the break in. Be vigilant just like that!"** (Matthew 24:43-44, The Message)

It is **your** job to be vigilant over your patch; others will support you, agree with you in prayer, help you – but it's not my job to protect your patch; **it's yours!**

Joyce

One Year Plan :	Psalm 119:1-56, John 11, Daniel 9 - 10
Two Year Plan :	Psalm 138, James 4, Isaiah 22 (Yr 1)
	Ezra 5 (Yr 2)

Strength and Peace

Weariness and worry are probably the two things that most undermine our quality of life and our health. Today's magazines and media are constantly seeking to give us the latest remedy or fix; and yet the psalmist states, **"The Lord gives strength to his people, the Lord blesses his people with peace."** (Psalm 29:11)

Real strength does not merely come out of our balanced lifestyle but from our relationship with God. The Apostle Paul's responsibilities were demanding and he had a very busy schedule, yet his testimony was, **"I can do all things through Christ who gives me strength."** (Philippians 4:13) At another time he said, **"For when I am weak, then I am strong."** (2 Corinthians 12:10) He knew how to draw strength from above.

Jesus describes peace as a gift, not the result of resolving all areas of conflict and stress. **"Peace I leave with you; my peace I give you."** (John 14:27)

In Galatians 5:22 we discover that peace is a fruit of the Spirit: **"But the fruit of the Spirit is love, joy, peace, patience, kindness, goodness, faithfulness, gentleness and self-control."**

And, Paul declares that peace comes through praise, prayer and thanksgiving: **"Rejoice in the Lord always. I will say it again: Rejoice! Do not be anxious about anything, but in everything, by prayer and petition, with thanksgiving present your requests to God. And the peace of God, which transcends all understanding, will guard your hearts and minds in Christ Jesus."** (Philippians 4:4-7)

We all need strength and peace; the question is: are we going to the right source?

As fatigue and anxiety seek to overwhelm, let us make God's promise, spoken by David, specific for our situation and say, **"Today, Lord, give me your strength and bless me with your peace."**

Charles

One Year Plan : Psalm 119:57-112, John 12, Daniel 11 - 12
Two Year Plan : Psalm 139:1-12, James 5, Isaiah 23 (Yr 1)
Ezra 6 (Yr 2)

Black Boots

I'm always glad when God answers personal 'little prayers; amazed at His ability to help me with the seemingly small and what might seem insignificant details of everyday life.

On a recent visit to my daughter's, my grandson aged five kept putting on my Ugg Boot type slippers. Whenever I couldn't find them, they were on his feet – far too big, but he just loved them! With Christmas in mind I asked, **"Would you like some boots like mine but in your size?" "Yes,"** he replied, **"but black."** Knowing the fickle nature of young children, I repeated the question at the end of my stay, and the reply was very definite: **"Yes and black."**

I began my search and could find nothing in either the right size, colour or price range (the ones from Australia were going to cost 'a King's Ransom'). I asked a friend to keep a lookout when she was shopping, to which she agreed, but added, **"Have you asked God to bring them to you?"** I hadn't, so right there and then I did just that.

A few days later I had arranged a trip to Costco with a friend who holds a card, as it is a place I seldom visit. You may have guessed already, for as I entered the store there in front of me was an enormous pile of Ugg Type Boots; they appeared to be all in adult sizes, but I began my search, and right in the middle was one pair of boots waiting for me in the right child's size – and at an amazing price!

I am so thrilled, and every time I think about this I am overwhelmed by a God who cares, who is so personal and who delights to see me and ultimately my little grandson rejoicing in **black boots**.

Psalm 35:27 says, **"May those who delight in my vindication shout for joy and gladness; may they always say, 'The Lord be exalted who delights in the well being of his servant.'"**

Do you have any 'little' prayers that need answering?

Joyce

One Year Plan : Psalm 119:113-176, John 13, Hosea 1 - 3
Two Year Plan : Psalm 139:13-24, 1 Peter 1, Isaiah 24 (Yr 1)
Ezra 7 (Yr 2)

The People Factor

There are some who believe becoming more like Jesus is achieved by living in a hut on the top of a mountain, near to God and separated from people! Wrong!

We grow in love by loving others and learning how to receive love. 1 John 4:20 says, **"If anyone says 'I love God,' yet hates his brother, he is a liar. For anyone who does not love his brother, whom he has seen, cannot love God, whom he has not seen."**

We learn forgiveness by learning how to handle offences. Peter asked Jesus, **"Lord, how many times shall I forgive my brother when he sins against me? Up to seven times?"** The answer was 'seventy times seven', which is another way of saying you never stop forgiving others because Jesus never stops forgiving you.

We grow in confidence because others encourage us. Hebrews 10:24 says, **"And let us consider how we may spur one another along toward love and good deeds."**

We need friends who will help us carry heavy burdens and difficulties, and we need to share the loads of others. Galatians 6:2 says, **"Carry each other's burdens, and in this way you will fulfil the law of Christ."**

People who irritate us and oppose us challenge us to do what Jesus said: **"Love your enemies, do good to those who hate you, bless those who curse you, pray for those who mistreat you."** (Luke 6:27-28)

Even when we see the splinter in someone else's eye, it helps us see the log that is in our own eye and take it out first before we can help the other person remove their splinter. (Luke 6:41-42)

The goal is to be like Jesus; the **'people factor'** is to help us get there. Value the people around you today, both their plusses and minuses!

Charles

One Year Plan : Psalm 120, John 14, Hosea 4 - 5
Two Year Plan : Psalm 140, 1 Peter 2, Isaiah 25 (Yr 1)
Ezra 8 (Yr 2)

The Cry that God Responds to

When a baby is crying, there is only one person who truly understands that cry. Because of the bond of intimacy, **Mum** understands when the cry becomes a desperate cry. She discerns the **"pick me up and cuddle me"** cry; the **"I want something but I'm not sure what"** cry; or **the grizzle** – that is the baby's way of expressing a general discontent. However, when that cry changes to a particular note and intensity – the mother knows – this means business! She will now drop everything to meet the need that is being expressed!

A friend of mine found a lump under her arm. She had already had treatment for breast cancer and surgery. Looking at it in the natural, this was not good. Her responsibilities were many and the thought of further medical treatment and all it could entail caused a cry from her heart to God. It was a desperate cry, beyond words. It came with such intensity and urgency. God heard and touched her body. At that touch, the lump was no longer to be found. She had cried to God for healing on many occasions and seen medical and surgical answers – but this time the cry came out of the depths with an intensity that reached heaven.

When the nation of Israel was in such severe bondage in Egypt, they cried out to God and He sent them a deliverer in Moses (see Exodus 3:7-9). Also, childless Hannah cried out to God in great anguish and grief, and God heard her and Samuel was born (see 1 Samuel 1:15-17).

Sometimes I'm like the baby who grizzles and goes back to sleep, and grizzles again; my cry is expressing some need or discontent but has not become desperate. It has yet to become **"Give me or I die"** or **"I will not let You go unless You bless me."**

In Hebrews 5:7 we read that **"Jesus offered up prayers and petitions with loud cries and tears to the one who could save him from death, and he was heard because of his reverent submission."** The cry was heard and the answer for Jesus was resurrection.

Joyce

One Year Plan : Psalm 121, John 15, Hosea 6 - 7
Two Year Plan : Psalm 141, 1 Peter 3, Isaiah 26 (Yr 1)
Ezra 9 (Yr 2)

Shouts of Joy

A friend of mine regularly leads tours to the Holy Land, and one of the special places they visit in Jerusalem is the Upper Room where Jesus celebrated the Passover with His disciples. On a recent visit, as his group arrived at the Upper Room, they burst into exuberant praise and great rejoicing, the Holy Spirit powerfully filled the room, and several of the group were prayed for and received a strong infilling of the Holy Spirit.

This great demonstration of loud praise to God greatly offended a group who were following them into the Upper Room. For them a pilgrimage to the Holy Land is a solemn and quiet affair, but is that what God is looking for?

I was reading Psalm 47 which says, **"Clap your hands, all you nations; shout to God with cries of joy ... God has ascended amid shouts of joy, the Lord amid the sounding of trumpets. Sing praise to God, sing praises; sing praises to our King, sing praises."**

When we visit Burundi in Africa, on Sunday morning we join with seven thousand other believers in sounds of loud and exuberant praise to God – I love it! I love the joyful abandon with which these people express their praise to God. I am sure God loves to hear their **shouts of praise.**

Psalm 100 gives a strong command to **"Shout for joy to the Lord, all the earth. Worship the Lord with gladness; come before him with joyful songs."**

Many of you reading this really need to **"make a joyful noise to the Lord"**. It is time to stop being like Holy Land pilgrims who believe that 'holiness = quietness'. Find somewhere where you will not shock the neighbours and let rip. It will do you good – and God will get a great kick out of it because He loves noisy praise.

Charles

One Year Plan : Psalm 122, John 16, Hosea 8 - 9
Two Year Plan : Psalm 142, 1 Peter 4, Isaiah 27 (Yr 1)
Ezra 10 (Yr 2)

Servants

I wonder if you read the beginning of the New Testament letters where the writer introduces himself. For example, **"Peter, a servant of the Lord."** Paul in most of his letters, introduces himself as a **"servant as well as an apostle"**. So, what does it mean to be a servant of the Lord?

Peter, addressing believers, says, **"Live as free men ... but also ... live as servants of God."** (1 Peter 2:16) There is an old prayer, part of which says, "...**whose service is perfect freedom."**

A servant is trained to obey commands. You and I are also called to follow instructions, not to make our own decisions or do our own thing. Deep within us we should have that unspoken attitude of **"Lord, what do you require in this situation?"**

If we are to obey instructions, we must first be sensitive to God's voice and listen to what He is saying in every situation. We are called to bring heaven's rule to earth – but often we are not sure what heaven requires.

Jesus said, **"Whoever serves me must follow me; and where I am, my servant also will be. My Father will honour the one who serves me."** (John 12:26)

Jesus calls us not only to be His willing servants, but also His friends – able to be directed by Him at any moment in time. Looking at His eyes, seeing and feeling His reactions, anticipating His desires, at all times in intimate communion with Him.

You can't have two masters. (Matthew 6:24) Today, reaffirm your allegiance to Jesus, King of Kings. Ask forgiveness for independent actions and look again to the Lord whose throne is in heaven but who has specific tasks for His servants on earth.

Joyce

One Year Plan : Psalm 123, John 17, Hosea 10 - 11
Two Year Plan : Psalm 143, 1 Peter 5, Isaiah 28 (Yr 1)
Zechariah 1 (Yr 2)

Setbacks or Stepping Stones?

When close friends of ours were unrighteously forced out of their teaching positions, we were perplexed and grieved that their years of devotion to education in this country should be rewarded with such treachery.

We spent time talking and praying and seeking the best way forward. Would this major setback cause them to sink into bitterness and consume them with endless legal battles? It was an extremely difficult time, but we have observed them move forward with faith and forgiveness.

To quote from a letter we have just received, **"People are sometimes surprised that we bear no resentment to those who planned our downfall at school. It is not surprising because we are all in God's hands. From God we can expect the best."**

Joseph spent thirteen years with what appeared to be one setback after another, but when he met his brothers who had been the cause of all the trouble he said, **"Do not be distressed and do not be angry with yourselves for selling me here, because it was to save lives that God sent me here."** (Genesis 45:5)

These brothers did not really believe that Joseph could act with such generosity of spirit, and when their father Jacob eventually died they expected revenge. Joseph had to reassure them once again: **"Don't be afraid. Am I in the place of God? You intended to harm me, but God intended it for good to accomplish what is now being done, the saving of many lives."** (Genesis 50:19-20)

Are you facing setbacks in your life at this time? Your enemy the devil would want to see disappointments and difficulties destroying you. But God wants to take every setback and turn it into a stepping stone.

Charles

One Year Plan : Psalm 124, John 18, Hosea 12 - 14
Two Year Plan : Psalm 144, 2 Peter 1, Isaiah 29 (Yr 1)
Zechariah 2 (Yr 2)

Be Like a Lizard

"A lizard can be caught with the hand, yet it is found in kings' palaces." (Proverbs 30:28) In the same way believers can find their way into strategic places as they individually follow God's plan for their lives.

Queen Esther, a simple Jewish girl, demonstrated that she had come to this royal position in order to rescue the nation of Israel.

Joseph, rejected by his brothers and separated from his family, found himself taken from prison and promoted to Prime Minister, enabling him to save millions from starvation, including his own family.

These are well known stories, but what about Ahikam, son of Shaphan, one of King Josiah's officials, who was sent to the prophetess Huldah and received a word from the Lord, which was to assure the King that he would not see disaster but die in peace (2 Kings 22:12-20)? Ahikam was also able to bring up a son Gedeliah, who was trusted enough by Nebuchadnezzar to be appointed governor over Jerusalem and because of this high position was enabled to save Jeremiah's life. (Jeremiah 39:14)

What about you? If you belong to Jesus, there is a destiny and purpose being worked out in your life, and you may find yourself in a situation where you have greater wisdom and integrity than possessed by anyone else around you.

We need to be known as people whose word can be trusted, people who cannot be bribed or intimidated. God also wants us to train our young people to value wisdom, resist foolish behaviour, have no skeletons in the cupboard, so He can also position them in places of influence and power.

Pauls says, **"Do everything without complaining or arguing, so that you may become blameless and pure, children of God without fault in a crooked and depraved generation, in which you shine like stars in the universe as you hold out the word of life."** (Philippians 2:15-16)

Why? So that God can have his people as salt and shining stars in today's society.

Joyce

One Year Plan : Psalm 125, John 19, Joel 1 - 3
Two Year Plan : Psalm 145:1-9, 2 Peter 2, Isaiah 30 (Yr 1)
Zechariah 3 (Yr 2)

Rebuke

Can you receive correction? Can you handle a rebuke from someone you respect? Can you hear truth about yourself, even from someone you find hard to respect?

If you can, then you can change – you can become a transformed person, and there is no limit to what you can become. If you cannot, you will remain stuck with what you now are.

Can you give a rebuke? Do you love your brother enough to speak the truth into his life? If you can rebuke without rancour, or to score points, you may be doing your friend the greatest favour.

There are many scriptures that contain the word **'rebuke'**. I find many of these very challenging, and I want to be someone who can receive a rebuke, and change. I also want to have enough love and courage to give a rebuke, and trust and believe that it can be creatively life-changing.

Here are some of those scriptures:

Proverbs 28:23: **"He who rebukes a man will in the end gain more favour than he who has a flattering tongue."**

Psalm 141:5: **"Let a righteous man strike me—it is a kindness; let him rebuke me—it is oil on my head. My head will not refuse it."**

Proverbs 9:8: **"Do not rebuke a mocker or he will hate you; rebuke a wise man and he will love you."**

Proverbs 15:31: **"He who listens to a life-giving rebuke will be at home among the wise."**

Proverbs 19:25: **"Flog a mocker, and the simple will learn prudence; rebuke a discerning man, and he will gain knowledge."**

Ecclesiastes 7:5: **"It is better to heed a wise man's rebuke than to listen to the song of fools."**

Why is this so important? Jesus said, **"Then you will know the truth, and the truth will set you free."** (John 8:32) Paul says in Romans that it is God's purpose that we should be conformed to the likeness of His Son. **That means that I need to constantly be willing to be challenged and to change.**

Charles

One Year Plan : Psalm 126, John 20, Amos 1 - 3
Two Year Plan : Psalm 145:10-21, 2 Peter 3, Isaiah 31 (Yr 1)
Zechariah 4 (Yr 2)

Let... Do Not Let!

What a strange heading! Few words, but they are commands to Christian believers which are given for their spiritual health and their own good.

Paul gave this command to the Colossian Church: **"Let the peace of Christ rule in your hearts ... and be thankful."** (Colossians 3:15)

There is a choice here; we can decide to be obedient and literally **let** peace have its way. There have been times, especially during conflict, when I would rather hold onto the circumstances that have caused me to lose peace than to **let** peace return. How foolish! – and yet how easy to do.

Jesus said, **"Do not let your hearts be troubled,"** (John 14:1) and later in John 14:27, He says, **"Peace I leave with you; my peace I give you."**

So what are you going to do? It's a choice to shut the door on trouble and fear and open the door to let peace in.

Paul adds to his instruction, **"...and be thankful."** At one time, I found myself alone in our home with my young children. They were all in bed as I sat watching the ten o'clock news and heard that a violent prisoner had escaped from jail and was on the loose in our vicinity. We were being instructed to make sure our houses were secure and warned not have any contact with this dangerous criminal. Our front door had a defective lock and was constantly blowing open in the wind – so you can imagine my churning emotions. However, I had to choose to keep fear out and let peace in. How did I do it? – With difficulty but through thanksgiving.

As I battled with this fear, right in the middle of the crisis, God spoke to me and said, **"Write a psalm of thanksgiving. Thank me; start with your own life and thank me for my goodness to you."**

As I meditated on God's faithfulness, His many acts of kindness, rescue and protection over many years ... **I fell asleep in peace and woke to a new day safe and untroubled.**

So **let** peace rule today, and **do not let** trouble and fear rob you ... and be thankful.

Joyce

One Year Plan :	Psalm 127, John 21, Amos 4 - 5
Two Year Plan :	Psalm 146, 1 John 1, Isaiah 32 (Yr 1)
	Zechariah 5 (Yr 2)

One Word

Joyce and I were taking a seminar in the Manchester area; our theme was **'Christ in You'** and we were enjoying teaching a very responsive group of folk. In one of Joyce's sessions, she suddenly diverted from her theme and said, "**Baptism... the Lord is showing me that there are some here who have never been baptised in water and have been resisting those who have tried to encourage them.**" The diversion lasted only for a few moments, and then Joyce continued with her teaching.

We later heard that at a Service of Baptism held in that church, three folk mentioned in their testimonies that Joyce's word had been the key that had made them decide to respond to the call to be baptised. It only took **one word** for God to get through and cause these people to respond, obey and move forwards in their walk with God.

This set me thinking about some situations in the ministry of Jesus. When the centurion was seeking healing for his servant, he did not feel worthy for Jesus to come into his house but said, **"Just say the word and my servant will be healed."** Jesus was astounded at his faith and replied, **"Go! It will be done just as you believed it would."** And his servant was healed at that very hour. (Matthew 8:5-13)

On another occasion a royal official came to Jesus and said, **"Sir, come down before my child dies."** Jesus replied, **"You may go. Your son will live."** The scripture continues, **"The man took Jesus at his word and departed."** When he arrived back home he found out that his son had been healed the moment Jesus had spoken those words. (John 4:46-54)

The **one word** Joyce spoke was responded to with obedience and had a profound effect on those who were baptised. When **one word** spoken by Jesus was responded to with faith, miracles happened.

Don't miss out on the <u>one word</u> that comes from God; it could change your life forever.

Charles

One Year Plan : Psalm 128, Revelation 1, Amos 6 - 7
Two Year Plan : Psalm 147:1-11, 1 John 2, Isaiah 33 (Yr 1)
Zechariah 6 (Yr 2)

Many Sons

The death of Jesus on the cross at Calvary releases you and me into the life which God intended Adam to live before he fell: a life of freedom, joy, authority over creation, fellowship with the Creator and so much more.

Paul writes in 1 Corinthians 2:8, **"None of the rulers of this age understood it, for if they had, they would not have crucified the Lord of glory."** Satan believed that he had caused the death of the **Son of God**, but in that moment, through Calvary, God opened up the way for the birth of **many sons**.

One night, I dreamed that I had to catch a chicken; it was carrying some sort of germ or disease, and I needed to capture it before it infected others. I set out to find it and thought I could identify the particular bird, but as I entered the wood in which I was searching, there wasn't just one chicken – it was full of identical birds. I was totally incapable of identifying the one I was searching for as they all looked the same!

Could satan have a similar problem? He crucified the Lord of glory – thinking that was the end – however, the resurrected Jesus is alive and living in many sons. God's plan is that Jesus, by His Holy Spirit, lives in all His children, changing them moment by moment to be **"conformed to the likeness of his Son"**. (Romans 8:29)

Some of you will have seen the children's book 'Where's Wally?' where you try to pick him out from the midst of crowds of identical beings. God's plan is to have an end time army of **many sons** doing the works of Jesus – being Jesus wherever they are!

No wonder Paul says, **"The whole creation waits in eager expectation for the sons of God to be revealed."** (Romans 8:19)

Are you one of those **many sons?**

Joyce

One Year Plan : Psalm 129, Revelation 2, Amos 8 - 9
Two Year Plan : Psalm 147:12-20, 1 John 3, Isaiah 34 (Yr 1)
Zechariah 7 (Yr 2)

Go – and Report Back

Jesus sent out his twelve disciples with a specific task. He gave them detailed instructions and the authority they needed to do the work. **They went out to preach the Kingdom of God and to heal the sick**. (Luke 9:1-6)

Later, Jesus sent out seventy-two others to go into the towns and villages, find a convenient place to stay and **to eat what was set before them, to heal the sick and to preach the Kingdom.** (Luke 10:1-12)

They were to go; they were to do what they had been asked to do; but they were also expected to report back. In Luke 10:17 it says, **"The seventy-two returned with joy and said, 'Lord, even the demons submit to us in your name.'"**

So what have you and I been sent to do today, this week, this year? Have you ever reported back? Have you told Jesus the results of your endeavours? Do you expect to achieve great things in the Name of Jesus?

If you aim at nothing, you will probably hit nothing!

Today, ask Jesus, **"What would you have me to do? What are you sending me to do at this time?"**

God has a special assignment just for you today. Listen to His voice and wait for His instructions. Then do what He is telling you to do.

It may be making a phone call or visiting someone. He might be telling you to write someone a letter or send an email. He may be asking you to lay hands on someone and heal them. It could be a great task or something small. So, just do it...

But remember: go and report back!

Joyce

One Year Plan : Psalm 130, Revelation 3, Obadiah 1
Two Year Plan : Psalm 148, 1 John 4, Isaiah 35 (Yr 1)
Zechariah 8 (Yr 2)

Beyond Understanding

At a Leaders' Lunch in Bristol we listened to Bill Johnson from Redding, California, who is the master of the one-liner. He gave us this very thought provoking statement: **"If you want the peace that passes understanding, you have to give up the right to understanding."**

Philippians 4:6-7 says, **"Have no anxiety about anything, but in everything, by prayer and petition present your requests to God. And the peace of God which passes all understanding will guard you hearts and your minds in Christ Jesus."** Worry is a tyrant that can prevent us from receiving not only God's peace but also His answers.

Whenever something difficult or tragic happens, we keep asking the question, **"Why?"** God sometimes chooses to withhold understanding. I don't know why, but I know that God has a bigger picture and He wants to support us, strengthen us and give us peace despite all that is happening.

Proverbs 3:5-6 says, **"Trust in the Lord with all your heart and lean not on your own understanding; in all your ways acknowledge him, and he will make your paths straight."** These verses make it clear and simple. Put your trust in the Lord, always give Him the first place in your life, lean on Him, and He has promised to make your path straight.

Our rational minds can hold us prisoner; they can block faith and prevent us leaning on God. Isaiah 55:9 says, **"As the heavens are higher than the earth, so are my ways higher than your ways and my thoughts than your thoughts."**

A walk of faith is not based on reason, but it opens up the way for you to live with **"the peace that is beyond understanding"** – live in it today!

Charles

One Year Plan : Psalm 131, Revelation 4, Jonah 1 - 4
Two Year Plan : Psalm 149, 1 John 5, Isaiah 36 (Yr 1)
Zechariah 9 (Yr 2)

The Temple of the Living God

King Solomon built a temple for his God, even though he knew, **"The heavens, even the highest heaven, cannot contain you. How much less this temple I have built!"** (1 Kings 8:27)

In 1 Kings 8:13 (The Message) Solomon says to God, **"I have built this splendid temple, O God, to mark your invisible presence forever."** God hides His glory in clouds and darkness to protect us. Moses, God's friend, could only view God's back. God placed him in the cleft of the rock and placed His hand over the entrance for his protection. Moses never spoke of that encounter – it was beyond words.

A cloud of glory accompanied the dedication of Solomon's temple, and the priests were unable to perform their service because of the cloud. Solomon prayed that God would fill this building, have his eyes and ears opened to the prayers prayed in the building and that whenever men's hearts were turned in faith towards it – in trouble or sickness, in war or whatever – God would hear and answer their cries. He also prayed that all nations would come to this temple to marvel at **"this presence"** which was beyond the architecture and design, beyond the gold and silver. They were to meet the One whose mighty hand and outstretched arm alone can perform miracles, answer prayer and cause true worship and reverential fear of God.

Paul, in 1 Corinthians 3:16, speaks of the Church being the temple of the living God and of our individual bodies also being a temple. (1 Corinthians 6:19) The enormity of linking these two thoughts has overwhelmed me. Is my body a splendid temple to contain the **"invisible presence"** of God? Is the Church (local, national or global) a place where God is known to dwell? A place where both individuals in need and world leaders can come to find answers or to marvel?

Will you cry out for God to come with His glory and inhabit you personally and also His Church? Will you pray that men may know the invisible but awesome presence of Almighty God, the King of Kings, coming to His temple?

Joyce

One Year Plan : Psalm 132, Revelation 5, Micah 1 - 2
Two Year Plan : Psalm 150, 2 John 1, Isaiah 37 (Yr 1)
Zechariah 10 (Yr 2)

Where are you Planted?

Psalm 92:12-13 says, **"The righteous [are] ... planted in the house of the Lord, they will flourish in the courts of our God."** These verses set me thinking. What does it mean to be **"planted in the house of the Lord"**? I am quite sure it does not mean that I should apply for the job of verger in my local parish church!

But it does mean that I should put down my roots in good soil. I need to wake up in an atmosphere of praise as Psalm 57:8-9 instructs: **"Awake, my soul! Awake, harp and lyre! I will awaken the dawn. I will praise you, O Lord, among the nations; I will sing of you among the peoples."**

I need to understand that thanksgiving is the best environment for receiving answers to prayer and dealing with anxiety, as Paul told the Philippians: **"Do not be anxious about anything, but in everything, by prayer and petition, with thanksgiving, present your requests to God."** (Philippians 4:6)

I need to read the Bible each day, not as a chore or a duty, but as encouragement to root growth in my life and to establish strength and resilience. Jesus said to His disciples, **"The words I have spoken to you are spirit and they are life."** (John 6:63)

I must also constantly live in an atmosphere of encouragement, as 1 Thessalonians 5:11 says: **"Therefore encourage one another and build each other up."**

Carefully check where you are planted, and what your life is producing – it could be fear, worry, criticism, self-pity, or just negativity.

A couple of years ago we made some raised beds in our garden so that we could grow and enjoy fresh vegetables – but we have had mixed results. When we ask the experts why, the first thing they say is, **"What are you putting into the soil?"**

I want to be **"planted in the house of the Lord"** because as Psalm 92:14 continues, **"They will still bear fruit in old age, they will stay fresh and green."** Good words for some of us who might not be as young as we once were!

Charles

One Year Plan : Psalm 133, Revelation 6, Micah 3 - 5
Two Year Plan : Proverbs 25:1-10, 3 John 1, Isaiah 38 (Yr 1)
Zechariah 11 (Yr 2)

Containers or Contents

We seem to be a society obsessed with packaging – presentation over product! We've all experienced the disappointment of sampling something that looked good, appeared to offer much and yet the contents were inferior.

God designs things very differently – the contents are infinitely more important to him, the container almost irrelevant.

Paul describes us as jars of clay containing treasure. 2 Corinthians 4:7 in the Message says, **"We carry this 'precious message' around in the unadorned pots of our ordinary lives. That's to prevent anyone confusing God's incomparable power with us."**

So who and what is the precious message – this treasure? It's Jesus – so what does He contain? **"He is the image of the invisible God ... In Christ all the fullness of the Deity dwells in bodily form."** (Colossians 1:15, 2:9)

During His days on earth the packaging confused the people; it looked so ordinary, so human. The contents were amazing: no one spoke with such wisdom; no one poured out such selfless love; no one exhibited such peace and joy. No wonder the people exclaimed, **"What manner of man is this?"** They were looking at a human package containing the very essence of the Godhead, not contaminated by sin and self, but fully God and fully man.

I have the same person living in me – heaven's treasure in an old clay pot! So do you. If you have Jesus living in you then you already have all you need for life and godliness (see 2 Peter 1:3).

I feel I've spent too much time looking for more, waiting for 'something' to come from heaven, from the special meeting, or the latest book. The Bible tells me that **"Christ in whom all the fullness of the Deity dwells"** has given to me that same fullness. (Colossians 2:9-10)

1. Pray today that you will value in a new way the treasure who is already inside of you.
2. Pray that you will listen to Him, talk to Him, and receive instructions and direction from Him.
3. What does He want to do today? Who does He want to meet? You have this treasure in you; carry Him carefully, aware that one word or one touch from Him can radically change people and situations.

Joyce

One Year Plan : Psalm 134, Revelation 7, Micah 6 - 7
Two Year Plan : Proverbs 25:11-19, Jude 1, Isaiah 39 (Yr 1)
Zechariah 12 (Yr 2)

DECEMBER

The Herrnhut Star

At the beginning of Advent we always hang an illuminated star outside of our front door. It originates from Herrnhut in Germany, which is the place from which the Moravian missionaries spread the light of Jesus all round the world through their pioneering work. I first saw these stars in the former East Germany more than twenty years ago. Just after Christmas I had left UK with a small team to speak at a retreat for a Lutheran Order of Sisters in Schoenebeck. Their Christmas decorations which were wonderful were still in place, and seeing my enthusiasm, and as a token of thanks, I was given several decorations including a star.

The star is such a powerful symbol. When Jesus was born in Bethlehem, God did not choose to announce His birth with a lot of words and declarations. He filled the sky with glory and took the shepherds by surprise before the angels announced the momentous event. God did not speak prophetic messages to the wise men but placed a star in the sky which they followed to Bethlehem.

The prophet Isaiah said, **"The people walking in darkness have seen a great light,"** and Jesus said, **"I am the light of the world. Whoever follows me will never walk in darkness, but will have the light of life."**

In the Psalms we read, **"The entrance of your word brings light."** This is a dark time of the year for those of us in the northern hemisphere; the shortest day will soon be upon us. The lights that fill our homes are comforting, adding brightness and fun to the festivities, but they will soon be taken down and packed away for another year.

Jesus gives us light and joy which cannot be extinguished; He sees the darkness within, and He longs to come into our place of need and fill it with His peace and light.

Paul wrote, **"For God who said, 'Let light shine out of darkness,' made his light shine in our hearts to give us the light of the knowledge of the glory of God in the face of Christ."** (2 Corinthians 4:6)

Charles

One Year Plan : Psalm 135, Revelation 8, Nahum 1 - 3
Two Year Plan : Proverbs 25:20-28, Revelation 1:1-8, Isaiah 40 (Yr 1)
Zechariah 13 (Yr 2)

"But How?"

After an angel had announced to Mary that she was to become pregnant with the Son of God, she exclaimed, **"But how?"** The angel's answer was a supernatural one, but essentially it is the same for every **"But how?'** question today! Luke 1:35 says, **"The Holy Spirit will come upon you, the power of the Most High will hover over you..."**

Every time you are faced with **"But how?"** remember: the Holy Spirit, the third person of the Godhead has chosen to be alongside to help you. He is the great **helper** sent by God the Father to be a help, to remind us of what Jesus taught, to show us all things, and to be with us so that we never feel abandoned or helpless. He is the expression of Jesus with us today, living inside us, always available to help, explain and instruct (see John 14:16-17).

I love His creative solutions. It should not surprise me that He who brought creative order out of chaos and brought light into darkness as He hovered over the formless earth should continue this today.

So what darkness are you struggling with? What practical answers do you need? When you come to the end of trying, reasoning and scheming, ask for divine resources and let the Holy Spirit answer your **"But how?"** questions and give you miracle answers. It may be a simple as, **"Holy Spirit, Maker of the universe, how do I remove this stain?"**, or it may be a far more complex and life-challenging situation.

The answer I believe is always the same – **"The Holy Spirit will hover over you"** – and miraculous insight, leading to practical solutions, will be the result. I feel very sad when I think of how often I have been slow to tap into His vast resources – and usually only when I have come to an end of my own!

Direct your **'but hows'** to the Holy Spirit and watch Him release divine answers and resources.

Joyce

One Year Plan : Psalm 136, Revelation 9, Habakkuk 1 - 2
Two Year Plan : Proverbs 26:1-9, Revelation 1:9-20, Isaiah 41 (Yr 1)
Zechariah 14 (Yr 2)

A Star

At this festive time of year stars feature very strongly. I was discussing with a friend how a star guided the Wise Men. What was it? Was it a single star? Did it move? Did they know where they were going? Matthew 2:9 says, **"...the star they had seen in the east went ahead of them until it stopped over the place where the child was."**

Perhaps God used a star to guide the Wise Men because the baby they had come to worship had been described as a **star**. Thousands of years earlier God chose a rather truculent prophet Balaam to foretell the coming of Jesus as a **star**. Numbers 24:17 says, **"A star will come out of Jacob; a sceptre will rise out Israel."** Jesus came to be the light of the world. **"The people walking in darkness have seen a great light,"** is the way Isaiah describes it. Wherever Jesus went He brought light, life and hope, and He still does. In Revelation 22:16 Jesus describes Himself when He says, **"I am the root and offspring of David, and the bright Morning Star."**

However, the verse that has really struck me is 2 Peter 1:19: **"And we have the word of the prophets made more certain, and you will do well to pay attention to it, as to a light shining in a dark place, until the day dawns and the morning star rises in your hearts."**

The most important star for us is neither the star the Wise Men followed nor the star foretold by the prophets but the **morning star that rises in our hearts.** As those who know and love Jesus, our darkness has been dispelled by His light, and in our hearts we have **the morning star** who fills us with light and guides and directs our lives.

Don't look at the sky or even into the manger; look into your heart and let His light excite you, fill you with joy and point you to a future full of hope.

Charles

One Year Plan : Psalm 137, Revelation 10, Habakkuk 3
Two Year Plan : Proverbs 26:10-19, Revelation 2:1-11, Isaiah 42 (Yr 1)
Esther 1 (Yr 2)

The Work of Angels

Luke 2:9 says, **"An angel of the Lord appeared to the shepherds, the glory of the Lord shone around them and they were terrified."**

Angels have always had a unique role in God's purposes; they heralded the birth of Jesus, and they are always available to work at God's command.

When Jesus was led into the wilderness to be tempted by the devil, He spent forty days fasting and repelled every onslaught of satan, and at the end when He was hungry and tired, Matthew 4:11 says, **"Then the devil left him, and angels came and attended him."**

Angels are sent by God to give help to His chosen ones who are in need. Hebrews 1:14 says, **"Are not all angels ministering spirits sent to serve those who will inherit salvation?"**

Peter was in prison. Acts 12:11 records, **"Peter came to himself and said, 'Now I know without a doubt that the Lord sent his angels and rescued me.'"**

Paul was in a storm. Acts 27:23 tells how angels helped: **"Last night an angel of God whose I am and whom I serve stood beside me and said, 'Do not be afraid, Paul...'"**

What Jesus said in Matthew 18:10 about children suggests that each has a 'guardian angel': **"See that you do not look down on one of these little ones. For I tell you that their angels in heaven always see the face of my Father in heaven."**

Psalm 91:11 tells us, **"The Most High will command his angels concerning you to guard you in all your ways."**

These heavenly beings dwell in the presence of God and worship Him day and night. They can cause awe, fear and wonder when they make themselves visible, but they also watch over you and can be available to you in your moment of crisis!

Joyce

One Year Plan : Psalm 138, Revelation 11, Zephaniah 1 - 2
Two Year Plan : Proverbs 26:20-28, Revelation 2:12-29,
Isaiah 43 (Yr 1)
Esther 2 (Yr 2)

An Amazing Child

Hundreds of years before the birth of Jesus, an amazing prophecy was spoken by Isaiah. The words are very familiar, particularly as we approach Christmas, but have you considered what they are saying?

"For to us a child is born, to us a son is given, and the government will be upon his shoulders. And he will be called Wonderful Counsellor, Mighty God, Everlasting Father, Prince of Peace." (Isaiah 9:6)

If we accept Him as our Lord and King, this is what we are promised:

"The government will be upon his shoulders ... of the increase of his government and peace there will be no end." He is the One who rules and reigns in all things, and He will bring order into our chaotic lives.

"Wonderful Counsellor" He has all wisdom, knowledge and compassion, and knows how to bring His counsel into our lives.

"Mighty God" He is our miracle-working God, who wants to answer our prayers and do things that are humanly impossible and to confirm His word with signs and wonders.

"Everlasting Father" In a world which is becoming increasingly fatherless, He is our totally reliable, loving and affirming Father. His promise is to be a Father to the fatherless, and if our earthly father has let us down and disappointed us, He never will.

"Prince of Peace" The peace that Jesus gives is not natural or subject to human limitations; it is perfect, and beyond our understanding.

Do not let pictures of a helpless baby deceive you; Jesus is all that this prophecy says and more. **He will be everything you need.**

Charles

One Year Plan : Psalm 139, Revelation 12, Zephaniah 3
Two Year Plan : Proverbs 27:1-9, Revelation 3:1-13, Isaiah 44 (Yr 1) Esther 3 (Yr 2)

Check your Obedience Levels

Would you like God to pour out His heart to you and make His thoughts known to you? Does this sound impossible? Proverbs 1:23 tells us this is exactly what He wants to do – **"If you had responded to my rebuke, I would have poured out my heart to you and made my thoughts known to you"** – we are the obstacles to this becoming a reality.

Our heavenly Father is longing to communicate with us; He is looking for obedient, tender hearts that will be responsive to His every word. Our love for Him is shown by our obedience to His commands, and He is looking for constant responsiveness to His written words and commands as well as the internal promptings of His Spirit.

Proverbs 1:24-25 records God's complaint:

- **You rejected me when I called.**
- **You gave no heed when I stretched out my hand.**
- **You ignored my advice.**
- **You would not accept my rebuke.**

God will not communicate His intimate thoughts and wisdom if we are so careless. I find myself overwhelmed by the implications of these verses. I have the possibility of hearing Almighty God pour out His amazing wise, creative thoughts, to be able to see and understand His loving heart, to receive His communications at this intimate level... and yet I can choose to live in my own limited way, with my own resources, doing my own thing! What a travesty! What a waste!

When I meditate on the implications of these verses, I set my heart to receive correction, to check my obedience levels, to ask for a circumcised, tender heart and ears – and that I will put into action everything I know and read in the Word of God.

I am looking for what Jesus described as **"the pearl of great price"** – intimate knowledge of the Most High. The price is committed obedience to his Word.

Don't be like those in Isaiah 65:2 where God says, **"All day long I have held out my hands to an obstinate people, who walk in ways not good, pursuing their own imaginations."**

Rather, **obey and God will pour out His heart to you.**

Joyce

One Year Plan : Psalm 140, Revelation 13, Ezra 1 - 2
Two Year Plan : Proverbs 27:10-18, Revelation 3:14-22, Isaiah 45 (Yr 1)
Esther 4 (Yr 2)

The Dynamic of God's Word

What happens to you when you open up the pages of the Bible? Are you going through the motions of a daily chore or are you liberating God's power and activity into your life?

Psalm 19:7-8 says, **"The law of the Lord is perfect, reviving the soul. The statutes of the Lord are trustworthy making wise the simple. The precepts of the Lord are right, giving joy to the heart. The commands of the Lord are radiant, giving light to the eyes."** When I read the scriptures, I expect to feel refreshed, revived, set free from weariness. I believe that God is going to give me wisdom, joy and understanding concerning the practical issues of life.

Psalm 119:9&11 says, **"How can a young man keep his way pure? ... I have hidden your word in my heart that I might not sin against you."** God's word is going to enable me to live in purity and give me resistance against sin.

Jesus said, **"The words I have spoken to you are spirit and they are life."** (John 6:63) There is a dynamic in God's word that does not exist in any other printed page, and the writers of the New Testament agree. Hebrews 4:12 says, **"The word of God is living and active. Sharper than a double-edged sword, it penetrates even to dividing soul and spirit, joints and marrow; it judges the thoughts and attitudes of the heart."**

When Paul was writing his last letter to Timothy he declared, **"All Scripture is God-breathed and is useful for teaching, rebuking, correcting and training in righteousness, so that the man of God may be thoroughly equipped for every good work."** (2 Timothy 3:16-17)

Come to God's word with faith and expectancy; you are holding dynamite in your hands which will destroy the work of the enemy; you are holding a book of healing which will minister peace and health to your whole being.

Charles

One Year Plan : Psalm 141, Revelation 14, Ezra 3 - 4
Two Year Plan : Proverbs 27:19-27, Revelation 4, Isaiah 46 (Yr 1)
Esther 5 (Yr 2)

How Brightly are you Shining?

"Those who are wise will shine like the brightness of the heavens, and those who lead many to righteousness, like the stars for ever and ever." (Daniel 12:3)

"Then the righteous will shine like the sun in the kingdom of their Father." (Matthew 13:43)

"John was a lamp that burned and gave light, and you chose for a time to enjoy his light." (John 5:35)

"Do everything without complaining or arguing, so that you may become blameless and pure, children of God without fault in a crooked and depraved generation, in which you shine like stars in the universe as you hold out the word of life." (Philippians 2:14-16)

Our son Craig and his family live in Bulgaria and work amongst Roma Gypsies, many of whom are living in spiritual darkness with no knowledge of Jesus, the Light of the World. At one particular time while Craig shared the good news of Jesus at a meeting, his daughter Gillian took a video of people listening to this gospel message for the first time. Craig began to pray for those who wanted a new life. As Gillian was panning the camera around the room, she captured the face of an old man at the moment he was receiving Jesus, and a new life was entering him by the Spirit of God. It was literally like a light being switched on: his face glowed; life came into him. It was visible, tangible, unmistakable and – dare I say it – should be normal.

We are called to be full of light, the shining ones, who give light where we live and work – and our light should be burning with increasing brightness – hence the question at the top of this page.

Are you burning brightly or growing dim?

Joyce

One Year Plan : Psalm 142, Revelation 15, Ezra 5 - 6
Two Year Plan : Proverbs 28:1-9, Revelation 5, Isaiah 47 (Yr 1)
Esther 6 (Yr 2)

Unsung Heroes

Consider this man. First he discovered that his fiancée was expecting a baby, not his, for which he faced public disgrace. He then escorted his heavily pregnant wife on a long journey to a place where the only delivery suite he could find was a stable. Next, he fled from a King who wanted to kill this newborn son, and eventually he returned to Nazareth, in response to a dream, and then used his skills as a carpenter to provide for his family's needs.

He believed the angel when told that the child his wife was carrying had been conceived by the Holy Spirit! He had no sexual relations with his wife until after the birth of her son. He provided a home for his family, brought Jesus up as if he was his own son, and trained him in the skills of carpentry.

Joseph is the unsung hero of the Christmas story, with the spotlight shining so much on Jesus and His mother Mary.

Nothing that Joseph said has been written down, and it would seem that he died before Jesus entered His public ministry. However, if he had not acted with faith and obedience, what would have happened?

Do not ever despise those who act in faithful obedience to God. The Church, the Body of Christ, contains a large number of folk who are seeking to hear God's voice, obey what He says, maintain their place of faith in difficult situations, and sometimes wonder, "What's it all about?"

If that is how you are feeling today, be encouraged and think of the example of Joseph. We know very little about him yet he was a most significant person.

Paul said, **"Now it is required that those who have been given a trust must prove faithful."** (1 Corinthians 4:2)

You may think that no-one sees your faithfulness and consistent following of Jesus – but God does!

Charles

One Year Plan : Psalm 143, Revelation 16, Ezra 7 - 8
Two Year Plan : Proverbs 28:10-18, Revelation 6, Isaiah 48 (Yr 1)
Esther 7 (Yr 2)

God is Kind, but He's Not Soft

"God is kind, but He's not soft" is how The Message records Romans 2:2. We often focus on God's goodness, love, grace, power, or His majesty, omnipotence and greatness. Today reflect on God's kindness. It is part of who He is – He always deals with us in a kind way. When correcting us He is able to be both stern and kind; that unique mixture of **"grace and truth"**.

When Jesus encounters Peter on the beach after the resurrection, He does not rub his nose in the dirt of his failure and sin; He talks with him about his future, based on Peter's relationship with Him at that moment. Peter is a broken man and needs restoration, and Jesus treats him with kindness; He points forward not backward.

You may find yourself in situations where human resources have run out – remember God is kind; He has no desire for you to fail, to be inadequate or embarrassed. He has promised to be with you and enable you so that in your weakness you experience His strength. (2 Corinthians 12:9)

"It is His kindness that leads us to repentance." "He does not treat us as our sins deserve." "He doesn't keep a record of wrong – or who could stand!" (Romans 2:4, Psalm 103:10, Psalm 103:3)

Jeremiah 9:24 speaks of how **"He delights in kindness"**, and God challenges us to treat each other as He does. In Ephesians 4:32, Paul encourages those he is writing to, **"Be kind to one another, tender-hearted, forgiving one another – as God in Christ forgave you."**

Kindness is one of the fruits of the Spirit alongside love, joy, peace, patience, goodness, gentleness, faithfulness and self-control – and I think it is greatly undervalued.

Proverbs 11:16-17 says, **"A kind-hearted woman gains respect ... A kind man benefits himself."** I am asking God's help to be kind to myself and to others and to really value God's kindness to me.

Joyce

One Year Plan : Psalm 144, Revelation 17, Ezra 9 -10
Two Year Plan : Proverbs 28:19-28, Revelation 7, Isaiah 49 (Yr 1)
Esther 8 (Yr 2)

Forgetfulness

There are things that we try very hard not to forget: family birthdays; where we parked our car in the multi-story; people's names at a party; shopping we promised to get on the way home!

However, there are things we would like to forget but cannot: failing the driving test; being fired from our job; losing a good friend over a stupid argument; feeling a failure in life.

We may think of forgetfulness as always bad – but it is not. God has the ability to forget our sins, so His acceptance of us in no way takes our past into consideration. In his letter to the Philippians, Paul also speaks of forgetfulness as something positive, when he says, **"Forgetting what is behind and straining toward what is ahead, I press on toward the goal to win the prize for which God has called me heavenward in Christ Jesus."** (Philippians 3:13-14)

Paul is commanding us to forget our past because the memory of failures and difficulties can dog our future path. Remembering our past sins can cause us to be loaded down with guilt. The weight of broken relationships can make us believe that no-one will ever like us again. That job that went all wrong can cast a shadow that says we can never succeed again.

When we come to God in faith and give Him our life, He not only forgives our sins but forgets them. **God told his people that his plan for them was to prosper them and give them a hope and a future.** (Jeremiah 29:11)

I believe that God can give us supernatural forgetfulness – to forget our past sin, to forget our disappointments, our failures, our broken dreams. God wants us to press on toward the goal He has for us.

God is a great redeemer and whatever may have blighted your path in the past, **forget – and press on into the future that God has planned for you.**

Charles

One Year Plan : Psalm 145, Revelation 18, Zechariah 1 - 3
Two Year Plan : Proverbs 29:1-9, Revelation 8, Isaiah 50 (Yr 1)
Esther 9 (Yr 2)

Be Like Mary

Everything was unusual: to see an angel would be amazing, but to have an angel speak to you and be told that you are **"highly favoured by God"**, going to have a son whose father is the **"Most High God"** and who is to **"reign forever"**... Wow!

We could expect Mary's natural reaction to be one of fear, but in her spirit she is not negative or fearful but curious. She questions, **"How will this be? I am a virgin."**

The angel answers:

- **The Holy Spirit will come upon you.**
- **The power of the Most High will overshadow you.**
- **For nothing is impossible with God.**

Mary's response is, **"May it be to me as you have said."**

God has made promises to you; perhaps they are things that could cause you to fear and question, **"How can this be?"**

The process for us to receive from God is no different:

- **A promise is made.**
- **The Holy Spirit overshadows us with His power.**
- **Our response is, "I agree with what you have said."**
- **And we proclaim, "Let it be to me as you have said."**

The process is: conception; birth; visibility – **"For nothing is impossible with God."**

"Blessed is she who has believed that what the Lord has said will be accomplished."

The full story is recorded in Luke 1:26-45.

Joyce

One Year Plan : Psalm 146, Revelation 19, Zechariah 4 - 6
Two Year Plan : Proverbs 29:10-18, Revelation 9, Isaiah 51 (Yr 1)
Esther 10 (Yr 2)

Peace and Joy

When God wanted to announce the imminent arrival of His Son, He sent an angel to Mary, gave a dream to Joseph, positioned a star for the Wise Men, but sent the heavenly host to the shepherds – why? God reserved the most spectacular display for these ordinary hardworking farmers. It shows that His gifts of love, joy and peace are for all people, not just a select few.

God's joy is supernatural and does not depend upon circumstances and events; it is a gift from heaven that will bring something powerful but unexplainable. Jesus said to His disciples just before He left them, **"Until now you have not asked for anything in my name. Ask and you will receive, and your joy will be complete."** (John 16:24)

Paul said, **"Do not be anxious about anything, but in every situation, by prayer and petition, with thanksgiving, present your requests to God. And the peace of God, which transcends all understanding, will guard your hearts and your minds in Christ Jesus."** (Philippians 4:6-7) Paul did not say that the circumstances would be instantly changed but that an unfathomable peace would be given.

The message from the angel and the heavenly host was,

"Glory to God in the highest heaven, and on earth peace to those on whom his favour rests."
(Luke 2:14)

Paul spoke a great prayer over the believers in Rome:

"May the God of hope fill you with all joy and peace as you trust in him, so that you may overflow with hope by the power of the Holy Spirit."
(Romans 15:13)

So my prayer for you is that you will be filled with the hope, joy and peace that come from a Father who loves, cares and wants the very best for you.

Charles

One Year Plan : Psalm 147, Revelation 20, Zechariah 7 - 8
Two Year Plan : Proverbs 29:9-17, Revelation 10, Isaiah 52 (Yr 1) Nehemiah 1 (Yr 2)

Stop!

STOP!

Especially if you are of the female gender

STOP!

Take a deep breath and pray as you slowly let it out! I expect you are extremely busy as you are in the middle of the Christmas Festivities.

Draw on heavenly resources right now. Activate your spirit and pray. Remember, joy and strength go hand in hand, and you need more than human resources when life gets busy.

Many times we are doing the 'Martha thing', and the Holy Spirit is gently whispering, **"STOP, look up and receive from me; let me help you; let me give you practical wisdom, order your day."**

It only takes a second to do this, and even if you do it sixty times in the next twenty-four hours it only adds up to one minute!

Wisdom has been described as the ability to know not only what to do and say but when and how to do it. Wisdom avoids stress.

So... **STOP and receive resources from heaven.**

Joyce

One Year Plan : Psalm 148, Revelation 21, Zechariah 9 - 10
Two Year Plan : Proverbs 30:1-8, Revelation 11, Isaiah 53 (Yr 1)
Nehemiah 2 (Yr 2)

Carrying Heavy Burdens

Pressure, stress, burdens, load, worry – do these the words only apply to 21st Century life? Or have they been with us since time began? Do we have to develop new techniques and therapies to cope, or can we apply ancient wisdom?

Over two thousand years ago David penned these words: **"Praise be to the Lord, to God our Saviour, who daily bears our burdens."** (Psalm 68:19)

Even in those days people had heavy burdens to carry. We have a choice: we can try to handle the demands of life in our own strength and with our own ability or we can find help from a source that is greater than ours.

Those who are followers of Jesus are encouraged to, **"Carry each other's burdens, and in this way you will fulfil the law of Christ."** (Galatians 6:2) The strength of Christian fellowship is to have those who will pray and support us through difficult times.

Paul promises **"...the peace of God which transcends understanding"** for those who will pray in times of anxiety. (Philippians 4:7)

One powerful promise written by David for those who are under pressure and carry heavy burdens is found in Psalm 55:22: **"Cast your burdens on the Lord and he will sustain you, he will never let the righteous fall."**

As I read Psalm 68, the phrase that struck me most powerfully was **"who daily bears our burdens"**. I constantly meet people who are living under tremendous pressure, carrying heavy loads and experiencing immense stress.

However, we have a God who understands and cares.

A well-known hymn says,

Oh, what peace we often forfeit!
O what needless pains we bear!
All because we do not carry
Everything to God in prayer.

Charles

One Year Plan : Psalm 149/150, Revelation 22, Zechariah 11 - 12
Two Year Plan : Proverbs 30:9-16, Revelation 12, Isaiah 54 (Yr 1)
Nehemiah 3 (Yr 2)

Anger

A friend of mine was having problems with angry reactions and angry thoughts. Anger was trying to dominate her life in a way that was not normal. Thinking about the problem only made it worse, and talking about it did provide some very reasonable answers as to why it was there but solved nothing.

When sharing this with a friend in church, she was given this advice: **"Stop focussing on the anger; look away, ignore the problem and focus on something positive."**

She made a decision; she chose to declare, **"This is not my anger, it isn't 'me'. I choose to look away; I choose to stop examining the why, what, how, and use my will to focus on something else."** Too simple? It worked for her.

Psalm 119:37 says, **"Turn my eyes away from worthless things."**

Hebrews 12:1-2 says, **"Let us throw off everything that hinders and the sin that so easily entangles, and let us run with perseverance the race marked out for us. Let us fix our eyes on Jesus, the author and perfecter of our faith..."**

2 Corinthians 3:18 says, **"And we all with unveiled face, beholding the glory of the Lord, are being transformed into the same image from one degree of glory to another."**

Anger is largely the result of injustice, disappointment and offence; however, being angry will never build you up – but it can destroy you. Choose to fix your eyes on Jesus, His love, His forgiveness and His purpose for a good future for you.

Joyce

One Year Plan : Proverbs 16, Isaiah 7:7-14, Zechariah 13 - 14
Two Year Plan : Proverbs 30:17-23, Revelation 13, Isaiah 55 (Yr 1)
Nehemiah 4 (Yr 2)

You are NOT Welcome Here!

We have been made aware in the media that many people feel our country has more than its fair share of asylum seekers. We are now at a time of the year when family breakdown and domestic violence reaches its peak, but we are also celebrating the birth of a baby whose parents were bombarded by these words:

"You are NOT welcome here!" There is **no room** at the **inn**!

We are all familiar with phrases such as these: **"I hate you!" "I don't want you living near me" "I don't want to have anything to do with you"**

The baby Jesus, whose birth we are celebrating, also received similar rejection and hatred when He lived on this same planet, and yet His sole purpose for coming was to reach out to His creation with...

LOVE – **"God so loved the world that he gave his one and only Son, that whoever believes in him shall not perish but have eternal life."** (John 3:16)

ACCEPTANCE – **"How great is the love the Father has lavished on us, that we should be called children of God! And that is what we are!"** (1 John 3:1)

FORGIVENESS – **"Be kind and compassionate to one another, forgiving each other, just as in Christ God forgave you."** (Ephesians 4:32)

The message of Christmas is love, acceptance and forgiveness.

We can love because He first loved us; we can accept the lonely and rejected because we have been accepted; and we can forgive because we have been forgiven.

What are going to be the dominant emotions in your heart this year? Hate? Rejection? Resentment?

Or... **love, acceptance and forgiveness?**

Charles

One Year Plan : Proverbs 17, Micah 5:1-5, Haggai 1 - 2
Two Year Plan : Proverbs 30:24-33, Revelation 14, Isaiah 56 (Yr 1)
Nehemiah 5 (Yr 2)

Changed Names!

Numbers 13:16 says, **"Moses gave Hoshea son of Nun the name Joshua"**; his new name means **'God saves'** and his old name Hoshea meant **'salvation'**. The name change took place just before the twelve tribal leaders were commissioned to enter Canaan and spy out the land.

There is a big difference between these two meanings. The old one suggests a generally good concept of salvation and victory, but the new one contains the unique ingredient that is essential – God. He is the One who saves, who gives victory. There is no might or power in Joshua, but there most certainly is in God.

For Joshua it must have been a significant moment to be given a name that was to be connected to his character and destiny. Many years before, Abram became Abraham and Sarai became Sarah. Changed names meant changed destinies; it was a special recognition that God had His hand on them and was intimately concerned with their lives.

It is with this knowledge that Joshua goes with the eleven others to spy out the new land God has promised to give them. When they report back they declare the land to be brilliant, beautiful and productive – but ten saw giants and were afraid. Joshua and Caleb saw possibilities and realities but knew that it was only with God's help and miraculous power that they could take the land.

Number 14:9 says, **"Do not be afraid of the people of the land, because we will swallow them up. Their protection is gone, but the Lord is with us."** There is no self-effort here; without God the task is fearsome and seemingly impossible, but Joshua's new name means 'God saves' and He will.

You and I have new names – mine is **'Joyce in Christ Jesus'**. I am not alone; God is for me, with me, in me. I have divine resources at my disposal. Life is much like Canaan land: full of giants but also full of opportunity. We can advance with God's help and resources or we can retreat through fear and weakness.

Today take a moment to reflect on the amazing privilege of being connected to Almighty God through Jesus and **ponder anew what the Almighty can do!**

Joyce

One Year Plan : Proverbs 18, Isaiah 9:1-7, Esther 1 - 2
Two Year Plan : Proverbs 31:1-9, Revelation 15, Isaiah 57 (Yr 1)
Nehemiah 6 (Yr 2)

Salt and Light

Have you felt the pressure of believing you ought to be sharing the gospel with someone and you were not able to get the words out of your mouth? Have you asked someone whether they were a follower of Jesus, and when they said, "No," you didn't know what to say next?

We have no record in the gospels of Jesus teaching His disciples how to witness. However, He did say, **"You are the salt of the earth,"** and, **"You are the light of the world,"** and He then went on to say, **"Let your light so shine before men, that they may see your good deeds and praise your Father in heaven."**

How do we become **salt and light**? I believe that it is to so live our lives with integrity, joy and grace that those looking on will see the light of Jesus in our lives; and then it is they who will ask the questions, not us.

Paul speaks about the believers in Corinth and says, **"You show that you are a letter from Christ, the result of our ministry, written not with ink but with the Spirit of the living God, not on tablets of stone but on tablets of human hearts."** (2 Corinthians 3:3)

I once heard this challenge: **"If you were arrested for being a believer in Jesus, would there be enough evidence to convict you?"**

Our testimony and witness is something we live 24/7, our families see it in the home, our colleagues see it at our work, and our friends see it in our leisure time. We never take time off from being followers of Jesus; we are on display all the time.

How salty are you, and how much light shines out from your everyday lifestyle? When was the last time someone asked you questions about your faith?

Perhaps we need less time on courses on evangelism and more time letting Jesus shine out from our eyes and our smiles.

Charles

One Year Plan : Proverbs 19, Jeremiah 31:7-18, Esther 3 - 4
Two Year Plan : Proverbs 31:10-20, Revelation 16, Isaiah 58 (Yr 1)
Nehemiah 7 (Yr 2)

Access to Wisdom

The Queen of Sheba made a special visit to King Solomon to see for herself if his reputation for wealth and wisdom was genuine. She may also have sought trade agreements and had other political agendas, but she was overwhelmed by all she experienced. She asked questions, poured out her heart, looked with wonder on all Solomon had achieved, but saw beyond the human to the evidence of God at work – recognising not only His love for Solomon but also His love for the nation of Israel in giving them such a wise and caring king. (2 Chronicles 9:1-12)

She honoured him during the visit with gifts from her own land – spices, gems, wood and gold – and Solomon reciprocated, so much so that she left with more than she came with. The visit involved a long journey; it was purposeful and she wasn't disappointed.

You and I have access to even greater wisdom. Jesus when speaking of Himself said, **"And now someone greater than Solomon is here."** (Matthew 12:42)

Paul describes Jesus in Colossians 2:3 as **"Christ, in whom are hidden all treasures of wisdom and knowledge"**. We do not have to travel thousands of miles to meet with superior wisdom. We can ask our questions, share our heart's longings, receive practical help and insight, and, like the Queen of the South, leave with more than we came with.

How? By spending time with Jesus, recognising Him as the source of all knowledge, and asking for His wisdom to be applied to our individual circumstances.

James 1:5 says, **"If any of you lacks wisdom, you should ask of God, who gives generously to all without finding fault, and it will be given to you."**

The result: **"Real wisdom, God's wisdom, begins with a holy life and is characterised by getting along with others. It is gentle and reasonable, overflowing with mercy and blessings, not hot one day and cold the next, not two-faced. You can develop a healthy, robust community that lives right with God and enjoy its results only if you do the hard work of getting along with each other, treating each other with dignity and honour."** (James 3:17-18, The Message)

Joyce

One Year Plan : Proverbs 20, Zechariah 9:9-17, Esther 5 - 6
Two Year Plan : Proverbs 31:21-31, Isaiah 9:1-7, Isaiah 59 (Yr 1)
Nehemiah 8 (Yr 2)

What Did You See?

When you hear of something amazing, you want to go and see it for yourself. The impact of what is seen can vary widely.

When the shepherds heard the announcement of the birth of Jesus, they immediately said to each other, **"Let's go to Bethlehem and see..."** The impact was powerful; they saw the baby and spread the word to the amazement of those who heard them. We then read, **"The shepherds returned, glorifying and praising God for all the things they had heard and seen."** (Luke 2:20) What they saw had a dramatic effect.

When Nathaniel heard that the Messiah had been discovered, he was sceptical. **"Can any good thing come from Nazareth?"** was his immediate reaction. **"Come and see,"** was Philip's response. He came, saw and declared, **"Rabbi, you are the Son of God; you are the King of Israel."** (John 1:49) What he saw changed his life.

Some Greeks, who had come to Jerusalem for the Passover Feast, had heard about Jesus. They came to Philip with a request, and said, **"Sir, we would like to see Jesus."** The response of Jesus was to challenge them with the cost of becoming a real disciple: **"Whoever serves me must follow me..."** plus other demanding statements. We never hear of the Greeks anymore.

What are you hearing this Christmas – the words of familiar Christmas Carols, the story of the baby lying in a manger? Look afresh at Jesus; what do you see? Do you just see the picture on a Christmas card, the baby at the centre of the Nativity scene? Or, do you see the One who can change your life and transform your future?

Take a fresh look at Jesus this Christmas; it will change your life.

Charles

One Year Plan : Proverbs 21, Luke 1:1-25, Esther 7 - 8
Two Year Plan : Song of Songs 1, Micah 5:1-5, Isaiah 60 (Yr 1)
Nehemiah 9 (Yr 2)

In the Bleak Mid-Winter

Our God, heaven cannot hold him,
nor earth sustain;
Heaven and earth shall flee away
when He comes to reign;
In the bleak mid-winter,
A stable sufficed the Lord God Almighty,
Jesus Christ.

Angels and archangels
may have gathered there,
Cherubim and seraphim thronged the air;
But His mother only, in her maiden bliss
Worshipped the Beloved with a kiss.

Mary worshipped. She knew she had been with no man; she knew that which was conceived in her womb was miraculous; she had not had intercourse; she believed that God had come to her – it was all beyond understanding but she worshipped because she knew the truth.

Cynics can argue and mock, but I choose to worship the One who is coming again as King of Kings, the Sovereign Lord God Almighty. *"When He comes to reign"*, heaven and earth will be made new, and it is only then they will be able to contain His Glory.

Those who worship now will welcome that day; resurrected ones will shout, **"Glory to the Kings of Kings and Lord of Lords."** Truly, **"heaven and earth will flee away when He comes to reign!"**

Let us be like Mary – worship the One who we know now in part. Like Mary, we have limited understanding of who Jesus is, but she kissed and worshipped a baby who one day would be Saviour of the world, and we now can kiss and honour the future King of Kings and Lord of Lords.

Let's do it this Christmas time!

Joyce

One Year Plan : Proverbs 22, Luke 1:26-56, Esther 9 - 10
Two Year Plan : Song of Songs 2, Luke 1:1-25, Isaiah 61 (Yr 1)
Nehemiah 10 (Yr 2)

The Light is Shining

I have already written about the beautiful illuminated Herrnhut Star I was given whilst visiting Germany. It was designed to hang outdoors from the beginning of Advent. I was thrilled when it was given to me as I had never seen anything like it in England.

As Christmas came around the following year, I proudly hung my star outside the house; there was nothing like it in our village, perhaps in the whole of the UK!

A couple of weeks later, I was preaching in Church about the uniqueness of Jesus being born into this world, and I stated the fact that God placed a star in the heavens to mark His birth.

To demonstrate how unique this all was, particularly seeking to communicate to the children, I offered a gift to anyone who was able to find my house – which was the only one in our village with a star hanging outside. I did not give them any clues because it is not a large community. I simply told them to find the house and knock on our door.

The gifts were placed ready and I waited for the doorbell to ring. It did – but not nearly as often as I had expected.

God placed a sign in the heavens to herald the birth of His Son. Not many followed the star – only a few wise men and some shepherds.

We are living in a dark world today, and the light is still shining. Jesus described himself as **"the Light of the World"**. He longs to enter the darkness of people's lives and bring light, joy and peace.

When John wrote his Gospel he said these words: **"The light still shines in the darkness and the darkness can never put in out."** (John 1:5)

The light is still shining; **let Him fill your darkness with His light.**

Charles

One Year Plan : Proverbs 23, Luke 1:57-80, Nehemiah 1 - 2
Two Year Plan : Song of Songs 3, Luke 1:26-56, Isaiah 62 (Yr 1)
Nehemiah 11 (Yr 2)

God's Beloved

Solomon was given his name by his parents, but God instructed His prophet Nathan to give the child an additional name – Jedidiah - which means **'God's beloved'.**

Imagine David holding this little baby, calling him by name; later on perhaps teaching him to use a sling and training him for the role he would eventually fulfil. Every time he used his name it spoke a powerful message. God loved Solomon and David and knew that name held strong significance for them both, as it carried a constant reminder of God's mercy and forgiveness.

Consider the circumstances surrounding Solomon's birth. The country is at war, and David, instead of being with the army, stays in Jerusalem. He fancies another man's wife, Bathsheba, and takes her secretly while her husband is on the front line. On discovering she is pregnant with his child, David tries to cover his tracks, fails, and then has Uriah, her husband, killed.

None of this is in **the public eye**, but God knows everything and is not pleased. When confronted by Nathan, to his credit David confesses to sin and expects to die. Nathan's word to him is terrible: David will live but the child will die. We can only imagine the turmoil David lived through, the thought of **'if only'** – the agony, the guilt, the shame and regret.

David spends time pleading with God for a different result, but the child dies. David accepts his responsibility and repents, as we read from Psalm 51. Later, when he and Bathsheba have another child, the message brought by Nathan to name the child **'God's beloved'** speaks of forgiveness and hope.

In Psalm 130:3-4 David writes, **"If you, Lord, kept a record of wrongs, who could stand? But with you there is forgiveness therefore you are to be feared or worshipped."** (The Message)

The devil constantly harasses God's children, trying to dig up our past, seeking to heap condemnation on us. The antidote is to keep speaking those words: **"God's beloved."** That is what you are in Christ – the old has gone, the new has come! Jesus calls you **friend, loved, chosen.**

Joyce

One Year Plan : Proverbs 24, Matthew 1:18-25, Nehemiah 3 - 4
Two Year Plan : Song of Songs 4, Luke 1:57-80, Isaiah 63 (Yr 1)
Nehemiah 12 (Yr 2)

Where is your Dwelling Place?

In the legal world of buying and selling houses we have some wonderfully old-fashioned words. We speak of a **'dwelling'**, of our **'abode'** and even where we are **'domiciled'**.

Where we live – **our dwelling** – should be a place of rest, peace, joy and safety. When we have been away for long time we will walk through our front door and say, **"It's wonderful to be back home."**

Moses said in Psalm 90:1, **"You have been our dwelling place throughout all generations,"** and in the next psalm we read, **"He who dwells in the shelter of the Most High will rest in the shadow of the Almighty. I will say of the Lord, 'He is my refuge and my fortress, my God, in whom I trust.'"** (Psalm 91:1-2)

Where is your dwelling? Are you dwelling in the presence of God? Or, are you dwelling in the middle of the stress and struggle of life's demands? There is a classic book entitled **'Practising the Presence of God'** by Brother Lawrence, which describes how a monk, whose chief responsibility was to work in the kitchen, learned to talk, commune and fellowship with God right in the middle of his daily responsibility. Right there in the middle of the mundane routine he found a **dwelling place** with God.

It is possible to live daily in the presence of God, to make Him your dwelling place. You can know the peace, joy and safety that come from His presence. In His presence you will hear His voice. In His presence you will receive His wisdom.

Jesus said these words: **"If you abide in me, and my words abide in you, ask whatever you wish, and it will be done for you."** (John 15:7) The **dwelling place** of God is also a place of answered prayer!

Where will your **dwelling place** be today?

Charles

One Year Plan : Proverbs 25, Luke 2:1-20, Nehemiah 5 - 6
Two Year Plan : Song of Songs 5, Luke 2:1-20, Isaiah 64 (Yr 1) Nehemiah 13 (Yr 2)

God Forgives our Sins, Not our Excuses

For a number of years I worked with Colin Urquhart, who is founder of Kingdom Faith Ministries in Sussex. For part of that time I travelled with Colin as he fulfilled his preaching commitments around the UK.

On one particular occasion, I was driving Colin's car which, unlike my own, had **automatic transmission**. It had been a great evening, God had been working powerfully in the lives of the people, many had been healed, and the prayer line never seemed to come to an end.

It was now very late as we headed for home, and I was trying to make as much haste as possible and still remain legal. We were approaching a T-junction and I was preparing for a rapid stop and a quick getaway, when I completely forgot about the **automatic** car and pushed both feet onto the brake pedal. The car stood on its nose, and we were all nearly catapulted through the windscreen. Once order had been restored I tried to explain why I had caused my passengers such shock and discomfort; Colin then looked towards me with a quizzical smile and said, **"God forgives our sins, not our excuses."**

I immediately realised what I had been doing and rapidly made my repentance speech. **"Will you all please forgive me; it was my bad driving and I am sorry."** Forgiveness was quickly given and we all had a good laugh, but I had learned a big lesson.

If we will not take responsibility for our mistakes, failures and sins, we cannot receive forgiveness. In our society today it seems that **blame shifting** is a disease. It may bring self-justification but it does not bring peace or forgiveness.

Check your heart; is there something that you need to ask God's forgiveness for today? You may need to ask someone else to forgive you. Remember, repentance and confession will set you free, excuses change nothing.

Charles

One Year Plan : Proverbs 26, Matthew 2:1-23, Nehemiah 7 - 8
Two Year Plan : Song of Songs 6, Revelation 17, Isaiah 65 (Yr 1)
Haggai 1 (Yr 2)

Investing in Relationship

One of our very young grandsons was relating to me by reaching out his chubby arms when he saw me and breaking into a beautiful smile. He was content in my arms for a short while but made it very obvious when Mum appeared that she was the one he really wanted – and back he went!

It took almost a year of interaction for him to learn to recognise and trust me, and yet I still can't say he knows me. It will take years before we interact at a deep level, are able to explore ideas and ponder things together.

Relationships are complex. How we relate, how connected we feel, depends on many factors. As circumstances change, so do our ways of relating. One thing which seems to be a common factor in developing any relationship is **time** spent in each other's presence.

You may be surprised at how quickly you re-connect with a long-time friend who you haven't seen for months – you just pick up where you left off. However, at some stage that relationship has had **time** invested in it.

It is unfathomable and almost inexplicable that God should place such value on His relationship with us. **"God demonstrates his own love for us in this: While we were still sinners, Christ died for us."** (Romans 5:8) God did this to bring us back into relationship with the Godhead. Your worth is defined by that priceless love – don't waste it. Spend time in worship and connect deeply: talk and listen; obey and be thankful.

Look back over this year and think about this all important relationship. Have you valued it or taken it for granted? Do you need to restore contact? The Father is watching for you, longing to see you, to hear your voice. Because having made you, restored you, redeemed you, He wants you to know Him and enjoy Him and to ultimately become **a friend of God.**

This takes time – **but is a privilege worth investing in!**

Joyce

One Year Plan : Proverbs 27, Luke 2:21-52, Nehemiah 9 - 10
Two Year Plan : Song of Songs 7, Revelation 18, Isaiah 66 (Yr 1)
Haggai 2 (Yr 2)

The Power of Lies – The Power of Truth

When the serpent tempted Eve in the Garden of Eden, his ploy was to undermine God's integrity by questioning the instructions He had given to them, saying, **"Did God really say..."** Satan's lie led to the first sin, and the tension between truth and lies has been at the very centre of life ever since.

In reality our lives are dictated and controlled by the words that we hear and believe. We may not be listening to a serpent, but words spoken over our lives by various people at different times mould us and shape us.

Negative words spoken by people of influence can become a curse over our lives. Parents tell their children, **"You'll never succeed; you'll always be a failure."** These words become a self-fulfilling prophecy. Words like **'trouble'**, **'ugly'**, **'hopeless'** may be heaped on our heads; they diminish us and will ultimately devastate our lives.

God's truth has the opposite effect. God said to Abraham, **"In blessing I will bless you, and multiplying I will multiply your descendants as the stars of the heaven and as the sand which is on the seashore; and your descendants shall possess the gates of their enemies."** (Genesis 22:17)

Jesus said, **"You will know the truth, and the truth will set you free"** (John 8:32)

What words are you living under – blessings or curses?

God says you are blessed; you have favour; you have a good future; you have peace that passes understanding; you are loved; you are forgiven; etc.

Add your own promises to that list and live and enjoy the Power of Truth today!

Charles

One Year Plan : Proverbs 28, John 1:1-18, Nehemiah 11 - 12
Two Year Plan : Song of Songs 8, Revelation 19, Ruth 1 (Yr 1)
Malachi 1 (Yr 2)

While you are Waiting, God is Working

Are there times when it seems that your prayers are being ignored? Remember, while you are waiting, God is working on your case. After Jesus had healed the man who had been waiting for thirty-eight years by the pool of Bethesda, He spoke to the Jews who were persecuting Him for doing good on the Sabbath, and said, **"My Father is always at work to this very day, and I too am working."** (John 5:17) God never stops working on behalf of those who love Him and look to Him. For the man by the pool it had been a very long wait, but God had not forgotten him.

In Habakkuk 2:2-3, when the prophet could not understand why things were going so badly for his nation, the Lord replied, **"Write down the revelation and make it plain on tablets so that a herald may run with it. For the revelation awaits an appointed time; it speaks of the end and will not prove false. Though it linger, wait for it; it will certainly come and will not delay."** God may have spoken clearly to you at some time in the past; you knew it was His voice. Wait; God is faithful; it will surely happen.

The Psalmist is equally confident of the consistent activity of God. **"He will not let your foot slip – he who watches over Israel will neither slumber nor sleep. The Lord watches over you..."** (Psalm 121:3-5) God never sleeps; He is always alert and aware of what is going on in your situation. He is working on your case even as you sleep. Don't lie in bed at night worrying; there is no point in both of you being awake!

Jesus also is acting on your behalf; in Hebrews 7:25-26 it says, **"Therefore he is able to save completely those who come to God through him, because he always lives to intercede for them. Such a high priest meets our need..."** Jesus is constantly presenting your case to His Father.

Keep your faith focussed on God – He has not forgotten you.

Charles

One Year Plan : Proverbs 29, Colossians 1, Nehemiah 13
Two Year Plan : Joel 1, Revelation 20, Ruth 2 (Yr 1)
Malachi 2 (Yr 2)